T0330252

Technological Leapfrogging and Innovation in Africa

Technological Leapfrogging and Innovation in Africa

Digital Transformation and Opportunity for the Next Growth Continent

Edited by

Ethné Swartz

Montclair State University, USA and University of Pretoria, South Africa

Caren Brenda Scheepers

Gordon Institute of Business Science, University of Pretoria, South Africa

Adam Lindgreen

Professor, Copenhagen Business School, Denmark and Extraordinary Professor, Gordon Institute of Business Science, University of Pretoria, South Africa

Shumaila Yousafzai

Nazarbayev University, Kazakhstan and Cardiff University, UK

Marianne Matthee

Gordon Institute of Business Science, University of Pretoria, South Africa

Edward Elgar
PUBLISHING

Cheltenham, UK • Northampton, MA, USA

Cover image: da-kuk on Getty

Published by
Edward Elgar Publishing Limited
The Lypiatts
15 Lansdown Road
Cheltenham
Glos GL50 2JA
UK

Edward Elgar Publishing, Inc.
William Pratt House
9 Dewey Court
Northampton
Massachusetts 01060
USA

A catalogue record for this book
is available from the British Library

Library of Congress Control Number: 2023913844

This book is available electronically in the **Elgar**online
Business subject collection
http://dx.doi.org/10.4337/9781800370395

ISBN 978 1 80037 038 8 (cased)
ISBN 978 1 80037 039 5 (eBook)

Printed and bound in Great Britain by
TJ Books Limited, Padstow, Cornwall

Contents

Contributors

Phil Alves specialises in applied competition and regulatory economics and takes a keen interest in trade policy issues, particularly as they relate to economic growth and development. He has worked at the South African competition authorities, the South African Institute of International Affairs, and in private consulting. The latter has focused on competition law, economic regulation, international trade disputes, and general commercial litigation.

Kieran Brown is Founder and Partner of Polis Consulting Group, working across Australasia and the South Pacific focused on corporate strategy, research and development management, and economic policy. He is a former Visiting Scholar of University of California Berkeley. Kieran is Adjunct Faculty at GIBS, University of Pretoria, and Visiting Lecturer at the University of Waikato New Zealand. He has consulted with government and global Fortune 500 clients on corporate strategy and innovation-related topics. His research interests are in the focused industrial and innovation policies, the micro foundations of firm performance and sustained competitive advantage, and their relationship with government research and development programmes.

Christopher Denecke is a Salesforce and data analyst at UMass Lowell with more than eight years of experience working with a variety of industries. He specializes in customizing Salesforce and creating useful reports and dashboards for all levels of users. Chris has worked with claim financial, audit, risk, sales, revenue, marketing, and higher education datasets throughout his career.

Arielle S. Emmett is a United States Fulbright Scholar and independent journalist-researcher who studied the Chinese in Kenya between 2018 and 2019. She has taught legal research, visual communication, science writing, journalism, and media history at Strathmore Law School, Nairobi, Universitas Padjadjaran, Indonesia, University of Hong Kong Media Studies Centre, and International College Beijing. Arielle was a contributing editor to *Smithsonian Air & Space* magazine for six years. Her first novel, *The Logoharp* will soon be published.

Alet C. Erasmus is a research associate at the Gordon Institute of Business Science, University of Pretoria. Her primary interest is consumers' decision making, particularly dealing with uncertainty and complex consumer decisions, and focusing on consumers' behaviour in different retail contexts. She supervises PhD and masters' degree studies, has presented her research at multiple international conferences, and has produced more than 60 international publications, including textbooks for secondary schools and tertiary institutions.

Frances Fabian is Associate Professor of Strategic Management and Entrepreneurship in the Department of Management, University of Memphis. She received her master's in public policy at the Kennedy School at Harvard University and PhD at the University of

Texas at Austin. Her research concentrates on decision making, knowledge, and the nature of environments, with a focus on culture in international environments and obstacles and motivators for entrepreneurship. Her research has been published in journals such as *Academy of Management Review*, *Strategic Management Journal*, and *Journal of Management Studies*. She has recently been applying her insights more directly to the African context and is preparing research to address the novel era ahead of us in regard to trade partners, entrepreneurship, technology, and host environments.

Nikitta Hahn is a Researcher at the Gordon Institute of Business Science (GIBS), the University of Pretoria. Her research focuses on economic development in the African context, particularly with regards to youth and female participation in the economy. Nikitta is involved with the writing of teaching case studies and white papers. She has completed her Master's in English Literature at the University of Johannesburg.

Adam Lindgreen is Professor of Marketing at Copenhagen Business School, where he heads the Department of Marketing. He is also Extraordinary Professor with the University of Pretoria's Gordon Institute of Business Science. Adam has published in *California Management Review*, *Journal of Business Ethics*, and *Journal of the Academy of Marketing Science*, among others. He is the recipient of the 'Outstanding Article 2005' award from Industrial Marketing Management and serves on the board of several scientific journals.

Joel Malen is Associate Professor at Waseda University, School of Commerce, Japan, and Director of the Waseda University Governance and Sustainability Research Institute. He received his PhD from the University of Minnesota. His research examines corporate environmental sustainability, focusing on the dynamics and macro-level implications of firm strategies for reducing impact on the natural environment.

Motshedisi Mathibe is a Senior Lecturer and Head of Department: Business Management and Entrepreneurship at the University of Pretoria's Gordon Institute of Business Science (GIBS). Her research interests are in the field of Social Entrepreneurship, Women Entrepreneurship, Informality, township Economy, and Base of the Pyramid markets. Her research interest is anchored around Sustainable Development Goals (SDGs): 4: Quality Education, 5: Gender Equality, and 8: Decent Work. Dr Mathibe is a mentor at The United Nation's Global Impact Young Sustainable Development Goals (SDGs) Innovators Programme. Here, she mentors and supports a team of young innovators in their efforts to frame a challenge, applying sustainable business and innovative concepts/ideas to create tangible business solutions with real market potential. In 2020 she co-published an award-winning case 'All Women Recycling: Staffing Challenges during a Global Pandemic'.

Marianne Matthee is Director of Research at the Gordon Institute of Business Science, University of Pretoria, where she is responsible for the school's research strategy and impact. She also teaches in the areas of macro economics, trade in Africa, and the environment of business. Marianne holds a PhD in international trade and has authored and co-authored numerous publications and cases. Her research interests are to understand the dynamics of exporting firms, international trade-related gender inequality, and opportunities for women entrepreneurs in export.

Michelle Montague-Mfuni is an Assistant Professor of Management at the Robins School of Business at the University of Richmond in the United States. She has an undergraduate degree in biochemistry from Harvard University, an MBA degree from the Darden School at the University of Virginia and a PhD in Management from the University of Memphis. Dr Montague-Mfuni harnesses previous multinational corporate executive experience (EY, Deloitte, Gemini, Citibank, Morgan Stanley, Salomon Brothers, and UBS Securities) to inform her research and teaching. For more than 21 years, she lived in South Africa where she was involved with the financial and strategic management consulting sector. Her research often utilises the African context to explore and expand strategic, international business, stakeholder, entrepreneurial, and family business theories.

Hugh Myres works as an executive coach both at the Gordon Institute of Business Science and in his own practice. He holds an MBA and master's of management in coaching and supervises students' research at MBA and MPhil levels.

Njuguna Ndung'u is Executive Director of the African Economic Research Consortium based in Kenya. He is Governor of the Central Bank of Kenya and has previously held positions at the University of Nairobi, the International Development Research Centre, and the Kenya Institute of Public Policy Research and Analysis. Njuguna has extensive policy, research, and teaching experience in macro economics, micro economics, econometrics, and financial development.

Alex Oguso is Senior Researcher at Kenya Revenue Authority's Strategy, Innovation, and Risk Management Department. He holds a PhD in economics from the University of Nairobi. He holds a master's degree in economics from the University of Nairobi. His research interests include financial sector development, macro-fiscal policy issues, and international trade/finance.

Ali Parry is Director of Trade Matters®, a company that provides research, consulting, and writing and editing services to academic institutions and other public- and private-sector concerns. She holds an MCom in International Trade from the North-West University in South Africa. She has been involved in the international trade sphere for more than 35 years, having previously worked at the South African Foreign Trade Organisation and the International Trade Institute of Southern Africa. She has participated in many local and international projects on trade and development, particularly in Africa, and has co-authored several articles, books and book chapters.

Liezl Rees is Head of the Centre for African Business at Johannesburg Business School (JBS), University of Johannesburg (UJ). In her role, she is involved in the writing of teaching case studies, journal articles, and white papers, and runs regular events and executive programmes which explore the context, challenges, and opportunities of doing business in Africa. Liezl is currently pursuing a doctorate specialising in Digital Transformation at the JBS, and has a Master's in Development Studies from the University of KwaZulu-Natal, South Africa.

Michele Ruiters is Senior Lecturer at the Gordon Institute of Business Science, University of Pretoria. She has a PhD from Rutgers, the State University of New Jersey, and a master's in commerce (development finance) from the University of Cape Town, South Africa. Her teaching and research interests include women's leadership, human behaviour, organisational behaviour, and diversity and inclusion.

Caren Brenda Scheepers is Professor of Contextual Leadership at the Gordon Institute of Business Science, University of Pretoria, South Africa. She holds a PhD in counselling psychology and is a professional credentialed executive coach. She teaches in the areas of contextual leadership, women's entrepreneurship, and organisational development towards strategy implementation. She has extensive management consulting experience in leadership and organisational development. Caren published in *Personnel Review, Diversity, Equity and Inclusion, European Business Review, Journal of Applied Management Studies* and *Gender in Management*. She has been receiving the 'Most Prolific Researcher' award amongst faculty at her school since 2018 and in 2020 received 'The Most Outstanding Contribution to the Case Method' from The Case Centre.

Ashley Elizabeth Sperbeck is an intellectual property associate at Morrison & Foerster LLP. She focuses her practice on domestic and international patent prosecution, as well as intellectual property due diligence, counselling, and portfolio management. She has extensive experience in several technical areas, including small molecule pharmaceuticals, medical devices, and life sciences. During her graduate studies at the University of Notre Dame, Ashley engaged in computational organic chemistry and drug design research in collaboration with the Dana Farber Cancer Institute of Harvard University Medical School.

Ethné Swartz is Professor of Management at the Feliciano School of Business, Montclair State University, United States. She is a Fulbright Scholar and a research associate at the Gordon Institute of Business Science, University of Pretoria. She received her PhD in management science from the University of Manchester, United Kingdom. She has co-authored a Sage text on research methods and her articles have appeared in *Long Range Planning, Risk Management: An International Journal, Journal of Applied Management Studies*, and *Leadership and Organisational Development Journal*, among others. She serves on the editorial boards of the *Journal of Developmental Entrepreneurship* and the *International Journal of Gender and Entrepreneurship*.

David Teece is Professor at the Haas School of Business at the University of California, Berkeley and is the faculty director of the school's Tusher Initiative for the Management of Intellectual Capital. He has authored over 30 books and 200 scholarly papers and is co-editor of the *Palgrave Encyclopedia of Strategic Management* and *Industrial and Corporate Change*. He is identified as the originator (with two of his graduate students) of the Dynamic Capabilities perspective in strategic management. He is also known for the 'Teece Model', a framework he developed to assist companies with their technology commercialisation strategies and business models.

Asmitha Tiekam is a dynamic, entrepreneurial-minded information technology management professional who has worked in various sectors such as Audit, FMCG, Manufacturing, Oil and Gas, and IT Software companies. Her areas of expertise lie in the fields of entrepreneurship, project management, information and application security, ERP solution delivery, governance, and strategy development. She graduated with an MBA from the Gordon Institute of Business Science in 2019. Asmitha also started up an e-commerce business during COVID-19 with fellow MBA colleagues to help small businesses trade digitally during the pandemic.

Paul M. Vaaler is Professor and John and Bruce Mooty Chair in Law and Business at the University of Minnesota's Law School and Carlson School of Management, where he has been a faculty member since 2007. He writes and teaches on how foreign investing firms and individuals manage risks in developing countries undergoing policy reforms. More information on Professor Vaaler is available at https://carlsonschool.umn.edu/faculty/paul-vaaler.

Wilma Viviers is a research professor in the TRADE research entity, a National Research Foundation-rated researcher, and the World Trade Organization Chair holder at North-West University in South Africa. She is also a member of the International Advisory Board of Nyenrode Business University in the Netherlands. She has received several awards for teaching and research excellence over the years. One of her most noteworthy achievements has been introducing the TRADE-DSM® (Decision Support Model) in South Africa and overseeing its rollout in several other countries. The TRADE-DSM® is a user-friendly tool that identifies high-potential export opportunities in different countries, thereby streamlining the market selection process.

Lyal White is an Associate Professor in Strategy at the Gordon Institute of Business Science (GIBS), the University of Pretoria. He is the founder of Contextual Intelligence and a Research Associate at the Brenthurst Foundation. Lyal offers strategic advice in international markets and people development in a cross-section of industries and cultures, with a particular interest in learning, leadership, and entrepreneurship. His commitment to learning and development extends to inclusive education through Edtech in partnership with Isizwe.com in low-income markets. Professor White serves on a number of boards, including the Association of African Business Schools and the Growth-Ten academic advisory board, and is widely published in news media, academic journals, and books. He is a regular commentator on radio, television, and social media.

Shumaila Yousafzai is Associate Professor of Entrepreneurship at Nazarbayev University, Kazakhstan, where she teaches entrepreneurship, marketing, and consumer behaviour. In her research, she focuses mainly on topics linked to contextual embeddedness of entrepreneurship, firm performance, institutional theory, and entrepreneurial orientation. She has published articles in various international journals, such as *Entrepreneurship Theory and Practice*, *Journal of Small Business Management*, and *Industrial Marketing Management*.

Ivy Zhang is Associate Professor of Accounting at the University of California, Riverside. Her research focuses on issues related to corporate governance, disclosure, and accounting choices. Ivy's work has been published in top accounting journals. She is a member of the Editorial and Advisory Review Board of *The Accounting Review* and has served as a reviewer for leading accounting, finance, management, and law journals and conferences.

Foreword

Kimberly Killmer Hollister

Technology leapfrogging and innovation are complex processes to undertake, especially during a period when there are fundamental realignments under way in globalisation, political forces, and the challenges of a pandemic. Yet, we are at an inflection point where Africa is emerging as an important continent demonstrating how eagerly its citizens are embracing technological change and how they have harnessed opportunities for economic progress. The pandemic provided a further push toward new technologies and business models that were already being sought by a population that had eagerly adopted innovations enabled by mobile phone technology and internet access. While the challenges of the twenty-first century are acute everywhere, it is in Africa where the reality is starkest, as we learned from the November 2022 COP27 Conference. If predictions by the World Economic Forum about Africa's youth population are accurate, we should, however, also regard Africa as providing huge opportunities. This volume argues we should acknowledge the challenges the continent faces while also seeing opportunity in Africa's people – their openness to innovation and desire to improve their lives. The various contributions speak to the spirit of the people who inhabit the diverse countries of the continent. The authors argue that academic researchers and educators must engage across disciplinary boundaries to collaborate and support knowledge dissemination about the possibilities of the liminal period we inhabit.

The premise of many of the chapters in the volume is that myriad challenges should not overshadow the great successes that have been realised in various African countries. Perhaps foremost is the example of Kenya, where M-Pesa was created as a mobile money solutions technology that has revolutionised the lives of ordinary people. One important voice from Africa is that of Njuguna Ndung'u, who served as a governor of the Central Bank of Kenya and helped shape the regulatory framework that enabled M-Pesa to take off. The same approach was used to launch M-Kopa, enabling people to access solar power, irrespective of where they live or whether they can access a conventional power grid. These are examples of technology leapfrogging that are innovative and instructive to those of us teaching innovation in the United States. M-Kopa's success in linking access to solar energy has expanded beyond energy into digital banking for vast numbers of the 'unbanked'. Other examples we learn about include companies such as Jumia in Nigeria, SweepSouth in South Africa, and the Ghanaian company, mPharma, which has brought mobile health services to unserved citizens in urban and rural areas. Business schools play a vital role in advancing an understanding of how innovations that occur in geographically distant locations might apply locally. As institutions, we want future generations of students and future leaders of business and society to be au fait with this Africa!

Above all, this volume lifts the veil on progress, such as Africa's rapidly developing entrepreneurial ecosystems, particularly entrepreneurial growth companies based in countries such as South Africa, Kenya, Nigeria, and Ghana. In order for Africa's companies and entrepreneurs to create the technology to leapfrog old or conventional tools, we need infrastructure investments but, crucially, education is also needed to build management capabilities to lead in a digital age. This is an argument well made by David Teece and his colleagues who skilfully apply the dynamic capabilities framework to the African context – leapfrogging presupposes that companies have skilled managers and workers to create, implement, and grow ventures. Chapters on intellectual property developments and raising investment capital further round out the volume and elucidate well the complexity of the region.

Universities and business schools are arguably among the most influential institutions in our society. By playing a key role in shaping the perceptions and skills of our future leaders, they can be powerful enablers of social entrepreneurship and innovation.

Montclair State University is an institution with a proud tradition of teaching pedagogy, having started as a 'normal school' chartered in 1908. By 1918, the institution had graduated 1,464 teachers to serve local schools in the region. After the Second World War, the university again lived up to its purpose of public service by educating those who were returning from the war. Our university leadership believes in the power of public universities to make a difference in the world, by providing transformational opportunities for students and engaging with our communities to develop solutions for critical challenges facing society. To that end, and embracing that purpose as a Hispanic-serving and the second-largest public university in New Jersey, we are committed to serving our community and advancing learner success – creating opportunities for innovation and impact.

The AACSB International-accredited Feliciano School of Business is focused on our mission: *to develop talent for a changing world*. We are committed to ensuring that our learners understand the challenges facing society both locally and globally, and how through their leadership they can advocate and create change through business. Across our programmes and disciplines, students are prepared to address how continued technological advancements are presenting unprecedented opportunities and challenges across the world. In part, this requires our students to become digitally and managerially equipped to craft successful career pathways, make sense of uncertainty, and embrace change. This is true also for students in Africa, where the context differs greatly, as we learn from chapters that discuss innovations in the homes of Africans, and the significant challenge of transforming education through the use of technology. Despite the different contexts that students face in Africa compared to those who live in North America, young people everywhere deserve an opportunity to thrive through access to education and basic services. There is no better time than the current technological era to collaborate to ensure we do justice to Africa and its hunger for change.

Montclair State University
November 2022

Foreword

Morris Mthombeni

The idea that nations can leapfrog their developmental shortcomings through a process of knowledge transfer has long interested scholars, especially those in the economics domain. Given Africa's uneven development patterns and myriad socioeconomic challenges, it is not surprising that the leapfrogging phenomenon would pique the interest of those who are determined to advance the dreams and aspirations of this vast, 54-nation continent. However, it is time to move beyond the 'Africa rising' rhetoric and take bold steps to ensure that African countries can take their rightful place alongside advanced nations, using the technological toolkits of the modern era.

Many books have been written about leapfrogging in a technological sense. However, what makes this book distinctive is that it takes the reader beyond first-order leapfrogging topics and adopts a systems-level approach. Using accepted theories and contemporary views as a foundation, the authors explore the leapfrogging phenomenon from various angles, including (in no particular order) inclusive growth, institutional logic and capacity, organisational design, leadership, ethics, human capital development, entrepreneurship, investment, access to resources, and the environment. While technology leapfrogging is frequently advanced as a solution for underdeveloped nations, of which there are many on the African continent, the core message in this book is that a technology-driven solution will only be effective if there is strategic alignment at the national, industry, and organisational levels.

In the chapter on dynamic capabilities, a strategic management concept developed in the Global North, the authors underscore the fact that managers in Sub-Saharan Africa face considerably more challenges than those for whom the concept was originally designed. While many of the top managers in Sub-Saharan African come prepared, having undergone high-level training at elite business schools, they nevertheless carry the burden of limited support owing to the paucity of middle managers throughout the region. This micro-level institutional constraint limits the number of opportunities that top managers can pursue, with deleterious effects on the potential to mobilise leapfrogging for the good of society. The authors offer important suggestions on how to address this and other institutional constraints, focusing on technology-rich investments in areas such as digital finance, green energy, and inclusive health services.

While the chapter on dynamic capabilities has policy implications at the country and organisational levels, the chapter on entrepreneurial growth in selected African countries shifts the focus to the agentic behaviours of entrepreneurs. The chapter also tackles what the authors correctly call the elephant in the room – the availability (scarcity) of data on entrepreneurship in Africa. The authors advocate evidence-based approaches and visualisation methods to investigate the leapfrogging phenomenon at a country level within the Sub-Saharan African context, with a view to better understanding the role of and challenges faced by entrepreneurs. The authors stress the importance of country-specific case studies as a source of context-rich data, from which policies can be formulated that are in tune with the needs of those entrepreneurs seeking a technology leapfrogging advantage. In this way, the authors put the spotlight on the path-dependent nature of entrepreneurship and its importance for development.

Given the development challenges confronting many countries in Africa, entrepreneurship is typically associated with the inclusive growth imperative. However, even technology leapfrogging is no panacea for the many economic, social, and environmental problems that are preventing African countries from keeping pace with their advanced-nation peers. The chapter on inclusive growth helps to convince the reader of the importance of structural transformation as a key driver of more expansive and sustained economic growth. The authors use both quantitative and qualitative (narrative-based) data to paint a cautiously optimistic picture of how each African country can lean into its strengths, such as labour cost advantages, to reform and revitalise areas of advantage and prepare the ground for systems-level technology leapfrogging. The authors lead the reader through an interesting discussion on the difference between 'path-creating leapfrogging' and 'path-skipping leapfrogging', while illustrating that patience and endurance must underpin the process. Policymakers therefore need to garner trust in themselves and the policies and initiatives that are aimed at bringing about an equitable digital ecosystem which will pay dividends over time (albeit unevenly).

Building on the concept of digital ecosystems, the chapter on the establishment of technology hubs stresses the importance of technological collaboration across African communities. The authors trace the growth of technology hubs in Africa, which today number over 644, according to a joint African Union and Organisation for Economic Co-operation and Development report. Given the growth of technology hubs, the high level of interest in them, and their potentially positive spill-over effects, the authors argue for the categorisation of such hubs to unleash their collaborative and developmental potential. To this end, the authors make an important contribution by devising a theoretical model on collaboration through technology hubs as well as a conceptual model on how African innovation ecosystems can leverage their respective strengths. In developing their theoretical and conceptual models, the authors build on a large body of knowledge pertaining to capabilities and identify and address various concerns surrounding the ability of technology hubs in Africa to overcome various obstacles to becoming leapfrogging springboards.

Any book providing insights on technology leapfrogging in Africa must have a chapter on financial leapfrogging, because the financial services sector has done more than any other sector to drive financial inclusion across the continent, using a wide range of technologies. From the standpoint of inclusive digital transformation in the financial services sector, the exemplar case in Africa is undoubtedly M-Pesa, which originated in Kenya and subsequently spread to many other countries. The M-Pesa case is the focus of the chapter on leapfrogging in finance, which underscores the importance of context when pursuing different technology development paths.

The chapter on the role of China in financial leapfrogging in Kenya will be of particular interest to readers, notably the divergent institutional logic of the Chinese and the Kenyans in this regard. Through this comparison, the authors illustrate the richness of context when analysing technology leapfrogging in different countries. Despite the success of M-Pesa and other fintech applications that have gained traction in Africa in recent years, the authors stress that a significant financial inclusion gap persists on the continent. There is still much to be done and much to learn about extending financial services to more Africans through technology leapfrogging, particularly in the areas of investment and systems development, lending, and payment facilities.

Towards the end of the book is an interesting chapter on how technology leapfrogging impacts people's home life. The chapter differs from the others in that it gently seduces the reader into reflecting on leapfrogging in an intimate, familiar setting. Using resource advantage theory, the chapter considers three types of leapfrogging – revolutionary, scattered, and coned – and discusses the relative impact of each on the home environment. The chapter draws a strong and definite link to the United Nations Sustainable Development Goals, using energy lifestyles and resultant paradoxes as the unit of analysis. The chapter also takes the discussion beyond the notion of the rational consumer to that of the contextual consumer who is culturally informed, especially in the African context. In this way, the chapter transcends the instrumental dimension and explores the normative dimension of technology leapfrogging.

The final chapter reminds us why we need technology leapfrogging in the education and skills development spheres, putting the spotlight on the shortage of competent teachers and the inadequacy of education and training infrastructure and methodologies in many parts of Africa. These shortcomings dampen the prospects of African countries developing their human capital and leveraging the many technology-based opportunities that will help them find a firmer socioeconomic foundation. The authors also question whether digital technologies can in fact help African countries to leapfrog their massive educational gap if the fundamental building blocks for an efficient and orderly society (which advanced nations almost take for granted) are not there.

I congratulate the authors on serving up an interesting cocktail of new insights and fresh perspectives on traditional theories and views and giving readers much to reflect on and be hopeful about. We need more books like this on Africa, for Africa, and by African scholars, working closely with their peers from the global academy. Africa's time is now; there is no time to waste.

Gordon Institute of Business Science, University of Pretoria, South Africa

Acknowledgements

The collaboration between the contributors to this volume is a testimony to the synergistic outcome of transdisciplinary research. We appreciate our contributors' perseverance during COVID-19 disruptions, and we hope this volume will support the post-pandemic recovery of Africa. As editors, we would like to acknowledge the following individuals and institutions:

- Arielle Emmet, who served as a developmental editor for several chapters in the volume.
- The peer reviewers for their valuable feedback.
- Kimberly Hollister, Dean of the Feliciano School of Business, Montclair State University, New Jersey and Morris Mthombeni, Dean of Gordon Institute of Business Science, University of Pretoria for the excellent forewords to the volume.
- A special thanks to Kieran Brown, who was a crucial first mover in supporting the concept for the book, by involving the Teece Dynamic Capabilities Model's team in applying this lens to view transformational pathway possibilities for Africa.
- The USA Fulbright Scholar awards afforded to Ethné Swartz, Paul Vaaler, and Arielle Emmett enabled personal intercontinental relationships between scholars and were important contributing factors toward the successful completion of this volume.
- We appreciate our institutions for their support, in particular, the Gordon Institute of Business Science for hosting Fulbright scholars and research fellows as well as the University of Pretoria and Montclair State University for encouraging international research collaborations.
- We are filled with gratitude towards so many local and international students, clients, and programme participants interested in contributing to a prosperous Africa and who are eager to develop themselves, their teams, businesses, and communities.
- We look forward to teaching the important principles of the alternative economic development pathways suggested in this volume, as well as their prerequisites and numerous case studies of innovation and entrepreneurship from Africa.

May this book bless Africa and contribute to the realisation of our people's potential towards prosperity, equality, and inclusion.

Introduction to *Technological Leapfrogging and Innovation in Africa*

Ethné Swartz, Caren Brenda Scheepers, Adam Lindgreen, Shumaila Yousafzai, and Marianne Matthee

INTRODUCTION

This edited research volume is the culmination of an idea rooted in a 2019 discussion at the Gordon Institute of Business Science (GIBS) in Johannesburg. That idea was to build on an initial presentation by two of this volume's co-editors, Caren Scheepers and Marianne Matthee, during which they observed the lack of research volumes that addressed technology leapfrogging in Africa. Ethné Swartz was a visiting Fulbright Scholar at GIBS in 2019 and, coincidentally, collaborated with Shumaila Yousafzai, who was also visiting Africa to collect data. Serendipitously, Adam Lindgreen was an extraordinary professor at GIBS at the same time, and drawn by our mutual interest in the rise of women entrepreneurs globally, but particularly across Africa, we agreed to edit a text that pooled our knowledge of entrepreneurship, economics, leadership, big data, and digital transformation, as well as financial inclusion. The objective was to build on work done by Marianne and Caren who presented in 2019 during the 79th Academy of Management Conference, entitled 'Can Africa make the leap? Contextual entrepreneurship in disruptive mobile technology for growth' (Matthee & Scheepers, 2019). We embarked on the writing of this volume that (happily) survived the effects of the Covid-19 pandemic on all our lives. We were also lucky that Arielle Emmet, a Fulbright Scholar in Kenya in 2019, contributed a chapter and served as a developmental editor for some chapters as the project advanced.

The co-editors are all committed to conducting research, teaching, and contributing to various communities in Africa, specifically Sub-Saharan Africa. Our vision was to contribute to a research volume that honestly observed what we were witnessing on the ground, as we live in communities touched by digital transformation and experience technological leapfrogging in towns, cities, and rural areas across Africa. We cast a wide net to involve as many researchers from the continent itself, and we are happy to have representation from many of the individuals who initially signed on to the project. Unfortunately, due to personal circumstances and exigencies imposed by the pandemic, colleagues who were to provide chapters on countries such as Tanzania and Ghana had to prioritize their personal health and career progression. Notwithstanding the headwinds faced, we hope that the volume provides readers and researchers with a sense of the transformation that is taking place in Africa. However, we are excited that authors from institutions in Kenya and South Africa contributed to this volume.

The 54 countries that constitute Africa south of the Sahara comprise many linguistically and culturally diverse countries. The United States (US) Library of Congress lists each of the countries (2010). The region starts at the southern tip with South Africa and ends in the north where the Sahara desert begins. Each country has a complex political and economic history, and we acknowledge that there are path dependencies that flow from such a history. We particularly acknowledge the impact of time, history, particularly colonialism, and political movements (Wadhwani et al., 2020) on Africa's growth and development.

AFRICA AND TECHNOLOGY LEAPFROGGING: CONTEXT IN 2019

Technological leapfrogging refers to the adoption of modern technologies in products and services, skipping over conventional and outdated distribution channels or means of service and product delivery. While Africa faces enormous challenges as it enters the twenty-first century and embraces the digital revolution, there also are potential opportunities. The continent's young and rapidly urbanizing population (Diop, 2017), coupled with the demands of a growing middle class, have brought the continent to the brink of explosive growth. Our context when envisioning this volume was the estimates by the World Bank report (2017a) that six sectors were critical for innovation to meet growth predictions: agriculture, education, energy, information and communication technology, finance, and governance. This report regarded leapfrogging in Africa as a necessity (Blimpo et al., 2017; Oranye, 2017) for economic progress.

Africa has one of the youngest populations in the world, and while educational outcomes have improved for young people, many economies experience mass unemployment, the rapid incorporation of women into market economies, the increasing importance of the informal sector, and an equally rapid development of technology solutions to persistent problems experienced by all citizens. For instance, Uber and other ride-hailing services have spread rapidly in Kenya and South Africa, and Nigerian startups have created new (and widely adopted) tech-enabled solutions to reduce counterfeit medicines (Lock, 2019). Similarly, entrepreneurs have created Africa-based platform businesses to solve intractable problems, such as domestic service employment (SweepSouth.co.za) and affordable technology education for schools (Obami.co.za). Sectors such as fintech, real estate, tourism, and education services are a hive of activity partly because of the lack of service provision for the poor and rural populations. Affordable technology solutions make possible, as Christensen et al. (2019) argue, ways to provide such services. This is not only because of disruptive technologies, but also because of a deliberate choice to focus on creating markets that address the needs of ordinary people. Although clean energy innovation has been uneven across economies, Africa has the potential to leapfrog straight to affordable renewable energy and solar mini-grids (Amankwah-Amoah, 2015; Batinge et al., 2017), with Kenya leading the way (Pilling, 2022a).

The journey of economic transformation coincides with a shift from pipeline businesses to platform businesses in the digital domain. Platform businesses provide the network effects that secure customers, engaging with customers in new ways and transforming the imperative of growth from supply-side economies of scale to demand-side economies of scale (Van Alstyne et al., 2016). This inverts the relationship that was extant with pipeline businesses. This view is consistent with our understanding of the development of dominant business models such as those for ride-hailing apps, many of which are being adopted in African markets. However, how do these business models fit the context and conditions in African markets? What are we learning from successful businesses that have emerged in the digital domain, and how are local startups taking account of customers' needs and wants? The 2018 Goalkeepers Report (Gates Foundation, 2018) shows that countries in Africa south of the Sahara face the challenge of extreme poverty but that the region is also home to a booming youth population with the potential to drive growth. In the context of the leapfrogging thesis, we wish to explore 'what if' scenarios of positive change that could result from investments in education, technology infrastructure, and business models that are appropriate to local conditions. As an example, Tracy Toefy and Caren Scheepers (2019) relate how SweepSouth.co.za has transformed the demand and supply of domestic workers in South Africa, leading to better conditions for domestic workers by placing upfront issues of human dignity and respect for labour of a largely female and unemployed workforce. Driven by values, the firm's leaders have pioneered a new way to think about domestic work, domestic workers, and accountability for the homeowners who make use of the domestic helpers who use the SweepSouth platform to source work and to innovate themselves (Cuthbertson, 2016).

The challenges in Africa are huge, but so are the potential opportunities. Saleh (2022) estimates that 460 million (one third of the population in the region) lived below the poverty line of \$US 1.90 a day. Yet, high rates of mobile phone adoption and use demonstrate the pent-up demand for access to services, and Leke et al. (2018) estimate that there are 122 million active mobile money accounts in Sub-Saharan Africa, more than in any other region of the world.

The World Bank (2018) estimates that Africa has approximately 95 million people who do not have a bank account or mobile money account, one of the definitions for those regarded as 'unbanked'. An encouraging trend is the increasing collaboration that is taking place between financial-sector technology businesses such as M-Pesa and the traditional banking incumbents. Africa's economic woes resulting from gaps or fragility in institutions/policies (World Bank, 2017a), technology, and infrastructure require 'out-of-the-box thinking', which some entrepreneurs are achieving through disruptive technological innovations, including mobile money and pay-as-you-go off-grid solar energy, which have even spread to other parts of the world. These African technological advancements have become Africa's best examples of leapfrogging over old technologies and business models. This is a contextual type of leapfrogging where appropriate application of digital technology manifests (and is enacted) within the African context, based on a granular understanding of customer needs. Moreover, this type of leapfrogging takes time and agency. For instance, Safaricom's success with M-Pesa was not immediate, launched initially as a solution for customers to access microfinance; the firm pivoted to mobile money instead (Cook, 2015), based on feedback from customers and a bottom-up innovation strategy (Amankwah-Amoah, 2015).

However, technology-driven leapfrogging requires good institutions and regulatory environments, investment in research and development, education, and infrastructure. Our multi-disciplinary focus encourages research on how to renew current theories to explain phenomena in the African context, aligned to the call of contemporary scholars to contextualize research in entrepreneurship (Baker & Welter, 2018). We must envision paths for inclusive growth in Africa at a macro (economy) level and micro (organizational) level to ensure participation from all in the economy and share the gains from growth in a more equitable manner (UNDP, 2017). This is especially important given the myriad challenges such as poverty and inequality. Africa's economic woes result from gaps in institutions/policies, technology, and infrastructure that require business models that work for African locations (Blimpo et al., 2017). Increasingly, Africa's tech innovators are at the forefront of its transformation (Oranye, 2017).

While some (Leke & Yeboah-Amankwah, 2018) stress that rapid technology adoption makes the continent a fertile arena for innovation, a caveat here is that there are limits to leap-frogging, and what technology can do (*The Economist*, 2016). The rapid spread of technology has raised hopes for Africa, but digital services cannot take the place of good governance to guard against corruption, which emphasizes the role of formal regulatory institutions (Pilling, 2018). Thus, while unlocking Africa's potential does depend on widespread technology adoption (World Bank, 2017a), Ménard and Shirley (2014, p. 12) observed that North's 1968 paper on political economy 'knocked technology [as a source of economic growth] off its throne'. North (1990, p. 110) explains that, 'Third World countries are poor because the institutional constraints define a set of payoffs to political/economic activity that do not encourage produc-tive activity'. North goes on to write that institutional change occurs when those economic or political entrepreneurs who have the bargaining strength to change institutions perceive 'that they could do better by altering the existing institutional framework on some margin. But their perceptions crucially depend on both the information the entrepreneurs receive and how they process that information' (North, 1990, p. 8).

THE INDUSTRIALIZATION AND LATECOMER 'CATCH-UP' DEBATE RELATED TO AFRICA

Africa is a comparative latecomer to the adoption of the internet. In 2019, the World Bank (Fukui et al., 2019) estimated that: 'approximately 45% of Africa's population is further than 10 km from fibre network infrastructure, which is a higher percentage than on any other con-tinent'. We have covered the barriers posted by a lack of internet infrastructure and last-mile access in several of the chapters in this volume. While the rate of adoption has increased dramatically across the continent, there is still much work required to ensure equitable access and digital inclusion, particularly given that Africa's abundance of land simultaneously creates the problem of bringing access points to distantly located populations.

As a region, Sub-Saharan Africa is highly underindustrialized. Nguimkeu and Zeufack (2019) argue that in non-oil-abundant countries, manufacturing value added is rising, but that resource-abundant countries had difficulties deepening their industrialization process. This 'curse of resources' is one of three barriers that Lee et al. (2021) discuss in their analysis of why emerging economies, especially middle-income economies, find it difficult to undertake sustainable structural change and to catch up with developed countries.

As mentioned in one of the chapters, South Africa is Africa's most industrialized country; the discovery of gold, diamonds, and mining of natural resources kick-started that journey in the 1860s. Stiglitz (2013) observed the region had a declining share of manufacturing to gross domestic product (GDP). Were this to continue, African countries would grow without the required transformation, and there is a danger that some could even deindustrialize. Faria (2022) estimates that by 2020, the service economy provided 41.6 per cent of African employ-ment. It is unclear if Covid-19 will have boosted manufacturing across the board, but at least there is now a debate about this pandemic showing the need to manufacture vaccines on the continent.

The above addresses a second barrier to catch-up (Lee et al., 2021), the negative effects of protecting intellectual property rights for firms in the global North on exports (and capacity development) in the global South. Technology transfer is an important mechanism to seed technological leapfrogging. Furthermore, higher global minimum standards established under the Agreement on Trade-Related Aspects of Intellectual Property Rights operate as a tax on developing countries. The health crisis caused by the Covid-19 pandemic has made the issue of intellectual property rights very visible and revealed Africa's vulnerability due to a lack of vaccine manufacturing locally. To their credit, African pharmaceutical manufacturers and scientists rose to the challenge, and in February 2022, Afrigen Biologics and Vaccines in South Africa replicated the Moderna vaccine. Large pharmaceutical firms (Pfizer, Moderna, and BioNTech) have agreed to support manufacturing facilities in Senegal and in Rwanda (Nature, 2022).

An important point of comparison between African countries is their rate of industrialization. Some (Signé, 2018) hypothesize that Africa's industrial revolution appears imminent. Signé (2018) argues that in the late 1990s and early 2000s the economic growth rates in Africa increased to high levels (see Figure 0.1) but that growth in manufacturing lagged; and by 2017, the manufacturing sector's share of Sub-Saharan Africa's total GDP was just under 10 per cent. If economies are to capitalize on the seeds of growth now visible in industries such as the pharmaceutical industry, industrialization in the context of twenty-first-century realities must factor in climate change, energy crises, supply chain conundrums, and access to the internet.

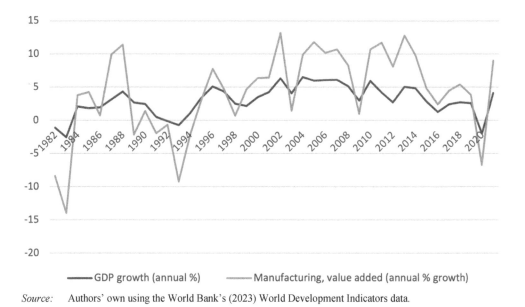

Source: Authors' own using the World Bank's (2023) World Development Indicators data.

Figure 0.1 *Annual GDP growth and growth in manufacturing output in Sub-Saharan Africa, 1995–2016*

The differences across African countries are also important to note. Figure 0.2 therefore illustrates the share of manufacturing value added in selected African countries.

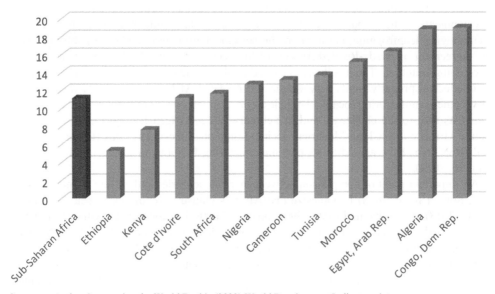

Source: Authors' own using the World Bank's (2023) World Development Indicators data.

Figure 0.2   Share of manufacturing value added in selected African countries

Africa is perceived as a 'latecomer' to technological innovation (Lee, 2019a). Theoretical and empirical evidence points to the advantages that 'latecomers' have over countries already industrialized. This includes the lessons that we can learn from the examples of the industrialized countries. The difficulty in closing the gap revolves around general challenges, as well as technology-specific challenges such as internet infrastructure and accessibility. Nonetheless, progress is under way as broadband internet penetration rates have increased from 0 to 19 million between 2000 and 2010 (Ojong, 2016). Elsewhere in this volume we show how this trend has continued, and heightened during the Covid-19 pandemic.

Schlogl (2020) describes the use of technology leapfrogging versus technology creeping in terms of how different domains are affected. According to Schlogl (2020), an example of technological leapfrogging in trade is the offshoring with technology transfers, compared to technology creeping when value-added erosion takes place due to global supply chain participation. Concerning the environment, technology leaping represents efficiency gains, green technology, as well as carbon decoupling, whereas technology creeping consists of growing energy consumption and electronic waste with a rise in emissions.

Added to the above line of argument on the lack of capabilities especially in Africa, the risks associated with technological leapfrogging (Lee, 2019b) are discussed in this volume. Gross (2019) offers an analysis of the dangers for Africa in shifting employment away from the least productive sector of agriculture. The overall productivity has not increased because employment is not increasing in manufacturing. Instead, employment has moved to low productive sectors such as service sectors and informal activities. Unfortunately, industrialization has declined in Sub-Saharan Africa since the 1970s. Moreover, the threat of being reliant on the resources sector with its highly volatile and declining commodity prices is a further reason for concern around Africa's long-term sustainable growth. Gross (2019) warns that these trends prevent Sub-Saharan African economies from diversifying.

An alternative might be for Africa to focus on other sectors than manufacturing, for example, faster convergence rates within service sectors, to enhance possibilities for catching up. Rodrik (2013), for instance, highlighted that the traditional or so-called natural structural transformation process would include manufacturing, whereas China is a formidable competitor with its cheap labour, and therefore latecomer countries could rather find an alternative path. The upgrading of the home market in turn will necessitate greater emphasis on income distribution and the health of the middle class as integral to a growth strategy. Since the convergence in the services sector is faster, it creates an opportunity for leapfrogging, which would require more social capabilities for absorption than technological capabilities (Ghani & O'Connell, 2014). Social capabilities include institutional quality, capacity of states, as well as education and social equality. Rodrik (2013) emphasizes in this regard that as an economy develops, the dualism between modern and traditional sectors disappears and economic activities become more complex across the board. For this reason, the region needs strong fundamentals since growth driven by structural transformation runs out of steam and falters without this foundational support.

Further research is required in exploring these alternative routes of structural transformation to enhance economic development. We must emphasize that context matters considering the heterogeneity that exists between African countries, and in several of the chapters we advance the contextualization framework as a lens through which to view leapfrogging.

THE CHAPTERS IN THIS VOLUME

Our volume opens with Chapter 1 as a reflection by David Teece, Kieran Brown, and Phil Alves on the management capabilities that are the bedrock of successful firms. They argue that for technology leapfrogging to occur, there is a need to close the management gap that exists at present. Sub-Saharan Africa is poised for growth, with large, dynamic populations in many of its economies. Technological and business advances in the rest of the world are available to African entrepreneurs to leapfrog past previous stages of business development. As governments attempt to clear various institutional and other hurdles to growth, they should not overlook the need to build and support the managerial capabilities of private firms. The authors briefly review the dynamic capabilities framework and then summarize the literature on management in Sub-Saharan Africa, including the current state of management education and support for entrepreneurs. They conclude with suggestions for a set of generic interventions that can be adapted to local conditions. First, firms must develop (and governments should encourage) development of firm-level dynamic capabilities. Second, we must reimagine how business school education is designed, and delivered. Third, we should build learning and mentoring networks, including international connectivity opportunities for firms. Finally, further research should be encouraged on fostering high-growth firms able to take advantage of leapfrogging technologies.

Entrepreneurial growth firms are the focus of Chapter 2, in which Ethné Swartz, Christopher Denecke, and Caren Scheepers explore the flows of risk capital (both venture capital and angel investments) into four African countries. They use investment data from Crunchbase to visualize how entrepreneurial firms are growing in local economies, transforming Africa through technology leapfrogging in four countries: Ghana, Kenya, Nigeria, and South Africa. The authors adopt a broad definition of entrepreneurship that includes individuals who enact agentic behaviours, as they pursue opportunities and solve problems in response to the contexts in which they operate. This equates to managers, startups, and other firm founders who are building firms in Africa, irrespective of the size of the firm. Using investment data from Crunchbase to construct a data set spanning the 2006 to 2020 period and providing visualizations of these economies based on new (or renewing) ventures in each of the four countries, the chapter harnesses visualization tools to provide a data-rich and contextual illustration to show what leapfrogging means in each of the countries. It suggests the possible trends for the firms that will become the future providers. Technological leapfrogging enables citizens of these countries to find modern ways of accessing services to live their lives. African firms are providing services that transform basic economic activities to improve efficiency and connectivity, including financial transactions, access to medical and food transaction and delivery tools, as well as the growth of e-commerce.

In Chapter 3, Marianne Matthee and Caren Scheepers demonstrate that the fourth industrial revolution offers myriad opportunities for countries to fast-track their growth and development by becoming more productive and competitive and by expanding employment, thereby giving their economies much-needed momentum. The Covid-19 pandemic demonstrated how quickly the world was able to adapt to virtual forms of communication and work, with technology playing a central role in this transition. However, the pandemic also exposed deep economic and technological divisions in the world, with many countries – particularly in Africa – currently at risk of lagging further behind as the fourth industrial revolution gathers speed. In the face of many countries' developmental shortcomings and relative digital isolation, the concept of technological leapfrogging is gaining ground. Matthee and Scheepers define technological leapfrogging as a process whereby countries or industry sectors 'skip' or streamline more traditional, protracted, and/or costly stages of development by leveraging emerging technologies with a view to achieving more rapid and cost-efficient results. Leapfrogging also affords entrepreneurs a better chance of scaling up their businesses and contributing meaningfully to the economy. Despite its benefits, technological leapfrogging will only be successful if the 'basics' are in place (a reliable energy supply, a sound education system, good physical and digital infrastructure, a coherent policy environment, among others) and the different stakeholders are aligned in their thinking. The authors further consider how technological leapfrogging could be a game changer for Africa as far as its inclusive growth and development prospects are concerned. They examine the link between economic growth and structural transformation, noting that the fourth industrial revolution offers innumerable opportunities for countries to accelerate their rate of growth, while also making it more inclusive. The authors discuss the concept of technological leapfrogging, and the circumstances in which it is most likely to occur, as well as the critical success factors that are required that drive it. The authors put Africa's digital ecosystem under the spotlight, critically evaluate the continent's digital preparedness, discuss how countries can leverage emerging technologies to narrow their digital divide, and create more broad-based and sustainable economies. As Africa is far from homogeneous, however, we emphasize that context matters. Thus, if technological leapfrogging is to gain traction in Africa, countries' unique characteristics and varying levels of development need to be taken into consideration.

In Chapter 4, Michelle Montague-Mfuni, Frances Fabian, and Caren Scheepers explore the expansion of intra-continental collaborations through African tech hubs. The authors argue that such collaborations, composed of technology hubs working together within and across countries, provide opportunities for creating pan-African innovation platforms. Using leading-edge technology capabilities, these platforms advance African imperatives for greater intra-continental cooperation and targeted alleviation of poverty. This chapter suggests a cat-egorization of African tech hubs that can help promote hub collaborations through designing effective structures. Specifically, the chapter proposes that technology hub collaborations are the ideal form for evolving technology innovation by providing 'ambidexterity' in managing exploration and exploitation capacities, as well as investing in spring-boarding opportunities. Technology hub collaborations develop synergistic value from shared identity and network relationships that promote Ubuntu ethics. As a result, members of tech hub collaborations benefit from drawing on expertise from firms devoted to explorative learning from advanced technology centres, as well as those focused on exploitation sensitive to African contexts. The authors propose a conceptual framework for advancing and advocating for the advancement of African tech hub collaborations, and offer practical examples of hub collaborations that helped provide effective responses to the Covid-19 pandemic.

In Chapter 5, Njuguna Ndung'u and Alex Oguso argue that leapfrogging in finance is one of the most critical and evident examples of the power of technological leapfrogging in Africa. This chapter pieces together discussions on the evolution of digital financial services in Africa that has pushed financial inclusion and leapfrogging in the financial sector in the continent. The innovation, growth, and success of retail electronic payment platforms starting from M-Pesa in Kenya in 2007 has unified this concept to a menu of digital financial services that is accessible, efficient, transparent, and safe. This has allowed provision of more information and practical solutions that have built a platform of avenues through which technology is leapfrogging financial development in Africa. Ndung'u and Oguso demonstrate that digital transformation in various sectors of the economy, supported by an efficient electronic payment system, will generate opportunities for the next diverse and sustainable growth frontier in African economies. Furthermore, the chapter argues that the digital revolution experienced across Africa could allow the countries to enhance the prospects of the fourth industrial revo-lution across the continent.

In Chapter 6, Michele Ruiters and Motshedisi Mathibe cover financial leapfrogging and gender lens investments for gender equality in Sub-Saharan Africa. The lack of gender equality has been a systemic issue in the business and investment community throughout its existence, but there is growing evidence that investing in gender equality will produce positive benefits. Conventional financial institutions are locked into path-dependent patterns in the way they service their clients, while financial-sector newcomers – impact-investing firms – can leapfrog conventional investment practices and act as catalysts for shifting informal norms and customs that negatively affect women as entrepreneurs, employees, and suppliers. Gender lens investing plays a critical role in guiding investments with the objective of women's empowerment and more equitable workplaces and communities. This chapter conveys new stories about how entrepreneurial firms are transforming African business through financial leapfrogging, and how investments promoting women-owned businesses will advance local and regional economies. While research on gender lens investing remains scant, this chapter explores the practical strategies for profitable gender lens investing, unpacking some of the investment opportunities within the infrastructure sector.

The impact of cultural approaches to time – context, political alliances, and investments in Africa – are discussed by Arielle Emmett in Chapter 7. The author spent nine months in Kenya teaching at a Kenyan University and collecting qualitative data among Kenyan and Chinese workers, employers, and other stakeholders. Emmett argues that there is a Chinese-Kenyan disconnect and that technological leapfrogging cannot be assessed in isolation from local context in Kenya, a nation known for its eye-catching infrastructure, tech startups, and prodigious reputation for government borrowing and graft. Emmett argues that technological leapfrogging facilitated by Chinese investment is simultaneously a prime mover and a distraction from Kenya's urgent need for social justice and economic reform. The chapter uses qualitative interviews with a range of Kenyans and Chinese to describe the impact of two infrastructure projects conceived as 'game changers': the Standard Gauge Railway and the LAPSSET Corridor originating in Lamu on Kenya's southeast coast. The chapter shows, using interview data collected during 2018–2019, how Kenyans and Chinese assess the benefits and negatives of these infrastructure projects based on labour impacts, divergent perceptions of time, time management, and investment payback. The chapter's narrative structure uses explanatory sub-themes, interweaving literature with interviews, and concludes with key questions regarding the future transformation of life for Kenyan citizens.

Alet Erasmus' contribution in Chapter 8 turns to the home and the double-edged sword that technological innovation is in that domain. In an era where technology is changing rapidly and significantly influences the way people live, changes in household technology – even on a basic level – have certainly not taken a back seat. Erasmus' chapter provides an overview of the relevance of changes in household technology, particularly in Africa, of how people perceive, appreciate, distrust, or even reject novel technologies designed to improve households' quality of life. Indications are that although technologies such as home appliances and electricity may cause excitement and can be a blessing in some households, they may, unfortunately, also cause concerns among those who are ill equipped to appreciate unfamiliar commodities in their homes and workplaces. Essentially, leapfrogging encompasses change fuelled by innovation, and although technological innovation mostly precedes leapfrogging, it is not the only determinant of its success (Gallagher, 2006; Tigabu et al., 2015). Equally important, the author argues, is the social impact of radical change, as a society needs to understand how it will benefit from any innovation relative to more familiar alternatives (Hackett, 2012; Tukker, 2005) so that they can embrace change rather than feel intimidated. In this chapter, we adopt a positive stance and indicate how access to electricity and other technological resources can improve people's living conditions and provide opportunities for African societies that are desperately seeking to advance. The concept of leapfrogging is introduced to indicate that technological change often occurs at a fast pace, even unexpectedly, with diverse consequences. The author frames the discussion on technological leapfrogging on the assumptions of resource advantage theory.

Remaining in the domain of the home and societal impact, Ali Parry and Wilma Viviers, in Chapter 9, consider whether digital technologies can assist Africa to leapfrog its education gap. The authors begin with the vision of Horace Mann (Duncan, 2021), that 'Education is the great equaliser of the conditions of men', and that education is widely regarded as both the bedrock of society and the springboard to professional and personal development. With a good education, many people – both younger and older – are able to recognize and exploit economic opportunities and find fulfilment in various forms of work and leisure activities. There is also a strong link between a country's level of economic development and the quality and equity of its education system. Yet, while school attendance in developing countries has risen steadily over the years, there is a significant educational gap between developed and developing countries. A marked educational divide is also evident within most developing countries (Winthrop & McGivney, 2017).

Of all the regions in the world, Africa is the furthest behind in terms of educational achievement, with Sub-Saharan Africa's performance being the most disappointing. Of the roughly 60 million children of primary school-going age in the world who for various reasons do not go to school, 54 per cent live in Sub-Saharan Africa (UNESCO, 2018). Moreover, only about 29 per cent of students in Sub-Saharan Africa complete secondary school, compared with 41 per cent in South Asia, 63 per cent in Latin America, 64 per cent in the Middle East and North Africa, and 73 per cent in East and Southeast Asia (Cilliers, 2021). Another alarming statistic is that only four out of every 100 children in Africa are likely to enrol for postgraduate studies as young adults (United Nations, 2018). Girls and women are often discriminated against when it comes to educational opportunities on the continent.

Among the factors that contribute to the parlous state of education in many African countries is a shortage of qualified and competent teachers and poor or non-existent infrastructure, which makes the process of teaching and learning very difficult. The debilitating effects of poverty on educational progress is a recurring theme. So, too, is the mismatch between school and university curricula and the knowledge and skills required by business. Clearly, conventional approaches to education on the continent need to undergo a paradigm shift – from the large-scale, government-funded education model to more focused initiatives aimed at producing cohorts of knowledgeable, skilled individuals capable of moving into in-demand jobs across all economic sectors. If Africa is lagging so far behind the rest of the world, should it be exploiting the technological leapfrogging phenomenon to catch up?

To many observers, Africa's mobile revolution in recent years is one of the clearest examples of leapfrogging in action. Bridging the gap in the financial services arena has broadened economic activity and helped to accelerate development in several African countries. Leapfrogging is also evident in sectors such as energy, health, and agriculture, where the use of data analytics and artificial intelligence is helping businesses to become more productive and to satisfy market demand more cost effectively (IFC & World Bank, 2019; Pilling, 2018).

There is no clear consensus, however, on whether education lends itself well to leapfrogging, particularly in Africa. After all, education is traditionally long term in nature, with knowledge acquired in a progressive, linear fashion, at least at the primary and secondary school levels. Moreover, many African countries still lack the basic requirements for productive, online learning experiences: a reliable electricity supply, appropriate telecommunications infrastructure, and accessible (including affordable) digital devices and internet services. The question therefore becomes whether digital technologies can help Africa to leapfrog its massive education gap, connect more people to quality jobs, and create societies that are more inclusive. The authors present a cross-section of views on the plausibility of leapfrogging in an educational context, and the implications for Africa, given its specific needs and circumstances. The authors provide selected examples of leapfrogging in the educational sphere and conclude with some policy recommendations.

Turning to South Africa itself, in Chapter 10, Asmitha Tiekam and Hugh Myres use qualitative data from senior managers in South African firms to ponder what leadership skills firms must foster to benefit from digital transformation. Digital transformation, with all its rapid new technological advances in disruptive technologies, is affecting the way we work and leadership in the workplace. Leaders have realized they now need new skills and new ways of leading. Africa is a continent of economic opportunity and has a large youth population. Digital transformation in Africa can help leapfrog the current legacy system challenges and leadership competencies through gaining the skills needed to accelerate digital transformation. This chapter explores the literature around digital transformation in Africa and South Africa, and various forms of leadership and digital leadership skills. The authors present their research with 17 South African digital leaders who carried out successful digital transformation projects in their organizations, and review the findings of the type of leader and digital leadership skills required for successful digital transformation. Complex Leadership Theory undergirds our theoretical approach and we explore whether adaptive leadership is relevant for the disruptive environment of digital transformation. The Skills Strataplex framework serves as a foundation to understand whether traditional leadership skills still apply. The authors conclude with a discussion of the Adaptive Digital Leadership Skills Model that we developed based on their research with South African digital leaders and suggest as a prerequisite there is a need for skills to carry out successful digital transformation of their firms.

Joel Malen, Paul Vaaler, and Ivy Zhang explore the concept of legal leapfrogging by firms in emerging markets in Chapter 11. They investigate how location choice carries implications for legal protections and access to capital, increasingly important for African high-growth firms such as Nigeria's Jumia (Pence, 2019), South Africa's Naspers, and its subsidiary Prosus. This issue is likely to become an increasing trend, as more growth firms that are African emerge and require access to capital markets. Many of these firms are technology based, and this year, the *Financial Times* published its inaugural list of the top 50 fastest-growing African firms (Pilling, 2022b), including many that enabled technology leapfrogging during the Covid-19 pandemic.

International management researchers commonly assume that firm location defines where it operates, but firms may also change relevant corporate governance standards – engage in legal 'leapfrogging' – by cross-listing shares in foreign countries where they have little or no operational presence. The authors ask why and how firms from emerging-market countries leapfrog legally to the US through cross-listing that 'bonds' them to US laws offering stronger protection to investors, particularly minority shareholding investors, and thereby fostering better managerial oversight, broader firm ownership, greater liquidity, and lower capital costs. The authors develop a cross-level theoretical framework to explain emerging-market firm tendencies to leapfrog legally as a function of three factors: (1) a firm's home-country legal system; (2) a firm's home-country rule of law strength; and (3) a firm's growth options. Analyses of US cross-listing tendencies from 1996 to 2007 among 7,453 firms from 22 emerging-market countries suggests that weaker home-country legal protection and more firm growth opportunities render shifts in legal presence more likely. These core findings prove robust to reasonable variation in model specification, estimation, and sampling strategies. The findings highlight the importance of broadening research about how and why firms vary location non-operationally as well as understanding how country-level institutions and firm-level characteristics influence such moves individually and in combination. That broadening would especially benefit business research on Africa, where countries offering weaker legal protection stunt domestic access to capital vital to domestic firms with high growth potential.

Continuing the focus on legal issues, in Chapter 12 Ashley Sperbeck explores how intellectual property regimes and innovations in infrastructure help to promote the growth of technological markets. The author argues that coastal countries in Sub-Saharan Africa such as Kenya, Nigeria, and South Africa have relatively sophisticated economies with direct access to trade and cultural exchange. The chapter begins with the assumption that capturing gains from investing in innovation is critical (Tidd & Bessant, 2013). After introducing forms of intellectual property, the author applies David Teece's research regarding 'appropriability' of technology as a framework for analysis. After assessing the strengths and weaknesses of these countries in view of Teece's framework, the author examines deterrents to technological innovation. Based on these concepts, she proposes a mathematical solution that predicts the ability of each of Kenya, Nigeria, and South Africa to contribute to Africa poised as one of the worlds' fastest-growing technological markets and a destination for 'technology tourism'.

Lyal White, Liezl Rees, and Nikitta Hahn close the volume with Chapter 13, which is based on key findings of a 2022 report they published in collaboration with the Institute for Social and Economic Research and Policy at Columbia University, the Academy of Political Science, and the Brenthurst Foundation. The authors incorporate key insights from that research, taking a retrospective view of key issues and developments in Africa that are important to the continent's post-Covid-19 pandemic recovery and trajectory. The continent must address five key developmental challenges exacerbated by the pandemic in order to accelerate recovery: pervasive inequality, a lack of statistical data, continental barriers to connecting with the digital economy, the impact of vulnerable informal business networks, and limitations in access to quality education.

Given the size of the continent and differences across sub-regions and countries, the chapter focused on five countries for in-depth analysis around these five areas of development, including Egypt, Ethiopia, Kenya, Nigeria, and South Africa. These are all significant countries in their respective sub-regions, carrying substantial weight in terms of economic size, population, and political influence in the broader African context. As was the case with Africa's economic growth and development before Covid-19, the continent's trajectory over the pandemic period and pathway to recovery have not been uniform across all countries and will continue to be uneven going forward. This is particularly true for the five countries in this chapter. The economic and political state of each country before Covid-19 will determine the pace and nature of their recovery in the long term. The authors argue that Covid-19 has exacerbated and highlighted the inequalities and widening divides prevalent in day-to-day life across the continent. This is particularly evident in the education sector – between those who can afford access to the internet and those who are disconnected from the rest of the world. Given the dynamic environment and rapidly changing Covid-19 landscape globally, this chapter relied on secondary research methods in order to access the latest pertinent information and data. This included the collection of information from respected internet data portals and databases, newspaper articles, online health and science journals, and special reports from organizations such as the World Health Organization and World Bank.

CLOSING REMARKS

We extend a special thanks to Edward Elgar and its staff, who have been most helpful throughout this entire process. We also warmly thank all of the authors who submitted their manuscripts for consideration for this book. They showed their desire to share their knowledge and experience with the book's readers and a willingness to present their research and their views for possible challenge by their peers. We also thank the reviewers, who provided excellent independent and incisive consideration of the anonymous submissions.

We hope that this compendium of chapters and themes stimulates and contributes to the ongoing debate surrounding the topic of technological leapfrogging in Africa. The chapters in this book can help to fill some gaps in what we know while stimulating further thought and action.

REFERENCES

Amankwah-Amoah, J. (2015). Solar energy in Sub-Saharan Africa: The challenges and opportunities of technological leapfrogging. *Thunderbird International Business Review*, *57*(1), 15–31.

Baker, T., & Welter, F. (2018). Contextual entrepreneurship: An interdisciplinary perspective. *Foundations and Trends® in Entrepreneurship*, *14*(4), 357–426.

Batinge, B., Musango, J. K., & Brent, A. C. (2017). Leapfrogging to renewable energy: The opportunity for unmet electricity markets. *South African Journal of Industrial Engineering*, *28*(4), 32–49.

Blimpo, M. P., Minges, M., Kouame, W. A., Azomahou, T., Lartey, E., Meniago, C., & Buitano, M. (2017). Leapfrogging: The key to Africa's development? From constraints to investment opportunities. World Bank Group, Third Investing in Africa Forum, Dakar, 25–27 September. http://documents .worldbank.org/curated/en/121581505973379739/pdf/119849-WP-PUBLIC-Africa-Leapfrogging -text-with-dividers-9-20-17-web.pdf. Accessed 22 December 2018.

Christensen, C., Ojomo, E., & Dillon, K. (2019). *The Prosperity Paradox: How Innovation can Life Nations out of Poverty*. New York: Harper Collins.

Cilliers, J. (2021). *The Future of Africa: Challenges and Opportunities*. Cham: Palgrave Macmillan.

Cook, T. (2015). M-Pesa 101. FSDKenya. http://fsd.circle.co.ke/wp-content/uploads/2015/08/M-PESA -customer-growth.png

Cuthbertson, A. (2016). SweepSouth wants to transform South Africa's domestic service industry. *Newsweek*, 30 November 30. www.newsweek.com/sweepsouth-south-africa-domestic-service -industry-pandor-525778. Accessed 15 September 2019.

Diop, M. (2017). Africa can enjoy leapfrog development. www.worldbank.org/en/news/opinion/2017/ 10/11/africa-can-enjoy-leapfrog-development. Accessed 8 January 2019.

Duncan, A. (2021). Education: The great equalizer. www.britannica.com/topic/Education-The-Great -Equalizer-2119678. Accessed 27 June 2023.

Faria, J. (2022). Employment in services in Africa 2010–2020. Statista. www.statista.com/statistics/ 1230875/employment-in-services-as-share-of-total-in-africa/#statisticContainer. Accessed 10 July 2022.

Fukui, R., Arderne, C. J., & Kelly, T. (2019). Africa's connectivity gap: Can a map tell the story? World Bank Blogs. https://blogs.worldbank.org/digital-development/africas-connectivity-gap-can-map-tell -story#comments. Accessed 5 June 2023.

Gallagher, K.S. (2006). Limits to leapfrogging in energy technologies? Evidence from the Chinese automobile industry. *Energy Policy*, 34, 383–394.

Gates Foundation. (2018). Goalkeepers: The stories behind the data 2018. www.gatesfoundation.org/ goalkeepers/report/2018-report/. Accessed 15 September 2019.

Gross, A.-K. (2019). Sub-Saharan Africa and the 4th Industrial Revolution: Technological leapfrogging as a strategy to enhance economic growth? Master's thesis, Lund University. https://lup.lub.lu.se/ student-papers/search/publication/8986790

Hackett, M. T. (2012). The everyday political economy of social enterprise: Lessons from Grameen Skakti in Bangladesh. PhD thesis, University of Adelaide. https://digital.library.adelaide.edu.au/dspace/bitstream/2440/83217/8/02whole.pdf

IFC & World Bank. (2019). Fresh ideas about business in emerging markets. IFCThoughtLeadership. Note 69, July. https://documents1.worldbank.org/curated/en/539371567673606214/pdf/The-Role-of-Artificial-Intelligence-in-Supporting-Development-in-Emerging-Markets.pdf

Lee, K. (2019a). *The Art of Economic Catch-Up: Barriers, Detours, and Leapfrogging in Innovation Systems*. Cambridge: Cambridge University Press.

Lee, K. (2019b). Economics of technological leapfrogging. Inclusive and Sustainable Industrial Development Working Paper Series, Working Paper 17/2019. United Nations Industrial Development Organization.

Lee, K., Ramanayake, S., & Wonkyu, S. (2021). Three barriers to structural changes and catch-up by the latecomers. In L. Alcorta, N. Foster-McGregor, B. Verspagen, & A. Szirmai (eds), *New Perspectives on Structural Change: Causes and Consequences of Structural Change in the Global Economy*. Oxford: Oxford University Press.

Leke, A., & Yeboah-Amankwah, S. (2018). Africa: A crucible for creativity. Lessons from the continents' breakout businesses. *Harvard Business Review*, November–December, 116–125.

Leke, A., Chironga, M., & Desvaux, G. (2018). Africa's overlooked business revolution. *McKinsey Quarterly*, November. www.mckinsey.com/featured-insights/middle-east-and-africa/africas-business-revolution. Accessed 5 June 2023.

Library of Congress. (2010). Library of Congress illustrated guide: Africana collections. www.loc.gov/rr/amed/guide/afr-countrylist.html. Accessed 21 July 2022.

Lock, H. (2019). Fight the fakes: How to beat the $200bn medicine counterfeiters. *The Guardian*, 5 June. www.theguardian.com/global-development/2019/jun/05/fake-medicine-makers-blockchain-artificial-intelligence. Accessed 5 June 2023.

Matthee, M., & Scheepers, C. B. (2019). Can Africa make the leap? Contextual entrepreneurship in disruptive mobile technology for growth. Academy of Management Conference Proceedings, Professional Development Workshop, Boston, MA.

Ménard, C., & Shirley, M. M. (2014). The contribution of Douglass North to new institutional economics. In S. Galiani & I. Sened (eds), *Economic Institutions, Rights, Growth, and Sustainability: The Legacy of Douglass North*. Cambridge: Cambridge University Press.

Nature. (2022). Editorial: Africa is bringing vaccine manufacturing home. *Nature*, 602(184).

Naudé, W. (2019, October). Three varieties of Africa's industrial future. IZA Institute of Labour Economics Discussion Paper Series, DP No. 12678. http://ftp.iza.org/dp12678.pdf

Nguimkeu, P., & Zeufack, A. G. (2019). Manufacturing in structural change in Africa. Policy Research Working Paper No. 8992. Washington, DC: World Bank Group.

North, D. C. (1990). *Institutions, Institutional Change, and Economic Performance*. New York: Cambridge University Press.

Ojong, N. (2016). Remittances, mobile phones and informality: Insights from Cameroon. *African Journal of Science, Technology, Innovation and Development*, 8(3), 299–308.

Oranye, N. (2017). *Taking on Silicon Valley: How Africa's Innovators Will Shape Its Future*. Nnamdi Oranye, self-published.

Pence, E. (2019). The real controversy about Jumia: Why did it list on the NYSE? Center for Strategic and International Studies, Blog, 13 June. www.csis.org/analysis/real-controversy-about-jumia-why-did-it-list-nyse#:~:text=It's%20no%20secret%20that%20Jumia,capital%20markets%20and%20stock%20exchanges. Accessed 5 June 2023.

Pilling, D. (2018). The big read innovation. African economy: The limits of leapfrogging. *Financial Times*, 13 August. www.ft.com/content/052b0a34-9b1b-11e8-9702-5946bae86e6d. Accessed 27 August 2022.

Pilling, D. (2022a). Africa resists pressure to put emissions before growth. *Financial Times Special Report African Development: Renewables*, 26 August. www.ft.com/content/c4ff5997-2b04-4f07-9252-12da0d2f8b02. Accessed 27 August 2022.

Pilling, D. (2022b). FT Ranking: Africa's fastest growing companies 2022. *Financial Times*, 2 May. www.ft.com/africas-fastest-growing-companies. Accessed 5 June 2023.

Rodrik, D. (2013, June). The past, present, and future of economic growth. Global Citizen Foundation Working Paper 1. www.law.nyu.edu/sites/default/files/upload_documents/GCF_Rodrik-working -paper-1_-6.17.131_0.pdf

Saleh, M. (2022). African countries with the highest share of global population living below the extreme poverty line in 2022. *Statista*, 15 July. www.statista.com/statistics/1228553/extreme-poverty-as-share -of-global-population-in-africa-by-country/. Accessed 27 August 2022.

Schlogl, L. (2020). Leapfrogging into the unknown. The future of structural change in the developing world. UNU-World Institute for Development Economics Research WIDER, Working Paper 2020/25. United Nations University.

Signé, L. (2018, September). The potential of manufacturing and industrialization in Africa: Trends, opportunities and strategies. Africa Growth Initiative at Brookings. www.brookings.edu/wp-content/ uploads/2018/09/Manufacturing-and-Industrialization-in-Africa-Signe-20180921.pdf

Stiglitz, J. E., Lin, J. Y., & Patel, E. (2013). *The Industrial Policy Revolution II: Africa in the 21st Century*. Basingstoke: Palgrave Macmillan.

Tidd, J., & Bessant, J. (2013). *Managing Innovation: Integrating Technological, Market and Organizational Change*, 5th Edition. Chichester: Wiley.

Tigabu, A. D., Berkhout. F., & van Beukering, P. (2015). Technology innovation systems and technology diffusion: Adoption of bio-digestion in an emerging innovation system in Rwanda. *Technological Forecasting & Social Change*, 90, 318–330.

The Economist (2016). Look before you leap. Referring to Schumpeter: The notion of leapfrogging poor infrastructure in Africa needs to come back down to earth. *The Economist*, 4 August. www.economist .com/business/2016/08/04/look-before-you-leap. Accessed 29 July 2022.

Toefy, T., & Scheepers, C. (2019). *SweepSouth South Africa: Contextually Intelligent Female Leadership of Entrepreneurial Domestic Services*. London, ON: Ivey Publishing.

Tukker, A. (2005). Leapfrogging into the future: Developing for sustainability. International *Journal of Innovation and Sustainable Development*, 1, 65–84.

United Nations. (2018). Africa grapples with huge disparities in education: Higher enrolment numbers mask exclusion and inefficiencies. www.un.org/africarenewal/magazine/december-2017-march -2018/africa-grapples-huge-disparities-education

UNDP. (2017). UNDP'S strategy for inclusive and sustainable growth. www.undp.org/content/dam/ undp/library/Poverty%20Reduction/UNDPs%20Inclusive%20and%20Sustainable%20Growth-final .pdf. Accessed 8 January 2019.

UNESCO. (2018). Accountability in education: Meeting our commitments. Global Education Monitoring Report Summary 2017/8. https://reliefweb.int/report/world/global-education-monitoring-report -20178-accountability-education-meeting-our

Van Alstyne, M., Parker, G., & Choudary, S. (2016). Pipelines, platforms and the new rules of strategy. *Harvard Business Review*, 94, 54–60.

Wadhwani, R. D., Kirsch, D., Welter, F., Gartner, W., & Jones, G. (2020). Context, time, and change: Historical approaches to entrepreneurship research. *Strategic Entrepreneurship Journal*, 1–17.

Winthrop, R., & McGivney, E. (2017). Can we leapfrog? The potential of education innovations to rapidly accelerate progress. Brookings. https://files.eric.ed.gov/fulltext/ED583015.pdf

World Bank. (2017a). *Africa's Pulse: Focus on Closing the Infrastructure Gap to Increase Growth*. Washington, DC: World Bank.

World Bank. (2017b). State of electricity access report 2017. Washington, DC: World Bank. www .worldbank.org/en/topic/energy/publication/sear. Accessed 15 September 2019.

World Bank. (2018). The global Findex database: Measuring financial inclusion and the fintech revolu- tion. www.worldbank.org/en/news/press-release/2018/04/19/financial-inclusion-on-the-rise-but-gaps -remain-global-findex-database-shows. Accessed 15 September 2019.

World Bank. (2023). World Development Indicators Data. https://databank.worldbank.org/source/ world-development-indicators. Accessed 27 January 2023.

1. Technology leapfrogging in Sub-Saharan Africa: jumping the management capabilities gap

David Teece, Kieran Brown, and Phil Alves

INTRODUCTION

Africa is often characterized as poised for growth.[1] Internet and smartphone penetration continues to spread, and sophisticated cloud computing infrastructure is available to firms on an as-needed basis. Thanks to developments like these, Africa's youthful entrepreneurs have the opportunity to leapfrog over traditional developmental stages, such as becoming suppliers to multinational firms, by deploying the latest technology and business models (World Bank, 2017). African economies face multiple challenges; but no matter what other improvements they make, their growth rates will remain low unless they can create a new crop of high-impact local firms capable of competing internationally and growing profitably.

The missing pieces of the puzzle are generally recognized to be top-down elements such as institutions, infrastructure, and finance—gaps that governments and their development partners can potentially fill. To the extent that human capital requirements are addressed, it is typically in the form of education and entrepreneurship, the need for both of which remains substantial. But this ignores a skills gap and a management capability gap that also need to be addressed, as this chapter will explain.

Leapfrog development depends not just on entrepreneurship (in the narrow sense of starting a business) but also on the capabilities and decisions of managers if it is to contribute to durable growth. Most policy initiatives assume that, once firms are created, they will be well run. In reality, the viability of firms that receive support must be assessed in terms of not only their business plan but also the underlying skills of employees and, in particular, the quality of the firm's management: the team's experience, personalities, technological knowledge, financial awareness, market research, and personal networks.

The concept of management capabilities is relevant to all firms, regardless of size. It is most associated with larger firms, in which managerial functions are shared across a team. In small firms, all managerial functions will often be carried out solely by the entrepreneur(s), but it is important to distinguish among the different roles that managers fulfill because, for example, the skill set to launch a business is distinct from the skills needed to manage and grow it.

---

[1] See, for example, the World Bank site "Poised for Growth: Africa's Development Future," May 9, 2019. www.worldbank.org/en/news/feature/2019/05/09/poised-for-growth-africa-s-development-future.

A more nuanced appreciation and understanding of the managerial function can provide vital support for pro-leapfrogging policies. After 1978, when China began liberalizing its economy, for example, it eventually discovered a need to introduce formal management training. From a handful of piloted MBA programs in 1991, China's business education has grown to more than 200 programs with tens of thousands of students (Zhang, 2013). But just increasing the raw output from schools is not enough because it takes time to develop high-quality management programs and time for new graduates to gain practical experience. China has no shortage of entrepreneurs, capital, or access to appropriate technology; yet its growth, as phenomenal as it has been, is generally considered to be hindered by a scarcity of experienced managerial talent (e.g., Lane & Pollner, 2008; Caye, Michael, Lee, & Nettesheim, 2012; Black & Morrison, 2019).

This chapter will open up the closed "black box" of the firm using the dynamic capabilities framework (Teece, 2017) to analyze how managers and management capabilities contribute to leapfrogging and growth. Capabilities, as used here, are based in both the organizational routines of a business and in the mental frameworks of its managers (Teece, 2012). "Ordinary" capabilities, which support operations, are critical for efficiency. They are necessary but not sufficient for establishing competitive advantage. Even more valuable are "dynamic" capabilities that support investment direction, organizational design, and strategy development. The core categories of dynamic capability are (a) sensing (outward strategic awareness and cognition), (b) seizing (asset orchestration), and (c) transforming (adaptation and resilience).

The chapter begins by briefly laying out the dynamic capabilities framework, with particular emphasis on the three roles that managers play. Next, we turn to Sub-Saharan Africa, noting that, while the potential for leapfrogging older stages of industrial development is high, firms attempting to adopt advanced technologies still face numerous constraints (Oluwatobi et al., 2020). While policy interventions often target external constraints, such as infrastructure and finance, they are less likely to address a hidden but potentially fatal weakness in management capabilities. We briefly review the literature on African management, which has focused primarily on the implementation of ordinary capabilities. We also discuss prior literature on management education and the management development programs that target entrepreneurs and leaders in smaller companies. In light of the current state of management capabilities (and abstracting from the specific conditions of individual economies), we suggest a set of management-oriented interventions. A final section offers some concluding reflections.

THE DYNAMIC CAPABILITIES FRAMEWORK AND THE ROLE OF THE ENTREPRENEURIAL MANAGER

The mainstream economic model of the firm combines undifferentiated "labor," "capital," and "technology" to produce the output of a "representative firm." This simplification has its place, but it treats all firms as exactly the same—and it's certainly no guide to running an actual business.

A big reason that firms aren't all the same, even if they are producing the same product, is that they are managed by individuals pursuing distinct strategies and possibly addressing different market segments. It has been well documented that firm performance varies greatly across firms even if they share the same business environment (e.g., Bloom, Lemos, Sadun, Scur, & Van Reenen, 2014). Thus, when considering potential firm responses to leapfrogging windows of opportunity, it is important to consider factors internal to the firm such as managerial capabilities. Underlying the capabilities of managers are the capabilities of the organization, which are rooted in its established processes, values, and culture—and thus unique to each firm.

Just as each country in Sub-Saharan Africa has its own social, political, and business culture, the organizational culture of the entrepreneurial firm is distinct. Firms are embedded in the surrounding culture and its norms and must adapt to them, at least to some extent. However, entrepreneurial management makes its own culture through a combination of leadership, vision, and incentive design. Entrepreneurially managed firms are also more likely to be connected to international networks, which provide yet another influence on their organizational culture. When corporations invest overseas, as in the case of apparel manufacturers in Sub-Saharan Africa, they are both embedded locally and influenced by their home-country cultures (Morris, Plank, & Staritz, 2016).

A company's culture—including its mission, values, and management style—tends to be longer lasting and harder to change than many other outputs of management and is therefore a critical component of organizational design. For strong dynamic capabilities, the culture should be entrepreneurial rather than bureaucratic—for example, ensuring that small, early failures lead to learning rather than blaming (Danneels & Vestal, 2020). Management in the most innovative businesses is open to thoughtful criticism that forces the holders of a consensus view to sharpen (or, in some cases, abandon) their thinking (Nemeth, 1997). For example, companies can often become more responsive and innovative by flattening management hierarchies and decentralizing decision-making authority. However, when they decentralize, they need to guard against an erosion of the authority for resolving conflicts among different parts of the company, each trying to go its own way in terms of investment, marketing, or duplicative services (Lee & Edmondson, 2017).

At the firm level, most capabilities are those needed for running the business day to day in line with its current business plan. These are *ordinary capabilities*—mere table stakes in the game of competition.

In the long run, though, the success of the firm in competitive markets depends on higher-level activities that enable a firm to direct its operations toward high-demand uses, develop the ordinary capabilities (processes and routines) required for new lines of business, and effectively coordinate (or "orchestrate") internal and external resources to address a shifting business environment. These are called *dynamic capabilities*, which can be summarized as three groups of activities: *sensing* new opportunities and threats, *seizing* new business pathways by adjusting the product mix and/or business model, and *transforming* the firm to accommodate new capabilities and remain resilient to unforeseen changes (Teece, Pisano, & Shuen, 1997; Teece, 2007).

Capabilities have become increasingly recognized in the literature on economic growth and development. Nobel laureate Amartya Sen used the concept, but focused on the individual (Sen, 1985). He recognized that individuals differ greatly in their abilities to convert a given set of resources into outputs. The dynamic capabilities framework expands this principle to embrace differences in how individual organizations harness individuals' joint efforts.

Economist John Sutton (2002) has noted the importance of firm-level capabilities to enhance product quality and reduce cost as drivers of economic growth. This is part of what we referred to as "ordinary capabilities," enabling a firm to compete in its existing market. Nelson and Pack (1999) come closer to a dynamic capabilities theory of development by emphasizing the role of innovation and learning.

Building (or strengthening) an absent (or weak) capability can be costly and time consuming. But, if the capability is necessary for the firm's operating environment, the investment will be worthwhile.

The quality of management is critical to determining whether a firm's dynamic capabilities are strong or weak. This is not something that can be measured by a single test. Management is highly dependent on context; what works well in one country or even one firm with a particular history may produce poor results elsewhere (Waldman et al., 2012). For example, an informal management style that would be welcomed in the United States would be more likely seen by employees as disqualifying in Egypt (Javidan, Dorfman, De Luque, & House, 2006).

In firms of any size, managers need to fill one or more of three main roles as presented in Table 1.1. Operational management focuses on the efficient execution of current plans through budgeting, staffing, and so on. This skill set, which corresponds to what most business schools teach, drives the firm's ordinary capabilities.

Table 1.1   *Three roles of managers*

	Operational role	Entrepreneurial role	Leadership role
Responsibility	Planning and budgeting	Sensing and seizing	Propagating vision and values
Activities	Organizing and staffing	Orchestrating resources	Aligning people with strategy
Levers	Controls, audits, and problem solving	Investing in research and development, developing new business models	Motivating people
Goals	Technical efficiency and predictable results	Competitive advantage	Unity of purpose

Source: Teece, 2016.

Entrepreneurial management involves the ability to sense opportunities and shifts in the business environment, to coordinate the resources to exploit promising new avenues, and to develop plans to adapt the firm's business model. These functions, which must be coordinated across all levels of larger organizations, are core elements of the dynamic capabilities of the firm.

Leadership is required for implementing the changes needed to keep the firm tuned to the needs and opportunities of the business environment. Leadership skills are needed to get others in the organization to share a strategic vision and to want to help the organization to succeed. Leadership is another core element of a firm's dynamic capabilities.

Entrepreneurial and leadership skills are difficult to teach, but they can be nurtured by mentors and other guides if they're already present to some degree (e.g., Kunaka & Moos, 2019). These two skill sets together make up *entrepreneurial management* in the dynamic capabilities framework.

The managerial capabilities of firms are critical for driving the innovation that undergirds growth in productivity and improvements in living standards. In the instance of technological leapfrogging, managerial capabilities are key to recognizing opportunities, developing a business model, and managing the risk associated with adopting a newer technology. Managers must also guide the asset orchestration, organizational design, product design, and brand building that can lead to sustained profitability.

This is relevant to firms of all sizes. Analyzing the inability of small-scale, micro, and medium enterprises (SMMEs)—despite their proliferation—to alleviate poverty in South Africa, Rambe and Mosweunyane (2017, p. 290) argue that SMMEs must be founded upon "a systematic integration of a strong entrepreneurial orientation, solid managerial capabilities, sustainable resourcing, commercialization of business activities, and capacity development of SMME managers' skills." This is hard to measure, but circumstantial evidence of entrepreneurial management can be found when companies make changes for the better. A recent study of management innovation (the adoption of new methods or new structures) in small and medium enterprises in Cameroon confirmed its positive impact on overall firm performance (Boubakary, Moskolai, & Njang, 2020).

LEAPFROGGING BY AFRICAN COUNTRIES: HIGH POTENTIAL, HIDDEN WEAKNESS

Africa Offers Potentially Fertile Ground for Leapfrogging

African countries are far behind the frontrunners in terms of development. Of the 54 countries on the continent, only six (Botswana, Equatorial Guinea, Gabon, Namibia, South Africa) have achieved upper-middle-income status, according to the World Bank.[2] Even these continental leaders seem to be stuck in a middle-income trap. For example, South Africa has been a middle-income country for over 70 years. By comparison, South Korea spent 26 years in the middle-income category before reaching high-income status (Felipe, Abdon, & Kumar, 2012).

The global economy has undergone major shifts since the rise of late industrializers such as South Korea. Globalization has facilitated greater access to technology and learning opportunities for latecomers but requires different strategies than the export-led growth used in the past. Leapfrogging past declining technologies and business models offers opportunities for African countries to catch up.

The African continent has been identified as the next big growth market. This is in part due to its relatively younger population, regional economic integration, and investment in infrastructure (George, Corbishley, Khayesi, Haas, & Tihanyi, 2016). In addition to these positive African trends, the availability of digital networks, the economic crises resulting from the COVID-19 pandemic, and a movement toward regionalization of supply chains offer windows of opportunity for African countries to close gaps, at least partially, with frontrunner economies. Private investments can "leapfrog" past older technology that African economies had only partially adopted and use current-generation technologies and infrastructure. The potential to adopt the latest technologies at the same time as developed countries gives Africa a fighting chance in the global economy—perhaps for the first time. New thinking about risk reduction in global supply chains raises the possibility that more stages of production will be relocated to African countries, leveraging hemispheric demand for goods and services in addi-

---

[2] World Bank, World Development Indicators. https://databank.worldbank.org/source/world-development-indicators.

tion to the minimally processed primary products, like oil, minerals, and timber, that currently dominate exports.

However, the mere existence of windows of opportunity is insufficient to support leapfrogging. Firms must be able to mount appropriate responses to the opportunities, including making the right technology choices, as there are often multiple options available at any given point in time. The entrepreneur must also be able to assess the market's potential demand for the goods and services produced with the adopted technologies (Lee & Malerba, 2017). Furthermore, the business environment must be conducive, including the availability of risk capital, support services, and physical infrastructure (Arnold, Mattoo, & Narciso, 2008).

The ideal is to foster high-impact startups. These are firms that bring innovations to market and grow rapidly, creating new wealth and new jobs (Acs, 2010). Such firms are a tiny fraction of all startups, but they transform industries and influence society (WEF, 2014). They represent the application of dynamic capabilities, and are able to sense openings, exploit new possibilities, and respond flexibly to unexpected challenges. For this type of entrepreneurial leapfrogging, ordinary capabilities are not a gateway to dynamic capabilities. They are a completely different skill set.

Another feature of high-impact startups is a relatively high failure rate. In the United States, national statistics show that about 20 percent of all new businesses fail within a year—and about 50 percent within five years.[3] Among venture capitalists, the rule of thumb is that nine out of ten venture-backed startups will fail (Patel, 2015). However, because these startups are aiming for high impact, the low success ratio still allows profitability for the investors across their whole portfolio because each success tends to be large.

There are many reasons venture-backed startups fail (CB Insights, 2021). High-impact startups typically fail because their plans did not work out fast enough to maintain investors' willingness to continue funding. It could be that market demand for the startup's innovation was overestimated or that inadequate market research had been done in the first place. In other cases, the startup may be one of several firms offering a solution to a particular problem, and one of its rivals finds success. Yet another potential problem is a flaw in the business model that the firm designed to balance the value captured against the value offered; the firm might have underestimated costs or overestimated customers' willingness to pay. An unfavorable regulatory development can also undermine a startup, such as when incumbent firms in an existing industry use their connections to stifle a disruptive startup.

In Africa, weak management capabilities are yet another contributor to the failure of high-growth startups. In a small online poll of members of an Africa-based startup community in 2011, the most common reason (29 percent of responses) cited for business failure was "poor execution" (White, 2011). The accompanying text notes that this suggests "that many entrepreneurs behind unsuccessful attempts fail to adapt or change their plans needed to meet a dynamic and changing marketplace." This can be seen in the detailed report (Omeje, 2021) about the failure of an ambitious blockchain-based startup uniting three young entrepreneurs from Angola, Ghana, and Nigeria. They tried for three years to find a viable business model (e.g., a cryptocurrency exchange). Their failure was attributed to a lack of technical knowledge, poor market research, and inadequate funding. The three entrepreneurs have moved on to other startup-related activities in the blockchain space and elsewhere.

---

[3]   www.bls.gov/bdm/us_age_naics_00_table7.txt.

Potential high-impact startups are risky wherever they are based. Fortunately, failure is integrated into the business models of a healthy entrepreneurial ecosystem, and failed projects should not be considered as wasted resources. They release new skills, information, and learning into the economy for use by other firms or for reapplication by the startup entrepreneur. Repeat entrepreneurs have been shown to have better outcomes in both venture-backed and standard startups, reinforcing the idea that entrepreneurial management capabilities are, at least to some extent, skills that can be acquired (Gompers, Kovner, Lerner, & Scharfstein, 2006; Lafontaine & Shaw, 2016).

In Sub-Saharan Africa, however, there can be barriers to serial entrepreneurship. A study in Ghana showed that social stigmatization of the failed entrepreneur, a devaluing of previous startup experience, and an unforgiving bankruptcy regime made serial entrepreneurship very difficult (Amankwah-Amoah, 2018).

Questions about the Business Environment

Sub-Saharan Africa has been experiencing a boom in startup activity despite the pandemic. The number and value of venture capital deals to fund African startups (including North Africa), which had been growing slowly for several years, suddenly jumped in 2021, from less than $2 billion to more than $5 billion (AVCA, 2022). The continent also features a growing roster of startup incubators and accelerators able to help guide ambitious entrepreneurs on their journey (Redford & Wolf, 2017; David-West, Umukoro, & Onuoha, 2018).

However, it is far from certain that Africa's entrepreneurial momentum will lead to higher growth now than in the past. Ajide (2022) showed that African entrepreneurship only leads to economic growth when it has a conducive institutional environment, including strong intellectual property protection and the rule of law. A well-known barometer of national business environments is the World Bank's "Doing Business" research.[4] It attempts to measure the "quality" of a country's legal and regulatory systems, seen as fundamental to the creation of healthy market-based economies (Besley, 2015). In 2020, Mauritius (13th) and Rwanda (38th) were the only two Sub-Saharan African countries in the top 50.[5]

One of the biggest barriers to doing business in much of Africa is corruption: the abuse of public services for private gain (Transparency International, 2022). This impacts many businesses directly, in the form of the need to pay bribes in some countries and in the inability to qualify for grants that are restricted to better-connected applicants. Large-scale corruption contributes in varying degrees to other major problems harming entrepreneurs, such as armed conflicts and the diversion of resources away from economic development. Various studies have demonstrated the relationship between weak economic institutions and low levels of entrepreneurship (e.g., Anokhin & Schulze, 2009; Dutta & Sobel, 2016).

The external constraints on entrepreneurs run much deeper than just the rules for starting and running a business. Insufficient availability of capital "has long been viewed as the most important constraint by both researchers and entrepreneurs in low- and middle-income countries" (Woodruff, 2018, p. 7). The 2018 Global Entrepreneurship Index confirmed that "Risk

---

[4]   See www.doingbusiness.org/en/doingbusiness.
[5]   New Zealand ranked first, Singapore second, and Hong Kong third. See the rankings here: www
.doingbusiness.org/content/dam/doingBusiness/pdf/db2020/Doing-Business-2020_rankings.pdf.

Capital" was the weakest of 14 dimensions of the entrepreneurial ecosystem in Sub-Saharan Africa (Acs, Szerb, & Lloyd, 2018, p. 12). It remains to be seen if the jump in funding in 2021 mentioned earlier represents a long-term trend. Incomplete markets for insurance present a related financial problem (Banerjee & Duflo, 2005). Inadequate or unreliable physical infrastructure, including the supply of basic inputs like electricity, also undermines startup activity (see, e.g., Blimpo et al., 2017).

Internal factors, especially the availability and quality of managers, have been less widely studied. Woodruff (2018) includes a review of the empirical literature on various initiatives carried out in Sub-Saharan African countries to develop entrepreneurial managers.

Current Status of Management Capabilities

Emerging economies need business managers and leaders with advanced capabilities. Firms operating in places like Sub-Saharan Africa have to overcome more challenges than counterparts in developed countries. A set of in-depth interviews with dozens of executives at large and small companies in Africa revealed a serious lack of middle managers able to analyze problems and make decisions (AMI, 2012, p. 17). Top executives typically trained at an elite school and had past business experience, but there was a shortage of trained middle managers capable of mediating between the vision and strategy of top management and the daily operation of the company (Lee & Teece, 2013). This was also true for potentially high-impact startups hoping to scale rapidly; and startups suffer from the additional bias of potential managers who prefer the security of a large employer (AMI, 2012, p. 12).

The literature on managerial capabilities in African countries is limited but growing. Studies typically identify poor management skills as just one among a litany of problems holding back African firms (e.g., Abor & Quartey, 2010). Empirical studies that undertake in-depth analysis of managerial capabilities often focus on developed and industrializing countries with very limited inclusion of African countries. Studies that include or focus on African countries generally confirm the impression that African businesses are, on average, poorly managed. For example, the Organisation for Economic Co-operation and Development World Management Survey, based on in-depth interviews with managers, includes seven African countries—Ethiopia, Ghana, Kenya, Mozambique, Nigeria, Tanzania, and Zambia—and shows that all these countries landed near the bottom of the ranking among the countries assessed. The average management score for African manufacturing firms is 2.32, as compared to 2.69 in Asia, 2.72 in Latin America, 2.97 in Europe, and 3.28 in North America (Scur & Lippolis, 2017). This is on a scale of 1 to 5, where 5 represents "best practice" for each of 18 different management activities.

Similar observations have been made in various other studies. From a survey of owners and managers of over 60 businesses in Nigeria, Tanzania, Uganda, and Zambia, Thompson, Shepherd, Welch, and Anyimadu (2017, p. 13) found that these countries are plagued by a "legacy of poor business management" and "a chronic need for more middle managers." A survey of senior managers found that key weaknesses in managerial capabilities in South Africa relate to the ability to lead change (Steyn & Bell, 2015). The lack of managerial skills, management behavior, and financial knowledge has been found to have a negative impact on the success, viability, and development of small businesses (Radipere & van Scheers, 2005).

Even in the agricultural sector, efficient management is critical for organizational sustainability (Louw, Louw, & Lategan, 2014).

Most empirical studies of management in Sub-Saharan Africa have focused on the efficiency of manufacturing firms, which means that they were concerned with operational, not entrepreneurial, management, which in turn involves ordinary, not dynamic, capabilities. There is no question that African manufacturers could benefit from a large-scale effort to improve their operational efficiency. In terms of policy, this is low-hanging fruit that could and should be harvested.

However, Africa's economies also need high-impact Silicon Valley-style startups like Nigeria's Paystack, a digital payment-processing firm that was acquired in 2020 by United States-based Stripe for more than $200 million as a way to enter the regional market.[6] Many such startups are needed because so few of them will succeed (as is true for ambitious startups worldwide). But as long as enough of them do, economic growth will result.

Current Status of Management Education

Although advances have been made in management education in African countries, including through growth in the number of business schools and continued efforts at raising quality, gaps still exist. While there are thousands of schools in Sub-Saharan Africa that teach business courses of some kind, a 2012 report from a management education consortium found that, of 76 MBA-granting institutions, only 39 were accredited internationally or nationally (AMI, 2012). Moreover, 12 of these top schools were in South Africa, leaving the rest of the subcontinent severely underserved.

Empirical research on the gaps in management education in African countries has found various challenges, including balancing global and local content in the curriculum (Honig & Hjortsø, 2018; Lee, Thomas, Thomas, & Wilson, 2018; Darley & Luethge, 2019). There are variations in the ways of doing business both within regions and within individual countries, calling for significant localization of content and methodology at business schools.

The appropriate balance of global and local content in management education in African countries is contentious in the literature. Kuada (2013) suggests that neither management practices based entirely on African cultural prescriptions, such as reciprocity, cooperation, and family, nor those based on Western management philosophy have been able to ensure efficient resource management on the subcontinent. The former has led to weak organizational loyalties while the latter is a poor cultural fit, manifesting in Africa as rigid management hierarchies. Kuada argues that a synergy must be found: "The overriding aim should be to raise the dynamic capabilities of all African employees and change the socially acquired state of inaction and perpetual helplessness prevailing in many organizations" (Kuada, 2013, p. 19).

Like many, if not most, business schools elsewhere, there is also a tendency to focus on ordinary rather than dynamic capabilities. Training in higher-order managerial capabilities such as problem solving, innovation, and entrepreneurial skills is limited (Temtime & Mmereki, 2011). This does not provide a solid foundation for leapfrogging.

---

6   "Stripe acquires Nigeria's Paystack for $200M+ to expand into the African continent," TechCrunch, October 15, 2020. https://techcrunch.com/2020/10/15/stripe-acquires-nigerias-paystack-for-200m-to-expand-into-the-african-continent/.

Other Management Development Programs

Some programs seek to cultivate entrepreneurs outside an academic setting. There is evidence that entrepreneurial talent can be identified by characteristics such as "fluid reasoning" and numeracy (Woodruff, 2018). However, the best way to convert raw ability into superior firm performance remains unclear.

Results from management training for micro and small businesses are mixed. Mano, Iddrisu, Yoshino, and Sonobe (2012) reported generally positive results from a randomized controlled trial with a small group of micro and small firms in Ghana, some of which participated in basic management training, such as information on starting or improving a business. Fafchamps and Woodruff (2017) report the detailed study of a business plan competition for small businesses with fewer than 15 employees, offering additional management training for the winners. In a one-year follow-up, they found no growth effect of the training after controlling for other factors likely to influence growth such as perceived ability and access to capital.

It may be that early-stage entrepreneurs need training to be better entrepreneurs, not just better managers. In a randomized trial in Togo, Campos et al. (2017) found that "personal initiative" training for the development of an entrepreneurial mindset produced better results than traditional training in operating a business.

Traditional management training has been shown to give a more significant boost to sales and employment in medium-size companies (e.g., Bloom, Eifert, Mahajan, McKenzie, & Roberts, 2013). Mentoring programs provide another promising avenue (Woodruff, 2018).

In larger companies, such as the growing number of Africa's emerging multinationals starting to look at cross-border mergers and acquisitions, the full dynamic capabilities framework provides useful guidance for management decision making (Degbey, Eriksson, Rodgers, & Oguji, 2021).

The cultivation of leadership and the ability to make strategic decisions is also critical. What works in developed economies will not necessarily translate directly to the African context where the cultural norms in many economies include paternalism, deference to authority, and an emphasis on harmony (Walumbwa, Avolio, & Aryee, 2011). While academic work in this area has been limited, there has been increasing attention among practitioners. A review of leadership development programs in health care covering 23 of the 46 countries in Sub-Saharan Africa showed a growing level of interest but found plenty of room for improvement in such programs (Johnson, Begg, Kelly, & Sevdalis, 2021).

INTERVENTIONS

Sub-Saharan Africa requires a paradigm shift in both firm-level management teams and in industrial policy, as well as in how they partner with one another.

Large or fast-growing small firms must ensure that they aren't forcing managers into the rigid pursuit of efficiency, but rather unleashing their ability to sense, innovate, and act. In smaller startups operating in relatively stable market niches, an emphasis on ordinary capabilities and training in management fundamentals, such as good accounting controls, may be the best means of helping them reach their potential. Research has confirmed that even the smallest firms, self-employed merchants, can benefit from managerial advice of a practical nature (Blattman, Fiala, & Martinez, 2014). Because of their limited market, they are unlikely to benefit from the responsiveness and mutability that an investment in dynamic capabilities could bring.

In more ambitious startups with better access to capital and other resources, investment in the cultivation of dynamic capabilities (as well as ordinary ones) is warranted. Policies in support of this could involve training in business model design, innovation management, hypothesis testing, research and development, and corporate strategy. Many of the building blocks of dynamic capabilities can be taught. Even entrepreneurial skills can be taught to some extent, although there is continuing debate over the methods and their real impact (e.g., Hindle, 2007).

For policymakers, a shift towards a capabilities-based view of growth and development could lead to programs more likely to empower firms and their managers. At the same time, policymakers must also improve their own dynamic capabilities in order to be better able to question and confirm the assumptions adopted by firms seeking support, to make effective use of resources, and to deliver excellent services.

Many types of intervention are possible, and they must generally be adapted to local conditions. General categories of intervention that we consider here are the following:

- Supporting the development of firm-level dynamic capabilities.
- Reimagining how business school education is designed and delivered (Teece, 2011).
- Building learning and mentoring networks, including international connectivity opportunities for firms.
- Encouraging further research on the fostering of high-growth firms able to take advantage of leapfrogging technologies.

Build Dynamic Capabilities at the Firm Level

Begin by designing and delivering a tailored program for a limited cohort of firms in strategic sectors such as digital finance, green energy, and health technology. The program should be developed and led by a cross-sector team and involve managers of private firms, researchers, experts, and policymakers. The primary task will be to establish a pilot program to help self-selected firms run internal diagnostic assessments of key aspects of dynamic capabilities, such as innovativeness, research and development orientation, and systemic alignment. Managerial profiles can also be assembled, with a view to identifying management capability gaps to be addressed by targeted interventions. Robust monitoring and evidence-based evaluation routines are needed to support the pilot to generate insights for future investments in the area. With stronger firm-level dynamic capabilities, the best firms will inspire the next firms, creating a virtuous cycle that will expand the economy's ability to leverage technological leapfrogging.

Reimagine Business School Education for the Twenty-First-Century Economy

The failure to produce graduates who can grapple effectively with Africa's cultural, economic, and technological issues stems in part from weaknesses common to most business schools, namely the failure to integrate across disciplines and to emphasize rigor over relevance. These issues account for why practitioners in most parts of the world are often disdainful of academic research and teaching and why corporate and technology recruiters are not entirely satisfied with new MBA graduates (Teece, 2011). Managers need to be able to think strategically and act in the face of uncertainty (Teece, Peteraf, & Leih, 2016). While academic freedom limits the ability of policymakers to influence curricula, the provision of incentives for partnerships between business and academia can help management programs learn about the needs of the business sector.

Develop Strong Mentoring and International Networks to Support High-Potential African Firms

The design of a tailored, multi-year mentoring program to provide coaching for founders and senior managers of African firms can support the development of managerial know-how and capabilities. Relationships with regional and global multinationals and global centers of technology excellence should be forged to expand awareness of external business cultures and opportunities.

Support Evidence-Based Research on Firm-Level Capabilities

The bulk of research on capabilities has taken place outside Africa. A research program that joins leading African business schools with international partners can help identify the capabilities most needed by different types of firms in the various economies of Sub-Saharan Africa. This is a long-term effort that will gradually inform the creation and improvement of future interventions.

SUMMARY AND CONCLUSION

In this chapter, we have sketched the dynamic capabilities framework—the leading paradigm in the field of strategic management—with particular attention to the roles played by managers. The combination of entrepreneurship and leadership that we call "entrepreneurial management" is required for the creation and development of high-growth, high-impact firms. Additional research is needed to understand how the dynamic capabilities framework applies in specific African societies. Swartz, Amatucci, and Marks (2019), for example, showed how the South African context has worked to constrain entrepreneurial activity.

Our review of the growing literature on management capabilities and management education in Sub-Saharan Africa found that neither is at the level it needs to be if these economies are to benefit from technological leapfrogging. The windows of opportunity presented by digital advances occurring on other continents will not remain open long before multinationals move in to exploit them. Risk capital is increasingly available to fund high-growth innovations; but it can't buy success. Success comes from building and exercising strong dynamic capabilities.

We have suggested targeted interventions to address management capability gaps at the firm level and, for the longer term, in business schools. A management upgrade is critical for turning Africa's leapfrogging firms into long-distance runners. Strengthening ordinary and dynamic capabilities will enhance Sub-Saharan Africa's productivity, innovation, and growth.

In firms of all sizes, the capabilities of managers are critical to firm performance. Management capabilities are hard to teach and take time to emerge. It is vital that policymakers take steps at once to expand the supply and quality of entrepreneurial managers for the sake of the economy's future growth.

ACKNOWLEDGMENTS

The authors are grateful to Greg Linden, Sibahle Magadla, Pamela Mondliwa, and Arielle Emmett for research support and many contributions and suggestions.

REFERENCES

Abor, J., & Quartey, P. (2010). Issues in SME development in Ghana and South Africa. *International Research Journal of Finance and Economics*, *1*(39), 218–228.

Acs, Z. J. (2010). High-impact entrepreneurship. In Z. J. Acs & D. B. Audretsch (Eds), *Handbook of Entrepreneurship Research*. Springer, pp. 165–182.

Acs, Z. J., Szerb, L., & Lloyd, A. (2018). Global Entrepreneurship Index 2018. Global Entrepreneurship and Development Institute. http://thegedi.org/wp-content/uploads/dlm_uploads/2017/11/GEI-2018-1 .pdf

Ajide, F. M. (2022). Entrepreneurship and productivity in Africa: The role of institutions. *Journal of Sustainable Finance & Investment*, *12*(1), 147–168.

Amankwah-Amoah, J. (2018). Revitalising serial entrepreneurship in Sub-Saharan Africa: Insights from a newly emerging economy. *Technology Analysis & Strategic Management*, *30*(5), 499–511.

AMI (2012). Catalysing Management Development in Africa: Identifying areas for impact. *African Management Initiative*. https://africanmanagersblog.files.wordpress.com/2016/04/ami-report-long .pdf

Anokhin, S., & Schulze, W. S. (2009). Entrepreneurship, innovation, and corruption. *Journal of Business Venturing*, *24*(5), 465–476.

Arnold, J. M., Mattoo, A., & Narciso, G. (2008). Services inputs and firm productivity in Sub-Saharan Africa: Evidence from firm-level data. *Journal of African Economies*, *17*(4), 578–599.

AVCA (2022). Venture capital in Africa report. African Private Equity and Venture Capital Association. www.avca-africa.org/media/2967/62644-avca-avca-venture-capital-in-africa-report-v13.pdf

Banerjee, A., & Duflo, E. (2005). Growth theory through the lens of development economics. In P. Aghion & S. Durlauf (Eds), *Handbook of Economic Growth* (pp. 473–554). North- Holland.

Besley, T. (2015). Law, regulation, and the business climate: The nature and influence of the World Bank Doing Business Project. *Journal of Economic Perspectives*, *29*(3), 99–120.

Black, J. S., & Morrison, A. J. (2019). Can China avoid a growth crisis? *Harvard Business Review*, *97*(5), 94–103.

Blattman, C., Fiala, N., & Martinez, S. (2014). Generating skilled self-employment in developing countries: Experimental evidence from Uganda. *Quarterly Journal of Economics*, *129*(2), 697–752.

Blimpo, M. P., Minges, M., Kouame, W., Azomahou, T., Lartey, E., Meniago, C., Buitano, M., & Zeufack, A. (2017). Leapfrogging: The key to Africa's development: From constraints to investment opportunities. World Bank Group. Report Number 119849 (Working Paper), September. http://documents.worldbank.org/curated/en/121581505973379739/Leapfrogging-the-key-to-Africas -development-from-constraints-to-investment-opportunities

Bloom, N., Eifert, B., Mahajan, A., McKenzie, D., & Roberts, J. (2013). Does management matter? Evidence from India. *Quarterly Journal of Economics*, *128*(1), 1–51.

Bloom, N., Lemos, R., Sadun, R., Scur, D., & Van Reenen, J. (2014). JEEA-FBBVA lecture 2013: The new empirical economics of management. *Journal of the European Economic Association*, *12*(4), 835–876.

Boubakary, B., Moskolai, D. D., & Njang, G. C. (2020). Managerial innovation and SME performance in Africa: The case of Cameroon. *Global Journal of Management and Business Research: A*, *20*(10), 15–28.

Campos, F., Frese, M., Goldstein, M., Iacovone, L., Johnson, H. C., McKenzie, D., & Mensmann, M. (2017). Teaching personal initiative beats traditional training in boosting small business in West Africa. *Science*, *357*(6357), 1287–1290.

Caye, J.-M., Michael, D., Lee, R., & Nettesheim, C. (2012). Four ways to stop worrying about talent in China. *BCG Perspectives*, May 10. www.bcg.com/publications/2012/globalization-people -management-human-resources-four-ways-stop-worrying-talent-china.aspx

CB Insights (2021). The top 12 reasons startups fail. www.cbinsights.com/research/startup-failure -reasons-top/

Danneels, E., & Vestal, A. (2020). Normalizing vs. analyzing: Drawing the lessons from failure to enhance firm innovativeness. *Journal of Business Venturing*, *35*(1), 105903.

Darley, W. K., & Luethge, D. J. (2019). Management and business education in Africa: A post-colonial perspective of international accreditation. *Academy of Management Learning & Education*, *18*(1), 99–111.

David-West, O., Umukoro, I. O., & Onuoha, R. O. (2018). Platforms in Sub-Saharan Africa: Startup models and the role of business incubation. *Journal of Intellectual Capital*, *19*(3), 581–616.

Degbey, W. Y., Eriksson, T., Rodgers, P., & Oguji, N. (2021). Understanding cross-border mergers and acquisitions of African firms: The role of dynamic capabilities in enabling competitiveness amidst contextual constraints. *Thunderbird International Business Review*, *63*(1), 77–93.

Dutta, N., & Sobel, R. (2016). Does corruption ever help entrepreneurship? *Small Business Economics*, *47*(1), 179–199.

Fafchamps, M., & Woodruff, C. (2017). Identifying gazelles: Expert panels vs. surveys as a means to identify firms with rapid growth potential. *World Bank Economic Review*, *31*(3), 670–686.

Felipe, J., Abdon, A., & Kumar, U. (2012). Tracking the middle-income trap: What is it, who is in it, and why? *Levy Economics Institute Working Paper* No. 715. Levy Economics Institute of Bard College. www.levyinstitute.org/pubs/wp_715.pdf

George, G., Corbishley, C., Khayesi, J. N., Haas, M. R., & Tihanyi, L. (2016). Bringing Africa in: Promising directions for management research. *Academy of Management Journal*, *59*(2), 377–393.

Gompers, P., Kovner, A., Lerner, J., & Scharfstein, D. S. (2006). Skill vs. luck in entrepreneurship and venture capital: Evidence from serial entrepreneurs. National Bureau of Economic Research Working Paper 12592. www.nber.org/system/files/working_papers/w12592/w12592.pdf

Hindle, K. (2007). Teaching entrepreneurship at university: From the wrong building to the right philoso-phy. In A. Fayolle (Ed.), *Handbook of Research in Entrepreneurship Education* (vol. 1, pp. 104–126). Edward Elgar Publishing.

Honig, B., & Hjortsø, N. C. (2018). Management education: Unique challenges presented by the African continent. *Africa Journal of Management*, *4*(2), 125–136.

Javidan, M., Dorfman, P. W., De Luque, M. S., & House, R. J. (2006). In the eye of the beholder: Cross cultural lessons in leadership from project GLOBE. *Academy of Management Perspectives*, *20*(1), 67–90.

Johnson, O., Begg, K., Kelly, A. H., & Sevdalis, N. (2021). Interventions to strengthen the leadership capabilities of health professionals in Sub-Saharan Africa: A scoping review. *Health Policy and Planning*, *36*(1), 117–133.

Kuada, J. (2013). Management education in Africa: Prospects and challenges. In I. Alon, V. Jones, & J. McIntyre (Eds), *Innovation in Business Education in Emerging Markets*. Palgrave Macmillan, pp. 9–28.

Kunaka, C., & Moos, M. (2019). Evaluating mentoring outcomes from the perspective of entrepreneurs and small business owners. *Southern African Journal of Entrepreneurship and Small Business Management*, *11*(1), a214.

Lafontaine, F., & Shaw, K. (2016). Serial entrepreneurship: Learning by doing? *Journal of Labor Economics*, *34*(S2), S217–S254.

Lane, K., & Pollner, F. (2008). How to address China's growing talent shortage. *McKinsey Quarterly*, *3*, 33–40.

Lee, K., & Malerba, F. (2017). Catch-up cycles and changes in industrial leadership: Windows of opportunity and responses of firms and countries in the evolution of sectoral systems. *Research Policy*, *46*(2), 338–351.

Lee, M. P., Thomas, H., Thomas, L., & Wilson, A. (2018). Blind spots in African management education: An examination of issues deserving greater attention. *Africa Journal of Management*, 4(2), 158–176.

Lee, M. Y., & Edmondson, A. C. (2017). Self-managing organizations: Exploring the limits of less-hierarchical organizing. *Research in Organizational Behavior*, 37, 35–58.

Lee, S., & Teece, D. (2013). The functions of middle and top management in the dynamic capabilities framework. *Kindai Management Review*, 1, 28–40.

Louw, L., Louw, M. J., & Lategan, F. S. (2014). Towards assessing managerial competencies and leadership styles required for successful game ranch management in the Eastern Cape, South Africa. *South African Journal of Agricultural Extension*, 42(2), 127–140.

Mano, Y., Iddrisu, A., Yoshino, Y., & Sonobe, T. (2012). How can micro and small enterprises in Sub-Saharan Africa become more productive? The impacts of experimental basic managerial training. *World Development*, 40(3), 458–468.

Morris, M., Plank, L., & Staritz, C. (2016). Regionalism, end markets and ownership matter: Shifting dynamics in the apparel export industry in Sub Saharan Africa. *Environment and Planning A: Economy and Space*, 48(7), 1244–1265.

Nelson, R. R., & Pack, H. (1999). The Asian miracle and modern economic growth. *Economic Journal*, 109(457), 416–436.

Nemeth, C. J. (1997). Managing innovation: When less is more. *California Management Review*, 40(1), 59–74.

Oluwatobi, S., Olurinola, I., Alege, P., & Ogundipe, A. (2020). Knowledge-driven economic growth: The case of Sub-Saharan Africa. *Contemporary Social Science*, 15(1), 62–81.

Omeje, C. (2021). The inside story of how an ambitious African cryptocurrency startup failed. *Quartz Africa*. https://qz.com/africa/2028642/why-startups-fail-founders-of-an-african-fintech-recount/

Patel, N. (2015). 90% of startups fail: Here's what you need to know about the 10%. *Forbes*. www.forbes.com/sites/neilpatel/2015/01/16/90-of-startups-will-fail-heres-what-you-need-to-know-about-the-10/

Radipere, S., & van Scheers, L. (2005). Investigating whether a lack of marketing and managerial skills is the main cause of business failure in South Africa. *South African Journal of Economic and Management Sciences*, 8(4), 402–411.

Rambe, P., & Mosweunyane, L. (2017). A poverty-reduction oriented perspective to small business development in South Africa: A human capabilities approach. *African Journal of Science, Technology, Innovation and Development*, 9(4), 289–302.

Redford, D. T., & Wolf, C. (2017). High-impact entrepreneurship and its importance in Sub-Saharan Africa. In D. T. Redford (Ed.), *Developing Africa's Financial Services: The Importance of High-Impact Entrepreneurship*. Bingley: Emerald Publishing, pp. 43–59.

Scur, D., & Lippolis, N. (2017). Management and industrialisation in Africa. OECD Development Matters. September 12. https://oecd-development-matters.org/2017/09/12/management-and-industrialisation-in-africa/

Sen, A. K. (1985). *Commodities and Capabilities*. North-Holland.

Steyn, C., & Bell, D. (2015). Management index report 2014/2015. Stellenbosch: Stellenbosch University Business School (Executive Education). www.academia.edu/50717356/Management_Index_Report_2014_2015

Sutton, J. (2002). Rich trades, scarce capabilities: Industrial development revisited. *Economic and Social Review*, 33(1), 1–22.

Swartz, E. M., Amatucci, F. M., & Marks, J. T. (2019). Contextual embeddedness as a framework: The case of entrepreneurship in South Africa. *Journal of Developmental Entrepreneurship*, 24(3), 1950018.

Teece, D. J. (2007). Explicating dynamic capabilities: The nature and microfoundations of (sustainable) enterprise performance. *Strategic Management Journal*, 28(13), 1319–1350.

Teece, D. J. (2011). Achieving integration of the business school curriculum using the dynamic capabilities framework. *Journal of Management Development*, 30(5), 499–518.

Teece, D. J. (2012). Dynamic capabilities: Routines versus entrepreneurial action. *Journal of Management Studies*, 49(8), 1395–1401.

Teece, D. J. (2017). Towards a capability theory of (innovating) firms: Implications for management and policy. *Cambridge Journal of Economics*, 41(3), 693–720.

Teece, D. J., Pisano, G., & Shuen, A. (1997). Dynamic capabilities and strategic management. *Strategic Management Journal, 18*(7), 509–533.

Teece, D. J., Peteraf, M., & Leih, S. (2016). Dynamic capabilities and organizational agility: Risk, uncertainty, and strategy in the innovation economy. *California Management Review, 58*(4), 13–35.

Temtime, Z. T., & Mmereki, R. N. (2011). Challenges faced by graduate business education in Southern Africa. *Quality Assurance in Education, 19*(2), 110–129.

Thompson, H., Shepherd, B., Welch, G. H., & Anyimadu, A. (2017). *Developing Businesses of Scale in Sub-Saharan Africa: Insights from Nigeria, Tanzania, Uganda and Zambia.* Royal Institute of International Affairs. https://www.chathamhouse.org/sites/default/files/publications/research/2017 -09-08-business-of-scale-africa-thompson-shepherd-welch-anyimadu-final.pdf

Transparency International (2022). CPI 2021 for Sub-Saharan Africa: Amid democratic turbulence, deep-seated corruption exacerbates threats to freedoms. www.transparency.org/en/news/cpi-2021-sub -saharan-africa-amid-democratic-turbulence-deep-seated-corruption

Waldman, D. A., Sully de Luque, M., & Wang, D. (2012). What can we really learn about management practices across firms and countries? *Academy of Management Perspectives, 26*(1), 34–40.

Walumbwa, F. O., Avolio, B. J., & Aryee, S. (2011). Leadership and management research in Africa: A synthesis and suggestions for future research. *Journal of Occupational and Organizational Psychology, 84*(3), 425–439.

WEF (2014). The Bold Ones: High-impact entrepreneurs who transform industries. *World Economic Forum.* www3.weforum.org/docs/AMNC14/WEF_AMNC14_Report_TheBoldOnes.pdf

White, B. (2011). Why do African startups fail? *VC4A.com.* https://vc4a.com/blog/2011/09/12/why-do -african-startups-fail/

Woodruff, C. (2018). Addressing constraints to small and growing businesses. London: International Growth Centre. https://chriswoodruff.qeh.ox.ac.uk/wp-content/uploads/2019/10/Woodruff-2018 -Review-paper.pdf

World Bank (2017). *Leapfrogging: The Key to Africa's Development?* World Bank. https://openknowledge .worldbank.org/bitstream/handle/10986/28440/119849-WP-PUBLIC-Africa-Leapfrogging-text-with -dividers-9-20-17-web.pdf

Zhang, W. (2013). Reaping the benefits of brain circulation: The impact of the overseas study and the returnees on the development of the management education in China. In I. Alon, V. Jones, & J. R. McIntyre (Eds), *Innovation in Business Education in Emerging Markets* (pp. 208–221). Palgrave Macmillan.

2. Following the money: leapfrogging through and with entrepreneurial growth companies in Ghana, Kenya, Nigeria and South Africa

Ethné Swartz, Christopher Denecke and Caren Brenda Scheepers

INTRODUCTION

African technology-based ventures are changing the economic landscape as their founders and managers identify and build solutions to meet the needs of local populations. This chapter uses investment data to visualize how entrepreneurial companies are growing in local economies, transforming Africa through technology leapfrogging in four countries: Ghana, Kenya, Nigeria and South Africa. We define entrepreneurship in line with the definition of Baker and Welter (2020), who argue that entrepreneurs are individuals who enact agentic behaviours while they pursue opportunities and solve problems. Specifically, 'entrepreneurs [are those individuals] … "doing context" in which they operate agentic responses to the environments they confront' (Baker & Welter, 2020, p. 50). For us, this equates to managers, startups and other company founders who are building companies in Africa, irrespective of the size of the company. This allows us to connect to Chapter 1 in this volume by drawing on the sensing, seizing and resource-orchestrating role of the entrepreneurial manager (Teece, 2014), irrespective of the size of the company.

The chapter uses data to elucidate investment in companies in these four economies – Ghana, Kenya, Nigeria and South Africa. Such a 'follow the money' approach is critical in moving us to think and theorize in context (Morris & Tucker, 2021). Each of the four countries has different needs, starting the transformation journey from unique cultural and economic contexts, with entrepreneurs identifying opportunities to solve local problems. These companies provide a glimpse of how 'intractable' social and development issues such as health needs, agricultural needs or financial inclusion can be used as the springboard for innovative solutions that can provide Africa with points of agency, and even distinction in the global entrepreneurship ecosystem.

Leapfrogging refers to the adoption of modern technologies in products and services, skipping over conventional and outdated distribution channels or means of service and product delivery. Africa's modernizing and urbanizing population needs to adopt responsible technology and innovative business models in line with critical areas such as agriculture, education, energy, information and communication technology, finance and governance. Research by the African Center for Economic Transformation shows that policies to promote growth must incorporate the lessons learned from prior decades when economic transformation did not always result in employment and economic inclusion (ACET, 2014). Post COVID-19, countries are adapting to the rapid pace of technological change mediated by safety, security and economic needs. Such change was already evident in the four paramount goals identified by the United Nations High Level Panel on development prior to changes unleashed by COVID-19:

1. Create opportunities for productive jobs that can help reduce inequality and reduce poverty.
2. Productivity gains must accelerate to sustain growth through efforts in agriculture, industry and services that fit the assets that are available in specific countries.
3. Environments must allow businesses to flourish and facilitate value chains that link to major markets locally and globally.
4. New production and consumption of goods and services that sustain the environment must be supported.

These goals are pursued contemporaneously with the Fourth Industrial Revolution, the global pandemic that has intensified digital transformation and a shift to services in African economies due to restructuring since 1990 (de Vries et al., 2015). Given the paucity of data sources for Africa generally (de Vries et al., 2015) and specifically on African companies that have developed technologies to facilitate leapfrogging, our aim with this chapter is to provide insight into the development of the technology sector in Africa, focusing specifically on those African countries for which data are available, notably, Ghana, Kenya, Nigeria and South Africa.

We provide visualizations[1] of these economies based on new (or renewing) ventures in each of these countries. We wanted this chapter to harness visualization tools to provide a data-rich illustration to show what leapfrogging means, for instance, in Ghana in contrast to South Africa. These two countries differ in size of geographic area, population size and industrialization but we wish to understand the manner in which their ecosystems are changing in relation to funding for companies and the needs of the local people. For instance, the innovative healthcare company, mPharma, was founded by a Ghanaian, Gregory Rockson, who returned to the country after studying in the United States (US). Motivated to start a company to make medication for ordinary Ghanaians easier and more affordable, Rockson was inspired by his experience growing up in Ghana and then seeing what is possible in the US – specifically, technologies to make e-prescriptions available while also reducing the cost of care (Njanja, 2022).

In contrast, South Africa's most important pharmaceutical company, Aspen Pharmacare, began life during British colonial rule of South Africa when an Irish pharmacist created a company, Lennons Ltd., in 1858, becoming a public company in 1898. Today Aspenpharma is an important pharmaceutical manufacturer, with a global footprint (Aspenpharma, n.d.). South Africa's early industrialization in the 1860s was spurred on by gold mining in the 1860s (Schwank, 2010) but its premature deindustrialization (Andreoni & Tregenna, 2021) is one of

---

[1]   All figures in this chapter may be obtained electronically by contacting the lead author for access to the online repository. Please use email swartze@montclair.edu for access.

the factors that inhibits economic growth in the country. For a longer history of the industrial development of the country, we refer readers to Schwank (2010) and Trapido (1971).

We acknowledge the differences among the four countries we investigate in this chapter while simultaneously allowing for and celebrating the innovative entrepreneurial solutions created by African startups and existing companies. The rest of the chapter is structured as follows. First, we discuss the theoretical framework for the chapter, incorporating political, social and historical factors that act as antecedents for entrepreneurial opportunities in Africa. Next, we discuss the methodological approach and this is followed by a section where we present secondary data that track investments in technology-based startups in Africa, drawing on data for four Sub-Saharan African nations, notably Ghana, Kenya, Nigeria and South Africa. We use the data to conduct a comparative analysis or snapshot of the transformations taking place in these four economies and juxtapose where investments are being made which the World Bank has identified as critical for growth.

THEORETICAL FRAMEWORK

Contextualization of Entrepreneurship

Contextualization of entrepreneurship research has advanced in recent years (Baker & Welter, 2018, 2020; Welter et al., 2019). Kolk et al. (2018) note the importance of context for research-ers who focus on Africa, with scholars selecting either context-bound (where comparison of empirics or theories apply across different context to aid research) or context-specific (where empirics or theories apply only to a specific context) frameworks. We first discuss the evolution in the domain, followed by specific dimensions of context and finally discuss the relevance of these dimensions for analysing African high-growth entrepreneurship.

Evolution of Domain

There are three recent and overlapping waves of contextualization in the entrepreneurship field. The first wave purposefully moved away from the Silicon Valley notion of entrepre-neurship by considering the why, what and how of entrepreneurship. The second wave took the agency of the individual entrepreneur into account by focusing on the more subjective elements and the construction and enactment of contexts. In the third wave, researchers were challenged to deepen their *theorizing* by broadening the domain of entrepreneurship research.

We aspire to contribute to these waves in our own unique way of offering context-specific accounts of building businesses and focusing on the embeddedness of these enterprises within their respective Sub-Saharan African countries. Illustrating the rich entrepreneurial diversity and novelty on the African continent enables us to add to the rising tide of contextualization in the entrepreneurship field.

All entrepreneurship takes place within specific contexts (Yousafzai et al., 2015), defined as 'the circumstances that form the setting for an event, statement, or idea, and in terms of which it can be fully understood' (Oxford Dictionaries online). In the original Latin meaning, context denotes the joining together, connecting or weaving together of something (Rousseau & Fried, 2001).

Scholars van Gelderen and Masurel (2012) offer an elaborate discussion on the interrelationship between entrepreneurs in general and context, showing that entrepreneurs involve, engage with and influence their contexts and as a result are able to discover, create and exploit opportunities. Teece, for example, argues that entrepreneurs exhibit both 'ordinary' capabilities, which support operations critical for efficiency, along with 'dynamic' capabilities, which support investment direction in the context of specific business climates, along with organizational design and strategy development. The core categories of dynamic capability are (a) sensing (outward strategic awareness and cognition), (b) seizing (asset orchestration) and (c) transforming (adaptation and resilience). All three capabilities remain critical to the leapfrogging mindset of any entrepreneur looking for next-generation market opportunities.

Along with Welter et al. (2014), we argue to move beyond the artificial separation of 'context' and 'individual' in entrepreneurship studies. Understanding entrepreneurship from only an individual perspective ignores the influences that cultural and societal norms have on the way entrepreneurship takes place (Welter, 2011).

Alongside Baker and Welter (2020), we promote the benefits of grounding our theoretical inferences more thoroughly in the places and circumstances of our empirical observations. Welter et al. (2019) interpret contextualizing theory as the application of situational and temporal boundaries to theories in entrepreneurship, which of course stimulates useful comparative research. The third wave of theorizing context holds the most challenge and potential for ground-breaking research, since it is asking broader and more challenging questions of entrepreneurship theories.

Contextual Dimensions

Johns' (2006, p. 386) influential work on context defines context as 'situational opportunities and constraints that affect the occurrence and meaning of organizational behaviour, and functional relationships between variables'. He draws a distinction between an omnibus context and a discrete context. An omnibus context is broad, encompassing the dimensions of who, when, where and why, whereas a discrete context refers to actual variables that affect behaviour or attitudes such as tasks, social and physical variables (Johns, 2006). Griffin (2007) considers the omnibus context as the lens through which variables in the discrete context can be observed.

Context has multiple sides and its dimensions cut across each other and may affect the entrepreneur to varying degrees. Welter (2011) describes 'where' entrepreneurship happens using four dimensions of context, namely business, social, spatial and institutional. Welter et al. (2014) frame context specifically along the 'where' and 'when' dimensions. The 'where' being institutional (regulatory and normative), social (networks, families, households, culture, beliefs, societal perceptions and biases) and spatial (the geography or place) contexts of entrepreneurship (Welter, 2011; Welter et al., 2014).

Referring specifically to women's entrepreneurship, Welter et al. (2014) emphasize the 'when' dimension in terms of the history of gender inequality, which is still prevalent and embedded in most societies today, and the temporal context (or time) in which entrepreneurship takes place. Gender is thus embedded in the context within which women operate.

Context is not static, as it changes over time just as circumstances and environments change (Johns, 2006). It is therefore essential to take note of how context changes over time and how this influences entrepreneurship (Baker & Welter, 2018). The temporal context thus reflects the study of the space in time that entrepreneurship happens (Zahra et al., 2014) and the fluidity of entrepreneurship as it changes over time (Baker & Welter, 2018). The case has been made for including history in analyses of strategy and entrepreneurship (Perchard et al., 2017). Focusing on the temporal context reveals the path-dependent nature of entrepreneurial choice (Jones & Wadhwani, 2006). Based on Joseph Schumpeter, Jones and Wadhwani (2006) critique the evolution of entrepreneurship research and provide a compelling argument that history does indeed matter.

Considering our four countries of focus, their histories, a city or region may encourage entrepreneurial activity by providing quality education in schools and colleges, including entrepreneurship training, or may discourage that same activity by having exorbitant business registration fees or a heavy burden of local regulation and bureaucracy, and therefore each national context is different. As a result, we support the Global Entrepreneurship Monitor's (2019) explanation of contextual variables' influence on entrepreneurship, namely that any decision to start and run a new venture will be taken in a specific context, encompassing a wide range of local and national conditions that may facilitate or hinder that new venture.

Dimensions Relevant to an African Entrepreneurial Context

Moving to the African entrepreneurial context, Swartz and Amatucci (2018) illustrated how political and historical contextual dimensions reveal factors that impact economic and legal outcomes in South Africa. In another study, Swartz et al. (2019) contribute a contextualization framework in understanding the low nascent entrepreneurship rate in South Africa that includes six dimensions illustrating contextual embeddedness. They include: social: personal and everyday life; business: ownership and economic power structures; spatial: geographic and environmental elements; institutional: legal, government and political structures; temporal: arc of development of phenomenon over time; and historical: colonial past, decolonization and modern history.

The authors advise that many other emerging markets, particularly those in Africa, require more research that fully explores the interplay of the six dimensions in shaping entrepreneurship. Indeed, the contextualization of theory should be applied rigorously to uncover the entrepreneurial 'story' for each country. This is particularly the case as we are at a pivotal point in history where so much appears to be possible as the rate of internet adoption increases across the continent. Allan (2021) suggests that Africa could approach parity with the rest of the world by 2030 when African internet users comprise 75 per cent of the population. The spillover effects in terms of economic participation and potential is important (see Chapter 5).

Digital Transformation in Africa

Digital transformation refers to a range of technologies transforming economic activities, issuing in changes to older ways of executing company activities (Majumbar et al., 2015). Older, analogue systems and processes are replaced by digital tools, including, at the most basic level, efficiency technologies (e.g., improving how a process is completed) as well as connectivity technologies (apps, social media, Internet of Things, etc.). More sophisticated technological forms include automation technologies (artificial intelligence (AI) and machine learning). Most of these changes result in a cascade of processes of *disintermediation* or *intermediation* in existing supply chains, based on innovating with business models and the removal or addition of intermediaries. As these processes unfold, Lanzolla et al. (2020) note that many unanswered questions remain in terms of how digital transformation is likely to affect jobs and transform innovation and organizations.

Most African economies and populations gained access to the internet comparatively late, starting from the late 1990s onwards. Interactive visualizations on the *Our World in Data* platform show that in the early 1990s, Africa had little internet penetration (Roser, 2018); by the start of the new millennium, this had begun to change, and penetration developed at different rates for different countries.[2] This lag (when compared to developed economies) has affected African economies both positively and negatively. For instance, African economies experienced relatively little fall-out from the implosion of web-based companies (dot-com bust) in the early 2000s because only a minority of people (estimated at 7 per cent) were online at the time, and mostly in the US, Europe and parts of Asia (Roser, 2018). However, African companies also missed out on early developments in online searches that reduced search costs and also provided access to (buy and sell) goods and services. The internet's shrinking of vast geographic distances is a critical issue in enabling market participation (Walton, 2022) for African entrepreneurs who are often distantly located from markets (Swartz et al., 2019). There is still a long way to go to ensure that connectivity in Africa is completed for the 'last mile' and some are concerned about a struggle for hegemony between Facebook and Google in these efforts as constituting 'digital colonialism' (Coleman, 2019). The high costs of infrastructure building to provide connectivity means that, at least for the moment, there is no alternative to the continent relying on Google (Alphabet) and Facebook (Meta) connecting the continent, via undersea cables, to the rest of the globe's internet pipes or satelites.[3]

Thus, current digital transformations in African economies occur at a unique inflection point in history. The World Wide Web is more than 30 years old and its inventor is calling for changes in its structure to increase privacy, security and data ethics (Berners-Lee, 2019). That original structure of the World Wide Web gave rise to technology giants in developed economies, all the while exploiting the convergence of information technology with data captured in areas such as agriculture and synthetic biology because of breakthroughs in genetic and medical research (Le Merle & Davis, 2017). Africa has to participate as an equal in shaping the way in which the internet is changing and being changed, or it will not benefit from the opportunity to set the rules of the game for the new types of companies spawned.

Many African countries, working collaboratively with the World Bank, have embraced changes in technology infrastructure and convergence of technologies by formulating strategies for how their economies can benefit from digital transformation (World Bank, 2020). For example, Kenya has emerged as a global leader in mobile money (GSMA, 2020). The World Bank (2019) estimates that e-commerce had grown at 40 per cent in Africa even prior to the

---

[2]   We highly recommend that readers use the interactive map available via Oxford University's *Our World in Data* site to view adoption rates for African countries compared to other parts of the world. The site is updated regularly and also provides historical data that contextualize Africa's lag. Available at: https://ourworldindata.org/internet#internet-access.

[3]   African companies such as Telkom Kenya, MTN and others are participating in these partnerships, but Meta and Google (Whitehouse, 2021) are key investors in infrastructure in the region.

pandemic. Furthermore, citing data from McKinsey, the World Bank (2019) assumes that the digital economy in Africa is likely to exceed $300 billion by 2025.

Of course, this forecast predates the pandemic and achieving these results depends on many factors and uncertainties. Yet, we see that these trends have been accelerated by the pandemic as companies adopted contactless commerce. Table 2.1 shows internet penetration data, as a percentage of population, from the World Bank for the four countries we focus on in this chapter. The most recent year for which data are available is 2020.

Table 2.1   *Internet penetration data and population size for Ghana, Kenya, Nigeria and South Africa by 2020*

Region and country	Individuals using the internet (% of population)	World Bank population estimates in 2020
Sub-Sahara	30	
Ghana	58	31,072,945
Kenya	30	50,221,146
Nigeria	36	206,139,587
South Africa	70	59,308,690

Source: World Bank (n.d.).

In summary, structural economic changes that began prior to 1990 reallocated workers in most African economies into services (logistics, domestic services and hotel, transportation and hospitality services) now coincide with the adoption and diffusion of digital tools. In fact, by 2015, about one-fifth of Africa's labour force worked in distributive services (de Vries et al., 2015). By 2020, it is estimated that employment in services in Africa constituted 41.6 per cent of total employment (Faria, 2022). This shift in the workforce accelerated during COVID-19 as structural change was reinforced during the pandemic as delivery of foods, medicines and consumer goods was necessitated during periods of lockdown (GSMA, 2021).

The remainder of our chapter focuses on our methodology, followed by findings about each of the four countries and significant investments in companies involved in digital transformation. We then discuss the implications of the growth of entrepreneurial companies in Africa and close the chapter with policy recommendations.

Methodology

Africa researchers face many obstacles when trying to source data on economic or entrepreneurial developments (Devarajan, 2013; Jerven & Johnston, 2015; Kolk & Rivera-Santos, 2018). Data availability and access determine 'what kinds of questions can be investigated', particularly regarding whether change (or poverty as in Jerven's paper) are conjunctural or structural in nature (Jerven, 2018, p. 452).

Data availability is the elephant in the room when writing about technological leapfrogging in Africa, despite the United Nations Sustainable Development Goal 17 (Partnerships for the Goals) specifying the achievement of statistical capacity (Target 17.18). The goal for developing nations is to collect data that can be disaggregated by variables relevant to the national context. Our *World in Data*'s SDG tracker (https://sdg-tracker.org/global-partnerships)

reveals that countries in Africa lag on this indicator, and our experience as researchers confirm the difficulty of disaggregating data. Although some advances are being made, the countries that we focus on (Ghana, Kenya, Nigeria and South Africa) lack country-based statistics on emerging technology companies.

Given the data access conundrum, we used a combination of research methods to source data for this chapter. Therefore, the methodological choice was entirely pragmatic in line with the exploratory nature of this research. First, we used up-to-date secondary data on emerging African technology-based and growth companies that obtained funding and sourced this from the big data company, Crunchbase.com. The platform is increasingly being used by researchers interested in following the development of startups, entrepreneurial or growth companies that secure investment. Crunchbase tracks data globally and the footprint for African companies has grown significantly. For a discussion of this trend in the datafication (Mayer-Schönberger & Cukier, 2013) of society as a whole, but particularly the implications for the global South, see Taylor and Broeders (2015).

We collected data for Ghana, Kenya, Nigeria and South Africa from the Crunchbase platform. The data included all company and funding data for the population of companies for each country through to December 2020. The data were exported into Excel and cleaned to remove double entries. Finally, the companies were classified based on industry. The data were then imported to Tableau and visualizations created.

In addition to creating our own dataset, we also used additional data from other sources now available on African entrepreneurial companies. Two such sources are available. First, we used the data compiled by Briter Bridges, which is a big data company that aggregates data on entrepreneurial companies and ecosystems, with a particular focus on Africa. Briter Bridges publishes maps and data for African countries and cities and the company has brought visibility to the changing ecosystems across the continent. A second useful compilation of data on African entrepreneurial ecosystems is the Substack newsletter entitled, *Africa the Big Deal*. Two entrepreneurs created the Substack newsletter as an entrepreneurial endeavour. Both of these companies provide access to their underlying database for a fee.

ANALYSIS AND DISCUSSION OF THE CRUNCHBASE DATA

We conducted an analysis in Excel and data visualization in Tableau, using the data we sourced from Crunchbase. Table 2.2 provides a summary of the types of dominant companies that attracted investment and listed on Crunchbase. Please note that these are the companies in each country listed on the Crunchbase platform that received investment of capital from external investors. Many investors were located outside of the African continent, and some were African.

Across all four countries, companies tend be located in one or two key geographic locations, regions or cities. The data displayed in the visualizations highlight investment by industry, geographic location and organization show that for all four countries, a few dominant organizations have attracted the most investment.

In Nigeria, the bulk of financial investment flowed into four sectors: financial services, e-commerce, telecommunications and mobile applications. The Crunchbase platform contained data for Nigeria, starting in January 1999. Figure 2.1 shows investment in Nigeria by industry and location in the country. Figure 2.2 shows the same data by industry, location and

Table 2.2   *Investments by country, sector and geographic location*

Country	Sectors attracting most investment	Areas in country attracting most investment
Kenya	Financial services, digital communications, logistics, internet infrastructure, energy, fintech, e-commerce, banking, food distribution, ag-tech, solar energy, agriculture, healthcase, renewable energy, real estate, transportation, construction	Nairobi, Kalifi Coast, Mombasa
Ghana	Healthcare, banking, mobile wireless, asset financing, e-commerce, wireless internet, internet platforms, financial services, software, digital platforms, fintech	Ridge Volta, Accra, Greater Accra
Nigeria	Financial services, e-commerce, telecommunications, mobile apps, venture capital, fintech, food and beverage, healthcare, energy, logistics	Lagos, Abuja, Agbara, Ogun
South Africa	Retail, e-commerce, telecommunications, automotive services, ag-tech, agriculture, insurance, broadcasting, healthcare, financial services, mining	Gauteng, Western Cape, Stellenbosch

organization. The two visualizations enable us to understand where in the country companies are located, which industries dominate and the companies receiving the lion's share of the funding.

The dominant financial services sector companies are distributed across a few geographic locations, including the Union Bank of Nigeria and Interswitch in Lagos, Diamond Bank, which has locations in Lekki and Lagos, Nigeria Enterprise Group (Ghana, Ebonyi) and a number of companies in the Abuja and Federal Capital Territory. Figure 2.2 shows that the Jumia Group is the dominant e-commerce platform based in Lagos, while telecommunications is dominated by IHS Towers, based in Lagos. Additionally, OPay (mobile apps), Origin Holdings (venture capital) and Hygeia Group (healthcare insurance) are in Lagos. Finally, Beloxxi is a food and beverage company based in Agbara and Ogun. In 2022, Nigeria is outpacing other African countries in its pace of innovation and ability to attract investment, according to the Africa-focused Substack newsletter, *Africa, The Big Deal* (Cuvellier, 2022). The reasons for Nigeria's attractiveness at present are complex and we should regard these data as a data point to consider in the continent's digital transformation process.

Turning to Kenya, we see more variety in sector investment. Recall that in Table 2.1 we showed that Kenya had the lowest internet penetration at 30 per cent, which equates to the average for Sub-Saharan Africa. Hence, it is intriguing to see the dominance of mobile communications evident in the visualization charts for Kenya. Once again, Figure 2.3 shows investment in Kenya by industry and location, while Figure 2.4 shows the same data but adds organizations that received the most funding.

Mobile communications companies located in Nairobi benefited from the bulk of investment, as evident in Figure 2.3. Safaricom was the beneficiary of most of the investment flow during this snapshot period that includes all Crunchbase-recorded investment transactions for Kenya from March 2006 to December 2020. Outside of this sector, financial services in Nairobi, and specifically Equity Group Holdings and Britam, received the most investment. Digital communications and energy are the other attractive sectors for investors, with Wananchi Group (digital communications) also located in Nairobi.

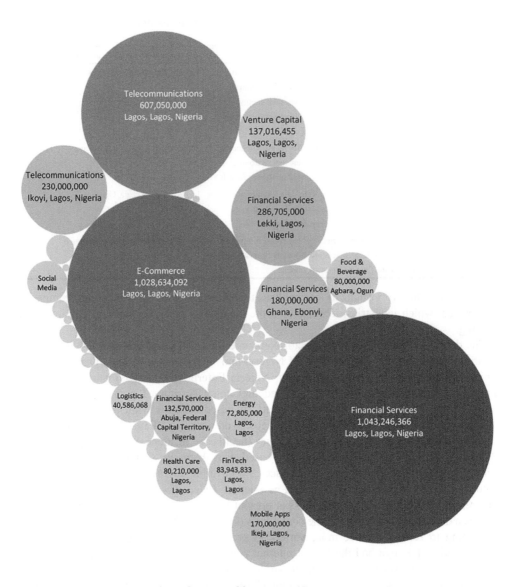

Figure 2.1   Investment by industry and location – Nigeria

Internet infrastructure investment lagged in terms of investment, as did food distribution and logistics, despite the success of companies such as Twiga Foods in food distribution. Of note for Kenya is the relative sophistication of companies such as Kenya Sendy, which uses machine learning and AI in logistics and MKopa investing in solar energy. While Nairobi clearly is the preferred location for most companies, agricultural technology companies such as Komaza.com is located on the Kilifi Coast. Solar and renewables, real estate, agriculture, healthcare, construction, edtech, finance and mobile are all sectors that received investment in smaller amounts so there are no dominant recipient companies.

Figure 2.2   Investment by industry, location and organization – Nigeria

Moving to Ghana, we see less variety in industry, with healthcare attracting most investment (see Figure 2.5) and with mPharma receiving the bulk of that investment, followed by Africa Health Holdings (see Figure 2.6). Please note that the visualizations for Ghana are based on the earliest investment listed in our Crunchbase data occurring in November 2001.

Other dominant companies include PEG (asset financing), Surfline Communications (mobile wireless), Zipnet (wireless internet) and Tigo (e-commerce). Ghana is a relative minnow in terms of population size and internet penetration, as evident in Table 2.1, and yet this country's transforming healthcare sector, illustrated by the company mPharma, has attracted significant investment (Njanja, 2022).

The second sector attracting investment is asset financing, followed by banking and e-commerce. PEG (www.pegafrica.com) provides pay-as-you-go solar energy and financing to customers who cannot easily connect to the electricity grid. The company was launched in 2015 by two founders with backgrounds in international development projects in the energy industry in Africa. Today the company is present in Ghana, Cote d'Ivoire, Senegal and Mali and employs 1,000 people. Surfline Communications is based in Accra and provides innovative communications devices and funding plans to enable consumers to access the internet.

Our final country of focus is South Africa. It is impossible to do justice to the country's complex history of entrepreneurial and growth companies in a chapter given the country's long and unsuccessful quest out of middle-income economy status (Andreoni & Tregenna,

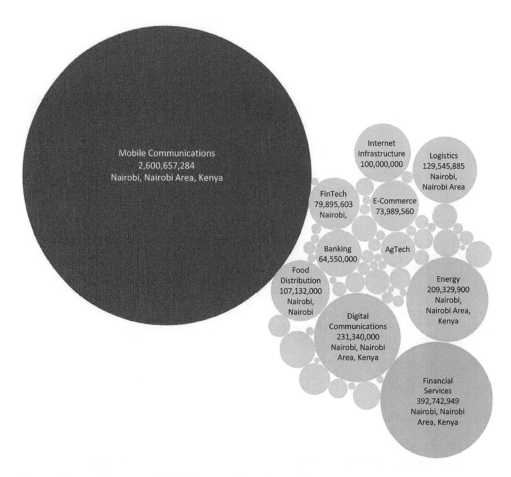

Figure 2.3   Investment by industry and location – Kenya

2021). Earlier in the chapter we commented on Aspen Pharmacare Holdings and contrasted its nineteenth-century roots in South Africa's colonial period to its growth into an important global pharmaceutical manufacturer. The country's complexity is best understood by reading contextually situated reviews (see Swartz et al., 2019), especially its poor performance with nascent entrepreneurship relative to other, less industrialized African economies.[4]

Some sectors of the economy were able to thrive and spawn companies engaged globally with the financial services company, Discovery Limited, a prime example of creating value

---

[4]   South African entrepreneurs of note include Johann Rupert who, in 1988, created Richemont.com, a Swiss-based luxury goods company that has its roots in South Africa. Rupert inherited ownership of the Rembrandt Group, a company founded in South Africa in the 1940s, spanning tobacco, wine and spirits, financial services and gold and diamond mining. Anton Rupert (father of Johann) built the group into the Remgro group which became influential across multiple sectors, including telecommunications. Today, Remgro remains headquartered in Stellenbosch, South Africa, while Richemont spun out the group's international assets listed on the Swiss stock exchange.

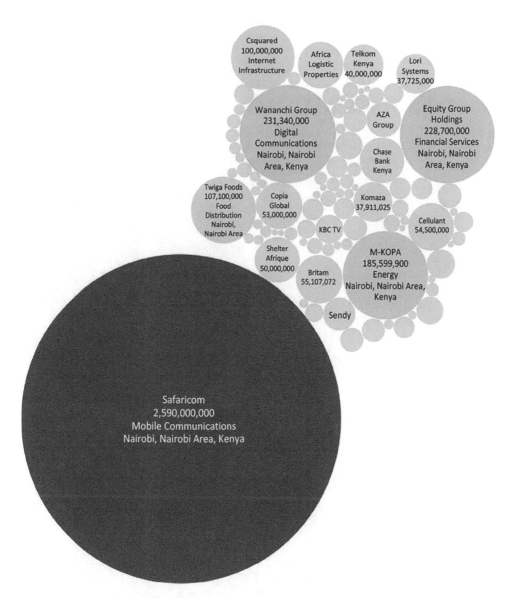

Figure 2.4   Investment by industry, location and organization – Kenya

through innovation in insurance, health and wellness in its country of origin. Discovery now operates in the United Kingdom, China and the US. Discussing the company's trajectory from a startup in the immediate post-Apartheid era to its global presence, founder Adrian Gore (2015) cites the poor healthcare conditions in South Africa as inspiring the initial challenge to sustainably finance health insurance. The visualizations in Figures 2.7 and 2.8 for South Africa show that most investment flows into established industry sectors such as pharmaceuticals,

Figure 2.5   Investment by industry and location – Ghana

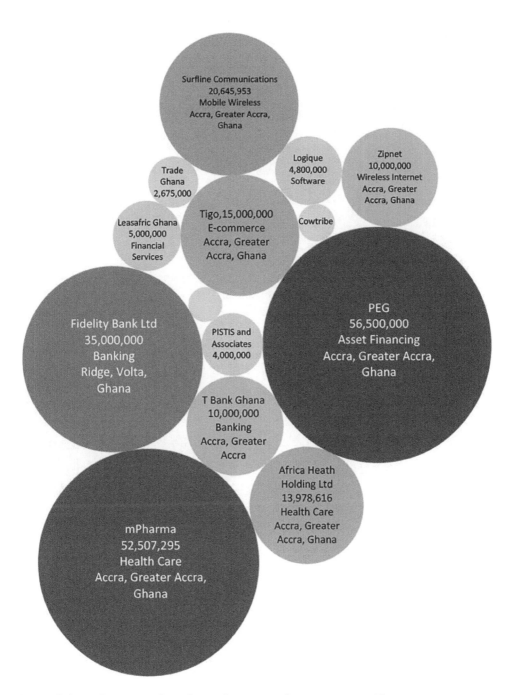

Figure 2.6   Investment by industry, location and organization – Ghana

mining, telecommunications and retail. Smaller investments flowed into logistics and food and beverage.

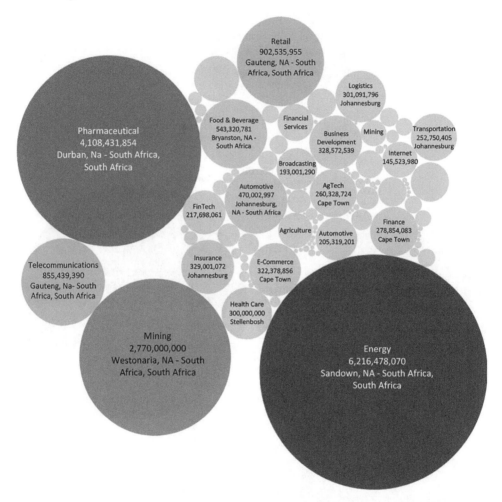

Figure 2.7   Investment by industry and location – South Africa

Investment in the energy sector, especially in Eskom, the state-owned power provider, dominates investment overall. South Africa's energy sector has seen innovation with solar energy for citizens who want freedom from the rolling electricity black-outs the country has experienced for years as Eskom struggles to manage itself profitably and sustainably. Solar companies in our Crunchbase data include the following: The Sunexchange, Solar MD, Distribution Power Africa and Wisolar.

Eskom produces nearly all of the electricity in the country and exports to neighbouring countries also. It has been beset by scandal and allegations of corruption involving the country's former president, Jacob Zuma, and the Gupta brothers, Indian-born entrepreneurs

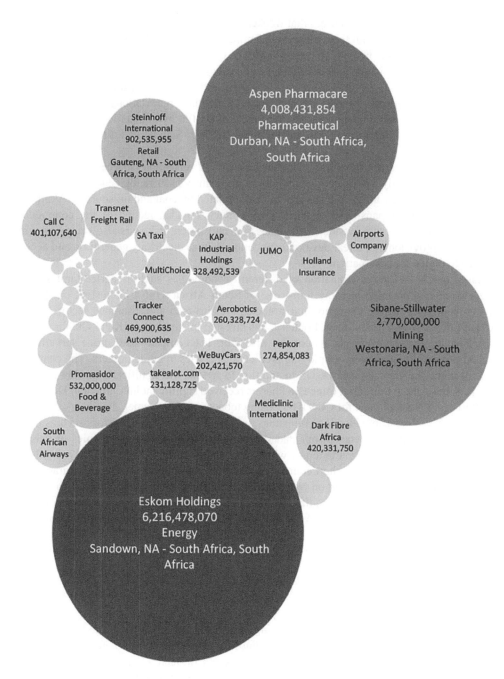

Figure 2.8   Investment by industry, location and organization – South Africa

accused of syphoning state resources that weakened Eskom (Cotterill, 2022). In June 2022, an agreement was reached with the United Arab Emirates to extradite two of the Gupta brothers to South Africa. Of note here is the country's Zondo Commission into government corruption and the role of the judiciary in South Africa in investigating and exposing poor governance. For those interested in the investigation, the reports are available via this government site: www.statecapture.org.za/. Myriad US and United Kingdom organizations were found to be complicit and calls have been made for the return of profits by companies such as Bain & Company, KPMG, McKinsey, SAP and the banks HSBC, Standard Chartered and Baroda (Hain, 2022).

South Africa does not have the abundant natural and renewable sources of energy that Kenya possesses. Only 5 per cent of electricity in the country is currently generated by renewables while the energy industry continues to be dominated by coal and oil sources (Akinbami et al., 2021). The expansion of electricity to a much broader section of the community post-Apartheid means that outside of the issues with corruption, Eskom is also struggling with the scale of provision and a real development conundrum as electricity generation and access are key to digital transformation.

Based on the unique combination of different technologies such as agricultural knowledge, drone and machine learning tools, one of South Africa's most interesting companies is Aerobotics, a software company that straddles the agri-tech and insurance sectors. South Africa's Naspers investment fund, Foundry, has invested in Aerobotics (Kene-Okafor, 2021), which has potential beyond just its country of origin. The company uses drone surveillance and AI to monitor farm crops, employing predictive analytics to guide farmers. The company has customers in Australia and the US in addition to serving the significant farming community in South Africa. Similarly, Cape Bio Pharms received significant investment in December 2020 to develop a rapid test for COVID-19 using tobacco plants (Daniel, 2020).

Despite investment in education companies not rising to the level of sectors such as pharmaceuticals, mining and retail in our data, entrepreneurial education companies of note in South Africa include GetSmarter.com, which was acquired by 2U.com in 2017 (Withers, 2017). GetSmarter focuses on short courses and its reach was global, making this attractive to 2U.com which is highly focused on North America, offering high-quality support to a range of universities to provide more traditional online degrees to customers. A second company of significance in education is SPARK Schools, a Gauteng-based provider of affordable, blended elementary school education in South Africa (Makgalemele, 2015). The company has benefited from $11.7 million in investment by the Omidyar Foundation and Pearson Education (Crunchbase, n.d.).

DISCUSSION

In terms of the types of African companies in our data set, the majority fit into the categories such as efficiency technologies (e.g., improving how a process is completed), connectivity technologies (apps, social media, Internet of Things and fin-tech, etc.) and automation technologies (AI and machine learning). Most of these facilitate processes of *disintermediation* or *intermediation* in existing supply chains, based on innovating with business models and use of creativity (Ladd, 2021). This suggests that entrepreneurs and investors are identifying these opportunities to serve populations largely untouched by innovations due to the relatively late arrival of internet access. However, some of these African startups are beginning to offer services globally. South Africa's Aerobotics provides services that combine technologies in agriculture, AI and drone technology to farmers in the US and Australia, while Andela is a human capital platform that connects job seekers from emerging markets with technology-based recruiters globally. The company has a large footprint across several African countries and a New York headquarters.

In line with our theoretical framework, our Crunchbase data suggest that while investments are flowing into entrepreneurial growth companies across all four countries, there are similarities and differences in the types of company in each country benefiting from that investment. South Africa and Ghana each experienced investment into pharmaceuticals and healthcare, but the nature of the companies differed greatly. The bulk of the funding in Ghana went into mPharma, essentially a pharmacy benefits management and distribution company, while in South Africa, Aspen Pharmaceuticals was the beneficiary of investment for pharmaceutical manufacturing, an industrial sector. Another example is that of Kenya, where financial services and digital communications companies were most attractive to investors. Overall, Nigeria[5] is the continent's most attractive destination for investment at present, with Jumia, Interswitch and others in financial technology finding willing investors from Africa and globally. For example, the top 100 African companies listed by Briter Bridges (2022) shows the dominance of Nigerian companies in terms of investment dollars raised and the number of companies in the list. Data from Cuvellier (2022) support this, showing that startups in Nigeria raised close to $1 billion in 2021 alone.

Our analysis did not include the gender of the leadership of companies in our data set. However, this is an important issue for African companies – only 7 per cent of the startups in data collected by Cuvellier (2022) on African startups have female CEOs and fewer than 1 per cent of these companies have single female founders or female-only founding teams. This is an important aspect of the transformation that we are witnessing and policy makers should be cognizant of the need to change the structural inequities at the root of the phenomenon. As Cilliers (2021) has pointed out, African governments will have to create the needed conditions for entrepreneurial companies to benefit from investment in information and communication technologies and more advanced transformational technologies. It is evident that some investment flows find fertile opportunity not only in startups but also in established companies. Our data for South Africa and Nigeria suggest that investors are seeing financial opportunities in traditional sectors such as electricity generation, mining, retail and banking.

CONCLUSION

In this chapter we have used a data snapshot of investment flows from a big data provider to offer a contextually situated view of how four African economies are changing. Companies receiving such investments are the future providers of services that enable citizens of these countries to find modern and technologically enabled ways of accessing services to live their

---

[5]   We are constrained by space to discuss the reasons for Nigeria's current attractiveness to investors, but the country is Africa's largest economy and its most populous country. Please see the US State Department report on the country for a fuller discussion: www.state.gov/reports/2021-investment-climate-statements/nigeria/.

lives. African companies are providing services that transform basic economic activities (Majumbar et al., 2015) that improve efficiency and connectivity; such tools facilitate financial transactions, access to medical and food transaction and delivery tools, as well as growth of e-commerce.

Of concern is the possibility that as African companies and consumers leapfrog the continent's lag in terms of internet adoption, a new digital colonialism is being born. The high costs of connecting all African citizens to the internet and implementing 'last-mile' connectivity means that we are now witnessing the Chinese government jockeying with US conglomerates for power in terms of investing in internet infrastructure (Hruby, 2021). The reality is that these are the powers with the ability to fund such investments, but we should be mindful of the associated costs.

The data we provided in this chapter, particularly for basic services (see Table 2.1 on the potential for growth in connectivity in our four countries of focus), mean that Africa is indeed a continent of potential growth, especially given its comparatively recent shift to services. The continent has a bright future if there is equitable access to resources and growth of the capabilities of Africa's people.

REFERENCES

ACET. (2014). *African transformation report: Growth with depth*. Accra: African Center for Economic Transformation.http://africantransformation.org/wp-content/uploads/2014/02/2014-african-transform ation-report.pdf

Akinbami, O., Oke, S., & Bodunrin, M. (2021). The state of renewable energy development in South Africa: An overview. *Alexandria Engineering Journal*, 60(6), 5077–5093.

Allan, N. (2021). The promises and perils of Africa's digital revolution. Brookings. 11 March. www .brookings.edu/articles/the-promises-and-perils-of-africas-digital-revolution/

Andreoni, A., & Tregenna, F. (2021). The middle-income trap and premature deindustrialization in South Africa. In A. Andreoni, P. Mondliwa, S. Roberts, & F. Tregenna (Eds), *Structural Transformation in South Africa: The Challenges of Inclusive Industrial Development in a Middle-Income Country*. Oxford University Press.

Aspenpharma. (n.d.). About Aspen. www.aspenpharma.com/history

Baker, T., & Welter, F. (2018). Contextual entrepreneurship: An interdisciplinary perspective. *Foundations and Trends® in Entrepreneurship*, 14(4), 357–426.

Baker, T., & Welter, F. (2020). *Contextualizing Entrepreneurship Theory*. Routledge.

Berners-Lee, T. (2019). I invented the World Wide Web. Here's how we can fix it. *New York Times*, November 24. www.nytimes.com/2019/11/24/opinion/world-wide-web.html

Briter Bridges (2022). 2021 Africa's rising 100. May. https://briterbridges.com/africa-rising-100

Cilliers, J. (2021). *The Future of Africa: Challenges and Opportunities*. Cham: Palgrave Macmillan.

Coleman, D. (2019). Digital colonialism: The 21st century scramble for Africa through the extraction and control of user data and the limitations of data protection laws. *Michigan Journal of Race and Law*, 24, 417–439.

Cotterill, J. (2022). Former South African leader Zuma handed control of Eskom to Guptas, says inquiry. *Financial Times*, April 29. www.ft.com/content/6ea582f8-3734-4830-b817-b8cf957381fa

Crunchbase (n.d.). SPARK schools. www.crunchbase.com/organization/spark-schools

Cuvellier, M. (2022). This is a man's man's man's world. Substack newsletter, January 25. https:// thebigdeal.substack.com/p/this-is-a-mans-mans-mans-world?s=w

Daniel, L. (2020). SA company gets R900 million to develop rapid Covid-19 test – using tobacco plants. *News24*, 27 December. www.news24.com/news24/bi-archive/sa-company-gets-r900-million -in-funding-to-develop-rapid-covid-19-test-using-tobacco-plant-2020-1

de Vries, G., Timmer, M., & de Vries, K. (2015). Structural transformation in Africa: Static gains, dynamic losses. *Journal of Development Studies*, 51(6) 674–688.

Devarajan, S. (2013). Africa's statistical tragedy. *Review of Income and Wealth*, 59(2), S9–S15.

Faria, J. (2022). Employment in services in Africa 2010–2020. *Statista*. www.statista.com/statistics/1230875/employment-in-services-as-share-of-total-in-africa/#statisticContainer

Global Entrepreneurship Monitor (2019). Global Entrepreneurship Monitor global report 2018/2019. www.gemconsortium.org/report/gem-2018-2019-global-report

Gore, A. (2015). How discovery keeps innovation. *McKinsey Quarterly*, May. www.mckinsey.com/industries/healthcare-systems-and-services/our-insights/how-discovery-keeps-innovating

Griffin, M. A. (2007). Specifying organizational contexts: Systematic links between contexts and processes in organizational behavior. *Journal of Organizational Behavior*, 859–863.

GSMA (2020). State of the industry report on mobile money 2019. www.gsma.com/sotir/wp-content/uploads/2020/03/GSMA-State-of-the-Industry-Report-on-Mobile-Money-2019-Full-Report.pdf

GSMA (2021). State of the industry report on mobile money 2021. www.gsma.com/mobilefordevelopment/wp-content/uploads/2021/03/GSMA_State-of-the-Industry-Report-on-Mobile-Money-2021_Full-report.pdf

Hain, P. (2022). Corporate corruption in South Africa demands global action in response. *Financial Times*, 6 February.

Hruby, A. (2021). Africa's digital infrastructure is the next playing field for great-power competition. Atlantic Council. www.atlanticcouncil.org/blogs/africasource/africas-digital-infrastructure-is-the-next-playing-field-for-great-power-competition/

Jerven, M. (2018). The history of African poverty by numbers: Evidence and vantage points. *Journal of African History*, 59(3), 449–461.

Jerven, M., & Johnston, D. (2015). Statistical tragedy in Africa? Evaluating the data base for African economic development. *Journal of Development Studies*, 51(2), 111–115.

Johns, G. (2006). The essential impact of context on organizational behavior. *Academy of Management Review*, 31(2), 386–408.

Jones, G., & Wadhwani, R. D. (2006). Schumpter's plea: Rediscovering history and relevance in the study of entrepreneurship. *Harvard Business School Working Paper*, 06-036. www.hbs.edu/research/pdf/06-036.pdf

Kene-Okafor, T. (2021). South African startup Aerobotics raises $17m to scale its AI-for-agriculture platform. *Techcrunch*, January 21. https://techcrunch.com/2021/01/21/south-africa-startup-aerobotics-raises-17m-led-by-naspers-foundry/#:~:text=Aerobotics%2C%0a%20South%20African%20startup,%245.6%20million%2C%20according%20to%20Aerobotics

Kolk, A., Rivera-Santos, M., & Rufin, C. R. (2018). Multinationals, international business and poverty: A cross-disciplinary research overview and conceptual framework, *Journal of International Business Policy*, 1(1).

Ladd, T. (2021). The Achilles' heel of the platform business model: Disintermediation. *Business Horizons*, 65(3).

Lanzolla, G., Lorenz, A., Miron-Spektor, E., Schilling, M., Solinas, G., & Tucci, C. (2020). Digital transformation: What is new if anything? Emerging patterns and management research. *AMD*, 6, 341–503.

Le Merle, M. C., & Davis, A. (2017). *Corporate Innovation in the Fifth Era*. Cartwright Publishing.

Majumbar, S., Guha, S., & Marakkath, N. (2015). *Technology Innovation for Social Change*. Springer.

Makgalemele, T. (2015). Igniting a spark for education in SA. *Finweek*, 30–32.

Mayer-Schönberger, V., & Cukier, K. (2013). *Big Data: A Revolution That Will Transform How We Live, Work, and Think*. Houghton Mifflin Harcourt.

Morris, M., & Tucker, R. (2021), The entrepreneurial mindset and poverty. *Journal of Small Business Management*. DOI: 10.1080/00472778.2021.1890096

Njanja, A. (2022). mPharma raises $35 million in round joined by Tinder co-founder's JAM fund, Bharti executive. Techcrunch. https://techcrunch.com/2022/01/05/mpharma-raises-35million-in-round-participated-by-tinder-co-founders-jam-fund-bharti-executive/

Perchard, A., MacKenzie, N. G., Decker, S., & Favero, G. (2017). Clio in the business school: Historical approaches in strategy, international business and entrepreneurship. *Business History*, 59(6), 904–927.

Roser, M. (2018). The internet's history has just begun. *Our World in Data*, 3 October. https://ourworldindata.org/internet-history-just-begun

Rousseau, D. M., & Fried, Y. (2001). Location, location, location: Contextualizing organizational research. *Journal of Organizational Behavior: The International Journal of Industrial, Occupational and Organizational Psychology and Behavior*, 22(1), 1–13.

Schwank, O. (2010). *Linkages in South African Economic Development: Industrialization without Diversification*. Peter Lang AG.

Swartz, E. M., & Amatucci, F. (2018). Framing second generation gender bias: Implications for women's entrepreneurship. *Journal of Developmental Entrepreneurship*, 23(1), 1850009.

Swartz, E. M., Amatucci, E., & Marks, J. T. (2019). Contextual embeddedness as a framework: The case of entrepreneurship in South Africa. *Journal of Developmental Entrepreneurship*, 24(3), 1–24.

Taylor, L., & Broeders, D. (2015). In the name of development: Power, profit and the datafication of the global South. Geoforum, 64, 229–237.

Teece, D. (2014). The foundations of enterprise performance: Dynamic and ordinary capabilities in an (economic) theory of firms. *AMP*, 28, 328–352.

Trapido, S. (1971). South Africa in a comparative study of industrialization. *Journal of Development Studies*, 7(3), 309–320.

van Gelderen, M., & Masurel, E. (2012). *Entrepreneurship in Context*. London: Routledge.

Walton, N. (2022). Digital platforms as entrepreneurial ecosystems and drivers of born-global SMEs in emerging economies. In V. Jafarai-Sadeghi & L.-P. Dana (Eds), *International Entrepreneurship and in Emerging Markets: Contexts, Behaviours and Successful Entry* (Vol. 1). Routledge Taylor & Francis Group.

Welter, F. (2011). Contextualising entrepreneurship: Conceptual challenges and ways forward. *Entrepreneurship: Theory and Practice*, 35(1), 165–184.

Welter, F., Brush, C., & De Bruin, A. (2014). The gendering of entrepreneurship context. *Institut für Mittelstandsforschung Bonn (Hrsg.): Working Paper*, 1, 14.

Welter, F., Baker, T., & Wirsching, K. (2019). Three waves and counting: The rising tide of contextualization in entrepreneurship research. *Small Business Economy*, 52, 319–330.

Whitehouse, D. (2021). Google to invest $1bn to back Equiano cable to increase Africa's Internet access. *The Africa Report*. www.theafricareport.com/133759/google-to-invest-1bn-to-back-equiano-increase-african-internet-access/

Withers, B. (2017). Was 2U Inc. smart in buying get smarter? *The Motley Fool*. www.fool.com/investing/2017/12/31/was-2u-inc-smart-in-buying-getsmarter.aspx

World Bank (2019). *Digital Economy for Ghana Diagnostic Report*. World Bank. License: Creative Commons Attribution CC BY 3.0 IGO.

World Bank (2020). Digital development. October 27. www.worldbank.org/en/topic/digitaldevelopment/overview

World Bank (n.d.). World Telecommunication/ICT Indicators Database https://data.worldbank.org/indicator/IT.NET.USER.ZS?locations=ZG and population data https://data.worldbank.org/indicator/SP.POP.TOTL?locations=ZA-KE-NG-GH

Yousafzai, S. Y., Saeed, S., & Muffatto, M. (2015). Institutional theory and contextual embeddedness of women's entrepreneurial leadership: Evidence from 92 countries. *Journal of Small Business Management*, 53(3), 587–604.

Zahra, S. A. (2007). Contextualizing theory building in entrepreneurship research. *Journal of Business Venturing*, 22(3), 443–452.

Zahra, S. A., Wright, M., & Abdelgawad, S. G. (2014). Contextualization and the advancement of entrepreneurship research. *International Small Business Journal*, 32(5), 479–500.

3. Technological leapfrogging in Africa: critical success factors to drive inclusive growth

Marianne Matthee and Caren Brenda Scheepers

INTRODUCTION

Africa has long grappled with the challenge of stimulating stronger and more inclusive economic growth while also implementing long overdue and sustainable improvements on the economic development front (Zeufack et al., 2022). Although several African countries have benefited from favourable commodity cycles, sometimes reflected in pleasing economic growth figures, their longer-term developmental efforts have been far from stellar – weighed down by fiscal constraints, lacklustre investment, infrastructure shortcomings and a widening skills deficit (Phillips, 2019). Moreover, periodic upturns in economic growth rates rarely translate into more *inclusive* growth, which implies that a larger proportion of the population productively participates in, and benefits from, a country's economic activities (Ianchovichina & Lundstrom, 2009).

Part of the challenge confronting Africa is the speed with which new and often more sophisticated technologies are being rolled out globally under the mantle of the Fourth Industrial Revolution (4IR) (Schwab, 2016), also called Industry 4.0. The 4IR phenomenon implies a fusion and interaction of technology across physical, digital and biological domains, which many African countries appear ill equipped to leverage (Gross, 2019). Thus, the question should be asked:

> What are the implications of today's technological or 'digital' era for the continent's inclusive growth and development prospects?

On the one hand, there is a strong risk that African countries will fall further and further behind their developing-country peers in other parts of the world through a lack of digital preparedness (Gross, 2019). On the other hand, there is scope for African countries to step up their economic momentum (Naudé, 2019) and do some catching up through the adoption of a strategy of 'technological leapfrogging' (Lee, 2019b).

In broad terms, technological leapfrogging refers to a process of using various technologies to skip or bypass some of the more traditional stages in a country's (or industry's) development (Lee, 2019a), thus allowing 'latecomers' to make up for lost time and create a stronger base for ongoing future development (Perez & Soete, 1988). However, leapfrogging should not be mistaken for a magic wand that makes fundamental problems go away, such as a dearth of qualified educators, dysfunctional infrastructure, weak financial controls or uneven digital connectivity (Cariolle & Carroll, 2020b; Pilling, 2018). It requires a firm foundation and scale to produce meaningful results. Africa is not a stranger to technological leapfrogging. Its so-called 'mobile revolution' – evidenced in the massive growth in mobile phone usage across the continent and the widespread side-lining of traditional fixed landline systems – is a well-known example (Cariolle & Carroll, 2020a). Yet leapfrogging has not gained meaningful traction on the continent, which can be attributed to a range of factors.

Africa is essentially at a crossroads: its economic future will largely be determined by the quality of its decisions today and how effectively it leverages digital technologies to ensure that growth (and particularly inclusive growth) is a planned outcome and not a random occurrence. In the next section we consider the importance of structural transformation for sustainable economic growth and how transformation means different things to different countries in Africa.

ECONOMIC GROWTH AND STRUCTURAL TRANSFORMATION

Structural transformation, an important source of sustainable economic growth, is a process whereby economic activity is reallocated from low-productivity to high-productivity sectors (Schlogl & Sumner, 2020). This is evidenced, for example, in the transition from agriculture to modern (urbanised), industrial-scale manufacturing and services, leading to a diversified, industrialised economic structure (Todaro & Smith, 2015). As the economy develops, with a progressive shift from agriculture (primary sector) to manufacturing (secondary sector) and services (tertiary sector), the contributions of these sectors to gross domestic product and employment grow (Naudé, 2019).

Rodrik (2013) notes that high growth rates are usually a consequence of rapid structural transformation, specifically industrialisation, and that industrialisation can take place even when fundamental capabilities are at a low level. Thus, poor countries can pursue structural transformation even in the face of limited skills and weak institutions. However, Primi and Toselli (2020) state that investment in education, skills development and infrastructure (both physical and digital) are essential prerequisites for developing countries to catch up with their more developed counterparts.

In Africa, the path to structural transformation will differ from one country to the next because each country has a unique character. For example, in countries such as the Cape Verde Islands, Mauritius, the Seychelles, Botswana and Lesotho, 'traditional' manufacturing capabilities (especially in less-automated sectors) can be developed because the countries offer a labour cost advantage (Naudé, 2019). An alternative path to structural transformation involves leveraging the technological opportunities presented by the 4IR (Schwab, 2016). This has been thrown into sharp relief over the past couple of years in the face of COVID-19. In their study on the relationship between information and communication technology (ICT) and economic growth, Solomon and Van Klyton (2020, p. 1) claim that 'the importance of digital technology has rarely been greater understood than during the 2020 global economic shutdown as a result of the COVID-19 pandemic'.

The influence of technology was theorised by Solow (1956) in his endogenous growth (or new growth) model. The endogenous growth model postulates that the degree to which capital and labour can drive economic growth is limited, whereas technology can produce boundless economic growth (Todaro & Smith, 2015). For example, investment in ICT boosts economic growth not only through capital deepening due to falling prices for ICT, but also through higher innovation levels resulting from business-to-business transactions (Signé, 2018), production spill overs and network externalities (Miller, 2001). Taking advantage of opportunities in the technological sphere can facilitate a resurgence in local manufacturing, with new high-tech start-up companies leading the development of extensive high-tech ecosystems (Naudé, 2019). New local industries, such as renewable energy, 3D printing and drone manufacturing, can be strong drivers of growth. Ghana's African Robotics Network, Uganda's Fundi Bots educational initiative and Egypt's EG Robotics entrepreneurial initiative are notable examples (Cariolle & Carroll, 2020a).

Regarding technology adoption, however, Naudé (2019) issues a word of caution: as the nature of manufacturing has evolved over time to embrace increasingly complex and efficient technologies (evidenced in multiple artificial intelligence and Internet of Things applications), African countries may not immediately experience the benefits of their structural shifts. It may take up to 15 years to allocate the necessary investment and create a conducive business ecosystem that starts delivering tangible results.

Clearly, in their efforts to bring about structural transformation as a driver of economic growth, African countries have an opportunity to use emerging technologies to ensure that such growth is more inclusive and sustainable (Zeufack et al., 2022). However, inducing such a paradigm shift is invariably complex, time consuming and expensive. In the next section, we look at the concept of technological leapfrogging and how it can be used to hasten the pace (and reduce the cost) of development in countries that otherwise risk being left behind.

CATCHING UP THROUGH TECHNOLOGICAL LEAPFROGGING

In his seminal study, Lee (2019b) explains that some countries are latecomers in the economic development process and might not follow developed countries' technological paths. They might even skip certain stages or create their own unique path that deviates from the 'norm'. A key enabler for these latecomers is making pre-emptive investments in emerging technologies. This allows them to catch up with their more advanced counterparts in new markets by bypassing the heavy investments made in earlier technological systems or stages – while also side-stepping some of the expensive mistakes that were made along the way.

There are several examples of countries in Asia that display the 'latecomer' effect (Gross, 2019), including South Korea (e.g., Samsung and LG) (Lee, 2019b; Lee et al., 2005) and China (e.g., Huawei). We contend that Africa is a 'latecomer' (Lee, 2019a) and that technology is an essential enabler for African countries to catch up as it fuels many exogenous opportunities that are ready to be seized (Perez & Soete, 1988).

In line with the Schumpeterian view, catching up with forerunners is most likely to occur when there is a shift in paradigms, which creates exogenous disruptions due to latecomers experiencing lower barriers to entry. Perez and Soete (1988) introduced this idea in their explanation of the imitator's lower cost curve. The authors assert that a key prerequisite for the lower cost curve of the imitator is the imitator's initial technical knowledge base in the relevant areas. Perez and Soete (1988) call the conditions for development paradoxical as previous capital is required to produce new capital, and previous knowledge and skills are necessary to absorb new knowledge and skills. Moreover, they argue that a certain level of development is required to create the agglomeration economies that make development possible.

From a development perspective, the danger for forerunners or incumbents is what Christensen (1997) calls the incumbent trap, where huge capital investment creates the risk of being locked in due to vested interests and even complacency. Forerunners are at risk of being challenged or displaced when new techno-economic paradigms are created with the advent of emerging industries. South Africa, for example, is widely regarded as the industrial leader in Africa and is the incumbent in certain industries, which makes it difficult to keep up with some newer and more technologically agile competitors.

The adoption of existing technologies is an important feature of the leapfrogging phenomenon (Lee, 2019a; Schlogl, 2020). Gross (2019) explains that developing countries are not bound by outdated technologies and can take the lead in the use of artificial intelligence, renewable energy, drones and other innovations. Lee (2019b) argues that diverse, 4IR-driven technologies can be a source of competitive advantage for companies when incorporated into their business models or product/service designs. This is particularly true for start-ups which typically have the least invested in existing, more traditional technologies. Indeed, start-ups with some absorptive capacity (Chaparro et al., 2020) and experience of technology are the most likely to leapfrog.

The above is called 'path-creating leapfrogging', which involves latecomers catching up through innovation (adopting more sophisticated technologies) and taking advantage of windows of opportunity. These windows offer a country scope to develop by adopting new, emerging technologies with a view to becoming a leader in those technologies, without the need for heavy initial investment in research and development. South Korea's leadership in the digital television sector is an example of this, although it should be noted that the country already had the capability to produce analogue televisions, which it then extended into the production of digital televisions (Gross, 2019; Lee, 2019b). Similarly, countries such as Malaysia, Indonesia, Thailand and the Philippines took over the technology production processes of more developed countries in East Asia, such as South Korea, Taiwan, Singapore and Hong Kong. In essence, the less-developed countries employed a system of leapfrogging to integrate regionally and join the global value chains (GVCs) of their more developed neighbours (Gross, 2019).

Another type of leapfrogging is 'path-skipping leapfrogging'. Here latecomers catch up by adopting sophisticated technologies that are available through international technological diffusion. Countries essentially skip certain stages on the traditional development path but remain on the same broad trajectory, such as moving from agricultural pursuits to services and skipping over manufacturing – a strategy that India has embraced to quite a large extent. Miller (2001) provides a number of examples of path-skipping leapfrogging in India which centred on the heightened use of the internet by businesses in the service industry that had benefited from a series of government incentives and were exempted from many onerous regulations and controls. Joshi (2017) refers to the 'great Indian leapfrog' where India never fully industrialised, but 'moved partially from an agricultural economy to a service economy'. In the Sub-Saharan African context, the widespread skipping of fixed landline phone technology in favour of mobile phone technology (helped by international technological diffusion) produced an important spill over – it paved the way for mobile money to take root and expand in several countries (Asongu & Asongu, 2018).

The above discussion highlights that technological leapfrogging (whether of the path-creating or path-skipping variety) will only deliver meaningful results if the industries and/or companies concerned have some existing technological knowledge and capacity and there is a supportive policy environment. In other words, leapfrogging cannot gain traction in a technological vacuum. In the next section, we outline some of the factors that are critical for the successful implementation of a technological leapfrogging strategy.

CRITICAL SUCCESS FACTORS FOR TECHNOLOGICAL LEAPFROGGING

Notwithstanding the fact that every country is different and has chosen a different developmental path, given its unique socioeconomic and political character and circumstances, a technological leapfrogging strategy is dependent on a number of critical enablers or success factors.

A favourable policy environment is essential if a country is to advance technologically (Zeufack et al., 2022), especially where a leapfrogging strategy is envisaged, which is designed to accelerate economic growth and development and narrow the digital divide. It is not enough, though, to have dedicated ICT policies and regulations (although these serve an important purpose). Rather, ICT strategies and plans should permeate all policy frameworks (economic, energy, education, health and so on) to reduce the risk of certain sectors and interest groups being left behind. This will go a long way towards fostering more inclusive societies.

Primi and Toselli (2020) assert that ICT policies need to be realistic and appropriate, matching a particular society's aspirations and needs. For example, hyper-connected smart factories are not within reach of countries in which industrialisation has not yet taken off. Primi and Toselli (2020, p. 386) advise developing countries to 'act fast and based on a clear understanding of the societies they aspire to become. In absence of visions, values, and choices, Industry 4.0 risks to become another, new, and even greater, source of development gaps within and between countries.'

Solomon and Van Klyton (2020) stress the importance of governments aligning their national workforces with the demands of a digitalising economy. 'The growth effects of ICT can be maximised through a skilled labour force and an enabling ICT environment … investment in human capital is an important policy consideration to improve the growth effects of ICT' (Solomon & Van Klyton, 2020, p. 12). A potential source of such investment is venture capital, which creates ripple effects by mobilising research and development, innovation and the creation of intellectual property assets. These, in turn, can generate additional wealth (Phillips, 2019). Phillips (2019) explains that venture capital not only covers finance but also mentorship, strategic guidance and network access.

Schwab (2016) predicted some challenges in relation to the 4IR, including growing inequalities between capital holders and labour suppliers, and short-term insecurities about substitution effects in the labour market and in the demand for skills. Accordingly, making it easier to do business and creating an investment-friendly environment are priorities for policymakers in developing countries (Gross, 2019). Public and private partnerships (together contributing to a national innovation system) can create opportunities for investment in emerging technologies and foster linkages with international knowledge holders, such as foreign universities and science hubs. At the same time, government and other stakeholders should guard against home-grown and/or nurtured technologies being eroded by foreign competition, as this could hamper the process of technological leapfrogging. For example, the Chinese government offered regulatory protection to Alibaba against the encroachment of Amazon in the Chinese market. Phillips (2019) advises African governments to formulate unified legal and policy responses in the face of interest from private equity investors in the technology space.

Infrastructure is at the centre of most discussions about economic growth and development, but it acquires special prominence in the context of the 4IR which demands ongoing investment and capacity building. Infrastructure is of critical importance to the transport, energy, telecommunications, banking and financial sectors (Cariolle & Carroll, 2020b). If it is inadequate, pockets of excellence (at best) will emerge with no real chance of scaling. In this regard, Pilling (2018) dismisses the notion that entrepreneurial innovations will compensate for a lack of infrastructure.

Undeniably, technology is only as good as its users and the way it is applied. Thus, a country's sociopolitical structures and technological capabilities are key determinants of whether or not technological leapfrogging will be successful (Gross, 2019). COVID-19 has highlighted the importance of digital literacy, with Lyons and Kass-Hanna (2021) concluding that digital literacy and financial literacy are key factors in building inclusiveness and financial resilience among at-risk groups, such as women and the youth. Another essential prerequisite for successful leapfrogging is absorptive capacity, which relates to existing production capacity and access to existing technologies from forerunners. Lee (2019b) stresses that latecomer firms should not attempt to leapfrog prematurely; they first need to build some absorptive capacity in their niche area.

In summary, the ability of a country to leverage the power of technological leapfrogging depends on there being a firm foundation in place in the form of conducive policy and regulatory frameworks, ongoing investments in infrastructure and human capital and realistic strategies that match the country's broad developmental needs and aspirations. Anything less has the potential to deliver disappointing results. In the next section, we analyse the status of Africa's digital ecosystem which, while showing encouraging signs in some quarters, is generally characterised by a deep digital divide.

AFRICA'S EMERGING DIGITAL ECOSYSTEM

While the rollout of fixed broadband had a significant impact on the global economy between 2010 and 2017, the impact was much more noticeable in less-developed countries, according to Katz and Callorda (2018). The authors state that a digital ecosystem (as defined by Chung et al., 2020) consists of an interconnected set of services through which users fulfil a variety of cross-sectoral needs under the banner of one integrated experience. A digital ecosystem positively contributes to economic growth and social well-being, with connectivity constituting its lifeblood. Katz and Callorda (2018) add that connectivity has transformative power in that it empowers people and creates an environment that nurtures innovation and triggers positive change in business processes and in the global economy. According to Cusolito et al. (2020, p. 101), 'adopting digital business solutions can have an impact on a company's sales and productivity, and through higher levels of production, on better jobs for more people'. One only has to think about how using an email service and having an online presence through a business website or social media can positively impact a firm's labour and capital demand, productivity and revenue-generating capabilities (Cusolito et al., 2020).

In 2018, Ban Ki-moon (as quoted in Pilling, 2018) wrote in the *Financial Times*: 'With the rapid development of the global digital economy and the availability of technology, the next generation belongs to Africa'. Indeed, it can be argued that given Africa's growing population and expanding middle class, digital technologies provide innumerable opportunities to unlock Africa's potential for rapid economic growth, job creation, expanded service delivery and regional and global trade. According to Asongu and Boateng (2018), the mobile phone revolution in Africa has transformed both industries and households by connecting colleagues, friends and family members in ways that were previously unimaginable, offering cost-effective business solutions to small and medium enterprises, enabling medical doctors and other specialists to consult from a distance and extending financial services to the previously unbanked. Zeufack et al. (2022), in turn, highlight how Africa's mobile revolution has improved access to financial projects, thus helping to drive greater financial inclusion. All these benefits suggest that digital adoption fosters inclusiveness.

At the heart of Africa's digital ecosystem is the extent of internet usage on the continent. It is estimated that Sub-Saharan Africa will have more than 130 million new mobile subscribers by 2025. Around half of these new subscribers will come from just five markets, namely Nigeria, Ethiopia, the Democratic Republic of the Congo, Tanzania and Kenya (GSMA, 2020).

Nearly half a billion people in Sub-Saharan Africa will be using the internet by 2025. One-third will come from Nigeria and Ethiopia (GSMA, 2020). Ethiopia is the fastest-growing economy on the African continent (after Nigeria) and aims to reach lower-middle-income status by 2025 (World Bank, 2022). Hjort and Poulsen (2019) report that the rollout of broadband internet connections has contributed to rapid job creation and a spike in economic activity in Sub-Saharan Africa. For example, the installation of subterranean internet cables along the African coast and the creation of a terrestrial cable network have increased the probability of an individual finding employment by 6.9 and 13.2 per cent, respectively (Hjort & Poulsen, 2019). Faster internet, in turn, helps to shift the focus of employment towards higher-productivity occupations.

Interestingly, too, the number of mobile money accounts in Sub-Saharan Africa increased from 469 million in 2019 to 500 million in 2020, with East Africa accounting for 'more than half of total registered accounts' (GSMA, 2020, p. 21). This promising trend prompted Visa (in April 2020) to partner with Safaricom to connect M-Pesa's 24 million (mobile money) accounts and 173,000 local merchants to Visa's global network. Mobile phone companies have tended to act as the pillar on which digital entrepreneurs have built their companies, which has led to the slow expansion of the market for digital services. Cariolle and Carroll (2020a) refer to instances in which some mobile network operators have engaged in infrastructure sharing to expand the reach of mobile networks and reduce the digital divide.

In Kenya, the growing popularity of mobile money has seen a spike in remittances to rural areas and a reduction in transaction costs, which has helped to reduce poverty in that country (GSMA, 2020). Suri and Jack (2016) found that improved access to mobile money services (linked to the rapid rollout of M-Pesa) increased household consumption and savings and moved 196,000 households out of extreme poverty (representing a 2 per cent reduction in the country's poverty rate), with the greatest impact felt in female-headed households. Furthermore, access to M-Pesa enabled 186,000 women to make the transition from agriculture as their main occupation to business and retail.

Bahia et al. (2020) showed that expanded mobile broadband coverage enhanced the labour market outcomes for women in Nigeria as well as the welfare of Nigerian households, particularly in impoverished, rural areas – where 'welfare' refers to higher levels of consumption and reduced poverty levels. In this regard, one year of mobile broadband coverage fuels a 6 per cent increase in household consumption and a 4.3 per cent reduction in extreme poverty (which rises to 6.9 per cent for two years of coverage). Bahia et al. (2020) emphasise that these gains are not only attributable to households participating in modern sectors of the economy; they also apply to poorer, rural households, such as those engaged in subsistence agriculture.

Senegal has seen rapid expansion in its fixed and mobile broadband internet infrastructure over the past 10 years, with the introduction of 3G coverage associated with a 14 per cent increase in total consumption in that country (Atiyas & Dutz, 2020). The positive effects are most noticeable among male-headed households in urban areas and among younger people, and are driven by better labour market outcomes, higher agricultural productivity and production and access to mobile money. Atiyas and Dutz (2020) also found that Senegalese firms that used more specialised digital technologies tended to generate higher profits than firms that used the generic smartphone, e.g., profits were 3.7 times higher when a digital inventory control system was used and 2.9 times higher when online banking was used. In addition, firms that used mobile money services to pay suppliers and receive payments from customers also tended to generate higher profits (Atiyas & Dutz, 2020).

Despite the promising picture painted above, Africa's digital ecosystem reveals a dichotomy in the form of a deep digital divide on the continent (Zeufack et al., 2020). For 800 million people in Africa, the internet remains unattainable (GSMA, 2020). Only 26 per cent of Africa's population, around 272 million people, have accessed internet-based services on a mobile device (compared to 56 per cent in East Asia, for example). Nearly half the African population live within the vicinity of a mobile broadband network, but have never accessed the mobile internet, while one-quarter of Africa's population do not live in the vicinity of such a network (GSMA, 2020). Achieving geographically dispersed digital inclusivity is a major challenge – as articulated in the analogy of the 'last-mile problem'. In the telecommunications sphere, end users in rural areas live some distance (i.e., the figurative 'last mile') from broadband internet infrastructure, which inhibits their ability to connect. Users in remote locations are often simply excluded as it is very expensive to facilitate access through additional infrastructure (Techopedia, 2021), making connectivity challenging in any country setting. In Africa, the last-mile problem is particularly acute.

Those who do have access to the internet face frequent connectivity problems. Moreover, the proportion of African firms that have access to a high-speed internet service is small, despite the potential of such a service to reduce business and transaction costs. For example, from April to June 2020, the average download speed for mobile internet in Sub-Saharan Africa was 17.4 megabytes per second (Mbps), compared to 29.7 Mbps in East Asia and the Pacific (Bezzina et al., 2019).

In Senegal, only 34 per cent of companies use the internet, while 20 per cent rely on a digital subscriber line. In addition, the number of secure internet servers per 1 million people was extremely low at 16.7 in 2018, compared to 35.9 in Rwanda, 219.1 in Kenya and 760.4 on average in Sub-Saharan Africa. Despite relatively good mobile penetration rates among the general population, Senegalese households are lagging behind their peers in Africa in the use of digital services, such as online payments (Bezzina et al., 2019). In general, Senegal's uneven digital adoption rates vary according to level of education, gender, age and digital literacy (Atiyas & Dutz, 2020).

Regarding data costs, Sub-Saharan Africa performs poorly alongside other developing regions. Figure 3.1 shows that the cost, to the bottom quintile of the population, of purchasing mobile data is particularly high in Sub-Saharan Africa, at 39 per cent of monthly income per capita. This simply entrenches the sharp economic divisions in the countries concerned. In addition, the figure shows that the cost of mobile data is much higher in Sub-Saharan African countries than in other developing countries, which negatively affects adoption rates in the region.

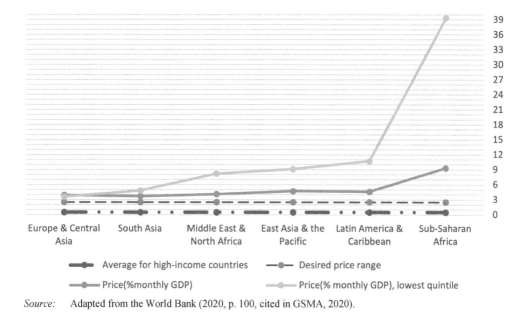

Source: Adapted from the World Bank (2020, p. 100, cited in GSMA, 2020).

Figure 3.1   *The cost of 1 gigabyte of data in developing countries across different regions*

Notwithstanding the positive trends in various areas, these have often come off a low base and many challenges remain. Africa (and Sub-Saharan Africa in particular) could be doing much more to capitalise on available technologies to mobilise broader internet usage and more diverse applications with a view to boosting inclusive growth and creating more future-ready economies.

To this end, Africa needs a more robust and inclusive digital transformation strategy to drive faster economic growth and job creation (Ghanem, 2020). Key elements in such a strategy would include a national ICT strategy, a conducive business environment, physical and ICT infrastructure, financial capital and an ICT skills base.

Figure 3.2 compares certain Sub-Saharan African countries in terms of these elements, as reflected in the International Telecommunication Union ICT Development Index report

(2021). According to the report, Senegal, Kenya and Ethiopia scored the highest in terms of national ICT strategy, while Ghana and South Africa scored the highest in terms of business environment. South Africa and Kenya scored the highest in terms of infrastructure readiness and financial capital. Unfortunately, all countries covered in the report fared badly in the area of ICT skills (Zeufack et al., 2021).

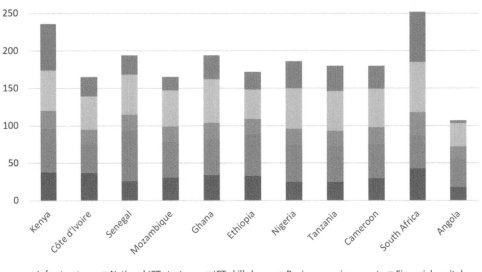

■ Infrastructure   ■ National ICT strategy   ■ ICT skills base   ■ Business environment   ■ Financial capital

Source: Adapted from Zeufack et al. (2021, p. 60).

Figure 3.2   ICT readiness in selected African countries

Undoubtedly, the opportunities available to Africa are as plentiful as the challenges that it currently faces. The fact that Africa has attracted strong interest from innovators, investors and development institutions is a clear sign of the continent's potential. In a crowded global technology market, Africa's growing population and expanding middle class are certainly exciting drawcards. However, an important question that should be asked is: Is Africa up to the leapfrogging challenge? In the next section, we consider some of Africa's technological leapfrogging success stories, offering a glimpse of how the continent's development prospects could improve if these innovations were replicated on a grand scale.

WHERE HAS AFRICA TECHNOLOGICALLY LEAPFROGGED?

The creative and forward-thinking use of innovative technologies has produced several pockets of excellence in Africa which, in overcoming market and institutional failures and reducing costs, constitute an impressive display of technological leapfrogging (Cariolle & Carroll, 2020b). We provide a few company-related examples below.

In Rwanda and Ghana, a private-sector start-up company, Zipline, in partnership with the Rwandan government, uses unmanned aerial vehicles or drones to deliver blood, medications and other supplies to medical centres within an 80 kilometre radius of each launching site. This overcomes the problem of infrastructural and logistical impediments facing the healthcare industry which would otherwise make distribution impossible. Cariolle and Carroll (2020a, p. 5) report that 'drone delivery overcomes obstacles such as underdeveloped market structures as well as the market failure of informational asymmetries between logistics providers and the healthcare industry that uses their services'. When the COVID-19 pandemic struck, Zipline began delivering COVID-19 test kits throughout Rwanda and Ghana.

Jumia, an e-commerce company based in Nigeria, was the first technology start-up in Africa to acquire unicorn status in 2016. Jumia, which has benefited from its access to the global venture ecosystem and seed capital from the German company, Rocket Internet (Cariolle & Carroll, 2020a), has already expanded into 18 other African countries. It offers a digital marketplace, a digital logistics platform and digital payment facilities that are linked to mobile money services. Jumia has leapfrogged 'missing financial infrastructures through partnering with major mobile money providers throughout Sub-Saharan Africa' (Cariolle & Carroll, 2020a, p. 3).

Another Nigerian company, Kobo360, has had success in leapfrogging missing transport infrastructure in the country. Kobo360, which calls itself the Uber for trucks, hosts a digital platform that enables truck drivers, owners and cargo shippers and recipients to interact online, formalise and optimise supply chains and reduce inefficiencies. It also offers an insurance service to its clients, including truck drivers. Founded in 2017, the company has already expanded into Kenya, Togo, Uganda and Ghana. Kobo360 is planning to offer a global logistics operating system, a block chain-enabled platform which will be an extension of its supply chain services (Cariolle & Carroll, 2020a).

Lynk, a labour market-matching company in Kenya, uses a two-pronged mobile and web-based platform to link skilled service providers to clients, thereby offering a solution to the poorly developed market structure. Lynk also offers a client and service provider evaluation and rating system on its platform. Lynk has partnered with training schools to recruit and on-board skilled informal-sector workers into its system, with the disbursement of payment for successful job placements taking place via M-Pesa within 24 hours of the completion of each job (Cariolle & Carroll, 2020a). In addition, Safaricom's e-commerce service, Masoko, has been integrated into the Lynk system (Cariolle & Carroll, 2020a).

The Investiv Group provides an example of innovation in the agricultural sector. This digital technology start-up company is in the business of precision agriculture, where unmanned aerial vehicles or drones are used to optimise crop management and overcome an underdeveloped market structure and informational asymmetries between products, grower cooperatives and clients (Cariolle & Carroll, 2020b). WorldCover, an agricultural insurance company, also makes use of M-Pesa in Kenya and MTB Mobile Money in Ghana to facilitate digital payments (Cariolle & Carroll, 2020a).

The diverse nature of Africa's leapfrogging success stories in several industry sectors is encouraging, showing that the technological seeds have been sown in a variety of places. But these seeds need to be nourished if they are to grow and ultimately bear fruit – certainly on a scale needed for Africa to narrow its digital divide and catch up with other, more technologically advanced regions. In the next section, we discuss some of the harsh realities facing Africa (including poverty, economic marginalisation and widespread educational shortcomings) which, if not seriously addressed, will continue to hamper efforts to boost technology adoption on the continent.

TECHNOLOGICAL LEAPFROGGING IN AFRICA: A REALITY CHECK

A superficial analysis may suggest that technological leapfrogging will be the 'saving grace' of Africa, which lags far behind many other regions in the world. However, we agree with Friederici et al. (2017) that a reality check is needed. Whether Africa can adopt a leapfrogging approach to generate quicker and more inclusive growth and make serious inroads in addressing developmental gaps and failures depends on whether and how scaling can take place. Furthermore, Rodrik (2013) points out that without some semblance of macroeconomic stability and property rights protection, new industries cannot emerge and leapfrogging efforts could end up being stillborn.

In Sub-Saharan Africa, populations that are excluded from public-service delivery are usually the same populations that are deprived of access to ICT services. Friederici et al. (2017) argue that, even though ICT has reduced the financial vulnerability and susceptibility to external shocks of poor households in South Africa, the poorest households might not benefit as much from these developments as those in other economic groupings. In an earlier section we highlighted the economically and digitally divided nature of most African countries, with poverty figures and economic exclusion weighing heavily on policymakers, businesses and ordinary citizens alike. The digital divide is most striking among those sections of the population that have low levels of education; yet unreliable and/or expensive internet access and generally limited technological experience and digital literacy affect other socioeconomic groups as well (Friederici et al., 2017). Another problem that technology companies in Africa face is the low level of willingness of users to pay for services.

All these factors make scaling challenging, especially for technology start-ups and entrepreneurs whose job is not to address national developmental shortcomings (energy, transport, schooling, among others) and market failures. Even Jumia reported losses for a number of years, citing challenges such as the company's dependence on call centres, warehouses and distribution centres which had their own operational problems.

Friederici et al. (2017) claim that the internet and other ICT innovations have not had the envisaged transformational impact on economic development in Sub-Saharan Africa. There are even indications that digital connectivity has exacerbated rather than reduced inequalities. For example, there is a large divide between rural and urban communities in terms of internet and mobile phone penetration and access to other ICT services (Cariolle & Carroll, 2020a). Moreover, Friederici et al. (2017) are of the view that digital entrepreneurs are 'not usually able to reach outside of their urban contexts because of insurmountable market fragmentation'.

On a broader scale, Friederici et al. (2017) warn that technological fixes might steer people's attention away from how the political economy in a country allocates power and wealth. For example, trying to address inequality through more widespread connectivity could take the focus away from the structural economic weaknesses that are the cause of widening inequality. 'Channelling resources into supporting entrepreneurs is a trade-off that shifts the burden of development away from building public institutions and tackling structural issues' (Friederici et al., 2020, p. 24).

In the African context, the recently launched African Continental Free Trade Area (AfCFTA) offers great potential for stronger economic integration, GVC participation and scaling – particularly in the technological arena which could be a source of innovative solutions to the current problems of limited and high-cost intraregional trade. At present, only 17 per cent of Africa's exports are destined for other African markets, compared to 59 per cent in Asia and 68 per cent in Europe (Kende-Robb, 2021). The market opening and market expansion benefits offered by the AfCFTA could be important inducements to engaging in technological leapfrogging by facilitating greater investment, technological diffusion and the sharing of expertise between African trading partners. This would allow the pockets of technological excellence seen in Nigeria, Kenya, South Africa and other countries to spread more liberally across the continent, assuming that the relevant legal and regulatory regimes are suitably accommodating.

In an era of growing isolationism, AfCFTA could become a model of technological cooperation that will help to drive leapfrogging on a grand scale. This is particularly important given that Africa has been significantly weakened by the effects of COVID-19. Baldwin (2008, 2011) asserts that entering existing supply chains is very important for latecomer industrialising countries. Lee (2019b) emphasises that while importing intermediate goods for the purpose of producing products for export appears to be good for competitiveness (because more exports are produced locally), such an approach (i.e., backward participation in GVCs) could in fact be a barrier to leapfrogging. What would be more leapfrogging friendly, he says, is focusing on upgrading local production capacity in order to move up the value chain.

For the effects of technological leapfrogging in Africa to be transformative, existing pockets of excellence need to be dramatically expanded and upscaled so that their value can be felt more broadly. However, this does not minimise the critical role played by the government in delivering essential services to keep the economy running efficiently while providing a supportive environment in which technological innovation is able to thrive.

CONCLUSION

The ability to adapt to technological change is an indispensable success factor in the world today. In fact, no country is immune to the rapid advances of new and increasingly accessible technologies. While this places enormous pressure on those countries that are developmental latecomers and are burdened by a deep digital divide, technological leapfrogging potentially offers the means to catch up and keep up with other, more developed countries.

In Africa, there is still only limited evidence of successful technological leapfrogging, although there are promising signs in several quarters. Countries like Nigeria, Ghana, Kenya and South Africa are able to boast several leapfrogging initiatives in the education, energy, health and agricultural sectors which have the potential to be scaled up, given the right preconditions. These include 'getting the basics right', such as ensuring reliable energy sources, reliable and cost-effective internet access, efficient infrastructure and logistics hubs and a sound education system that is accessible to all. These are all fundamental to the smooth running of an economy and cannot be bypassed or glossed over – although various forms of technology can make them more efficient and inclusive. Another precondition is that there is a conducive policy environment evidenced in sound ICT-specific and cross-cutting policies and regulations, an investment-friendly business environment, an open trade regime and the political commitment to support leapfrogging in designated sectors – with a strong emphasis on boosting digital access and digital literacy.

Certain scholars have expressed the opinion that technological leapfrogging is possible even from a low developmental base – in other words, it is not only the domain of advanced countries or industries (Lee, 2019a; Naudé, 2019). The implication here is that African countries at different stages of development have the opportunity, through technology adoption, to leapfrog into more productive and job-enhancing economic spaces without having to commit huge amounts of time or money to their development. Nevertheless, having the 'basics' in place and sufficient absorptive capacity are important building blocks in this process.

Essentially, the secret to technological leapfrogging in Africa will be the ability to replicate the many industry- and company-based success stories on a much wider scale so that the benefits can be diffused throughout the population. This in turn will create new generations of capable entrepreneurs who will be powerful forces driving their countries' economies.

REFERENCES

Asongu, S. A., & Asongu, N. (2018). The comparative exploration of mobile money services in inclusive development. *International Journal of Social Economics, 45*(1), 124–139.

Asongu, S., & Boateng, A. (2018). Introduction to special issue: Mobile technologies and inclusive development in Africa. *Journal of African Business, 19*(3), 297–301.

Atiyas, İ., & Dutz, M. (2020). *Digital technology use among informal micro-entrepreneurial firms: Productivity, profits, exports and inclusive jobs outcomes in Senegal* (Policy Research Working Paper 9573). World Bank Group.

Bahia, K., Castells, P., Cruz, G., Masaki, T., Pedrós, X., Pfutze, T., Rodríguez-Castelán, C., & Winkler, H. (2020). *The welfare effects of mobile broadband internet: Evidence from Nigeria* (Policy Research Working Paper 8298). World Bank Group.

Baldwin, R. (2008). Managing the noodle bowl: The fragility of east Asian regionalism. *Singapore Economic Review, 53*(3), 449–478.

Baldwin, R. (2011). *Trade and industrialization after globalization's 2nd unbundling: How building and joining a supply chain are different and why it matters* (NBER Working Paper 17716). National Bureau of Economic Research.

Bezzina, J., Muller, A., Khoury, Z., & Seck, M. T. (2019). *Country diagnostic of Senegal* (Digital Economy for Africa (DE4A)). World Bank Group.

Cariolle, J., & Carroll, D. (2020a). *Advancing digital frontiers in African economies: Lessons learned from firm-level innovations* (Archives, ID: 03118738). HAL.

Cariolle, J., & Carroll, D. (2020b). *The use of digital for public service provision in Sub-Saharan Africa* (Archives, ID: 03004535). HAL.

Chaparro, X. A. F., Kozesinki, R., & Camargo, A. S. (2020). Absorptive capacity in start-ups: A systematic literature review. *Journal of Entrepreneurship, Management and Innovation, 17*(1), 57–95.

Christensen, C. M. (1997). *The innovator's dilemma: When new technologies cause great firms to fail.* Harvard Business School Press.

Chung, V., Dietz, M., Rab, I., & Townsend, Z. (2020, 11 September). Ecosystem 2.0: Climbing to the next level. *McKinsey Quarterly*.

Cusolito, A. P., Lederman, D., & Peña, J. (2020). *The effects of digital-technology adoption on productivity and factor demand: Firm-level evidence from developing countries* (Policy Research Working Paper 9333). World Bank Group.

Friederici, N., Ojanperä, S., & Graham, M. (2017). The impact of connectivity in Africa: Grand visions and the mirage of inclusive digital development. *Electronic Journal of Information Systems in Developing Countries, 79*(2), 1–20.

Friederici, N., Wahome, M., & Graham, M. (2020). *Digital entrepreneurship in Africa: How a continent is escaping Silicon Valley's long shadow*. Massachusetts Institute of Technology Press.

Ghanem, H. (2020, 7 February). *Shooting for the moon: An agenda to bridge Africa's digital divide.* Brookings Education.

Gross, A.-K. (2019). *Sub-Saharan Africa and the 4th Industrial Revolution technological leapfrogging as a strategy to enhance economic growth?* Master's thesis, Lund University. https://lup.lub.lu.se/student-papers/search/publication/8986790

GSMA (GSM Association) (2020). *The mobile economy: Sub-Saharan Africa 2020.* www.gsma.com/mobileeconomy/wp-content/uploads/2020/09/GSMA_MobileEconomy2020_SSA_Eng.pdf

Hjort, J., & Poulsen, J. (2019). The arrival of fast internet and employment in Africa. *American Economic Review, 109*(3), 1032–1079.

Ianchovichina, E., & Lundstrom, S. (2009). *Inclusive growth analytics framework and application* (Policy Research Working Paper 4851). World Bank.

International Telecommunication Union (2021). *Measuring digital development facts and figures 2021.* www.itu.int/en/ITUD/Statistics/Documents/facts/FactsFigures2021.pdf

Joshi, A. M. (2017, 17 December). *The great Indian leapfrog.* IMD.

Katz, R., & Callorda, F. (2018). *The economic contribution of broadband, digitization and ICT regulation.* ITU Publications.

Kende-Robb, C. (2021, 9 February). *Six reasons why Africa's new free trade area is a global game changer.* World Economic Forum.

Lee, K. (2019a). *The art of economic catch-up: Barriers, detours, and leapfrogging in innovation systems.* Cambridge University Press.

Lee, K. (2019b). *Economics of technological leapfrogging* (Inclusive and Sustainable Industrial Development Working Paper Series, Working Paper 17/2019). United Nations Industrial Development Organization.

Lee, K., Lim, C., & Song. W. (2005). Emerging digital technology as a window of opportunity and technological leapfrogging: Catch-up in digital TV by the Korean firms. *International Journal of Technology Management, 29*(1–2), 40–63.

Lyons, A. C., & Kass-Hanna, J. (2021). A methodological overview to defining and measuring 'digital' financial literacy. *Financial Planning Review, 4*(e1113), 1–19.

Miller, R. (2001). *Leapfrogging? India's information technology industry and the internet* (International Finance Corporation Discussion Paper 42). World Bank.

Naudé, W. (2019, October). *Three varieties of Africa's industrial future* (IZA Institute of Labour Economics Discussion Paper Series, DP No. 12678). http://ftp.iza.org/dp12678.pdf

Perez, C., & Soete, L. (1988). Catching-up in technology: Entry barriers and windows of opportunity. In G. Dosi, C. Freeman, R. Nelson, G. Silverberg & L. Soete (Eds), *Technical change and economic theory* (pp. 458–479). Pinter Publishers.

Phillips, O. (2019, 28 February). The leapfrog model: Venture capital as a cure to Africa's funding paralysis. *SSRN.* https://papers.ssrn.com/sol3/papers.cfm?abstract_id=3366908

Pilling, D. (2018, 13 August). African economy: The limits of 'leapfrogging'. *Financial Times.* www.ft.com/content/052b0a34-9b1b-11e8-9702-5946bae86e6d

Primi, A., & Toselli, M. (2020). A global perspective on Industry 4.0 and development: New gaps or opportunities to leapfrog? *Journal of Economic Policy Reform, 23*(4), 371–389.

Rodrik, D. (2013, June). *The past, present, and future of economic growth* (Global Citizen Foundation Working Paper 1). www.law.nyu.edu/sites/default/files/upload_documents/GCF_Rodrik-working-paper-1_-6.17.131_0.pdf

Schlogl, L. (2020). *Leapfrogging into the unknown: The future of structural change in the developing world* (UNU-World Institute for Development Economics Research WIDER, Working Paper 2020/25). United Nations University.

Schlogl, L. & Sumner, A. (2020). *Disrupted development and the future of inequality in the age of automation.* Palgrave Macmillan.

Schwab, K. (2016, 14 January). *The Fourth Industrial Revolution: What it means, how to respond.* World Economic Forum.

Signé, L. (2018, September). *The potential of manufacturing and industrialization in Africa: Trends, opportunities and strategies*. Africa Growth Initiative at Brookings.

Solomon, E. M., & Van Klyton, A. (2020). The impact of digital technology usage on economic growth in Africa. *Utilities Policy, 67*, 101104, 1–12.

Solow, R. M. (1956). A contribution to the theory of economic growth. *Quarterly Journal of Economics, 70*, 65–94.

Suri, T., & Jack, W. (2016). The long-run poverty and gender impacts of mobile money. *Science, 354*(6317), 1288–1292.

Techopedia (2021, 16 November). *Last mile technology*. www.techopedia.com/definition/26195/last -mile-technology

Todaro, M. P., & Smith, S. C. (2015). *Economic development* (12th ed). Pearson.

World Bank. (2022, 21 April). *The World Bank in Ethiopia*. www.worldbank.org/en/country/ethiopia/ overview#1

Zeufack, A. G., Calderon, C., Kambou, G., Kubota, M., Korman, V., & Canales, C. C. (2020, October). *An analysis of issues shaping Africa's economic future* (Africa's Pulse, No. 22). World Bank Group.

Zeufack, A. G., Calderon, C., Kambou, G., Kubota, M., Korman, V., Canales, C. C., & Aviomoh, H. E. (2021, April). *An analysis of issues shaping Africa's economic future* (Africa's Pulse, No. 23). World Bank Group.

Zeufack, A. G., Calderon, C., Kabundi, A., Kubota, M., Korman, V., Raju, D., Girma, A. K., Kassa, W., & Owusu, S. (2022, April). (Africa's Pulse, No. 25). World Bank Group.

4. Advancing technological hub collaborations to promote transnational African communities

Michelle Montague-Mfuni, Frances Fabian, and Caren Brenda Scheepers

INTRODUCTION

Recent decades have seen the rise of hundreds of regional innovation ecosystems throughout the African continent (Kelly & Firestone, 2016). These technology hubs vary widely in advancement, sponsorship (e.g., government, university, corporate), and stability (Hernández-Chea, Mahdad, Minh, & Hjortsø, 2021). Recognizing the value of both these large and small home-grown, micro-innovation hubs, many African countries have been promoting an impressive number of tech hubs. For example, by 2017 the top four countries hosted almost two dozen or more hubs – South Africa (54), Egypt (28), Kenya (27), and Nigeria (23) (Workman, 2017). More recently, an Afrilabs and Briter Bridges report (2019), as well as the African Union Commission and OECD (2021), identified a total of 644 tech hubs across Africa. In Figure 4.1 we share the World Bank's (Kelly & Firestone, 2016, p. 3) illustration of the innovation hubs across the continent. Not surprisingly, relatively new literature on African technology hubs has focused on documenting the prolific growth rate in hub establishment and the implications for leapfrogging traditional institutions such as universities in building knowledge that can be transformed into value (Atiase, Kolade, & Liedong, 2020).

Existing categorizations for understanding these hubs vary widely. Country-level emphases naturally arise due to the ability to draft policies promoting hubs (Asongu & Odhiambo, 2020). Alternatively, a 2016 World Development report (drawing from the population of 117 tech hubs identified in Kelly & Firestone, 2016) stressed the institutional sponsorship of the hub in its analysis: e.g., government-led, civil society-led, academic institution-led, and/or hybrid. Elhoussamy, Weheba, and Rizk (2020) applied a comparable differentiation based on private-sector tech, university-based, and government-run tech hub categories in their comparison study on the technology hubs in Egypt.

Other researchers defined African tech hubs by three legal categorizations: (1) collaboration hubs; (2) company hubs; and (3) country hubs (De Beer, Millar, Mwangi, Nzomo, & Ruthenberg, 2017). Similarly, Afrilabs identified hubs with a combination of approaches: by sponsor (non-governmental organization, private, academic, government program, association) and by their structure (accelerators, corporate ventures, co-working spaces, hackerspaces, incubators, maker spaces, and technology parks) (Afrilabs & Bridges, 2019).

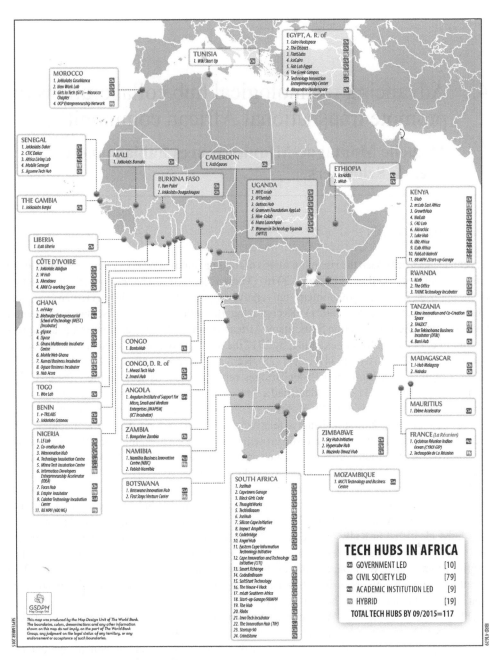

Source: Kelly & Firestone (2016, p. 3).

Figure 4.1   Technology hubs across Africa

Missing from these approaches is a categorization schema that can highlight the collaborative potential for different hubs to effectively work together. Given the vast scalar opportunities inherent in technology and the daunting need for greater continental investment, we offer a theoretical model to answer the question:

How might African technology hub collaborations contribute to connecting and expanding relevant technology advancements across Africa?

Our proposed conceptual model rests on three capabilities unique to hub collaboration-level dynamics, reflecting how collaboration among hubs offers distinctive advantages in handling both exploration and exploitation demands to direct ongoing management, drive investments, and encourage cooperative behaviors. These three capabilities encompass (1) *ambidexterity*, that is, the ability to exploit state-of-the-art technology while managing exploration through absorptive capacity (March, 1991; O'Reilly & Tushman, 2004; Koryak, Lockett, Hayton, Nicolaou, & Mole, 2018); (2) *springboard advantages* (Luo & Tung, 2018), that stress the value of home-based markets and operations while incorporating leapfrogging investments in innovation from external sources that can drive disruptive innovation; and (3) *synergies* that improve Pan-African integration from a relational emphasis consistent with those found in a conventional network synergy (Hernandez & Shaver, 2019), but draws from the African Ubuntu tradition (Pérezts, Russon & Painter, 2020). Considering these perspectives in concert, technology hub collaborations that link diverse innovation hubs can serve as fundamental players in pan-African integration. These collaborations marshal capabilities for leading-edge technology knowledge while shepherding resources to reflect African values and imperatives.

Research continues to link innovative firms to overall economic growth rates, increased skilled labor, enhanced academic research, and venture capital presence in regional development (Freeman, 2002; Qureshi, 2005; PricewaterhouseCoopers, 2017). The African Union Commission and OECD (2021) report that the COVID-19 crisis could push some 23 million Sub-Saharan Africans into extreme poverty and, therefore, the potential contribution of innovative firms is a necessity for Africa's future. The digital economy has been predicted to increase the African continent's gross domestic product (GDP) by $300 billion by 2025 and thus provide jobs to alleviate the disproportionate ratio of three to four available employees for every available job position (Bayuo et al., 2022). In particular, technology hub collaborations can provide both direct and indirect benefits by raising the return of firms already deriving value from hub colocation, with the additional value of other hubs that specialize in different parts of the value chain or that complement innovation across the exploration/exploitation divide. Of special note here is that these effects can produce relevant technologies faster and closer to markets while heavily rewarding the firms financially – offering extensive rent capture in the regions where the hub collaborations are located (Bresnahan, Gambardella, & Saxenian, 2001).

Both outcomes are especially compelling for the evolution of the African economy. Two African examples presented in a 2022 study include: (1) between 2010 and 2019, the technology sector contributed more to Nigeria's GDP than its resource-rich oil and gas sectors; and (2) the information communications technology (ICT) sector was approximately 8 percent of Kenya's GDP, creating nearly 250,000 jobs in 2021 (Bayuo et al., 2022). In the sections below, we provide a general background on the nature of technology hubs and review the special value of moving toward hub collaborations. We then elaborate our model on the essential role technology hub collaborations are likely to play in producing disruptive innovations customized to Africa. These innovations can promote profitable pan-African economies of scale.

We next offer practical insights on African technology hub collaboration, followed by theoretical concerns around the value of such hub collaboration, and then offer our proposed conceptual framework. We then hone in on the springboard effect in international expansions across Africa and, finally, we conclude the chapter with a discussion of implications of our proposed model for technological hub collaboration.

PRACTICAL INSIGHTS ON AFRICAN TECHNOLOGY HUB COLLABORATION

Friederici (2018) reviewed the growth of Africa tech hubs and the representations of hub ideals against some observed realities. Conducting 133 qualitative interviews in six African hubs in Ghana, Rwanda, and Zimbabwe, the study found that hub missions are often vague, though they do indeed tend to share three main assets: (1) services (training or events); (2) location workspace; and (3) entrepreneurial support. What is often unclear is the stated intent of how startup ventures are to be created or supported, e.g., whether directly or indirectly, and the missions often lack any distinction between internal and external tech communities. These network communities often have a local, national, regional, and sometimes international component of knowledge-sharing in addition to a shared workspace and training. In the face of this ambiguity in mission, measuring impact and performance is complex and not straightforward. Friederici (2018) proposed the view that African hubs act as a facilitator of "supportive technology social structures." From this vantage point, a key next question asks what technology social structures they should support.

A simple answer would hearken to the importance of creating a pan-African capacity to absorb and innovate new global technologies, customize them to local markets, and respond swiftly to new priorities. Such initiatives would incorporate a growing professional class that can span national borders and improve the capability to counter isolation and conflict on the continent. Due to their constrained size and location, though, no single hub is capable of marshaling all of the necessary resources. Consequently, numerous hub collaborations, some quite advanced, have already arisen throughout the African continent. Many were initially sponsored by multinational tech companies, while others represent smaller scale, micro-innovation hubs (Murphy, Carmody, & Surborg, 2014).

In one review, Cunningham, Cunningham, and Ekenberg (2014) performed a comparison of innovation ecosystems in Kenya, Tanzania, and Uganda. They first delineated an impressive list of innovation stakeholders, critical success factors, and specific challenges in developing-country contexts. Innovation stakeholders included entrepreneurs, private entities, venture capitalists, public organizations, government, universities, research and development groups, local communities, multinational corporations (MNCs), training consultants, marketing gurus, international development/funding sectors, and legal consultants, in addition to the actual end-user participation in innovation hubs (Cunningham et al., 2014; Bastos de Morais, 2015). They then identified four critical success factors for these partnerships: (1) public policy coordination; (2) level of socio-economic diversification; (3) level of technological adoption; and (4) the innovation stakeholders' commitment. The researchers further noted that influential country context variables included country size, maturity, growth potential for the innovation ecosystem, accessibility to education and skills training, and importantly, leadership to align interventions with public policy (Cunningham et al., 2014).

These advantages well align with McCormick's (1999) model that stresses the dynamic and adaptive advantages of hub collaborations. Specifically, McCormick (1999) highlights three main benefits of African enterprise hub collaboration: (1) collective efficiency that enhances firms' competitive advantage; (2) collaboration that facilitates growth in small steps; and (3) cooperation that eases the ability to respond to opportunities and crises.

Similarly, Bell and Albu (1999) argued that hub collaboration can help evolve knowledge systems in developing countries to improve their longer-term competitiveness. Intriguing recent examples arise from COVID-19 responses by African tech hubs. In one case, a United Kingdom (UK)–Nigeria tech hub launched a series of intervention programs that had three main goals: (1) support Nigeria's tech ecosystem; (2) mitigate the COVID-19 impact on startups; and (3) improve skills capacity within Nigeria's digital sector (Adarmola, 2020). The UK–Nigeria tech hub first conducted a survey on startups and investors to understand how COVID-19 affected them. They then provided recommendations to the Nigerian National Information Technology Development Agency Presidential Tech4 COVID-19 committee. This committee of government and technology executives was set up to assess and relieve the negative impact of COVID-19 on the Nigerian technology sector. Another intervention initiative of the UK–Nigeria tech hub was "Hub Upskill (COVID-19)" to enable tech hub managers to transition their services to a virtual delivery format. The UK–Nigeria tech hub also hosted numerous COVID-19 virtual roundtables to discuss and brainstorm issues within Nigeria's tech communities (Nigerian News Direct, 2020).

Other examples of how African tech hub collaborations can move from a geographical country focus to a value chain focus (Pananod, Gereffi, & Pedersen, 2020) are illustrated in recent responses to the COVID-19 crisis. 54Gene, an African genomics startup with offices in Lagos, Nigeria and Washington, DC, USA launched a $500,000 fund to expand testing sites in Nigeria (Unah, 2020). Through the provision of mobile laboratories in 40-foot containers fitted with equipment, 54Gene was able to rapidly support testing in three different states of Nigeria (Ogun, Kano, and Abuja). In a second example, pan-African initiative Quip created a national asset register that is now operating in Nigeria and Kenya, with initiatives to extend coverage to Ghana and Ethiopia. Quip documents the availability of respirators, ventilators, and intensive care unit beds, and identifies volunteer engineers that can be deployed to fix broken machines. Finally, Africa's largest innovation incubator, CcHub based in Lagos and Nairobi, has coordinated efforts with Kigali-based Design Lab to fund and support teams working on solutions to COVID-19 outbreaks on the African continent (Jackson, 2019).

Bastos de Morais (2015), the founder of the African Innovation Foundation, describes an innovation ecosystem as a "living, functioning, ever-evolving mechanism that supports the continuous creation of new products and services to meet evolving market needs." However, Cunningham and colleagues (2014) zeroed in on the impact of addressing the existing fragmentation across East African ecosystems as a central priority needing to be addressed. In their research they outlined ten existing deficiencies, as depicted in Table 4.1.

These fragmentation deficiencies are not only limited to their impact on East Africa, but on the entire continent. Boston Consulting Group (BCG) outlined that the fragmented market of 54 countries, each with different and complicated regulations, scarce human and financial

Table 4.1   *Examples of fragmentation deficiencies*

Deficiency description
Structural obstacles exist arising from a skills deficit in university graduates
Limited participation by experienced professionals constrains effectiveness of majority graduate/undergraduate student-based innovation hub users
Lack of differentiation in innovation hub advantages
Weak management capacity and service delivery
Needed increases in public and private funding to support training and mentoring efforts
A shortage in affordable assistance to entrepreneurs
Dearth of venture funding accessibility (bank loans, government-sponsored enterprise loans and seed capital from venture capitalists)
Lack of alignment between research and innovation with policy priorities
Lack of African cross-border links (e.g., AfricaConnect)
Poor advocacy by education/public sectors to entrepreneurship opportunities given hub focus on quality professional services and products

Source: Adapted from: Cunningham et al. (2014).

capital, and low consumer purchasing power, also contribute to African tech startup obstacles (Maher, Laabi, Ivers, & Ngambeket, 2021).

Akshay Grover, the chief executive officer of Cellulant, one of the oldest and largest digital payment companies in Africa, describes 257 payment methods (mostly bank accounts, but also approximately 60 mobile money wallets and a very low usage of credit and debit cards) that exist on the African continent and prove to be a costly challenge for African retailers (Mureithi, 2022). Grover mentions that each African digital market is at a distinct stage of development (Mureithi, 2022). Cellulant is a Kenyan company pursuing cross-border money collection across Africa and represents an initiative to overcome this deficiency. By reducing this avoidable tech hub fragmentation, collaboration can provide scalar opportunities, making hubs an ever stronger technological force for the region and in global markets.

In another example, JUMO, a Ghana-based mobile financial services platform, tech hub collaborations are facilitated currently in South Africa, Kenya, and Europe while servicing Ghana, Tanzania, Kenya, Uganda, Zambia, Cote d'Ivoire, and Pakistan. The firm currently plans further expansions in Nigeria, Cameroon, and Benin. This entrepreneurial example of win-win collaboration is based on creating automated algorithms that can review multiple Africa telecom customer payment patterns, and then develop credit information for banks to provide these customers with consumer loans (Maher et al., 2021; Intelligent Banking Technology, 2022). JUMO provides a second tech hub example of addressing African tech fragmentation by marshaling resources to improve hub effectiveness and entrepreneurial innovation.

A final third example shows how the integration of policies, technologies, and innovation across hubs can contribute to a dynamic COVID-19 response through ongoing coordinated events across hubs. The Zimbabwean tech hubs TechVillage and ImpactHub Harare have been regularly collaborating with the Stimulus Innovation Center in Harare, Zimbabwe to host design challenges every two weeks around issues arising from the pandemic. One critical tactic is crowdsourcing ideas from local innovators (AEIP, 2020). In the next section we provide a framework for how technology hubs can collaborate across African borders.

THEORETICAL CONCERNS ON THE VALUE OF HUB COLLABORATIONS IN THE AFRICAN CONTEXT

There is considerable ambiguity about the proper lexicon for describing an innovation eco-system (Oh, Phillips, Park, & Lee, 2016; Hernández-Chea et al., 2021). We define it here as a web of interrelated actors and entities (e.g., firms, entrepreneurs, industrial infrastructure) that seeks to develop and exploit value-added technological innovation. At its root, though, innovation systems encompass the understanding that increasingly specialized and differen-tiated organizations in society need to link with integrated networks to produce successful innovation (Hage, Mote, & Jordan, 2013). When these networks consist of a set of co-located firms, we refer to them as a "technology hub" which can specialize on any of a variety of dimensions (Kelly & Firestone, 2016), but whose spatial co-location offers identifiable bound-aries for investors in government, technology, and financial markets to regularly evaluate and analyze their progress. Such business communities are especially critical in nascent markets (Santos & Eisenhardt, 2009), where commonalities can help in forming the alliances needed to demarcate market boundaries.

Promoting collaboration networks that link across hubs is key to raising the geographically limited role of hubs to a unified level that can play a central role in improving pan-African integration. Saxenian and Hsu (2001), for instance, examined how collaboration across hubs can be valuable in building populations of technical communities with shared professional backgrounds that can then transform into a transnational "community." More specifically, cross-border engagements that share information, trust, and contacts can lead to the develop-ment of less asymmetric power relations, and that can foster budding technology hub collabo-rations to grow and stabilize. This is exemplified in the startup JUMO, where African telecoms (MTN, Airtel, Telenor) partnered with large African banks (MANSA BANK, Letshego, Econbank, ABSA) and high-profile investors (Goldman Sachs, Leapfrog Investments, Brook Asset Management, Athena Capital Advisors) to operate multiple tech hubs in South Africa, Kenya, and Europe and provide services in more than seven African countries.

A brief review of related global research provides a variety of insights on factors driving the formation and development of hub collaborations. Santos and Eisenhardt (2009) detailed the formation of nascent market boundaries; Adner and Kapoor (2010) outlined how ecosystems arise and impact innovation adoption; Hallen and Eisenhardt (2012) outlined mechanisms for network tie formation; Weiss and Gangadharan (2010) modeled ecosystem structure and growth; and Autio and Thomas (2014) more recently investigated implications for innovation management. Shared across all of these treatments is a recurring role for path dependencies that arises among the interactions in innovation, ecosystem performance, and market growth.

Researchers have highlighted the worrying status of Africa in relation to participating in the increasingly necessary global knowledge-based economies (Asongu & Odhiambo, 2020). Past strategies created disappointing results, specifically dependencies from investing ever more in regional university training but then relying on MNC investments to build a knowledge-based economic infrastructure.

Given the burgeoning rise of African "tech hubs," though, the spillover from a stable and mobile professional labor force community that can span borders offers many attractive benefits. Empirical evidence demonstrates that the higher the internet speed in an African country, the larger the positive effects on skilled employment rates – and to a lesser degree, increases extend to the employment of less educated workers as well (Hjort & Poulsen, 2019). Highlighting that fast internet is an outcome of increased knowledge production investments, a World Bank study indicated that knowledge production is significantly and positively associated with ensuing job creation (Choi, Dutz, & Usman, 2020). Specifically, a commonality of successful technology hub collaborations is that their long-term investment in skilled labor can be key to the building of a pan-African professional community that will contribute to a more valuable continental labor pool. The Tony Blair Institute for Global Change cites the example of 300,000 jobs created in Kenya since 2007 due to the growth of mobile money solutions – indicating how jobs can be indirectly created through digital innovations and uplift whole regional African economies (Bayuo et al., 2022). Technology companies such as Google have also trained more than 100,000 African professionals, and Microsoft sponsors an African Development Centre in Nigeria and Kenya; however, such programs are fragmented throughout the African continent (Bayuo et al., 2022). Further collaboration amongst regional African tech hubs can assist in upskilling across the continent, create mobile transfer opportunities, and thus retain existing talent.

The rise of African tech hubs spawning hundreds of startups and transdisciplinary skills offers an effective method for leapfrogging into the competitive knowledge economy. This phenomenon can thus also compensate for the slower process that relies on building new university systems (Atiase et al., 2020). MNC alliances with these hub collaborations can create systematic interactions that enhance technological learning, which in turn becomes a primary mechanism for developing countries' local firms to accumulate technological capabilities (Alfaro-Urena, Manelici, & Vasquez, 2019).

An example of this collaborative potential is exemplified in the Tshimologong Digital Project created in 2017 in the inner-city Braamfontein precinct of Johannesburg, South Africa. Originally formed to commercialize research projects of Wits University students, this initiative was supported by JP Morgan Chase, as well as local (City of Johannesburg and Gauteng Provincial) governments. The Tshimologong Project has incubated more than 105 startups and 172 entrepreneurs and partners with IBM Research Africa, ABB, Microsoft, Cisco, and Accenture. Local South African companies also play a key role, including Telkom, Airports Company South Africa, and international agencies such as Agence Francaise de Developpement and Institut Francais. This African hub provides skills development opportunities, incubation, acceleration programs, and market access (Tshimologong – Digital Innovation Precinct, n.d.). Importantly, for MNC investments to be valuable in this vein, the strategic intent must go beyond seeking relatively cheap labor (Dunning & Lundan, 2008); hence, the availability of strategic assets arising from technology hub collaboration implies mutual gains for spurring true technological learning and embeddedness (Lall & Narula, 2004). Simply put, MNCs create an occasion for industrial upgrading in less advanced economies (Saxenian & Hsu, 2001), and will themselves be rewarded by improved demand and supply derived from the existence of tech hub collaborations.

Another example of the value of MNC deployment of tech hub resources includes Morocco's Akwa Group, an oil and gas conglomerate that collaborated with BCG Digital

Venture to develop Kenz'up, a regional loyalty app platform for its customers (Maher et al., 2021). This example allowed the firm to sidestep the MNC's internal administrative red tape that can limit innovation (Maher et al., 2021) by creating its own internal business incubator. The ensuing app was able to service more than 1 million users in less than six months.

In addition to MNCs benefiting from technology hub collaborations, Jahanbakht and Mostafa (2022) refer to the important role that developing country firms (DCF) can play in the radical innovation of global value chains (GVCs) for frontier markets such as Africa. These DCFs regularly experiment to alter their downstream value chains in order to address their demand and supply-side challenges and opportunities. Jahanbakht and Mostafa (2022) found that these pioneering DCFs entered multiple African host countries, and in the process ended up connecting these countries with their transformed GVCs. These pioneering DCFs would likewise benefit as well from being connected to multiple technology hubs and especially those that are collaborating across regions.

Labor mobility is key for building greater pan-African integration. Expatriates with prior established hub collaboration experience can aid in new hub collaboration formation in emerging markets through their social ties that form through recruiting. These actors can also form important components for future transnational communities (Saxenian & Hsu, 2001). Such value has been documented in other emerging markets. Ciravegna (2012) for instance, surveyed 150 entrepreneurs in Costa Rica and found evidence supporting technological learning via social ties (Granovetter, 2005).

Because technology hub collaborations can be significant drivers of value in the contemporary global economy, they are also the subject of extensive policy prescriptions (Braunerhjelm & Feldman, 2006). Bresnahan et al. (2001, p. 27) went so far as to list the following policies as key determinants for success in innovation ecosystems: "invest in education, have open market institutions, tolerate and even encourage multinationals, and tolerate and even encourage a brain drain." Notably, the collaborative processes across innovation hubs is underemphasized; while these other factors may serve as credible processes to encourage African innovation ecosystems, the potential for technology hub collaborations to work in greater concert can contribute substantially to the development of pan-African capabilities.

PROPOSED CONCEPTUAL MODEL

Our proposed conceptual model stresses three needed capabilities for effectively deploying resources to the hub collaborative level: (1) the ability for exploration to learn new innovations; (2) the ability for exploitation to implement relevant innovations; and (3) a recognition of the value of an Ubuntu ethics that recognizes the social value of building this pan-African structure. The imperative for both exploration and exploitation in organizational learning (March, 1991) is a key point in creating a type of "ambidexterity" for survival that we use to anchor our view. An exploration imperative in tech hub collaboration strategy stresses the resources to search for new opportunities, often via knowledge-generating, investigative coalitions; it is key to adaptation and renewal and requires the expertise to absorb new knowledge.

Exploitation, on the other hand, pragmatically stresses that garnering knowledge is insufficient for innovation without mechanisms to exploit, or implement, the knowledge into a value-generating system. A central imperative is tailoring the innovation to the African context; this should generate disruptive innovations to not only poorly working existing

African infrastructure, but also disrupt static developed world applications that allow emerging market multinationals to effectively "springboard" their assets to build their competitiveness.

Finally, innovation is not the end in itself. The tech hub collaboration process can create a formal mechanism for producing both formal and informal relational synergies. Drawing from an Ubuntu ethics perspective, working in cross-continent tech hub collaborations can help build an identity for a pan-African professional class that can create new relational ties while diffusing the exploration and exploitation capacities to new hubs. We expand on these three ideas below as depicted in Figure 4.2.

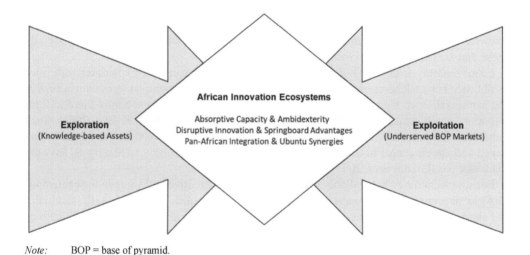

Note: BOP = base of pyramid.

Figure 4.2   Conceptual model of how African innovation ecosystems can leverage strengths

MANAGING ABSORPTIVE CAPACITY THROUGH AMBIDEXTERITY

Given the heavy barriers in successfully managing ambidexterity within a firm in even the most advanced economies (O'Reilly & Tushman, 2013), emerging multinational firms need to pursue ambidexterity with an eye to the potential advantages their unique context can provide (Meyer, Mudambi, & Narula, 2011). Ambidexterity involves the simultaneous process of pursuing two distinct goals which may appear to be competing to achieve firm success (Luo & Tung, 2018). Thus, emerging market multinational enterprises may be forced to incorporate local cultural norms and needs while concurrently utilizing global resources. Accordingly, it is not surprising that a majority of entrepreneurs are likely to pursue incremental innovation rather than de novo disruptive innovation (Robson, Haugh, & Obeng, 2009). Anecdotally, a recent music rap song asked francophone African countries to develop their own "CFA Franc monetary unit" that is untied to France (Chiwanza, 2018) – these local imperatives resonate with how expanding financial alternatives need to harness the ability to customize and tailor pan-African advantages. The song reflects ground-level recognition that a unified regional currency can create global negotiation strength, but such unification should be separate from a former colonial power.

Absorptive capacity represents the aptitude to appreciate, incorporate, and administer external expertise to cultivate new innovations. Pursuing new partnerships, especially with mature tech economies, can enhance the exploration advantage across at least three domains: function, structure, and attribute (Lavie & Rosenkopf, 2006).

A functional alliance recognizes the exploration value of alliances centered on research and development, such as the Nigerian startup Andela's alliances with Microsoft for training engineers (Gaffey, 2016). Such alliances are critically necessary for the development of local tech hub collaboration resources. Exploration through a functional alliance offers the potential for a tech hub to establish a network collaboration with a partner it has not previously engaged and build its own resource. The structure advantage of hub collaborations is especially essential to counter the asymmetric power differentials that small tech firms face in pursuing partnerships (Sawers, Pretorius, & Oerlemans, 2008). Finally, by adopting attribute exploration, firms in the tech hub collaboration can pursue a novel association that introduces an organization characteristic that is different from a hub collaboration's existing partners.

An example of how African partners can extract unique value from their partners can be inferred from Ado, Su, and Wanjiru's (2017) study that described the dynamics of 29 joint ventures between African and Chinese firms. They noted that the overwhelming motivation for African companies was their interest in learning and knowledge transfer – whereas the Chinese motivation appeared to be profit and resource based. Through the employment of informal mechanisms with colleagues on WhatsApp and Facebook, evidence indicated a high potential for African nationals' learning to transfer to not only the joint-venture parent firm, but also to other hub collaboration partners, and theoretically, throughout transnational communities.

Technology hub collaborations provide a mechanism for creating the capacity to perform both exploration and exploitation imperatives simultaneously. Lavie and Rosenkopf (2006) documented the tendencies for firms to balance exploration and exploitation in their alliance formation over time. As technology hub collaborations represent the capabilities inherent in a set of firms, we postulate that this exploration/exploitation balance is implemented across firms (rather than time) with some firms emphasizing the exploration imperatives while others pursue exploitation opportunities. With the former, absorptive capacity to integrate new knowledge is central; in the latter, a finely honed recognition of the continental prospects is key to foment disruptive innovation.

INVESTING IN DISRUPTIVE INNOVATION WITH SPRINGBOARD ADVANTAGES

Relatedly, the springboard theory of international expansion outlines the unique strategies that emerging market multinational enterprises employ in their globalization, in particular by pursuing and acquiring compensatory assets from mature markets (Luo & Tung, 2007). With their formulation, Luo and Tung (2007) noted several motives applicable to African tech hub collaboration asset-seeking from abroad: saliently, to compensate for competitive and latecomer disadvantages, launching counterattacks to global rival footholds in home markets, and bypassing domestic institutional constraints. In their extension of the theory, Luo and Tung (2018) discuss at greater length the upward spiral of development which recognizes key process paths that are especially relevant to tech hub collaboration potential for spanning the continent: in particular, the transfer of strategic assets to home countries, and the accentuation of home-centered upgrading of capabilities.

Technology hub collaborations can take these alliance-driven initiatives to help gain socio-political legitimacy (Santos & Eisenhardt, 2009). Specifically, a central feature of innovation adoption has been the need to educate customers that the innovation adoption is viable. Biogas technology for energy, which we expand upon later below, has faced an uphill battle in acceptance until a full cycle of sales and management was designed in a "hub" form (World Bank, 2019). Technological knowledge can then be spread to other countries on the continent more efficiently than it would through incremental, domestically constrained innovation centered around single firms. In particular, there is the potential to "leapfrog" older technologies and skip to creating new technological solutions (Amankwah-Amoah, 2015; Welsch et al., 2013). An exploitation imperative for tech hub collaboration strategy stresses the search for applications of existing innovations to new contexts. Specifically, the exploitation component refers to the modification of "old certainties" (March, 1991). Periodic collaborations that employ and expand established products and services are a conventional form of exploitation (Lavie & Rosenkopf, 2006). But in nascent markets, exploitation can include existing research which applies "soft power strategies." Soft power strategies, for instance, have the capacity to manipulate situations and to exploit natural inclinations by utilizing illusion and asynchronous timing advantageously (Santos & Eisenhardt, 2009).

Disruptive innovation occurs when a smaller company with few resources can change an industry and successfully outperform incumbent businesses (Christensen, Raynor, & McDonald, 2013). Such innovation often erupts from an incumbency disadvantage; successes in mature markets, for instance, can serve as blinders to customizing innovation that is sensitive to regional needs. These blinders can further act as a form of inertia, to the extent they are entrenched within established mature market ecosystems that have responded to pressures to reduce uncertainty and risk (Lavie & Rosenkopf, 2006).

African technology hub collaborations, on the other hand, are likely to be apprised of the basic building blocks of local economies. This knowledge provides relevant measures of supply and demand forces, as well as a recognition of the critical workings of the societal infrastructure. Their contextual awareness not only responds appropriately to the level of ICT in the local networked economy, but this awareness can aid in closing the digital divide via unorthodox innovation (Ifinedo, 2005). The knowledge in African technology hub collaborations accumulates from both experience and perception, thus allowing them to develop strategies customized to meet local needs with available resources from a "blank slate." An example described in Littlewood and Kiyumbu (2018) would include the provincial hub in Kenya that helps tech enthusiast members to work on projects with businesses and provides finders/facilitation services to link expertise to targeted needs.

The springboard perspective also recognizes the role of emerging market multinational enterprise interactions with mature markets for exploitation. In Luo and Tung's (2018) springboard theory, along with the value of ambidexterity, they elaborate two other concepts: amalgamation and adaptability.

Amalgamation refers to the creative competence that emerging market multinational enterprises utilize to develop tailored solutions to cost-sensitive consumers by combining all available resources and improvising for any institutional deficits. A powerful example would be the creation of M-Pesa in Kenya, which simplifies payment services via mobile phones and negates the significant travel and logistical requirements involved in brick and mortar-type banks in many communities (Mbiti & Weil, 2013). The innovation first arose from the multinational South African company Vodafone initially responding to a UK development arm's request: they needed help with the narrow goal of providing a mechanism for the repayment of microloans. Distribution and branding were essential, so Vodaphone turned to Kenya's network operator Safaricom to roll out the product. Immediately it became apparent people were using it in more ways, specifically to transfer money to other contacts (TechChange, 2022). This history illustrates a number of key elements: the international profile of the initial project; the dependency on local expertise and knowledge; and the ensuing "leapfrogging" of the technology to surpass existing alternatives. The program's founder, Michael Joseph of Safaricom, noted the unique positioning of mobile providers to serve the very poor, based on the very different incentive of gaining customer loyalty; he noted that banks, which still want to enter the space, rely on the wrong incentives and that this makes them nonrespondent and overpriced. Today M-Pesa's unique solution of a mobile phone-based financial service, it is currently operating in Kenya, Tanzania, Mozambique, DRC, Lesotho, Ghana, Egypt, Afghanistan, and South Africa. In 2022, Safaricom partnered with Visa to make virtual M-Pesa GlobalPay cards that allow African customers to enter Visa's e-commerce system of 100 million merchants across 200 countries (Vodafone, 2022).

Finally, adaptability refers to the resourcefulness and resilience of emerging-market multinational enterprises to acclimate to unexpected market changes. This aptitude prevails due to high institutional complexity and volatility within the emerging market environments (Kano, Narula, & Surdu, 2021). A salient example can be found in the advancement of biogas technologies. In response to national policy programs, a considerable network of firms is involved in implementing biogas technologies across a wide set of countries (Kenya, Uganda, Ethiopia, Tanzania, Rwanda, Cameroon, Burkina Faso, and Benin) to address both waste management problems and energy deficits (Roopnarain & Adeleke, 2017). Past obstacles have been viability, property rights, costs, and notably a lack of communication. In 2018, a titled "hub" model was adopted to promote and market biogas in Kenya. This creates a full cycle of sales and service by first identifying a target cooperative or microfinance institution, and then supporting the model with Biogas Extension Service Providers, who link to the larger Kenya Biogas Program, and, importantly, set up both a call service center and quality service provider consultants to assess functionality (World Bank, 2019). The knowledge learned in smaller programs like these is then transferred to larger pan-African initiatives such as the Africa Biogas Partnership Programme.

DISCUSSION OF IMPLICATIONS: PAN-AFRICAN INTEGRATION

We propose a conceptual model for how existing and potential technology hub collaborations on the African continent are best positioned to amalgamate knowledge and transfer these resources across hub collaborations through transnational communities. At the same time, we make the strong caveat that the continent should not be oversimplified; the many highly distinct cultures, countries, and companies tolerate little overall generalization.

For that reason, we do not endorse a "one-size-fits-all" approach (Ojo, 2016). The activation of transnational communities to transfer knowledge and help implement improved technology hub collaboration survival does not conceptualize a "United States of Africa" policy for the technology and innovation sector. Rather, through accentuating the benefits of African collaboration that is currently reflected in initiatives such as the African Continental Free Trade Area and the African Union goals, we propose that moving to the hub collaboration level of analysis is an important first step.

Recognizing Africa holds many socio-economic dilemmas (such as skills deficiencies, informal economies, weak institutional structures, and the need for poverty reduction), local forms and expressions still vary greatly throughout the continent (Toivanen, Mutafungwa, Hyvönen, & Ngogo, 2012). We propose that these differences and the ability to harness transnational communities drawing from many technology hub collaborations can enable a strong pan-African market advantage. A formal network structure that links multiple technology hubs through events, projects, and other interactional goals can enhance pan-African communication. Collaborations across technology hubs can utilize the recombinant nature of the innovation process to reinterpret solutions for new contexts (Weiss & Gangadharan, 2010). Put simply, an innovation has to be understood (exploration), but then taken apart and repurposed (exploitation) by participants with a stake in the future of the innovation (professional pan-African community).

We emphasize that more static categorizations of technology hubs and firms (along dimensions like educational/private/nonprofit/industry) diminish the ability to recognize how such hubs connect and bring value to each other. Therefore, we offer the alternative framework of categorizing firms and hubs based on their emphasis on exploration (centered on basic research and development and openness to international knowledge transfer) and exploitation (with its engineering emphasis on prototyping customizable innovation to the African context). These functions naturally link sequentially, potentially forming a more permanent network that allows the tech hub collaboration to serve as an analog to high-level GVCs.

CONCLUSION

In sum, it has been critical to move the research on technology and innovation in Africa up a level of analysis to their role in the quickly expanding co-located technology hubs. However, we argue here, it is as important to move up another level to depict how hubs that differentially specialize in exploration and exploitation can create synergistic technology hub collaborations linking these capacities across countries and regions. Specifically, by focusing on how firms in a tech hub serve as part of a greater network of sequential value-added functions, we can encourage managerial decision makers to better incorporate this network role in their strategic decisions.

Such a view is consistent with recent research integrating global strategy – a dynamic concept – with its important structural foundation of GVCs: "By understanding how firms are embedded in a broader value chain network, managers have to take into consideration the firm's positioning along the value chain in their strategic decision making" (Pananond et al., 2020, p. 422). Similarly, research must focus on how firms can form long-lasting value-added roles within the exploration–exploitation continuum and should encourage not only greater collaboration but also more efficient resource allocation.

From a practical perspective, business schools interested in technology hubs and collaboration formation could promote these models across Africa in three important ways. First, research projects involving schools from the different regions in Africa could assist in building indigenous theory on technology hub collaboration development by challenging contemporary management thinking in the West. The African Academy of Management could play an important role in facilitating these research projects. Second, business schools could initiate conferences to enable sharing of knowledge on critical success factors enabling technology hub collaborations. Third, professors can discuss the opportunity that the African Continental Free Trade Area offers technology hub collaborations, teaching case studies on effective cross-country collaborations that enhance pan-African prosperity and integration.

REFERENCES

Adaramola, Z. (2020). Nigeria: COVID-19 UK–Nigeria tech hub to engage start-ups on economic challenges. *Daily Trust*, June 12. https://allafrica.com/stories/202006120429.html

Adner, R., & Kapoor, R. (2010). Value creation in innovation ecosystems: How the structure of technological interdependence affects firm performance in new technology generations. *Strategic Management Journal*, *31*(3), 306–333.

Ado, A., Su, Z., & Wanjiru, R. (2017). Learning and knowledge transfer in Africa–China JVs: Interplay between informalities, culture, and social capital. *Journal of International Management*, *23*(2), 166–179.

Africa-Europe Innovation Partnership (AEIP) (2020). Discover the AEIP Tech Hub Network COVID-19 initiatives. May 6. https://africaeurope-innovationpartnership.net/news/discover-aeip-tech-hub-network-covid-19-initiatives

African Union Commission & OECD (2021). Africa's development dynamics: Digital transformation for quality jobs. www.oecd-ilibrary.org/docserver/0a5c9314en.pdf?expires=1644238471&id=id&accname=guest&checksum=20454432CFA55AA3CCA159BF81234668

Afrilabs & Briter Bridges (2019). Building a conducive setting for innovators to thrive. A qualitative and quantitative study of a hundred hubs across Africa. www.afrilabs.com/wp-content/uploads/2019/11/AfriLabs-Innovation-Ecosystem-Report.pdf

Alfaro-Urena, A., Manelici, I., & Vasquez, J. P. (2019). The effects of joining multinational supply chains: New evidence from firm-to-firm linkages. *NBER Working Paper*, April.

Amankwah-Amoah, J. (2015). Solar energy in sub-Saharan Africa: The challenges and opportunities of technological leapfrogging. *Thunderbird International Business Review*, *57*(1), 15–31.

Asongu, S. A., Odhiambo, N. M. (2020). Building knowledge-based economies in Africa: A systematic review of policies and strategies. *Journal of the Knowledge Economy*, *11*, 1538–1555.

Atiase, V. Y., Kolade, K., & Tahiru, A. L. (2020). The emergence and strategy of tech hubs in Africa: Implications for knowledge production and value creation. *Technological Forecasting and Social Change*, *161*, 120307.

Autio, E., & Thomas, L. (2014). Innovation ecosystems. In M. Dodgson, D. Gann, & N. Phillips (eds), *The Oxford handbook of innovation management* (pp. 204–288). Oxford University Press.

Bastos de Morais, J. C. (2015). What if African nations operated as one big innovation ecosystem? *IT New Africa*, May 6. www.itnewsafrica.com/2015/05/what-if-african-nations-operated-as-one-big-innovation-ecosystem/#!prettyPhoto

Bayuo, B., Bamford, R., Baah, B., Mwaya, J., Gakuo, C., & Tholstrup, S. (2022). Supercharging Africa's startups: The continent's path to tech excellence. Tony Blair Institute for Global Change, February 15. https://institute.global/policy/supercharging-africas-startups-continents-path-tech-excellence

Bell, M., & Albu, M. (1999). Knowledge systems and technological dynamism in industrial hub collaborations in developing countries. *World Development*, *27*(9), 1715–1734.

Braunerhjelm, P., & Feldman, M. P. (eds) (2006). *Cluster genesis: Technology-based industrial development*. Oxford University Press.

Bresnahan, T., Gambardella, A., & Saxenian, A. (2001). "Old economy" inputs for "new economy" outcomes: Cluster formation in the new Silicon Valleys. *Industrial and Corporate Change*, *10*(4), 835–860.

Chiwanza, T. H. (2018). "The CFA franc will die and we will dance at its funeral": Time to abandon the "colonial remnant"? *The African Exponent*, June 25. www.africanexponent.com/post/9013-is-it-now -time-to-abandon-the-cfa-franc-which-is-regarded-a-remnant-of-colonialism

Choi, J., Dutz, M. A., & Usman, Z. (eds) (2020). *The future of work in Africa: Harnessing the potential of digital technologies for all*. World Bank Publications.

Christensen, C., Raynor, M. E., & McDonald, R. (2013). *Disruptive innovation*. Brighton, MA: Harvard Business Review.

Ciravegna, L. (2012). *Promoting Silicon Valleys in Latin America: Lessons from Costa Rica*. Routledge.

Cunningham, P. M., Cunningham, M., & Ekenberg, L. (2014). Baseline analysis of 3 innovation ecosystems in East Africa. In *2014 14th International Conference on Advances in ICT for Emerging Regions* (pp. 156–162). IEEE, December.

De Beer, J., Millar, P., Mwangi, J., Nzomo, V., & Rutenberg, I. (2017). A framework for assessing technology hubs in Africa. *New York University Journal of Intellectual Property and Entertainment Law*, Ottawa Faculty of Law Working Paper No. 2017–18, *6*(2).

Dunning, J. H., & Lundan, S. M. (2008). *Multinational enterprises and the global economy*. Edward Elgar Publishing.

Elhoussamy, N., Weheba, N., & Rizk, N. (2020). Power relations, innovation, scaling, and knowledge governance at three Egyptian tech hubs: An initial exploration. Working Paper 21, January 6, The American University in Cairo. https://openair.africa/power-relations-innovation-scaling-and -knowledge-governance-at-three-egyptian-tech-hubs-an-initial-exploration/

Freeman, C. (2002). Continental, national and sub-national innovation systems: Complementarity and economic growth. *Research Policy*, *31*(2), 191–211.

Friederici, N. (2018). *Hope and hype in Africa's digital economy: The rise of innovation hubs. Digital Economies at Global Margins*. MIT Press.

Gaffey, C. (2016). Silicon Lagoon: Africa's tech revolution heads west. *Newsweek*, November 29. www .newsweek.com/2016/12/09/nigeria-startups-yaba-lagos-mark-zuckerberg-525824.html

Granovetter, M. (2005). The impact of social structure on economic outcomes. *Journal of Economic Perspectives*, *19*(1), 33–50.

Hage, J., Mote, J. E., & Jordan, G. B. (2013). Ideas, innovations, and networks: A new policy model based on the evolution of knowledge. *Policy Sciences*, *46*(2), 199–216.

Hallen, B. L., & Eisenhardt, K. M. (2012). Catalyzing strategies and efficient tie formation: How entrepreneurial firms obtain investment ties. *Academy of Management Journal*, *55*(1), 35–70.

Hernandez, E., & Shaver, J. M. (2019). Network synergy. *Administrative Science Quarterly*, *64*(1), 171–202.

Hernández-Chea, R., Mahdad, M., Minh, T. T., & Hjortsø, C. N. (2021). Moving beyond intermediation: How intermediary organizations shape collaboration dynamics in entrepreneurial ecosystems. *Technovation*, *108*, 102332.

Hjort, J., & Poulsen, J. (2019). The arrival of fast internet and employment in Africa. *American Economic Review*, *109*(3), 1032–1079.

Ifinedo, P. (2005). Measuring Africa's e-readiness in the global networked economy: A nine-country data analysis. *International Journal of Education and Development using ICT*, *1*(1), 53–71.

Intelligent Banking Technology (n.d.). JUMO. https://jumo.world/

Jackson, T. (2019). Nigerian tech hub launch calls for COVID-19 solutions. *Disrupt Africa*, March 19. https://disrupt-africa.com/2020/03/nigerian-tech-hubs-launch-calls-for-covid-19-solutions/

Jahanbakht, M., & Mostafa, R. (2022). The emergence of GVCs for frontier markets: Insights from the African mobile telecommunications industry. *Africa Journal of Management*, 1–24.

Kano, L., Narula, R., & Surdu, I. (2021). Global value chain resilience: Understanding the impact of managerial governance adaptations. *California Management Review*, 00081256211066635.

Kelly, T., & Firestone, R. (2016). How tech hubs are helping to drive economic growth in Africa. World Bank Group, background paper for the *World Development Report 2016 Digital Dividends.* https://thedocs.worldbank.org/en/doc/895381452529897772-0050022016/original/WDR16BPHowT echHubsarehelpingtoDriveEconomicGrowthinAfricaKellyFirestone.pdf

Koryak, O., Lockett, A., Hayton, J., Nicolaou, N., & Mole, K. (2018). Disentangling the antecedents of ambidexterity: Exploration and exploitation. *Research Policy, 47*(2), 413–427.

Lall, S., & Narula, R. (2004). Foreign direct investment and its role in economic development: Do we need a new agenda? *European Journal of Development Research, 16*(3), 447–464.

Lavie, D., & Rosenkopf, L. (2006). Balancing exploration and exploitation in alliance formation. *Academy of Management Journal, 49*(4), 797–818.

Littlewood, D. C., & Kiyumbu, W. L. (2018). "Hub" organisations in Kenya: What are they? What do they do? And what is their potential? *Technological Forecasting and Social Change, 131,* 276–285.

Luo, Y., & Tung, R. L. (2007). International expansion of emerging market enterprises: A springboard perspective. *Journal of International Business Studies, 38,* 481–498.

Luo, Y., & Tung, R. L. (2018). A general theory of springboard MNEs. *Journal of International Business Studies, 49*(2), 129–152.

Maher, H., Laabi, A., Ivers, L., & Ngambeket, G. (2021). *Overcoming Africa's tech startup obstacles.* BCG Global, April 12. www.bcg.com/publications/2021/new-strategies-needed-to-help-tech-startups -in-africa

March, J. G. (1991). Exploration and exploitation in organizational learning. *Organization Science, 2*(1), 71–87.

Mbiti, I., & Weil, D. N. (2013). The home economics of e-money: Velocity, cash management, and discount rates of M-Pesa users. *American Economic Review, 103*(3), 369–374.

McCormick, D. (1999). African enterprise clusters and industrialization: Theory and reality. *World Development, 27*(9), 1531–1551.

Meyer, K., Mudambi, R., & Narula, R. (2011). Multinational enterprises and local contexts: The opportunities and challenges of multiple embeddedness. *Journal of Management Studies, 48*(2), 235–252.

Mureithi, C. (2022). *Why Africa's digital payment landscape is still highly fragmented.* Quartz, April 4. https://qz.com/africa/2149097/why-africas-digital-payment-landscape-is-still-highly-fragmented/

Murphy, J. T., Carmody, P., & Surborg, B. (2014). Industrial transformation or business as usual? Information and communication technologies and Africa's place in the global information economy. *Review of African Political Economy, 41*(140), 264–283.

Nigerian News Direct (2020). *COVID-19: UK–Nigeria tech hub to launch intervention programmes for start-ups.* June 10. https://nigeriannewsdirect.com/covid-19-uk-nigeria-tech-hub-to-launch -intervention-programmes-for-start-ups/

O'Reilly, C. A., & Tushman, M. L. (2004). The ambidextrous organization. *Harvard Business Review, 82*(4), 74–83.

O'Reilly, C. A., & Tushman, M. L. (2013). Organizational ambidexterity: Past, present and future. *Academy of Management Perspectives, 27*(4), pp. 324–338.

Oh, D. S., Phillips, F., Park, S., & Lee, E. (2016). Innovation ecosystems: A critical examination. *Technovation, 54,* 1–6.

Ojo, T. (2016). Global agenda and ICT4D in Africa: Constraints of localizing "universal norm." *Telecommunications Policy, 40*(7), 704–713.

Pananod, P., Gereffi, G., & Pedersen, T. (2020). An integrative typology of global strategy and global value chains: The management and organization of cross-border activities. *Global Strategy Journal, 10,* 421–443.

Pérezts, M., Russon, J. A., & Painter, M. (2020). This time from Africa: Developing a relational approach to values-driven leadership. *Journal of Business Ethics, 161*(4), 731–748.

PricewaterhouseCoopers (2017). Disrupting Africa: Riding the wave of the digital revolution. www .pwc.com/gx/en/issues/high-growth-markets/assets/disrupting-africa-riding-the-wave-of-the-digital -revolution.pdf

Qureshi, S. (2005). How does information technology effect development? Integrating theory and practice into a process model. University of Nebraska, Omaha Faculty Proceedings and Presentations, 40. https://digitalcommons.unomaha.edu/isqafacproc/40/

Robson, P. J., Haugh, H. M., & Obeng, B. A. (2009). Entrepreneurship and innovation in Ghana: Enterprising Africa. *Small Business Economics*, *32*(3), 331–350.

Roopnarain, A., & Adeleke, R. (2017). Current status, hurdles and future prospects of biogas digestion technology in Africa. *Renewable and Sustainable Energy Reviews*, *67*, 1162–1179.

Santos, F. M., & Eisenhardt, K. M. (2009). Constructing markets and shaping boundaries: Entrepreneurial power in nascent fields. *Academy of Management Journal*, *52*(4), 643–671.

Sawers, J. L., Pretorius, M. W., & Oerlemans, L. A. (2008). Safeguarding SMEs dynamic capabilities in technology innovative SME-large company partnerships in South Africa. *Technovation*, *28*(4), 171–182.

Saxenian, A., & Hsu, J. Y. (2001). The Silicon Valley–Hsinchu connection: Technical communities and industrial upgrading. *Industrial and Corporate Change*, *10*(4), 893–920.

TechChange (2022). The Story of M-Pesa, interview with founder Michael Joseph. www.techchange .org/work/the-story-of-m-pesa-2/

Toivanen, H., Mutafungwa, E., Hyvönen, J., & Ngogo, E. (2012). *Pro-poor social and economic opportunities in the African ICT innovation ecosystem: Perspectives and case study of Iringa, Tanzania.* VTT Technical Research Centre of Finland.

Tshimologong – Digital Innovation Precinct (n.d.). https://tshimologong.joburg/

Unah, L. (2020). Nigerian tech steps up to boost coronavirus testing. *African Business magazine*, June 4. https://africanbusinessmagazine.com/sectors/technology/nigerian-tech-steps-up-to-boost-covid-19 -testing/

Vodafone (2022). M-Pesa goes global with new virtual Visa card. www.vodafone.com/news/services/ mpesa-goes-global-with-new-virtual-visa-card

Weiss, M., & Gangadharan, G. R. (2010). Modeling the mashup ecosystem: Structure and growth. *R&D Management*, *40*(1), 40–49.

Welsch, M., Bazilian, M., Howells, M., Divan, D., Elzinga, D., Strbac, G. … & Brew-Hammond, A. (2013). Smart and just grids for sub-Saharan Africa: Exploring options. *Renewable and Sustainable Energy Reviews*, *20*, 336–352.

Workman, D. (2017). African Countries with the most tech hubs ranked. *IT News Africa*, June 23. www .itnewsafrica.com/2017/06/african-countries-with-the-most-tech-hubs-ranked/

World Bank (2019). The power of dung: Lessons learned from on-farm biodigester programs in Africa. World Bank Group Agriculture. https://documents1.worldbank.org/curated/en/468451557843529960/ pdf/The-Power-of-Dung-Lessons-Learned-from-On-Farm-Biodigester-Programs-in-Africa.pdf

5. Digital technology and innovation in Africa: leapfrogging in finance

Njuguna Ndung'u and Alex Oguso

INTRODUCTION

In the last two decades, Africa has experienced a rapid growth in digital transformation and innovation. The outcome has been a major transformation of African business operations and processes. So far, the evidence that seems to be emerging shows that digitization has helped to reduce the costs, increase market information flow, formalize capital, increase productivity, and promote efficient financial services and efficient e-government services in Africa. Evidently, technology and innovation have become important drivers of contemporary economic growth and development. Specifically, mobile phones/internet, sharing economy, artificial intelligence/machine learning/big data analytics, blockchain/distributed ledger technology, and cloud computing are revolutionising the financial sector around the world and moving to other sectors of the economy (CCAF & MicroSave, 2018). These technologies have stimulated the development of fintech (financial technology) – technology-enabled solutions disrupting traditional financial services and challenging incumbent service providers (Disrupt Africa, 2021).

According to the World Bank (2017), high interest spreads, general risk aversion, high concentration in certain sectors, short tenure of financial products, and inadequate products have characterized the African financial system. Thus, the banking sub-sector in Africa tends to have high levels of liquidity but provides a small amount of lending to small and medium-size enterprises (SMEs). Even in countries where the banking sector is vibrant, the bulk of lending is to the government, signalling lending risk in the market. The International Finance Corporation (2018) noted that despite Africa's financial development gap relative to other regions, Africa has led the world in innovative financial services. Financial innovation across Africa, spearheaded by fintech startups and traditional financial services providers, is leapfrogging the financial sector development in the region. This is opening huge financial potential that is still largely untapped. The rapid growth in use of mobile phone-based financial transactions or what is generally referred to as 'mobile money' in Africa shows the region's fast adoption of modern technologies in financial products and services, skipping over conventional and traditional banking systems – leapfrogging in the financial sector. As affirmed by Ndung'u and Signé (2020), this has influenced inclusive finance, enabling the unbanked to enter the formal financial market through retail electronic payments platforms and virtual savings and credit platforms. The banks have enabled this after the realization that the retail electronic payments platform, spearheaded by M-Pesa, was an efficient technological tool to manage micro savings and deposit accounts without a physical visit to the bank.

The rest of this chapter is as follows: the next section discusses the evolution of digital financial services (DFS) in Africa, which began with the M-Pesa technological platform in Kenya. This is followed by a summary of the current financial inclusion profile and gaps in the continent using selected indicators. The chapter then provides a detailed discussion of leapfrogging in the financial sector in Africa, in line with the six areas of fintech taxonomy. A conclusion follows with a summary of key points and a brief discussion on whether the fourth industrial revolution is feasible in African economies.

EVOLUTION OF DIGITAL FINANCIAL SERVICES IN AFRICA

This sub-section discusses the innovative stages of DFS evolution in Africa, with a focus on the M-Pesa technological platform in Kenya and the replication of the developments across Africa. Following a pilot project, M-Pesa was launched in March 2007 as a bank product in partnership with a telecommunications company. This innovative development has since undergone four stages (Ndung'u, 2018). The first stage is where the mobile phone technological platform was used for electronic money transfers between users (person to person, person to government, and government to person), and later for retail electronic payments and settlement in real time. The emergence of a retail electronic payments system was a game changer – it has been efficient, effective, transparent, and safe. This allowed adoption at the individual transactions level and navigation across all market segments, including the informal markets.

In the second stage, the platform integrated with commercial banks, micro finance, savings and credit cooperative organizations, and insurance companies. The virtual savings accounts introduced became a platform for managing micro-deposits and micro-savings accounts and an electronic payments platform: payment of utility bills, payment of insurance premiums, and settlement of insurance claims. The banks could then easily provide accounts for the unbanked, pushing the financial inclusion frontier in Kenya. Consequently, commercial banks in Kenya built mountains of deposits, provided them with the capacity to intermediate, and expanded their networks across the country and the East African region. In the subsequent expansion after launching bill payment services in 2009, Safaricom collaborated with 25 banks and over 700 businesses to facilitate fund deposits, bank transfers, and the regular payment of utility bills, insurance premiums, loan instalments, and all other transactions. Other mobile network operators (MNOs) followed with similar products and competitive services. In addition, others moved to mobile virtual network operations (MVNOs) – a communications service provider that does not own the wireless network infrastructure over which it provides services to its customers. The businesses using the e-commerce platforms to reach customers who eventually make their payments through DFS have grown. Additionally, most utility companies have embraced electronic payments. Consequently, sustainable business models have developed on the digital platform across all sectors of the economy.

The third stage is where the mobile phone financial services platform developed from a virtual savings account to a virtual credit supply platform. M-Shwari, launched in November 2012 through a strategic partnership between the Commercial Bank of Africa and Safaricom, became the virtual savings and credit supply platform in Kenya at this stage. This is a virtual bank account that is linked to an M-Pesa account such that savings can be transferred from the M-Pesa transactions account to an M-Shwari savings account as well as making with-drawals. In addition, credit applications can be made and received on the M-Shwari plat-form. After 40 months of operations, M-Shwari had over 15 million customers. It has now expanded to Tanzania as M-Pawa, to Uganda and Rwanda as MoKash, and to Cote d'Ivoire as Momo-Kash. Generally, a wide range of operators, including leading MNOs in Africa such as Orange, Airtel, Tigo, and MTN, have developed similar products. In March 2015, Safaricom collaborated with Kenya Commercial Bank to roll out KCB M-Pesa – a mobile phone-based savings, credit supply, and retail payments transaction platform. In addition, other products such as M-Kesho, Tangaza, and Mobicash have led to increased access to credit and improved savings in the continent. The novelty of this stage is the use of transactions and savings data to generate credit scores, using them to price short-term micro credit and assess credit risks. This in effect has revolutionized the collateral technology in the banking sector that previously required fixed assets as the form of collateral. The old collateral requirement inhibited growth in the credit markets in Africa. Transactions on the virtual platforms have generally become the entry point for financial services, with the informal markets also using these formal finan-cial services.

The fourth stage is the developments of cross-border payments and international remit-tances as well as improvements in the regional payments system. Previously, money transfer companies (such as Western Union) expensively delivered international remittances into bank accounts, while others delivered remittances through Hawala (Aron, 2017). Safaricom in Kenya was one of the first movers in international remittances via mobile money. Aron (2017) noted that, in late 2015, Safaricom in collaboration with MoneyGram, an international transfer company, launched international remittances via mobile money enabling the remittances from over 90 countries worldwide into individual M-Pesa accounts.

Indeed, the evolution of DFS in Africa provided means of managing bank accounts at minimal cost and thus enabled commercial banks to reach more customers and grow moun-tains of deposits. Recall the years when the banks set minimum balances for deposit and savings accounts, it meant that those with low and irregular flow of income would remain unbanked. In addition, a trip to the bank was an expensive exercise. The digital banking plat-form has solved these financial service access constraints. Subsequently, strong commercial banks have emerged, leveraging the digital platform to manage micro accounts, build deposits, and extend financial services to previously unbanked and underserved populations. Currently, Sub-Saharan Africa (SSA) leads the world in mobile money accounts per capita, mobile money outlets, and volume of mobile transactions. Figure 5.1 compares the number of 30-day active mobile money accounts across the world.

Figure 5.1 shows that the 30-day active mobile money accounts in SSA have increased tremendously in the last decade, from 1.89 million in December 2008 to 159.24 million in December 2020. As of December 2020, there were over 300 million 30-day active mobile money accounts globally. In the other regions, there were 66.14 million accounts in South Asia, 51.80 million accounts in East Asia and the Pacific, 15.60 million accounts in Latin America and the Caribbean, 4.12 million accounts in Europe and Central Asia, and 3.26 million accounts in the Middle East and North Africa. Compared to other regions, SSA had 53.0 per cent of the 30-day active mobile money accounts, followed by South Asia at 22.0 per cent.

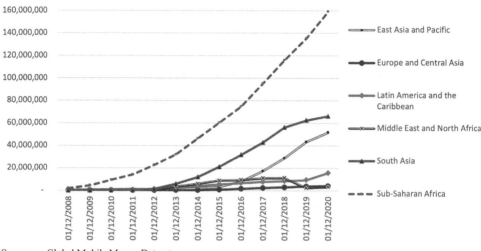

Source: Global Mobile Money Dataset.

Figure 5.1   Mobile money accounts (active, 30-day agents)

The 2017 Global Findex survey showed that SSA was the global leader in the use of mobile phone-based banking accounts and money transactions. About 21 per cent of adults in the region have a mobile money account – nearly half have only a mobile money account, while the other half have a financial institution account as well. Mobile money accounts are particularly widespread in Kenya, where 73 per cent of adults have one, as well as in Uganda and Zimbabwe, where about 50 per cent have an account (Demirgüç-Kunt et al., 2018). The growth in active mobile money agents' network, shown in Figure 5.2, provided support to the growth in active mobile money accounts in SSA.

These figures show that as of December 2020, the SSA region had the highest number of active mobile money agents, which grew from 5,682 in December 2008 to 2.46 million. Globally, the number of active mobile money agents grew from 51,167 to 4.75 million in the same period. This shows that the mobile agents in SSA were 52 per cent of the global total as of December 2020. Apart from SSA, South Asia had a significant growth of active mobile money agents from 1,295 in December 2008 to 1.25 million in December 2020, while those in East Asia and the Pacific grew from 42,638 to 820,032. The other regions recorded relatively slow growth. As of December 2020, the active mobile money agents were 97,691 in Latin America and the Caribbean, 64,211 in the Middle East and North Africa, and 48,375 in Europe and Central Asia. These were far fewer than the number of active mobile money agents in Kenya alone, which the Central Bank of Kenya (2021) reported to be at 294,706 in April 2021 – this was approximately a 96,000 per cent growth from Kenya's 307 active mobile money agents in March 2007 when M-Pesa was launched. The growth in active mobile money agents in SSA shows the increase in financial access points across the continent, which has improved the financial inclusion profile of the region.

Finally, this spectacular adoption of DFS introduced changes in the monetary policy frameworks in most of the African region. The monetary policy framework was based on the

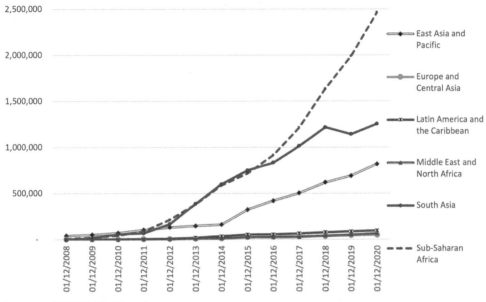

Source: Global Mobile Money Dataset.

Figure 5.2 *Global mobile money agents (active, 30-day agents)*

base money as an intermediate target to control broad money. Thus, to achieve the target for inflation required a check on the path of growth of private-sector credit. This relied on two assumptions, that the velocity of money was constant and that the ratio of broad money to base money, that is, the money multiplier, was constant. The first impact was a decline in the use of cash substituted with electronic units of cash. Since these electronic payment platforms were in commercial banks, then outside money moved to banks as inside money and the preference of cash declined over time. This implies that the velocity of money declined. In addition, the ratio of broad money to base money, the money multiplier, was rising. This did not imply that the central banks were losing control of the money supply process, but rather that innovation in the financial market was evident. The monetary policy framework used in Kenya was thus obsolete (the use of base money as an intermediate target to control broad money and achieve their inflation target would never work) and had to change with the changing realities in the banking sector and perhaps the totality of the financial market.

FINANCIAL INCLUSION PROFILE IN AFRICA

Evidence is emerging that the success of retail electronic payment systems is driving the financial inclusion profile in Africa, especially for women and low-income earners. The success story seems to revolve around the binding constraints on financial services that digital evolution is helping to overcome. Among the binding constraints that sustained financial exclusion in Africa were levels of income, the irregular flow of that income, and the physical distance to a bank branch or financial service point. In one stroke, DFS seem to be solving these binding constraints and turning the tables from financial exclusion to financial inclusion. These have pushed the frontier of financial inclusion in Africa, as evidenced by the 2017 financial inclusion profile of selected SSA countries shown in Figure 5.3.

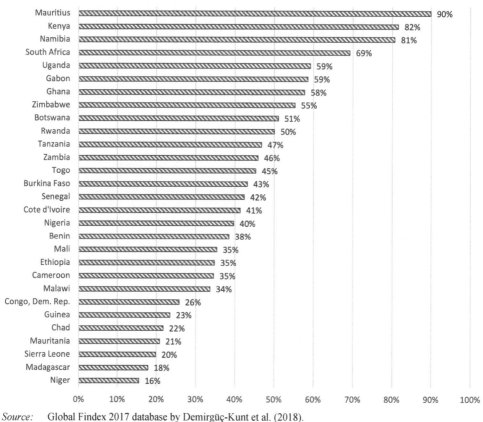

Source: Global Findex 2017 database by Demirgüç-Kunt et al. (2018).

Figure 5.3   Financial inclusion profile for selected SSA countries, 2017 (% age 15+)

Figure 5.3 shows that despite the DFS revolution in Africa, in 2017 there was still a significant financial inclusion gap in the region. Out of the 29 African countries, only ten had a financial inclusion index above 50 per cent. The top countries with a financial inclusion index of over 80 per cent were Mauritius (90 per cent), Kenya (82 per cent), and Namibia (81 per cent). Demirgüç-Kunt et al. (2018) pointed out that, apart from South Africa, the number of female adults included was lower than that of male adults included in all the African countries – with Morocco, Mozambique, Rwanda, and Zambia having a double-digit gender gap. However, following the mobile financial services revolution in Africa, the gender gap in financial inclusion seems to have generally reduced. The spread of mobile money accounts has created new opportunities to better serve women, poor people, and other groups traditionally excluded from the formal financial system (Demirgüç-Kunt et al., 2018). Indeed, any effort to increase overall account ownership in the African economies needs to prioritize financial inclusion for women and the poor. The digital financial instruments allow women and the poor to participate in financial transactions, savings, and credit with instruments that cannot be encroached. Evidently, the financial inclusion picture that has emerged in Africa is consistent with the fact that mobile phone financial services have allowed accelerating financial inclusion where new financial services and products have emerged – encouraged by innovation and a sound regulatory environment, and new effective, transparent, and efficient delivery channels.

LEAPFROGGING IN THE FINANCIAL SECTOR

Table 5.1   Examples of fragmentation deficiencies

Deficiency description
Structural obstacles exist arising from a skills deficit in university graduates
Limited participation by experienced professionals constrains effectiveness of majority graduate/undergraduate student-based innovation hub users
Lack of differentiation in innovation hub advantages
Weak management capacity and service delivery
Needed increases in public and private funding to support training and mentoring efforts
A shortage in affordable assistance to entrepreneurs
Dearth of venture funding accessibility (bank loans, government sponsored enterprise loans, and seed capital from venture capitalists)
Lack of alignment between research and innovation with policy priorities
Lack of African cross-border links (e.g., AfricaConnect)
Poor advocacy by education/public sectors to entrepreneurship opportunities given hub focus on quality professional services and products

Source: Adapted from Cunningham et al. (2014).

DFS have spread rapidly in the developing world, 'leapfrogging' the provision of formal banking services by solving the problems of weak institutional infrastructure and the cost structure of conventional banking (Aron, 2017), and the binding constraints that sustained financial exclusion in the countries. Particularly, the growth of fintech in Africa in the last decade has enabled leapfrogging in its financial sector. Despite the Covid-19 pandemic, Disrupt Africa (2021) showed that fintech startups in Africa grew by 17.3 per cent from 491 reported in 2019 to 576 in 2021. However, this was a slow growth as compared to the 63.1 per cent recorded between 2017 and 2019. The top six countries, that is, South Africa, Nigeria, Kenya, Egypt, Ghana, and Uganda, performed particularly well, contributing 85.4 per cent of startups (492 companies) in 2021. This is up from 81.7 per cent in 2019; which had been a decline from 88.4 per cent in 2017. CCAF, World Bank, and World Economic Forum (2020) noted that fintech has responded to the Covid-19 pandemic by implementing changes to their existing products, services, and policies. The most prevalent changes across all fintech verticals being 'fee or commission reductions and waivers', 'changes to qualification/on-boarding criteria', and 'payment easements'. Table 5.1 shows the fintech taxonomy highlighting the wide range of financial products and services that have revolutionized the financial sector in Africa.

Improved Banking Infrastructure

Digitization has revolutionized the front-office and back-office operations of the financial institutions. This includes back-end architecture and information systems that enable any financial institution to record, manage, and analyse transactions. Digitization has presented opportunities to banks to roll out an electronic Know Your Customer (KYC), which has helped reduce bank fraud and corruption in the sector. Disrupt Africa (2021) showed that there are currently 22 startups active in the security and identity space, helping to secure financial transactions and assisting with KYC and due diligence processes in Africa. Although this constitutes only 3.8 per cent of fintech companies in Africa, this was a 51.7 per cent growth on the 14 startups reported in 2019. These developments have helped to reduce banks' overhead costs. Figure 5.4a shows the trend in bank overhead costs to total assets across Africa regions.

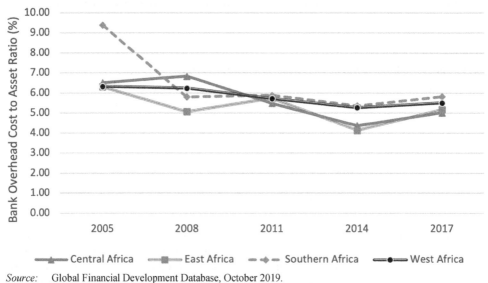

Source: Global Financial Development Database, October 2019.

Figure 5.4a   *Bank overhead costs to total assets*

Figure 5.4a shows that there has been a general decline in bank overhead costs as a ratio of the total assets since 2005, with significant drops noted in the Southern Africa region. The continent achieved these through innovative, automated, personalized, and relevant marketing outreach based on the preferences and needs of users, automated customer service through chatbots, and digitized protocols to review risk and fraud on a real-time basis, among others. As the overhead costs reduced, the banks have been able to expand their branch networks and grow their accounts, as shown in Figures 5.4b and 5.4c, respectively.

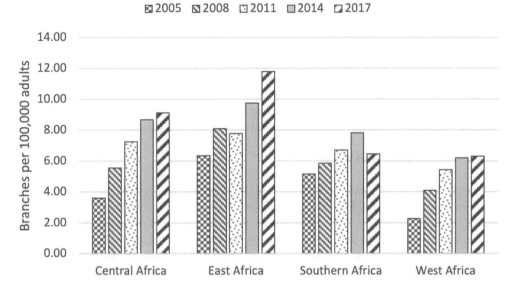

Figure 5.4b   Bank branches per 100,000 adults

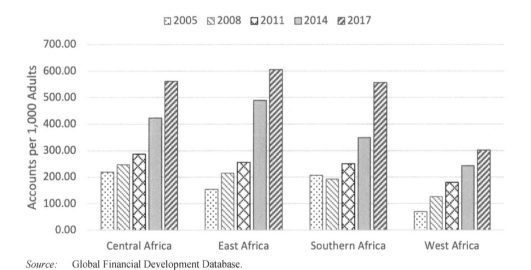

Source: Global Financial Development Database.

Figure 5.4c   Bank accounts per 1,000 adults

As demonstrated by Figure 5.4, the growth in branch networks slowed towards 2017 while bank accounts have continued to grow significantly. This is because fintech has enabled the banks to adopt new business models that offer expanded DFS to customers, thus generating new revenue streams. Evidently, the banks are slowly moving away from brick-and-mortar branch networks and adopting agency banking in addition to offering digital banking services. Disrupt Africa (2021) also reported the emergence of open banking fintech startups in Africa, with only six startups reported in the open banking space in 2021. The most established venture – South Africa's truID – opened its doors in 2017. Disrupt Africa (2021) defines open banking as a practice that provides third-party financial service providers with open access to consumer banking, transaction, and other financial data from banks and non-bank financial institutions through the use of application programming interface and data aggregation services. Moving into the future, the innovation will reshape the banking industry.

Digital Payments and Remittances

Disrupt Africa (2021) showed that there were 206 payment and remittance startups active in Africa in 2021, growing by 24.1 per cent from 2019. This accounted for 35.8 per cent of fintech ventures in Africa in 2021. Payments are the largest segment of fintech in Africa, with mobile money or person-to-person transfers being the most common area of payments (CCAF & MicroSave, 2018). Figure 5.5a shows the percentage of adults who made digital payments in SSA regions in 2014 and 2017. On the other hand, Figure 5.5b shows the percentage of adults who sent domestic remittances through a mobile phone in SSA regions in 2014 and 2017.

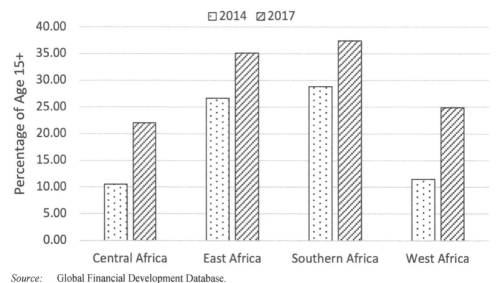

Source:　Global Financial Development Database.

Figure 5.5a　　*Made digital payments*

Figure 5.5 shows a significant increase in the number of adults making digital payments and those sending domestic remittances through mobile phones in all the regions. On top of the

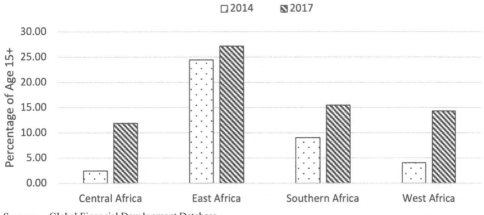

Source: Global Financial Development Database.

Figure 5.5b   Sent domestic remittances through a mobile phone

domestic remittances, CCAF and MicroSave (2018) showed that in 2017, the flow of international remittances in Africa was US$585 billion, which had more than doubled in the previous ten years. Digital's share of the global remittance flow is increasing fast, however, under the impetus of legacy companies shifting volumes to digital channels as well as digital-first startups. As pointed out by Oranye (2018), the latter are undercutting traditional remittance fees in some corridors, with legacy companies fighting by lowering traditional fees. There is a limit to how far legacy companies can go in this regard without undermining their margins completely, but the result is that technology will win and lower transfer costs of remittances. PricewaterhouseCoopers (2016) noted that the use of cryptocurrencies such as Bitcoin is currently reducing the cost of remittances to and from Africa.

Blockchain-focused incubators are beginning to appear across the region. Disrupt Africa (2021) reported 42 blockchain startups in Africa in 2021, constituting 7.3 per cent of the total fintech ventures. This was a decrease from the 45 startups reported in 2019 (Disrupt Africa, 2021). The uptake of blockchain across the continent remains uncertain considering the warnings issued by a number of central banks in the recent past. Blockchain generates a permanent record of each transaction and information exchange between the transacting parties (PricewaterhouseCoopers, 2016). This has important applications in banking and trading businesses as well as greater transparency in government. Over the next years, blockchain technology could upend how businesses and marketplaces in Africa operate completely.

Digital Lending and Real-Time Credit Risk Assessment

In the period prior to 2007, before the launch of M-Pesa in Kenya and the ensuing digital revolution in the financial sector, obtaining a short-term loan from the banks was costly. The costs included high interest rate charges, collateral requirements, out-of-pocket costs such as physical travel to the point of service, and opportunity costs due to time spent on the long application process and documentation (Gubbins & Totolo, 2018). In addition, there were separate costs for valuation of the collateral and legal charges to perfect the collateral. Some consumers, especially small businesses, could not meet the collateral requirements to access bank loans. Thanks to the digital revolution in the financial sector in Africa, an efficient platform of financial services is slowly developing in the region. In these developments, the transactions data and savings are used to generate credit scores for short-term virtual credit, thus revolutionizing the collateral technology that has inhibited growth in the credit markets in Africa. The virtual credits are processed, disbursed, and repaid remotely, without the need for customers to visit bank branches or outlets.

According to Disrupt Africa (2021), there were 134 lending and financing startups in Africa in 2021, constituting 23.3 per cent of the continent's fintech companies. This was a growth of 42.6 per cent on the 94 ventures operating in the lending and financing space in 2019, which in turn was up 44.6 per cent on 2017 (Disrupt Africa, 2021). The lending and financing startup growth has enabled the development of a number of fintech products in this space. For example, the development of virtual savings and credit products that began with M-Shwari in Kenya in November 2012 was replicated across five African countries. At the beginning of M-Shwari, it was clear that savings data, transactions data, and the tiered KYC would safeguard the credit supply platform in Kenya as well as generate appropriate credit scores to enable a pricing mechanism of short-term credit. This is an innovation unheard of before. Table 5.2 provides a summary of some virtual savings and credit products that have developed across Africa.

Table 5.2 shows that there is a general increase in digital savings and deposits in all the five countries. To qualify for an M-Shwari loan in Kenya and an M-Pawa loan in Tanzania, a customer should have an active M-Pesa account for at least six months, save on M-Shwari/M-Pawa and actively use the mobile money services. Similarly, to qualify for a MoKash loan in Rwanda and Uganda, a customer should be an MTN mobile money subscriber for at least six months, save on MoKash and actively use other MTN services. To access MoMoKash loans in Cote d'Ivoire, a customer should have an MTN mobile account, be well identified, and be an active MoMoKash user. The table also shows an increase in total loan amount disbursed in all the countries. This perhaps reflects the important role that the virtual credit supply products are playing as alternative sources of finance in Africa. The frequency of short-term loans is amazing in this product platform. In view of the increasing demand for short-term micro credit, application-based fintech lenders have also emerged. However, in most jurisdictions, they are not regulated and are not mandated to report to the credit reference bureaus like the Telco-facilitated bank virtual savings and credit products. Several startups (such as Tala and Branch) offering credit through apps have emerged. The M-Pesa transaction messages are used to determine a borrower's eligibility and loan limit. Borrowing from the Tala and Branch business model, more of such virtual credit supply platforms have mushroomed in Africa. These include Saida, Haraka, Okash, Pesa Pata, Pesa na Pesa, Zidisha, and Kiva in Kenya.

Evidently, the digital financial platform has transformed the intermediation process between borrowers and lenders. Advanced data analytics has revolutionized credit risk assessment by using alternative data sources to assess the credit risk of a borrower. As pointed out in CCAF and MicroSave (2018), new fintech lenders have emerged that use varied forms and combinations of non-traditional data – mobile call data records, user location and movement patterns, psychometric data, bill payments, internet browsing patterns, and social media behaviour. These companies analyse the data with artificial intelligence, machine learning, and big data

Table 5.2   *Example of virtual savings and credit products developing in Africa*

	M-Shwari (Kenya)	M-Pawa (Tanzania)	MoKash (Uganda)	MoKash (Rwanda)	MoMoKash (Cote d'Ivoire)
Launched	November 2012	May 2014	August 2016	February 2017	January 2018
Number of customers (as of June 2019)	28.8 million	8.6 million	5.5 million	1.3 million	2.1 million
Interest on savings (per annum, up to)	6.65%	5%	5%	5%	7%
Loan limit	Based on the M-Pesa transactions history, savings and past loan repayments	–	UGX 1,000,000	Rwf 300,000	100,000 CFA francs
Repayment duration	30 days	30 days	30 days	30 days	30 days
Facilitation fee	7.5%	9%	9%	9%	–
Total deposits as of June 2018 (US$ million)	140.20	8.04	1.48	0.51	–
Total deposits as of June 2019 (US$ million)	166.60	7.79	1.98	1.06	7.84
Average savings as of June 2018 (US$)	5.97	1.09	–	0.65	–
Average savings as of June 2019 (US$)	5.82	0.91	0.36	0.81	2.51
Total loan amount Disbursed as of June 2018 (US$ million)	2,771.63	56.43	19.81	4.11	–
Total Loan Amount disbursed as of June 2019 (US$ million)	3,749.71	69.52	50.27	13.46	6.87
Average usage per day (as of June 2019)	16,333 customers	2,953 customers	6,189 customers	1,399 customers	9,037 customers

Source: Commercial Bank of Africa.

analytic algorithms to develop new ways to assess the creditworthiness of consumers and the SMEs. These have offered an opportunity for alternative sources of finance that are convenient, efficient, and affordable to the unbanked, the underbanked, and SMEs when compared to traditional banks. These have resulted in a more stable bank-lending deposit spread (Figure 5.6a) and an increase in access to credit by the private sector (Figure 5.6b) across the Africa regions.

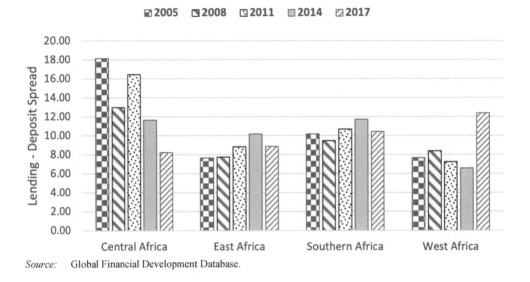

Source: Global Financial Development Database.

Figure 5.6a   Bank-lending deposit spread

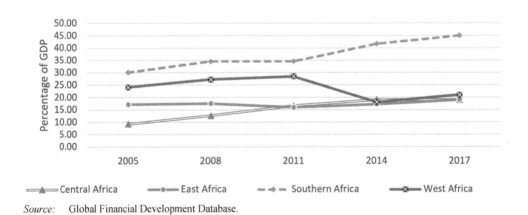

Source: Global Financial Development Database.

Figure 5.6b   Domestic credit to private sector

Figure 5.6a shows a reduction in bank-lending deposit spread in 2017 in all the regions except West Africa. This is evidence of an improved intermediation process between the borrowers and lenders across Africa. Consequently, there has been improved access to domestic credit by the private sector players in the continent. Figure 5.6b shows that was the case for all the regions, except West Africa that experienced a drop in 2011 to 2014. However, this improved after 2014. Generally, this section argues that African economies will attain a more inclusive growth by enhancing households and SMEs' access to finance through alternative digital finance platforms. This will be supported by the developing alternative financial platforms across Africa and improved access to domestic credit by SMEs.

Investment and Savings

Developing domestic capital markets is crucial for deepening the financial market and for generating alternative sources of funding for investment across Africa. The World Bank (2017) argued that most African stock markets are quite thin, with low levels of liquidity, and there is relatively low private equity penetration. Currency markets in many SSA countries remain risky and are devoid of liquid, long-term investment instruments. The increasing demand for investments has provided a ground for the development of Investtech in Africa. Disrupt Africa (2021) reported that Investtech startups in Africa grew by 18.5 per cent from 2019 to 77 in 2021. This accounted for 13.4 per cent of fintech companies in Africa but was a slow growth compared to the 242 per cent growth recorded between 2017 and 2019.

According to the Cambridge Centre for Alternative Finance (CCAF) (2020), online alternative finance models are developing in Africa. These are donation-based crowd funding, crowd-led micro-finance models, revenue-share models, real-estate crowd-funding models, person-to-person business-lending models, reward-based crowd funding, equity-based crowd funding, and balance sheet business-lending models. CCAF (2020) showed that in 2018, person-to-person consumer lending was the dominant model across the African continent, with a 53 per cent market share, followed by balance sheet business lending at a 22 per cent market share. CCAF (2020) reported that the alternative finance market across Africa raised US$209.1 million in 2018, which represented a substantial increase of 102 per cent from the 2017 volume of U$103.8 million. There was a sporadic improvement from US$ 44.4 million in 2013, to US$ 181.6 million in 2016, before the drop reported in 2017 (CCAF, 2020). This growth is partially due to the continued growth of African-based platforms, which CCAF (2020) attributes to an improved regulatory environment for the domestic fintech ecosystems as new firms are established and, more crucially, existing firms are better able to grow and expand. Figure 5.7 shows the trend in total alternative finance market volume in the African regions from 2016 to 2018.

Figure 5.7 shows that the overall regional leader by market share in 2018 was East Africa, with a 58 per cent market share – an 18 per cent increase from their 40 per cent market share in 2017 (with Kenya as the primary engine for the region's growth). Southern Africa (led by South Africa) had the second largest market share, with a 21 per cent market share, followed by West Africa (led by Nigeria) at 14 per cent (US$29.4 million). By contrast, Central Africa had a mere 7 per cent market share, with a negligible volume of only $1 million reported in North Africa.

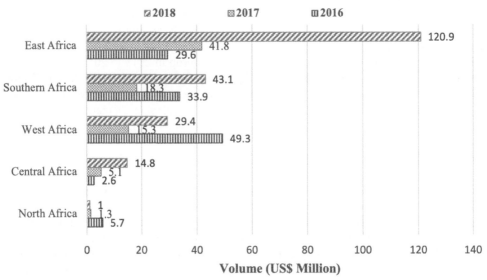

Figure 5.7   *Total online alternative finance market volume by region in Africa*

Insurtech

In most African markets, the insurance penetration rate is still exceptionally low (below 2 per cent) (Deloitte, 2017). The high complexity of financial products, the cumbersome claims process, and trust in insurance products linked strongly to low levels of financial literacy among consumers are some of the reasons for this low penetration rate. To overcome these challenges and to capture the largely unserved market in Africa, insurtech (a subset of fintech) is transforming the way insurance is bought and sold, how it assesses and quantifies risk, how consumers understand and manage their risk exposure, and disbursement of claims. Disrupt Africa (2021) showed that in 2021, there were 57 startups active in the insurtech space in Africa, accounting for 9.9 per cent of the total fintech. However, this has stagnated from the 2019 numbers largely due to the adverse effects of the Covid-19 pandemic on economic activities across the continent.

Micro-insurance services are developing across the continent following the recognition of the importance of insurance for low-income households. These are characterized by individually tailored policies and use of alternative data to determine the price of the premium (CCAF & MicroSave, 2018). The new insurance platforms are increasingly mobile-based and use USSD and SMS as their main channels of communication. In addition, the insurer works with aggregators, such as banks and MNOs, to leverage its impact and to offer its products to a larger customer base (Leach, 2018). The mobile phone is rapidly becoming the key instrument in information flow, marketing, selling, and delivering insurance products to low-income customers.

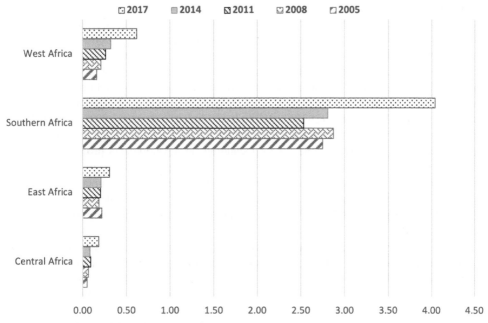

Source: Global Financial Development Database.

Figure 5.8a   Life insurance premium volume to GDP (%)

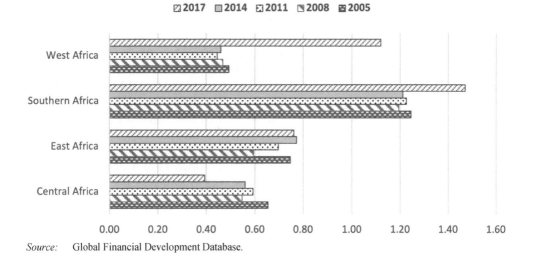

Source: Global Financial Development Database.

Figure 5.8b   Non-life insurance premium volume to GDP (%)

Moreover, person-to-person insurance has emerged, which allows individual users to pool their premiums together to insure each other against risk, creating a social risk-sharing network. This is becoming common with 'last expense covers' in Kenya, where family members and friends pool their premiums to cover funeral expenses. Other financial leapfrogging examples include the relatively rapid take-up of risk index insurance in some African countries (World Bank, 2017). For instance, due to the need for on-site farm visits, the traditional agriculture insurance market largely fails to meet smallholder farmers' demand for affordable insurance. As argued by the World Bank (2017), satellite-based index insurance, when combined with mobile technology for registration and claims settlement purposes, has huge potential to meet the needs of these farmers. Together, these technological developments provide avenues to reduce information costs, increase transparency, as well as enable greater trust and enforcement of contracts (International Monetary Fund, 2019). Consequently, the uptake of insurance products is slowly increasing across Africa, as indicated by the life insurance premium volume to gross domestic product (GDP) (Figure 5.8a) and non-life insurance premium volume to GDP (Figure 5.8b).

Figure 5.8a shows that there was a slight increase in life insurance premium volume to GDP over the decade prior to 2017. However, this is still below 1 per cent in all the regions except Southern Africa, which increased from 2.75 per cent in 2005 to 4.04 per cent in 2017. On the other hand, Figure 5.8b shows that non-life insurance premium volume to GDP was below 1.5 per cent in all the regions despite the significant increase noted in West and Southern Africa. This seems to have stagnated in the East Africa region and dropped in the Central Africa region.

Market Provisioning

Market provisioning entails regulatory technology, cybersecurity, and trading platforms. Regulatory technology enables companies to meet their regulatory and supervisory compliance requirements more efficiently (CCAF & MicroSave, 2018). The innovations in the financial sector have also led to a continuous evolution of regulation and supervision to keep pace with the innovations in the marketplace. The digital platform has enhanced the capacity of the various financial-sector regulators in Africa to monitor, evaluate, and ensure compliance. This has improved the space for the formulation of an effective and forward-looking monetary policy and allowed improvements in the anti-money laundering/counter-terrorist financing regime in some of these countries. The lessons are clear: a poor regulatory environment can be a major obstacle to innovations in the market and will constrain the speed of financial inclusion. Digitization has also brought with it other challenges that include cybercrimes, whose prevention remains a challenge to the regulators in Africa. Most African countries lack a comprehensive cybercrime legal framework to deal with cyberattacks, malware, spam, and phishing.

Summary Points on Digital Financial Services and the Emergence of Fintech

1. *A retail electronic payments system has emerged that is effective, efficient, transparent, and safe*: retail electronic payments is an easier entry point for financial services that has the capacity to formalize informal market transactions. Those retail payment platforms are

operated from commercial banks. An electronic payments platform is a game changer – fintech can roll out new products across all sectors.

2. *Financial inclusion, development, inclusive finance, and poverty reduction seem evident*: banks now have a technological platform to manage micro accounts and to reach out to customers cost-effectively, and virtual savings, credit supply platforms, and strong banks with intermediation capacity have emerged. This allows the formulation of an effective and forward-looking monetary policy and DFS platforms, it also allows improvements in the anti-money laundering/counter-terrorist financing regime. Finally, women can save in instruments that cannot be encroached. Being efficient savers, female-headed households can escape cycles of poverty. In Kenya, 2 per cent of Kenyan households were lifted from poverty (Suri & Jack, 2016).

3. *Fintech have rolled out sustainable business models cutting across all economic sectors*: some examples from Kenya and East Africa are: One Acre Fund raised productivity and incomes for smallholder farmers in East African countries; M-Kopa on domestic solar energy supply in Kenya and Tanzania; water-vending machines for urban slums for poor households in Nairobi; M-Tiba on financing health services in Kenya; and M-Akiba on investments in government securities in Kenya.

4. *Fintech is developing tax payments platforms and revenue administration to minimize leakages.*

5. *Fintech is designing platforms for e-government services that are effective and easy to reach, as well as in government social protection programs.*

6. *During the Covid-19 pandemic, some African countries, like Kenya, with digital capacity were able to develop a targeted social protection program support the vulnerable households using the digital payments platform.*

CONCLUSION: AFRICAN ECONOMIES ARE LEAPFROGGING IN FINANCE – IS THE FOURTH INDUSTRIAL REVOLUTION FEASIBLE IN AFRICAN ECONOMIES?

In this chapter we have shown that retail electronic payments platforms have emerged in Africa. They are effective, efficient, transparent, and safe, creating an easier entry point for formal financial services and leapfrogging of the financial sector across the continent. The most important outcome is that once digitization has taken root in the economy, it allows for the development of sustainable business models to support a particular market segment or productive activity with ease and with positive results across all other sectors of the economy.

However, the major concern to policymakers is the prospect of the fourth industrial revolution in African economies. The continent still lags behind both developed and other developing countries in several indicators essential for the fourth industrial revolution, especially in infrastructure, technology access, and education (Ndung'u & Signé, 2020). The digital revolution being experienced across Africa could allow countries to develop their own unique development path that will skip certain historical development stages by taking the lead in innovation and technologies such as drones, robotics, artificial intelligence, and renewable energies. The traditional and historical narrative, looking at developed economies' stages of development, is that manufacturing – the 'smokestack industry' – is regarded as the key driver of structural transformation in Africa. However, there has been an emergence of 'industries without smokestacks' such as the services industry, agro-processing firms, and horticultural firms that have benefited from technological change and productivity growth.

A further opportunity is that small-scale manufacturing in Africa may become more competitive and efficient because of the emerging technologies. As noted by Prisecaru (2016), new innovative producers have rapid access to digital platforms of research and development, marketing, and distribution and they may quickly improve the quality, price, and distribution of their products/services. On the other hand, consumers are more and more involved in the production and distribution chains and they may easily connect to suppliers by means of digital technological platforms. Naudé (2017) argued that additive manufacturing (3D printing) has the potential to open opportunities for entrepreneurs to enter manufacturing in Africa – it has promising applications for agricultural industrialization, for example. A recent project that piloted additive manufacturing in this regard is the 3D4AgDev project, funded by the Bill and Melinda Gates Foundation and GIZ and supported by the University of Galloway. This project uses 3D printing to provide women smallholder farmers with technology to design and develop their own labour-saving agricultural tools whereby local tool manufacturers (artisans, blacksmiths) can copy plastic prototypes and develop their own modifications.

There are several factors that are essential to enhancing the prospects of the fourth industrial revolution in African economies. First, transformative regulatory technology is required to nudge the market in appropriate and optimal paths without stifling innovation. This regulatory technology requires adequate capacity and capability to regulate, protect, and create partnerships that will encourage sustainable and tractable innovations. The economies in Africa need to enhance collaboration between the regulators, fintech and players in finance (banks), and manufacturing (entrepreneurs) sectors. This will enable the regulators to reinvent the regulatory framework, ensuring they truly understand the dynamic nature of the current digital developments so the regulatory environment will enhance investment in robust interoperable electronic payments platforms. Policymaking processes will need to shift from a focus on individual problems to an interdisciplinary approach that treats problems as interrelated. This will help to check the disruptions that may come with digitalization and the fourth industrial revolution. State and institutional capacity will be required to cope with market innovations and dynamism – developing institutions that regulate the market and those that protect markets with the capacity to nudge them to the appropriate optimal path of development.

Second, African economies require adequate infrastructural development across the continent. In the information and communication technology sector, African countries will have to close the connectivity gap – defined in terms of the extent of internet access and speed – with more advanced economies. Development of connectivity infrastructure for mobile phones and internet such as the fibre optic network is essential for the fourth industrial revolution. A good example is the presence of a fibre optic network in Kenya. This allowed the development of the core infrastructure for the electronic payments platform. Other forms of physical infrastructure will also accelerate efficiency in production. Newfarmer et al. (2018) have shown that with lower transport and communication costs, countries with suitable agro-ecological conditions can potentially produce high-value products, such as perishable horticultural products, which formerly needed to be produced near their point of consumption. Also, scalability of the digitization process, interoperability of retail electronic payments platforms, market conduct, and competition are challenges that require feasible market solutions. The retail electronic payments were developed individually with first-mover advantage, but now they should allow for an interoperable platform that will use connectivity to enlarge the market, lower unit costs, and provide room for more innovative solutions and scalability, while at the same time seamless and transformative regulatory technology will drive developments and innovations to the next level. There is a need to enhance MNO and MVNO interoperability, agent network interoperability, and agency banking interoperability across Africa. These solutions are endogenous to the market supported by across-the-board regulatory and state capacity (see Ndung'u, 2019).

Third, increased participation of Africa in the global value chains, a significant driver of labour productivity, mainly through agro-industrial and horticultural value chains, tourism, and business and trade services enhances the prospects of the fourth industrial revolution in the continent. Participation in the global value chain creates an avenue through which countries can industrialize at a much earlier stage of development, as lead firms choose to offshore fragments of the production value chain to countries where labour is cheaper or where other locational advantages confer a competitive cost advantage (Newfarmer et al., 2018). It may also allow suppliers in developing countries to meet standards and regulations that allow access to rich-country markets; it may permit imports under privileged tariff treatment for intra-firm trade; or it may facilitate the use of network technology that would not otherwise be available (Newfarmer et al., 2018). Finally, the service industry is also becoming important in African economies. Much of manufacturing is undergoing a process of servicification while at the same time service-sector firms have become larger, providing a range of specialized services such as engineering design work, legal services, and accounting (Newfarmer et al., 2018). Evidently, services in Africa are taking up the role of the primary source of within-sector productivity growth as services accounted for more than 50 per cent of labour productivity growth in several African countries.

In conclusion, physical infrastructure will be required so that fintech can develop core infrastructure that will ignite the vibrancy M-Pesa-type products has created in the financial system to move other sectors of the economy and ignite production efficiency downstream, and value addition and new markets upstream. This vibrancy can be pushed downstream to other sectors of the economy when fintech, blockchain, and distributed ledger technologies become more acceptable and easily accessible. The digital economy will still have to take the centre stage upstream with all its promise. Governments will need to continue developing appropriate capacity that will support these developments and nudge them to the optimal development path. In the end, the technological developments will coordinate the development discourse.

REFERENCES

Aron, J. (2017). 'Leapfrogging': A survey of the nature and economic implications of mobile money. *Centre for the Study of African Economies Working Paper WPS/2017-02.* https://econpapers.repec.org/paper/csawpaper/2017-02.htm
CCAF (Cambridge Centre for Alternative Finance). (2020). The global alternative finance market benchmarking report: Trends, opportunities and challenges for lending, equity, and non-investment alternative finance models. www.jbs.cam.ac.uk/wp-content/uploads/2020/08/2020-04-22-ccaf-global-alternative-finance-market-benchmarking-report.pdf
CCAF (Cambridge Centre for Alternative Finance) & MicroSave. (2018). Fintech in Uganda: Implications for regulation. www.jbs.cam.ac.uk/wp-content/uploads/2020/08/2018-ccaf-fsd-fintech-in-uganda.pdf
CCAF (Cambridge Centre for Alternative Finance), World Bank, & World Economic Forum. (2020). The global Covid-19 fintech market rapid assessment report. www3.weforum.org/docs/WEF_The_Global_Covid19_FinTech_Market_Rapid_Assessment_Study_2020.pdf

Central Bank of Kenya. (2021). National payments system statistics. 2 June. www.centralbank.go.ke/national-payments-system/mobile-payments/

Cunningham, P. M., Cunningham, M., & Ekenberg, L. (2014). Baseline analysis of 3 innovation ecosystems in East Africa. *2014 14th International Conference on Advances in ICT for Emerging* Regions. IEEE, December, pp. 156–162.

Deloitte. (2017). Unlocking new markets: Digital innovation in Africa's insurance industry. www2.deloitte.com/content/dam/Deloitte/za/Documents/financial-services/za_Digital-Insurance-101017.pdf

Demirgüç-Kunt, A., Klapper, L. Singer, D., Ansar, S., & Hess, J. (2018). The global findex database 2017: Measuring financial inclusion and the fintech revolution. World Bank. https://globalfindex.worldbank.org/sites/globalfindex/files/2018-04/2017%20Findex%20full%20report_0.pdf

Disrupt Africa. (2021). Finnovating for Africa 2021: Reimagining the African financial services landscape. https://disruptafrica.gumroad.com/l/razjs

Gubbins, P., & Totolo, E. (2018). Digital credit in Kenya: Evidence from demand-side surveys. Financial Sector Deepening Trust Kenya. https://fsdkenya.org/wp-content/uploads/2021/aws/Archive%20data%20FSD/12-06-07_FinLandscapes_demand-side_survey.pdf?_t=1610970301

International Finance Corporation. (2018). Shaping the future of Africa: Markets and opportunities for private investors. www.ifc.org/wps/wcm/connect/701a29a9-0740-400c-bb86-3d64e5d0a11a/Africa+CEO+Forum+Report_FIN3_Web-lores.pdf?MOD=AJPERES&CVID=m9z19ct

International Monetary Fund. (2019). Fintech in Sub-Saharan African countries: A game changer? Departmental Paper Series No. 19/04. www.imf.org/en/Publications/Departmental-Papers-Policy-Papers/Issues/2019/02/13/FinTech-in-Sub-Saharan-African-Countries-A-Game-Changer-46376

Leach, J. (2018). Digital insurance: Managing the risks that really matter. In J. Sharp, L. Gronbach, & R. Villiers (eds), Digital finance in Africa's future: Innovations and implications. International Colloquium, Johannesburg, 22–26 October. www.up.ac.za/human-economy-programme/article/2707793/colloquium-on-digital-finance-in-africas-future-innovations-and-implications

Naudé, W. (2017). Entrepreneurship, education, and the fourth industrial revolution in Africa. *Institute of Labour Economics Discussion Paper No. 10855.* https://ftp.iza.org/dp10855.pdf

Ndung'u, N. (2018). Next steps for the digital revolution: Inclusive growth and job creation in Kenya. *Brookings Institution Working Paper No. 20.* www.brookings.edu/wp-content/uploads/2018/10/Digital-Revolution-in-Africa_Brookings_AGI_20181022.pdf

Ndung'u, N. (2019). Digital technology and state capacity in Kenya. *Centre for Governance and Development Policy Paper 154.* www.cgdev.org/publication/digital-technology-and-state-capacity-kenya

Ndung'u, N., & Signé, L. (2020). The fourth industrial revolution and digitization will transform Africa into a global powerhouse. Foresight Africa, Brookings Institute. www.brookings.edu/wp- content/uploads/2020/01/ForesightAfrica2020_20200110.pdf

Newfarmer, R. S., Page, J., & Tarp, F. (2018). Industries without smokestacks and structural transformation in Africa: Overview. In R. S. Newfarmer, J. Page, & F. Tarp (eds), *Industries without Smokestacks: Industrialization in Africa Reconsidered* (pp. 1–26). Oxford University Press.

Oranye, N. (2018). Market research about African remittance flows: The mobile money landscape in Africa matter. In J. Sharp, L. Gronbach, & R. Villiers (eds), *Digital Finance in Africa's Future: Innovations and implications*. Johannesburg: International Colloquium, Johannesburg, 22–26 October. www.up.ac.za/human-economy-programme/article/2707793/colloquium-on-digital-finance-in-africas-future-innovations-and-implications

PricewaterhouseCoopers. (2016). Disrupting Africa: Riding the wave of the digital revolution. www.pwc.com/gx/en/issues/high-growth-markets/assets/disrupting-africa-riding-the-wave-of-the-digital-revolution.pdf

Prisecaru, P. (2016). Challenges of the fourth industrial revolution. *Knowledge Horizons – Economics*, 8(1), 57–62.

Suri, T., & Jack, W. (2016). The long-run poverty and gender impacts of mobile money. *Science*, 354(6317), 1288–1292.

World Bank. (2017). Leapfrogging: The key to Africa's development? From constraints to investment opportunities.   https://openknowledge.worldbank.org/bitstream/handle/10986/28440/119849-WP -PUBLIC-Africa-Leapfrogging-text-with-dividers-9-20-17-web.pdf?sequence=1&isAllowed=y

6. Financial leapfrogging and innovative financing in sub-Saharan Africa: gender-lens investments for gender equality

Michele Ruiters and Motshedisi Mathibe

INTRODUCTION

Institutional decision making and choices require specialized study. Political theorist Theda Skocpol (1985) argued that institutions have their own interests that make them rule makers, referees and enforcers. North (1990) identified institutions as cultural and procedural entities in which norms are created and formalised based on beliefs, values and culture. North (1990) further defines institutions as 'formal' or 'informal' where the former have clear rules of engagement and the latter are defined by cultural and social repetition. This chapter explores how formal institutions, particularly development finance institutions (DFIs) and some commercial banks, have changed to ensure that they address the needs of women in the economy, especially women entrepreneurs. The chapter uses North's institutional theory to explore the developments that have taken place to facilitate gender mainstreaming in financial institutions.

THEORETICAL FRAMEWORK

Institutional theory explores the use of informal (culture) relationships within formal rules and regulations that result in a particular way of organising the world and the way individuals are situated within institutions. Scott (2013) explores three dimensions of institutional force, namely regulatory, normative and cognitive forces that build on North's (1990) concept of formal institutions.

Institutions have interests manifested through regulations (Skocpol, 1985; North, 1990; Scott 2013). But regulations reflect gender biases which result in gender inequalities (Zhang, 2020). To correct these imbalances, some institutions, for example the European Investment Bank, the Asian Infrastructure Investment Bank, the French Development Bank and the African Development Bank (AfDB), have introduced gender-mainstreaming policies that could result in new legal and procedural changes, gender-sensitive decision-making processes and a change in attitudes towards financing women-owned businesses (Moore, 1994).

Feminist economics and gendered institutional analyses have explored the gendered nature of economies and institutions (Bangani and Vyas-Doorgapersad, 2020). Due to the structure of global and national economies, women's labour force participation lags that of their male counterparts (WEF, 2020) and women experience disproportionately higher barriers in accessing resources and opportunities than men to participate in the workforce and benefit from that participation (Buvinic and Furst-Nichols, 2016). More recent data show a 0.76 gender parity in women's economic participation in the African economy but record that this employment is in 'low-paid, subsistence jobs in the informal economy' (Moodley et al., 2019). In the post-Covid-19 period, these statistics have worsened as more women than men lost their jobs because of lockdown (Aoyagi, 2021).

Gender-Lens Investing: A Leapfrogging Financing Initiative

In 2009, Jackie Van der Brug and Joy Anderson coined the term gender-lens investing (GLI) in relation to a trend they witnessed in gender equity investors (Gender Smart Investing, n.d.). In 2010, the European Bank of Reconstruction and Development launched the first loss guarantee fund for women entrepreneurs in Turkey and the United Nations launched Women's Empowerment Principles (Gender Smart Investing, n.d.). Since then, GLI has become an approach that enables impact investors to make strategic and inclusive decisions that yield more equitable gender outcomes and a stronger portfolio company performance (Aidis et al., 2022).

In 2013, the AfDB established its Special Envoy of Gender under the leadership of Geraldine Fraser-Moleketi. The AfDB later finalised the gender strategy that aimed to mainstream gender equality across its business. The Canada-African Development Bank Climate Fund, launched in 2021, will provide concessional loans to 'climate change-related projects with a strong gender-responsive component' (AfDB, 2021). The Development Bank of Southern Africa (DBSA), a Green Climate Fund (GCF) implementation partner, has also introduced gender mainstreaming into its lending, particularly in relation to climate-related projects (DBSA, n.d.).

In addition to providing access to resources, GLI could also drive social/political and economic change by promoting gender-aware policies in companies and financial value chains while improving policy enablement (Maheshwari et al., 2019). African companies such as EY, Tiger Brands, Credit Bank PLC and Kenya Breweries Limited have committed to gender equality through their business practices (Business Engage, 2021). These companies have intentionally and strategically adopted gender-aware policies because economic and social attitudes have changed over time (North, 1990) and become mainstream best practice.

There is an increasing demand to incorporate standardized metrics to measure GLI outcomes. In 2017, the Global Impact Investing Network's definition identified two main approaches to GLI. The first approach focused on promoting women-owned businesses and female beneficiaries and the second focused on supporting gender equality within business operations (regardless of ownership). The second approach addressed gender from pre-investment activities (e.g., sourcing and due diligence) to post-deal monitoring (e.g., strategic advisory and exiting). For investors, this approach examined companies in terms of their vision or mission to address gender issues and their organizational structure, culture, internal policies and workplace environment. It included the use of data and metrics for the gender-equitable management of performance and to incentivise behavioural change and accountability (see Global Impact Investment Network, 2019 for more detail). The decision to adopt GLI strategies can be motivated by different aims and goals. We summarise the case for GLI from three different standpoints: (1) the social justice case; (2) the business case; and

(3) the case for small and growing businesses (Aidis et al., 2022). This chapter delves deeper into understanding the latter.

The Case for Small and Growing Women-Led Businesses

Few studies have demonstrated the benefits of gender-inclusive practices specifically for small and growing businesses. Research shows that the more gender equality and representation there is in a firm, the better the growth prospects for that firm (Zhang, 2020). Calvert Impact Capital, an impact-investing firm and an early adopter of GLI strategies, identified positive effects from GLI in its global portfolio. Its Africa investments include the Solar Energy Transformation Fund in sub-Saharan Africa and Asian countries, a sustainable mobility investment in South Africa and an environmental fund with Criterion Africa Partners. Kenya Women Holding, a financial institution in Kenya, adopted GLI to fully mainstream women in their workplace equity, funding decisions and access to capital initiatives (Biegel and Nyong'o Madison, 2017).

A recent performance analysis found that, on average, companies with the highest percentage of women on boards and in leadership positions outperformed those with the least. Other research has identified negative effects of implicit gender bias, sexual harassment, groupthink and gender stereotyping on businesses regardless of size or sector (Braun et al., 2017; Chan et al., 2008; Keplinger et al., 2019; Rock and Grant, 2016). Companies and workgroups with the lowest prevalence of gender-based harassment are often those with the greatest gender balance (ICRW, 2018). These findings are relevant for small and growing businesses. Unequal opportunities for women can also directly affect a company's bottom line by diminishing its image with employees, consumers and supply chains (Business for Social Responsibility, 2019; Aidis et al., 2021).

The value of making investment decisions that have a positive impact and benefit women can manifest in numerous ways. Many of these outcomes often have complementary and compounding effects on the strength and long-term success of an investment or business:

> Mainstreaming a gender perspective is the process of assessing the implications for women and men of any planned action, including legislation, policies, or programs, in all areas and at all levels. It is a strategy for making women's as well as men's concerns and experiences an integral dimension of the design, implementation, monitoring and evaluation of policies and programs in all political, economic and societal spheres so that women and men benefit equally, and inequality is not perpetuated. The ultimate goal is to achieve gender equality. (ECOSOC 1997/2 agreed conclusions, in UNIDO, 2014)

Focus of the Chapter

This chapter aims to highlight the role innovation can play in increasing women's access to capital and products and services that potentially fall within the mandate of public and private financiers. The chapter will provide a roadmap for building on each of these categories.

The rest of the chapter is structured as follows. The first section provides an overview of the state of entrepreneurship and leapfrogging in Africa, conveying new stories about how entrepreneurial companies are transforming African business through financial leapfrogging. Second, the chapter makes the business case for gender mainstreaming in financial institutions and argues that the economy will benefit from the inclusion of successful women-owned businesses. Third, it explores some of the gender-lens investments, then discusses practical strategies for investments. Finally, the chapter unpacks some of the investment opportunities within infrastructure sectors and the innovative projects in those sectors. It concludes with recommendations on how innovative financial inclusion of women-owned businesses could ensure economic development.

LITERATURE REVIEW

State of Entrepreneurship and Leapfrogging in Africa

Leapfrogging refers to the adoption of modern technologies in products and services, skipping over conventional and outdated distribution channels or means of service and product delivery. Africa's modernizing and urbanizing population needs to adopt innovative business models and technology in line with critical areas such as agriculture, education, energy, information and communications technology (ICT), finance and governance.

A Gap in the Ecosystem Regarding Women Entrepreneurs

Current debates on gender equality in society, the economy and politics have moved away from targets aiming to increase the number of women involved in boards, parliaments, management, supply chains, etc. to the actual value addition that gender diversity brings to the economy. By adding an analysis that pays attention to how women-owned businesses access finance and the financial products they need, investors identify gaps in the financial market, tailor and strengthen their products and strategically address the needs of 'invisible' market sectors that may be underserved or undervalued. By making financing programmes sensitive to gender equality, the economic outcomes both for women and men – and for investors – can be improved. Studies by the World Bank and the International Monetary Fund show that fostering gender equity could grow gross domestic product by 2–3.5 per cent (Alliance for Financial Inclusion, 2016).

The framework for analysing GLI data shows differences from conventional investment decision making (Anderson and Miles, 2015). Simply put, the lens used to determine investment decisions changes to include women-owned businesses and becomes more focused on gender inclusion. Data suggest that women-owned and women-led companies in Africa account for less than 1 per cent of the total funds raised in 2021. In contrast, male founders of start-ups raised 99 per cent of funding received in 2021 while male-led companies raised 93 per cent of total funding. This discrepancy shows the unequal access to finance based on gender. Financial institutions require collateral or security for loans, which many women in Africa and other emerging markets lack; women-owned businesses either do not have the capital that banks require to underwrite loans or their lower education rates limit their understanding of financial products and how to access them (Ulwodi and Muriu, 2017). The business case for gender-lens investments becomes stronger as women entrepreneurs increase in number and in size of business (Mastercard Index of Women Entrepreneurs, 2022).

Influencing Financial Institutions' Investment Frameworks

Emerging markets and DFIs have the opportunity to contribute greatly to new investments in innovative areas of growth; for example, technology, small business leapfrogging and under-represented businesses. Innovative financing technologies such as mobile money firms M-Pesa and Safaricom have created applications that move money faster, more cheaply and more inclusively in developing countries. In a similar way, targeted DFI investments review conventional investment decisions and make them more inclusive by, for example, framing women-owned businesses as an investment class and market opportunity. DFIs could adopt gender-lens perspectives to maximise investment and growth opportunities. This will result in the following:

- Increased access to capital, particularly beyond the microfinance and grants categories.
- Development of financial products and services that address the needs of women who need finance for businesses that redress gender inequality.
- Promotion of workplace equity to achieve greater and effective representation of women at executive and senior levels in companies and to meet women's time, social and health needs within the workplace.
- Use of finance as a transformative tool by including gender analysis to determine where the greatest development impact can be achieved. The relevant DFIs review existing policies and practices to ensure that a gender lens is applied to infrastructure financing.

Why Gender Finance?

The Sustainable Development Goals (SDGs) commit the United Nations member states to gender equality generally (SDG 5) and in the economy (SDG 8), calling for 'sustained, inclusive and sustainable economic growth, full and productive employment and decent work for all' (United Nations, 2018) Much needs to be done to ensure that the sector becomes more representative in terms of operators, owners and builders, and more gender aware in how the infrastructure is used by men and women.

In the past, financial institutions offered ostensibly non-gendered products that were intended to meet the needs of a generic clientele. Economies were structurally designed for men and men's labour (Stotsky, 2006), with little allowance for women's care work or the contributions women make to formal economies. Women and women-owned businesses have lagged in their access to finance and growth, struggling to raise money that suits their business needs.

This chapter provides an overview of an innovative financing value chain for women-led and women-owned businesses in South Africa. Research, undertaken by the Bertha Centre (Ivankovic and Essa, 2021) at the University of Cape Town on the full financing value chain, includes public, private and other sources of finance. A 2015 McKinsey Global Institute Report calculates that women's equal participation in the economy could potentially contribute $12 trillion to the global economy.

Women-owned businesses have struggled with accessing different sources of finance, including venture capital, equity (Alsos et al., 2006), debt and loans (Cowling et al., 2019). These strategies recognise the importance of including gender considerations into financing decision making. Currently, international best practice has targeted the recipient in their policies and impact intentions, thereby highlighting the experiences of women, youth and other marginalised communities in the development finance sector. For example, the GCF requires a gendered analysis of projects applying for finance from the facility. Further, several financial institutions have opted for gender-lens financing where women and women-owned projects are given high priority in their financing decisions.

METHODOLOGY

The chapter relies on desktop research of DFIs, private investors and women-owned businesses. Institutional theory provides an understanding of institutional norms, regulations and culture.

ANALYSIS AND DISCUSSION

Institutions have been coerced into adopting gender-lens frameworks because the international financing environment has changed with the advent of the SDGs and gender mainstreaming. Global recognition of a business case for women's financing has also motivated financiers to change their regulations and norms for financing women-owned businesses, resulting in an institutional and cultural change. Examples of these are initiatives from the GCF and the Global Environmental Facility (GEF) that require a gender focal point to be included on every project they finance.

GENDER-LENS FINANCING IN THE VALUE CHAIN

The accepted definition of gender mainstreaming means that gender is considered at every point of the infrastructure financing cycle:

- project identification;
- project preparation;
- financing decisions;
- project implementation; and
- monitoring and evaluation.

The DFI models include gender mainstreaming at all stages of the infrastructure investment value chain. DFIs recognise that an opportunity exists in gender-lens financing, but their systems need to change in order to redefine their concept of risk, collateral, repayment terms and size of project. The assumption is that women-led or women-owned projects require additional work because they are relatively new to the infrastructure space. This is not a simple task as it does require an ideological shift from finance as a tool for economic development to finance as a tool for equitable and sustainable development.

The argument that women are new to infrastructure can be contested by bodies such as South African Women in Construction, South African Women in Transport, Women in Oil and Energy in South Africa and the more recently established African Women in Energy and Power. The main concern these bodies have is that they are continually falling short of the financing requirements because DFIs do not have suitable products to finance women-led and women-owned businesses that often fall on the smaller end of the infrastructure scale.

Unfortunately, hard data are lacking since African institutions do not have a history of collecting data (De Vries et al., 2015).

Many women-owned businesses in Africa have had to resort to using their own savings or relying on development programmes that support their businesses through services and training. One such business belongs to a woman entrepreneur, Martha Radebe of South Africa, who started her business, Soma Solutions, without financing. This ICT consulting company offers solutions to small and medium enterprises and government departments in South Africa. Radebe solely grew Soma Solutions from one employee to 15 staff members within three years (2017–2019). Radebe was exposed to the ICT sector from an early age as she attended meetings with her brother, who owned a technology company. Radebe noticed there was a lack of women representatives in the industry and decided to address this gap. She obtained her tertiary qualification and job experience in ICT and started working in the industry to gain experience. Soma Solutions now partners with different organisations and enterprises to offer ICT solutions and services to its clients.

In 2008, she registered a consulting company as a side hustle, but did not receive any financing despite numerous attempts. Radebe's experience is not uncommon as the average rejection rate for women-owned small and medium enterprises is around 44 per cent, with women-owned businesses being 2.5 times more likely to have 100 per cent of their projects rejected by banks (Janse van Vuuren, 2022). Instead, Radebe used her savings to grow her business. Radebe registered for the Enterprise Supply Development programme through Accenture Enterprise Development, where she received coaching and profiling for herself, her business and her staff members. The programme got Radebe to appreciate the importance of personality profiling and how it could make or break a business.

In addition, enterprise supplier development programmes assisted Soma Solutions; the first was the Innovator Trust which Radebe joined in 2017. The trust offered to pay for Radebe to study ICT at the Gordon Institute of Business Science but she refused, believing she was already more than qualified. Instead, she requested assistance in growing her business and the trust assigned her to Shanduka Black Umbrellas, where she drafted a business plan. Despite Radebe's refusal to attend specific training programmes, she had monthly meetings with Shanduka Black Umbrellas to report on turnover, business challenges, successes and business proposals she sent out. The Shanduka programme ran for three years, and Radebe graduated in June 2020. Radebe demonstrated her high-impact entrepreneurial ability by growing Soma Solutions' revenue to over 70 per cent year on year from 2017 to 2019.

Gender and the DFI Infrastructure Mandate

Certain infrastructure sectors and financing processes lend themselves to a gender-lens approach better than others. For example, the water, education and health sectors are more likely to include gender-based services; less likely are transport and energy. Programme gaps can be eradicated by making gender-aware investments available. Table 6.1 provides a list of how gender could be included in each stage of the infrastructure project's life cycle. Table 6.1 is an example of how gender mainstreaming can inform gender-aware strategies for DFIs.

Table 6.1   *Gender checklist for infrastructure sectors*

Sector	Indicator
Energy	Monitor disaggregated energy needs of women and men.
	Ensure inclusion of women-owned/led businesses in the tender process.
	Support the development of sources of energy that might be more beneficial to women users (especially in rural areas); for example, renewable energy for cooking, lighting and heating.
	Identify links between energy and other sectors to facilitate equitable access to water and sanitation (pumping, lighting and processing); transport (nodes and routes used by women for business and social roles); energy sources for ICT to be rolled out for all in urban and rural areas.
	Ensure participation of women in every phase of the project.
	Develop financial products that meet the needs of women-owned/led businesses in the energy value chain, particularly in renewables.
Transport	Improve disaggregated data on how women and men use transport modes.
	Identify time use of transport for social roles and responsibilities.
	Ensure women and men are included in every stage of the project.
	Provide financial products that meet the needs of women-owned/led businesses to crowd in smaller contractors.
Water and sanitation	Monitor disaggregated data on women and men's water use and needs.
	Ensure inclusion of women-owned/led businesses in the tender process.
	Ensure women and men's participation in decision-making structures linked to the project.
	Identify access needs for women (location, distribution, etc.) in the water and sanitation sectors (including maintenance and recycling).
	Identify entry points for women-owned/led businesses in the project value chain.
	Provide financial products that meet the needs of women investors and women-led/owned businesses.
ICT	Monitor disaggregated data on the needs of women and men in relation to the project.
	Determine the barriers to women's participation in the ICT project (time, access, skills, social roles, finance, etc.) and identify ways to mitigate them.
	Ensure participation of women in the planning, preparation, tender and implementation phases of the project.
	Document project outcomes and address the gendered needs identified in the planning phase.

Source: Adapted from AfDB (2009).

GENDER-LENS FINANCIAL PRODUCTS

The Criterion Report on the State of the Field of Gender Lens Investing (2015) identifies a few important vehicles in the impact investment sector. This section highlights other products that supply finance for larger projects in infrastructure.

An interesting set of questions has been developed over the years by people working on impact investments. It is beneficial to reproduce the timeline and adapted relevant questions before specifying products individually (see Box 6.1).

BOX 6.1   SELECT QUESTIONS: IMPLEMENTING VEHICLES

These questions show the maturation of the field over time, from the first year where the conversation focused on simply getting something to the market to more recent conversations adapting to the needs of scale.

The Express Lane to Investible Deals

- If the capital is readily available, where can we simply create a product?

Design of Gender-Lens Investment Products

- What are the characteristics of the ideal women-focused venture or debt fund? What are the constraints in that design that are most common?
- How do we design for impact?
- How can we include leaders with deep knowledge of gender-biased business systems but less knowledge of finance in the process of design?

Implementation Muscles: Building Products and Vehicles for Gender-Lens Investing

- Which is more common/effective: introducing gender into an existing product or vehicle or building a new vehicle around gender? Why?
- What kinds of products have worked in the past?
- What are the sustainable models for products?

Products at Scale/for Scale

- How do gender-lens products get visibility within platforms overall?
- When gender-lens investing sits within a broader environmental, social and governance framework, is it okay if gender sits largely in governance?
- How do we learn from other fields, or make linkages to other fields that have already built investment vehicles on platforms at scale (e.g., climate change)?

Source: Adapted from Anderson and Miles (2015).

We will return to the questions in Box 6.1 in the section that looks at products some DFIs provide to women. The products below map a few options for products that have been developed effectively in the market over the years.

Impact/Social Investing

These products include socially responsible investing, which entails investors determining sectors that they would prefer to invest in based on the 'do no harm' principle. No-go sectors include social taboos such as the tobacco, alcohol and coal industries.

Examples of companies and products in these markets include:

- African Women's Development Fund provides grant-making services for women-focused organisations.
- Affirmative Finance Action for Women in Africa aims to bridge the $42 billion financing gap facing women in Africa.
- African Women Leadership Fund Initiative funds women-owned and operated investment funds and companies across Africa.

- Calvert Foundation's Women Investing in Women Initiative provides loans to women in Africa and other developing markets to access clean energy.
- Triodos Sustainable Trade Fund provides finance to farmers in Africa, Latin America and Asia whose cultivation practices are more sustainable.
- Women's World Banking Capital Partners, a 'wholesale' investor that makes direct equity investments in women-focused financial institutions.
- Abrazo Capital, a South Africa-based investment company that does impact and social investments.
- Women's Development Bank, an investment bank set up to finance women in Africa.
- Alitheia Partners and the Identity Group, women-led investor companies investing in women on the African continent.
- Women in Infrastructure Development, a South Africa-based women-owned investment and project development company that provides support to women-owned small and medium businesses.

Social Impact and Gender Bonds

The Organisation for Economic Co-operation and Development (OECD) defines social impact bonds as an innovation financing mechanism in which governments or commissioners enter into agreements with social service providers and investors to pay for the delivery of pre-defined social outcomes. In reality, the term 'bond' is more of a misnomer. In financial terms, SIBs are not real bonds but rather future contracts on social outcomes. They are also known as payment-for-success bonds (United States) or pay-for-benefits bonds (Australia) (Galitopoulou and Noya, 2016, p. 4).

Social or gender bonds can raise funds 'easily' but need to be rated favourably by the ratings agencies, offering a secure return on the investment, and be socially attractive to investors. South Africa has had experience with social bonds, particularly in the Western Cape where the Provincial Departments of Social Development and Health committed R25 million in outcome funding for three social impact bonds for maternal and early childhood outcomes. The Bertha Centre for Social Innovation and Entrepreneurship at the University of Cape Town Graduate School of Business facilitated the bond.

Investors may invest in an intermediary that then structures, coordinates and manages risk. Social service providers are selected and tasked with the delivery of the service or programme to the targeted population. Independent evaluators measure and evaluate the programme, determine if the objectives are met and report to the relevant government department that pays the intermediary for the work done. The intermediary finally provides investors with returns on their investments. This is not a grant system but rather works like a normal investment but with specific outcomes.

Gender bonds are more aligned to traditional bonds where money is raised on the open market to finance gender-based programmes. Gender bonds have become more common in recent years, as shown in the information below:

- The Asian Development Bank issued a ten-year gender bond at the end of 2017 to 'increase women's presence in society' that Japan's Dai-ichi Life Insurance will support with an investment of $89.9 million (10 billion yen) (Nikkei Asia, 2017). The expected yield is 0.9 per cent.

- In 2016, the Banco del Estado de Chile issued the second offering (US$147 million) of its ten-year fixed-rate Women Bond on the Japanese market, which shows that there is an appetite for these bonds. The initial offering came in at US$94.2 million.
- In 2017, the National Australia Bank launched a five-year A$500 million gender equity bond with a return of 95 basis points over the bank bill swap rate and an AA minus rating by S&P and Fitch and Aa2 by Moody's.
- In September 2017, the AfDB announced its intention to launch a social bond programme that will be guided by four components: use of proceeds process for project evaluation and selection, management of proceeds and reporting (AfDB, 2017). The social projects should fall within the AFDB's mandate, have well-defined expected social outcomes and impacts and lead to significant poverty reduction, job creation and inclusive growth across age, gender and geography. The AfDB's initial plan to launch a gender bond was put on hold because of this holistic bond strategy.
- In 2018, the World Bank's five-year Sustainable Development Bond was launched in Canada at CAD1 billion. The bond was launched to raise finance to meet the SDG programme. The issuer rating was Aaa/AAA (Moody's/S&P) with a coupon price of 2.25 per cent.

The International Finance Corporation (IFC) (2017) has a social bond cash flow diagram that maps out how social bonds could operate in real terms. Figure 6.1 describes the process that begins with investors investing cash into the social bond, which is funnelled into a General Liquidity Account. A portfolio of eligible projects is created based on the objectives for the social bond. Loans are then disbursed from the General Liquidity Account to intermediary financial institutions (in the case of the IFC) or directly to applicants (if a small financial institution is managing the bond) and to eligible projects. As the loans are repaid, the payments are then returned to investors as Fixed Coupon Payments.

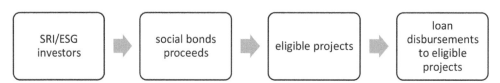

Note: ESG = environmental, social, and governance; SRI = socially responsible investment.
Source: IFC (2017).

Figure 6.1   International Finance Corporation social bond proceeds cash flow diagram

Blended Finance

Blended finance, 'the strategic use of development finance for the mobilization of additional finance towards sustainable development in developing countries' (OECD DAC, 2018), is a useful vehicle for gender products. It allows DFIs to catalyse or crowd in additional sources of finance from other partners. Table 6.2 sets out some of the blended finance options available to DFIs.

Table 6.2   *Instruments used in blended finance*

PF blending instrument	Justification for use
Grants ('investment grants')	Fund-specific costs and activities that decrease overall project costs and increase chances of success. Involves grants for equipment, project preparation and equity grants to move projects along.
Technical assistance	Technical assistants can lower the high transaction costs and risks for new investors by being involved directly in the running of the project. DFIs can finance impact studies and improve the likelihood of success.
Loan guarantees	Protect investors against losses and/or improve the financing costs because government or DFI guarantees reduce borrowing costs.
Structured finance – first loss capital	Absorbs risks by making the public entity the first to take losses that may occur should the project incur losses.
Equity investment	Equity ownership provides funding for the project and also demonstrates viability and other comfort for investors.

Source: Adapted from Pereira (2017).

In the 2017/2018 period, the commitment of OECD Development Action Committee members to gender equality was at 42 per cent of all commitments (OECD, 2020). By the following period, the commitments had marginally moved to 2018/2019 blended finance targeted at gender as a primary focus (5 per cent) and finance as a secondary focus (40 per cent), accounting for less than 50 per cent of targeted funds (OECD, 2021). This growth has been encouraging, but there is more to be gained from increasing investments in women-focused programmes.

Blended finance can be used with facilities that have been structured to finance gender lens projects. The blending can represent equity, debt, concessional financing or various iterations of other finance. What most gender-lens projects require is early-stage financing, which means that grants could be used for project preparation, and debt and equity could be blended to produce the best financial product for the sector. DFIs manage several projects for other partners, which makes them ideally placed to suggest alternative sources of financing to gender-lens projects, particularly for project preparation. GEF and GCF sources could be blended with DFI financing to bring down the cost of the project overall.

Blended finance has targeted certain SDGs very effectively, but the gender goal (SDG 5) has not had much traction in the private-sector space, particularly from investment funds. There are various development finance facilities that address gender, but private-sector funds have not been as successful in highlighting gender programmes' financing needs because they argue that the cost is too high and the projects are too small in financial terms, that women are perceived to be high risk and that women-owned businesses are not likely to scale and become economically powerful.

By packaging GLI programmes and projects in ways that highlight how women access them compared to men, financiers from the private sector could support gender mainstreaming, especially in infrastructure. For example, if a water and sanitation or energy project was structured using a gender lens, finance could be sourced from the public and private sectors to finance those niches.

Project Finance

Project finance provides an ideal structure for gender-lens financing because it isolates project income, shares risk among the stakeholders or partners and the project is financed off the balance sheet. Gender-lens projects, due to the nature of the businesses being supported, will be smaller in quantum than the usual DFI loans. The exposure to the DFI is less but the reputational risk of failure in development projects is high.

The project finance model will need to ensure that all partners are involved in the ideation stage through to the monitoring and evaluation stages. Special purpose vehicles (SPVs) would be ideal for ring-fencing income for loan repayments and to protect the company against bankruptcy or failure. Granted, the nature and size of the gender-lens projects might not warrant an SPV, but it would be good practice to ensure that financial loans are protected from risk.

Figure 6.2 explains the project finance model with an SPV, as described above. The stakeholders do not have to be numerous, but they do need to be included in the decision-making process from start to finish, particularly minority or vulnerable groups. The main objective of this process is to ensure that the outcomes are sustainable and lead to equitable development.

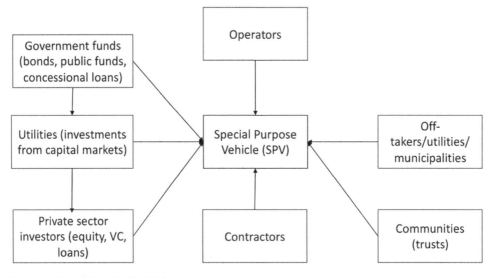

Source: Adapted from Bathia (2011).

Figure 6.2   *General model of the structure of project finance*

The challenge for GLI in this context is that the project sizes might not warrant a project finance approach; moreover, the model might be too onerous for projects the gender programme aims to support. Also, there might not be enough partners involved to structure a project with numerous contractors and off-takers. This means that financiers will have to take on the risk of providing a project loan. An additional challenge is that equity might be difficult to obtain. Projects may rely on too much debt, thereby making them too risky. If the

DFI does project finance with gender-lens investments, it would need to provide a structure on a project-by-project basis. A one-size-fits-all approach will not work.

Gender and Climate Finance

GEF (UNIDO, 2014), GCF (2019) and the Climate Investment Funds (ADB, 2016) have been at the forefront of promoting GLI in projects that design mitigation and adaption responses to climate change.

These funds can be accessed either by financiers to use in conjunction with other sources of finance; for example, loans, public–private partnerships, equity, other grant funds and so forth. An opportunity exists here for other DFIs to blend their existing finance products with the climate facilities.

GCF and GEF have incorporated gender considerations across their entire project life cycle. DFIs have committed to gender mainstreaming because of the requirements of climate change facilities (GCF, 2019). Some DFIs have already incorporated gender mainstreaming successfully. The Asian Development Bank has prepared a sample tip sheet for gender mainstreaming in climate change (Box 6.2).

BOX 6.2   SAMPLE TIP SHEET FOR GENDER MAINSTREAMING IN CLIMATE CHANGE

Mitigation and Gender Equality

Clean energy projects:

- Provide clean energy that benefits women specifically, including lighting for women's spaces and safety.
- Provide women with clean energy for productive activities, including agricultural production, if possible, with lower tariffs.
- Increase the involvement of women in clean energy-related businesses.
- Increase the involvement of women in demand-side management.

Adaptation and Gender Equality

Climate-resilient infrastructure projects:

- Provide infrastructure features or elements that specifically benefit women, such as climate-proofed market structures, roads women use for mobility and access to services, disaster shelters and water and sanitation systems.
- Involve women in the design of new infrastructure, specifically in their siting and location, to harness women's local knowledge for climate change adaptation.

Urban planning projects:

• Involve women in urban plans for climate resilience.

Source: Adapted from ADB (2016).

PRACTICAL STRATEGIES

This section will look at strategies for GLI that will provide significant development impact and footprint in their mandated area of investment.

Criteria for Investing

Different tools can set out project eligibility for financing. By utilizing a carefully constructed tool, the institution determines what it wishes to finance and how it finances women-led and women-owned projects. The goal is to finance high development impact and financially sustainable projects playing a catalytic role in Africa's development. Table 6.3 outlines some of the considerations for eligibility criteria.

Table 6.3   Potential criteria for gender-lens investments

Criteria	Gender lens explanation
Mandate	Women-owned or women-led project
Financial viability	Gender-sensitive financial product adapted to fit needs of project and project owner
Risk appetite	Adjusted risk rates to suit smaller projects
Investment value	Smaller than a mainstream infrastructure project
Strength of the sponsor	Track record of sponsor in sector (years of working towards financial viability)
Profitability	Financial profitability (but not the main driver)
Data quality/ready for appraisal	Status of the project paperwork, time frame in months to project readiness (project preparation support available)
Alternative solutions that meet the objective of the project	Maintenance, rehabilitation of existing infrastructure, partnerships, consortiums, technical assistance

Source: Adapted with permission from the Development Bank of South Africa's Project Assessment Tool: Improving the Efficiency of the Project Pipeline. The bank no longer uses this tool (2013).

Options for Gender-Lens Investing

A few African countries have achieved good results under the SDGs and in particular SDG 5 for the achievement of gender equity. The World Economic Forum ranks Africa as a global and regional leader in promoting gender equity, with Rwanda and South Africa leading the continent (WEF, 2022). Rwanda has made commitments to reduce the gender gap in ICT by 2026, placing it as one of the world leaders (UN Women, 2022).

SheTradesZA, a global investment partner with a chapter in South Africa and is focused on financing women-led and women-owned initiatives, estimates that there is a shortage of $300 billion for these businesses and 75 per cent of women-led businesses have poor or no access to finance (2021). Investments are required in all the main business sectors where innovation could leapfrog conventional financing options.

Four options identified earlier for gender investing are available to public and private funders:

* investing in gender-diverse projects with 51 per cent women ownership;
* investing in women-owned/women-led enterprises;
* investing in projects that have mainly women beneficiaries; and
* adapting an existing project into one that is gender sensitive.

The difference in the approach to GLI compared to 'business-as-usual' investing is that public- and private-sector investors could frontload support for gender-lens projects to ensure that they are planned sufficiently and made bankable. The institutions have the option of financing new projects (brown field) or retrofitting existing projects to make them more gender sensitive. Retrofitting usually applies when new technologies change the way projects are developed or made 'green' and climate sensitive. For retrofitting, innovative financial products can set one financier apart from others as they find new ways to finance projects.

Investing in gender-diverse projects with 51 per cent women ownership
Project sponsors would need to prove the 51 per cent ownership when applying for finance under the gender-lens financing programme. In this way, project financiers limit the abuse of fronting where women are placed in leading roles but are not instrumental in the decisions of the company. South Africa's Broad Based Black Economic Empowerment policy framework would set out the requirements for the companies that are majority owned by women.

Investing in women-owned/women-led enterprises
Again, ownership needs to be verified and should not be fronted ownership to meet the requirements. Women-owned/led projects will be identified through careful consideration of the mandate fit, viability of the project and the development impact of the project in the long run. Female suppliers or contractors would need to be included in this product offering because women struggle to find finance for their businesses. The finance provided could extend from microfinance to large investments that cover significant infrastructure projects.

Investing in projects that have mainly women beneficiaries
Some sectors avail themselves to gender mainstreaming more easily than others. Projects in water and sanitation, energy and ICT could have direct women beneficiaries if they are structured to benefit women specifically. For example, a water project in a rural area would benefit women directly by reducing their water collection times and by improving their health and living conditions. ICT, seen to be a leapfrogging sector, is ideally positioned to bring more women into the sector if suitable finance is made available.

Adapting an existing project that could be made gender sensitive
A mainstream infrastructure project could be adapted to include gender-sensitive criteria such as including women as equity holders, in the maintenance and operations of new projects, and ensuring that part of the project directly benefits women. The project will be considered for financing if the added gender-sensitive portion fits the investor's mandate and sector focus.

GENDER INVESTMENT OPPORTUNITIES WITHIN INFRASTRUCTURE SECTORS

Gender-lens investments will be subject to the due diligence and appraisal that other infrastructure projects are subjected to. Since construction is one of the main industries that has many women-owned businesses, investors could consult South African Women in Construction to determine what women working in construction need. The other networks for women in power – energy, oil and gas and logistics – could also provide information on the needs of each network.

Energy

The Department of Mineral Resources and Energy Small Independent Power Producers programme is an ideal approach to gender-lens investments, particularly with established women-owned/led businesses belonging to organisations like Women in Oil and Energy in South Africa and African Women in Energy and Power. Investors have access to the project pipelines if they contact these networks. The Solar Turtle[1] project, a mobile energy platform with mounted solar panels on a shipping container, is an example of a disruptive energy project ripe for financing earmarked for the energy sector. Another direct opportunity is in the REIPPP 5th window which includes gender as a requirement for the power producers. Partners include Women in Oil and Energy in South Africa, African Women in Energy and Power, Women's Entrepreneurial Access Centre in Zambia, Women in Infrastructure Development and other private-sector investors.

ICT

ICT4All, a global programme aimed at reducing the technology gap around the world, offers an opportunity to bring women into the ICT sector as suppliers and financiers. For example, the ICT and energy sectors could be combined to finance ICT provision with renewable energy. ICT4All's Structured Project division is currently exploring a Northern Cape pilot project providing networking coverage to communities, with private ICT service providers carrying much of the costs. The South African Women in ICT Forum is the ideal partner for collaboration in this sector. South African partners include ICT networks like WomeninTechZA, DOTNXT, GirlCode, the Ministry of Science and Technology and women investment companies including ICT financing such as the Graça Machel Trust, FinMark and Identity Group. Importantly, mobile and internet usage have a significant positive relationship with poverty reduction, therefore, it is imperative that the ICT sector continues to find ways to grow women-owned businesses in Africa (Kelikume, 2021).

---

[1]   www.solarturtle.co.za.

Women in Technology

The Women in Tech ZA[2] platform was established to raise awareness of women working in the technology sector and to highlight gender disparities. Its founder, Samantha Perry, aims to positively impact the gender gap in the tech sector and establish groundwork from which future generations of women will benefit.

Water and Sanitation

Water and sanitation have the most direct links to women. Women benefit the most as users of water and sanitation services. New water-financing models show that there are opportunities to bring women in as suppliers of water services, particularly in relation to water pumps, water-recycling plants and the maintenance of water infrastructure. South Africa has a Women in Water Empowerment Programme that was launched in 2016 and supports 90 women-owned companies. The programme has an Entrepreneurship Incubator Project that includes:

* full-scale dam projects (small and large) and large upgrades;
* sanitation projects;
* river rehabilitation projects; and
* the Rehabilitation of Canals programme.

The Women in Water Empowerment Programme can unlock suitable projects for financing in the medium to long term. For instance, 'point-of-use' programmes provide water in small projects to move water financing away from bulk applications. These smaller projects provide an opportunity for the DBSA to support women-owned companies while maintenance programmes are more effective in projects divided into women-run services. Partners could include the Women in Water Empowerment Programme, the Department of Water, United Nations Development Programme and UN Women.

Transport

Transport projects are generally mega in scale, but smaller women-owned and operated construction and finance companies can participate. Women in logistics could also be brought into the value chain as delivery grows exponentially. Women in Logistics and Transport South Africa and South African Women in Transport make strategic linkages in the sector.

FINANCIAL PRODUCTS

Project Preparation and Grants

One of the biggest needs in financing women-led projects and businesses is for financing in the start-up phase. Preparation funds therefore are important to develop early-stage projects

---

[2]   https://womenintech.co.za/blog/.

that meet the gender-lens criteria. To build the project pipeline effectively from inception to financing, women should be considered, but not as 'remedial' recipients of grants and loans.

Innovative financial products using technology have created new opportunities. One such example is the East African-based myAgro and Mobile layover financing platform established by Anushka Ratnayaka in 2011. myAgro is committed to empowering smallholder farmers, especially women, to reduce poverty and increase food security. The financing platform is based on prepaid seed purchases on a model similar to prepaid airtime. Farmers buy scratch cards to top up their mobile myAgro accounts. The product is referred to as a *mobile layaway*, which incorporates a savings-based prepaid model for seeds, fertilizer and training with 240 farmers. Some farmers are able to prepay for their seeds six or twelve months before the sowing season. Since 2011, myAgro has expanded to Mali, Senegal and Tanzania and serves over 89,000 farmers.

This innovative financial model changes the norm of buying seeds in bulk with cash or credit that most small farmers do not have access to. myAgro affords small farmers the opportunity to prepay for a few seeds at a time through a system that allows them to accumulate sufficient seed over an extended period.

Early-Stage Investments and Equity Holdings

DFIs provide significant investments with 'patient finance' which fills an important gap in financial products for entrepreneurs. Many entrepreneurs do not have access to early-stage finance, which would mostly be sourced from angel funders or early-stage investors willing to finance projects based on their long-term potential to earn. One example of a private-sector long-term financer is the Flying Doctors Healthcare Investment Company.[3] Started by Dr Ola Brown in 2019, and based in Lagos, Nigeria, Flying Doctors is Africa's leading healthcare and wellness-sector investment firm relying on impact investing for social good. The Flying Doctors Healthcare Investment Company promotes entrepreneurship and proactiveness by offering financial support and providing business opportunities, consultations and mentorship, networking opportunities and more. This is a relationship model that relies on impact investing for social good. In September 2020, FD Investment Company announced its intention to raise $1 billion for African healthcare projects in three tranches over four years. Flying Doctors is currently worth $70 million and provides early-stage venture capital with an investment partner, Greentree, for tech start-ups worth $80 million.

Public finance is not generally used for early-stage or even equity finance, which means that the private sector provides much of the equity required by small businesses. This could result in the business being owned by the investors and the owner losing control. There are, however, reputable companies, such as the Africa Trust Group in South Africa that provides project preparation investments for early-stage companies. Lupiya in Zambia offers business support and working capital loans for women-owned businesses in Zambia. One of the earlier investment houses is the Women's Development Bank and Investment Holdings[4] in South Africa providing finance to women-owned businesses and opportunities for investors to join. These are women-led and managed investment institutions. They aim to increase their hold-

---

3   http://fdinvestmentcompany.com and www.investafrica.com/personel/dr-ola-brown.
4   www.wdbinvestments.co.za/about/.

ings in women-owned businesses that are financed by them. The Women's Development Bank was established by Zanele Mbeki and a few economically powerful women in 1991 to provide South African women with much needed investment funds for small businesses. It filled a gap in the market and provided finance to financially excluded women.

Gender Bonds

The bond markets rely on the ratings of an agency or the state's ratings in the case of a state-owned entity such as the DBSA. The AfDB initially planned to float a 'gender bond' but then decided to float a social impact bond instead. In a 2020 research report on the viability of gender bonds in sub-Saharan Africa, FSD identifies four areas of focus for new bond issuers (Battista et al., 2020):

- availability of a project pipeline;
- economic viability of the project;
- enabling factors related to policies and regulations; and
- issuer and sponsor credibility.

In 2018, the IFC's Banking on Women Program, along with Goldman Sachs' 10,000 Women initiative and the Women's Entrepreneur Opportunity Facility, issued its first emerging market gender bond in Turkey. The IFC, a member of the World Bank Group, invested $75 million in a bond issue by Turkey's Garanti Bank – the first private-sector gender bond in emerging markets. The Agence Française de Developpement provided technical support to Turkey to improve gender equality within the economy. The IFC initiated a $200 million privately placed gender bond in a bank in Indonesia in 2020 for women's economic empowerment.

Blending (Public and Private Funds)

DFIs have access to various facilities combined with their usual project funds. Blending has become popular in DFI circles to ensure that sufficient quantity is raised and that the cost of finance is reduced through the blending of concessional and conventional sources of finance. By creating a gender-lens asset class, private investors can collaborate with public institutions to create financial packages that contain grant and loan components structured for women-owned or women-led businesses. The energy sector lends itself to this kind of collaboration because of the innovative sources of finance being offered by the GCF and the GEF.

Government Programmes

Gender mainstreaming has been recognized as a strategy to bring more women into the economy by supporting women's entrepreneurship. The private sector requires stable regulatory frameworks as well as an enabling environment to provide funding to targeted businesses. The role that government could play here is to instruct policy makers to lift barriers to entry and increase financial inclusion.

The South African government held its inaugural Women's Economic Assembly in October 2021 where the President, Cyril Ramaphosa, set out the programme for meaningful gender equality in the country. Policy requires that at least 40 per cent of government procurement should go to women-owned businesses, and that the private sector matches that allocation. The government's gender initiatives are commendable with different loci of control. It will be necessary for the presidency to centralise the management and oversight of those initiatives to ensure that they are implemented and benefit the women business owners who have much to contribute to economic and social growth.

CONCLUSION

The gender-mainstreaming strategy offers clear targets and implementable approaches to bring more women into the formal economy. Women's networks across all sectors have begun the work to identify project pipelines; therefore, the onus is on the public and private sectors to provide suitable financial products in collaboration with recipients. The great gap in financing lies in the start-up phase of business where entrepreneurs cannot find the initial funds to launch their businesses. This is the riskiest phase of the business. Therefore, as in large infrastructure projects, the financial value chain could provide patient finance to de-risk the projects while private investors provide additional support, especially with working capital. The concern is that these projects are smaller in value than the usual investment projects, but commitment to gender mainstreaming will support investment decisions designed for benefit in the longer term.

Project preparation, from private- and public-sector financiers, will need to provide businesses with the kind of support they need to make their project 'bankable' or attractive to investors. It is recommended that government and the private sector identify new gender lens-financing products offering concessional finance from partners, project preparation finance, operational finance and/or a blend of various sources of finance through partnerships. Ideally, gender-lens financing should have its own products that deal directly with the needs of women-led and women-owned businesses.

Gender mainstreaming for financial projects for women-owned and women-led businesses requires a new way of doing business. It requires new financing models and the use of ICT to provide more financial access to women-owned businesses. The perception of women as high-risk lenders also needs to be changed through institutions advertising their gains through gender-lens investments and the reliability of women in repaying their loans. More has to be done to bring women into the formal economy.

ACKNOWLEDGEMENTS

We thank the reviewers, Libby Dreyer, Caren Scheepers and Ethné Swartz, for their comments and input on the draft.

REFERENCES

ADB (Asian Development Bank) (2016). Building gender into climate finance: ADB experience the with climate investment funds. www.climateinvestmentfunds.org/sites/default/files/knowledge-documents/gender-climate-finance.pdf
AfDB (African Development Bank) (2009). Checklist for gender mainstreaming in the infrastructure sector. www.afdb.org/fileadmin/uploads/afdb/Documents/Policy-Documents/Checklist%20for%20Gender%20Maintstreaming%20in%20the%20Infrastructure%20Sector.pdf

AfDB (African Development Bank) (2017). Social bond framework. www.afdb.org/fileadmin/uploads/ afdb/Documents/Generic-Documents/AfDB_Social_Bond_Framework.pdf

AfDB (African Development Bank) (2021). Canada and African Development Bank sign CAD 133 million gender lens Climate Fund for Africa.

Aidis, R., Eissler, S., Etchart, N. and Truzzi de Souza. R. (2022). Taking small steps together: Incorporating a gender lens approach for small and growing businesses – a case study. *Journal of Sustainable Finance & Investment, 12*(3), 724–751.

Alliance for Financial Inclusion (2016). Policy frameworks to support women's financial inclusion. www.afi-global.org/wp-content/uploads/publications/2016-08/2016-02-womenfi.1_0.pdf

Alsos, G. A., Isaksen, E. J. and Ljunggren, E. (2006). New venture financing and subsequent business growth in men- and women-led businesses. *Entrepreneurship Theory and Practice, 30*(5), 667–686.

Anderson, J. and Miles, K. (2015). State of the field of gender lens investment: A review and a roadmap. The Criterion Institute. www2.unwomen.org/-/media/files/un%20women/grb/resources/criterion %20institute_2015_gender%20lens%20investing.pdf?vs=3708

Aoyagi, C. (2021). Africa's unequal pandemic. International Monetary Fund, Finance and Development. www.imf.org/external/pubs/ft/fandd/2021/07/africas-unequal-pandemic-chie-aoyagi.htm

Bangani, A. and Vyas-Doorgapersad, S. (2020). The implementation of gender equality within the South African Public Service (1994–2019). *Africa's Public Service Delivery and Performance Review, 8*(1), 353.

Bathia, A. (2011). SPV (Special Purpose Vehicle). Infrastructure project finance blog. http:// infrastructure-projectfinance.blogspot.co.za/2011/04/spv-special-purpose-vehicle.html?_sm_au_= iHV67HSWFkPMSqBP

Battista, G., Bukuru, M., Musili, D., Oyofo, I. and Calder, R. (2020). Viability of gender bonds in SSA: A landscape analysis and feasibility assessment. FSD Africa and UN Women. www.fsdafrica.org/wp -content/uploads/2020/09/Gender-bonds-report-27.08.20-2.pdf

Biegel, S. and Nyong'o Madison, I. (2017). Five ways to advance gender lens investing in Africa. https:// socialimpact.wharton.upenn.edu/news/five-ways-advance-gender-lens-investing-africa/

Braun, S., Stegmann, S, Hernandez Bark, A. S., Junker, N. M. and van Dick, R. (2017). Think manager – think male, think follower – think female: Gender bias in implicit followership theories. *Journal of Applied Social Psychology, 27*(7), 377–388.

Business Engage (2021). Status of gender on JSE-listed boards 2020, 4th research report. https://issuu .com/gendermainstreaming/docs/annual_report_2020_p7_1_

Business for Social Responsibility (2019). The state of sustainable business in 2019: Results of the 11th Annual Survey of Sustainable Business Leaders. www.bsr.org/reports/BSR-Globescan-State -Sustainable-Business-2019.pdf

Buvinic, M. and Furst-Nichols, R. (2016). Promoting women's economic empowerment: What works? World Bank. https://openknowledge.worldbank.org/handle/10986/27699

Chan, D. K.-S., Chow, S. Y., Lam, C. B. and Cheung, S. F. (2008). Examining the job-related, psycho-logical, and physical outcomes of workplace sexual harassment: A meta-analytic review. *Psychology of Women Quarterly, 32*(4), 362–376.

Cowling, M., Marlow, S. and Liu, W. (2019). Gender and bank lending after the global financial crisis: Are women entrepreneurs safer bets? *Small Business Economics, 55*, 853–880.

DBSA (Development Bank of Southern Africa) (n.d.). How sustainable infrastructure contributes to gender mainstreaming in South Africa. www.dbsa.org/article/how-sustainable-infrastructure -contributes-gender-mainstreaming-south-africa

De Vries, G., Timmer, M. and de Vries, K. (2015). Structural transformation in Africa: Static gains, dynamic losses. *Journal of Development Studies, 51*(6), 674–688.

Galitopoulou, S. and Noya, A. (2016). Understanding social impact bonds. Organisation for Economic Co-operation and Development (OECD) Working Paper Series. www.oecd.org/cfe/leed/ UnderstandingSIBsLux-WorkingPaper.pdf

Gender Smart Investing (n.d.). The history of gender lens investing. www.gendersmartinvesting.com/a -history-of-gender-lens-investing

GCF (Green Climate Fund) (2019). Gender policy. www.greenclimate.fund/sites/default/files/document/ gcf-gender-policy.pdf

Global Impact Investment Network (2019). Gender lens investing initiative. https://thegiin.org/gender-lens-investing-initiative/

ICRW (2018). Coalition for Women's Economic Empowerment and Equality. www.icrw.org/publications/guiding-principles-coalition-for-womens-economic-empowerment-equality/

IFC (International Finance Corporation) (2017). Social bonds: Introduction and impact report. www.ifc.org/wps/wcm/connect/173785cf-5361-4159-b196-a30ba1a280a1/IFC+Social+bonds+impact+report_FINAL.pdf?MOD=AJPERES

Ivankovic, K. and Essa, E. (2021). Understanding social entrepreneurs in South Africa: Experiences, gaps and opportunities. The Bertha Centre, University of Cape Town. https://res.cloudinary.com/do95jfmcf/image/upload/v1624300757/website/publications/210607_BC_Early_Stage_Funding_Report_V3-compressed_nxdwrk.pdf

Janse van Vuuren, L. (2022). Apply a gender lens to trade finance. Cenfri. https://cenfri.org/articles/applying-a-gender-lens-to-trade-finance/

Kelikume, I. (2021). Digital financial inclusion, informal economy and poverty reduction in Africa. *Journal of Enterprising Communities: People and Places in the Global Economy*, *15*(4), 626–640.

Keplinger, K., Johnson, S. K., Kirk, J. F. and Barnes, L. Y. (2019). Women at work: Changes in sexual harassment between September 2016 and September 2018. *PLoS ONE*, *14*(7), e0218313.

Maheshwari, P., Gokhale, A., Agarwal, N., Makena, A. and Borthakur, S. (2019). The global landscape of gender lens investing report. www.intellecap.com/wp-content/uploads/2019/02/The-Global-Landscape-of-Gender-Lens-Investing.pdf

Mastercard Index of Women Entrepreneurs (2022). How targeted support for women-led businesses can unlock sustainable economic growth. www.mastercard.com/news/media/phwevxcc/the-mastercard-index-of-women-entrepreneurs.pdf

Moodley, L., Kuyoro, M., Holt, T., Leke, A., Madgavkar, A., Krishnan, M. and Ainktayo, F. (2019). The power of parity: Advancing women's equality in Africa. McKinsey Global Institute. www.mckinsey.com/featured-insights/gender-equality/the-power-of-parity-advancing-womens-equality-in-africa

Moore, H. (1994). *A passion for difference*. Cambridge: Polity Books.

Nikkei Asia (2017). ADB to issue first gender bond at $90m: Japan, Dai-ichi Life invests in women empowerment products. https://asia.nikkei.com/Politics-Economy/Economy/ADB-to-issue-first-gender-bond-at-90m

North, D. (1990). *Institutions, institutional change, and economic performance*. Cambridge: Cambridge University Press.

OECD (2020). Aid focused on gender equality and women's empowerment. www.oecd.org/development/gender-development/Aid-Focussed-on-Gender-Equality-and-Women-s-Empowerment-2020.pdf

OECD (2021). Development finance for gender equality and women's empowerment: A 2021 snapshot. OECD DAC Network on Gender Equality. www.oecd.org/development/gender-development/Development-finance-for-gender-equality-2021.pdf

OECD DAC (2018). Making blended finance work for the Sustainable Development Goals. http://dx.doi.org/10.1787/9789264288768-en

Pereira, J. (2017). Blended finance: What it is, how it works and how it is used. Oxfam. www-cdn.oxfam.org/s3fs-public/file_attachments/rr-blended-finance-130217-en.pdf

Rock, D. and Grant, H. (2016). Why diverse teams are smarter. *Harvard Business Review*, 4 November.

Scott, W. R. (2013). *Institutions and organizations* (4th ed.). New York: Sage.

SheTradesZA (2021). She Trades brochure. Department of Small Business Development. www.dsbd.gov.za/sites/default/files/docu/SheTradesbrochure-Oct2021.pdf

Skocpol, T. (1985). Bringing the state back in: Strategies of analysis in current research. In Evans, P. B., Reuschemeyer, D. and Skocpol, T. (eds), *Bringing the state back in*. Cambridge: Cambridge University Press, pp. 3–38.

Stotsky, J. (2006). Gender and its relevance to macroeconomic policy, a survey. International Monetary Fund Working Paper WP/06/233. www.imf.org/external/pubs/ft/wp/2006/wp06233.pdf

Ulwodi, D. W. and Muriu, P. W. (2017). Barriers of financial inclusion in sub-Saharan Africa. *Journal of Economics and Sustainable Development*, *8*(14), 66–81.

UN Women (2022). Bridging the gender digital divide in Africa: UN Women Rwanda connects youth with policy influencers, private sector and government to discuss gender biases and more involvement in STEM fields. https://africa.unwomen.org/en/stories/news/2022/10/bridging-the-gender-digital-divide-in-africa-un-women-rwanda#:~:text=This%20gender%20digital%20divide%20was,to%2062per%20cent%20of%20men

UNIDO (United Nations Industrial Development Organization) (2014). Draft guide on gender mainstreaming for energy and climate change projects. www.thegef.org/sites/default/files/documents/UNIDO-Draft_Guide_on_Gender_Mainstreaming_for_Energy_and_Climate_Change_Projects.pdf

United Nations (2018). The 17 goals. https://sdgs.un.org/goals

WEF (2020). Global gender gap report 2020. World Economic Forum. http://reports.weforum.org/global-gender-gap-report-2022

WEF (2022). Global gender gap report 2022. World Economic Forum. http://reports.weforum.org/global-gender-gap-report-2022

Zhang, L. (2020). An institutional approach to gender diversity and firm performance. *Organization Science, 31*(2), 439–457.

7.   Two kinds of time: the Chinese–Kenyan infrastructure disconnect

Arielle S. Emmett

INTRODUCTION: BORROWING TO LEAP AHEAD

A sense of possibilities, of "time enough" to reap future reward, remains a huge risk for societies entertaining both technological advancement and crushing corruption. In Kenya, especially, an evolving East African economy known for its tech-hub start-ups, eye-catching infrastructure, much of it built and financed by the Chinese, and a prodigious reputation for local government borrowing and graft (Ndii, 2018a; Dickson, 2021; Olander, 2021), the idea of "progress" emerges in public narratives with conflicting, often angry, interpretations (Taylor, 2020).

To intellectuals, citizen activists and the poor – more than a third of Kenya's population still lives in extreme poverty, defined as US$1.90 or less a day, according to the World Bank (2018) – society is shaped like an hourglass sifting two kinds of time. For the rich and middle class, which includes cabinet and county ministers and business elite, tech innovators, salaried employees, trained professionals, and the street smart, time is rushing, hurtling forward, reshaping society and individuals with both dangers and opportunities. For the rural poor selling vegetables on the roadside, or casual day workers carrying water in jugs or buckets of sewage to dump into the streams flowing beside Nairobi's seven slums, time is more like a treadmill. One day is much like another, grinding slowly and repeating its patterns, past to present. The future barely exists. At the same time, corruption at every social level disrupts opportunities to envision and act productively toward a better future (Schifrin, 2016).

Add to this mix the Chinese migration to Kenya in recent years and a time clock vastly accelerated by China's more than US$9 billion in loans (2010–2018) to Kenya for massive infrastructure projects – ports, highways, railroads, skyscrapers, transmission lines, hospitals, stadiums, and dams (Dickson, 2021; Olander, 2021).[1] Both Chinese and Kenyan officials expected these projects to boost trade and local employment, open markets to allow China

---

[1]   From 2010 to 2018, Kenya borrowed just under US$9 billion from China with almost two-thirds of those loans funding transportation projects like the Standard Gauge Railway. Kenya's debt to China stood at US$737 million in 2014, the first year of President Uhuru Kenyatta's presidency, before increasing 766 percent to US$6.4 billion in December 2020 (Olander, 2021). According to the University of Nairobi's Wandeda Dickson (2021, para. 1): "Kenya's overall public debt increased from 48.6% of GDP at the end of 2015 to an estimated 69% of GDP at the end of 2020 … The ballooning public debt has been partly driven by large spending on infrastructure projects and by the COVID-19 global shock in 2020."

to move its exports throughout the African continent while obtaining local raw materials such as timber, rare earths, and oil and gas. However, a perceptual disconnect now exists – a sense of rapid time and progress advanced by Chinese officials and Kenyan elites who embrace the Chinese presence, and those Kenyans who equate "debt trap," labor exploitation, eco-homicide, and "China" in similar, unsavory terms.

This chapter examines how and why these perceptual discrepancies exist, and what implications they have for technological leapfrogging, debt repayment, and overall economic and social improvements in Kenya, by now considered China's main maritime gateway and import/export hub to the African continent.

Of special focus in this chapter is an examination of two controversial megaprojects. The first, a diesel-powered standard gauge railway (SGR), was built and financed with loans of US$3.24 billion from China's Export-Import Bank (Nyabiage & Elmer, 2020; Skidmore, 2022). As the first national train to be built in Kenya since the now dilapidated narrow-gauge British meter railway was constructed beginning in 1896, SGR, a wider gauge rail, is built to support heavy cargo loads and passenger traffic, extending 480 km and connecting the southern port city of Mombasa to Nairobi, the capital. The second phase, a US$1.5 billion track extension from Nairobi to Naivasha, a popular tourist destination, was completed in 2019. But the Chinese refused to finance another US$3.68 billion for a third phase of SGR intended to link Naivasha to the port city of Kisumu on Lake Victoria and eventually Malaba on the eastern Uganda–Kenya border (Olingo, 2019; Mureithi, 2020). Chinese officials apparently misjudged the railway's viability, its high cargo fees (currently twice that of trucks carrying cargo in Kenya), and poor business performance; revenues from first-year operations came to less than 50 percent of projections and provided less than half of operating costs (Skidmore, 2022). Further, Kenya's struggle to repay its debts to China has raised the specter of an SGR loan default; in worst-case scenarios, the southern port of Mombasa, which the Kenyan government put up as SGR loan collateral without ensuring sovereign immunity, could be subject to Chinese seizure.[2]

To the south east, the second megaproject, LAPSSET (Lamu Port–South Sudan–Ethiopia Transport) for which the China Communications Construction Company is the primary contractor, was originally estimated at US$24.5 billion. It remains unfinished and stalled by security issues, most recently attacks by suspected al-Shabaab militants (Kitimo, 2022).

LAPSSET centers on a brand-new Kenyan seaport located in Lamu on the Indian Ocean about 240 km north east of the primary port of Mombasa (LAPSSET, n.d.). Launched in 2009 during the Mwai Kibaki administration in Kenya, LAPSSET, if completed, will constitute an international "corridor" of planned port, rail, highway, oil pipelines, airports, resorts, power plants, and fiber optic cables designed to boost trade and communications between China, South Asia, the underdeveloped Kenyan north (e.g., Isiolo, Turkana), along with oil-rich South Sudan, Ethiopia, and Uganda (LAPSSET, n.d.). However, many of LAPSSET's intended international partners have withdrawn support, and Kenya has seen surrounding countries like Uganda and Rwanda cancel or interrupt plans to build connecting railways. Further, a dramatic fall in international oil prices since 2014, civil strife in South Sudan and Uganda, and the

---

[2]   "As collateral, Kenya was required to set up a special reserve account and to waive sovereign immunity for the port of Mombasa, making the latter vulnerable to seizure by Chinese creditors should Kenya default" (Skidmore, 2022, para. 16).

discovery that Kenya's oil reserves in Turkana are apparently insufficient to support commercialization have cast doubts on the regional plan (Mohammed, 2019).[3] Environmentalists charge that LAPSSET damages both culture and livelihood in the coastal region as the project cleared away extensive mangrove forests providing breeding grounds for fish (Chome, 2020). Port construction affected 5000 fishermen after the majority of fishing channels closed. Within Lamu County, a UNESCO World Heritage site, more than 3000 indigenous people were reportedly exiled from use of their land without government compensation (Praxides, 2015).[4]

Questions about SGR and LAPSSET's future value continue to occupy the lion's share of public discussion in Kenya. As of spring 2022, while government officials led by Jubilee President Uhuru Kenyatta laud these projects, critics argue that the government's "moonshot mentality" is nothing more than a "debt-spinning mirage," robbing the country of real socio-economic transformation (Marete, 2019).

One aspect of this debate, perhaps a less visible factor, is a cultural view of *time* – or more properly, time perception and management envisioned as a yardstick of socio-economic risk and reward. Having benefitted from years of economic prosperity and industrialization at home, the Chinese *perceive* the value of their African strategy in a long-term horizon – decades and beyond – a horizon they believe will pay benefits not only to themselves but also to East Africans, specifically markets, employment levels, and quality of life. The majority of Kenyans, on the other hand, are struggling to live in the moment. Churchill Otieno, an editor at *The Daily Nation*, one of Kenya's leading newspapers, put it this way: "There's a survival approach to life here in that everyone is busy trying to live today. Not a lot of people are taking the long-term view" (personal communication, October 18, 2018).

BACKGROUND: CHINESE CATALYST FOR CHANGE

The Chinese represent a huge catalyst for change in East Africa. Decades before President Xi Jinping's 2013 announcement of the Belt and Road Initiative (BRI), China's vision of an infrastructure corridor extending to 65 countries and reaching 60 percent of the world's population, the Chinese were migrating to Kenya to seek opportunity in small businesses – mostly in food service, textiles, and trade in cheap consumer goods (Newcomb, 2020). Later, private Chinese companies and some state-owned firms brought their construction skills and technical expertise; in the 1980s Kenyan President Daniel Arap Moi paid several trips to China which resulted in comparatively modest trade agreements and a Chinese renminbi loan of KSh1.18 billion to build the Moi International Sports Complex (Newcomb, 2020).

---

[3]　"Kenya discovered commercial oil in 2012 in its Lokichar basin, which Tullow Oil estimates contains an estimated 560 million barrels in proven and probable reserves. Tullow has said this would translate to 60,000 to 100,000 barrels per day of gross production." However, "it is proven the world over that a refinery would make money only when it has refining capacity of at least 400,000 barrels a day, Andrew Kamau, principal secretary at the petroleum and mining ministry, told reporters." See www.reuters.com/article/us-kenya-oil/kenya-says-crude-oil-capacity-insufficient-for-refinery-idUSKCN1Q80JZ.

[4]　In 2018, the Kenyan High Court ordered the government to pay US$17 million in damages to 4600 people whose lives and livelihoods were harmed by port construction (Chome, 2020). A startling environmental win occurred in 2020, when local activists defeated a bid in court by Kenya's Amu Power, the Industrial and Commercial Bank of China, and two Chinese state-owned companies to build a gigawatt coal-fired plant on the Lamu County mangrove coast just 20 km from the city's Old Town (Shi Yi, 2021).

Succeeding Moi, President Mwai Kibaki in 2005 accompanied a Kenyan trade and investment delegation to hold talks with China's then President Hu Jintao. This resulted in a five-part agreement with grants for infrastructure and energy, extended air services, and support for classifying standards for industrial products (Newcomb, 2020). In addition, the Chinese provided grants and loans for the Northern and Eastern Bypass roads (KSh8.5 billion and KSh21.6, respectively) and the Thika highway upgrades (US$100 million, roughly KSh11 billion) (People's Daily Online, 2009). Even after the post-election ethnic violence in 2007–2008, which resulted in more than 1100 Kenyan deaths and displaced 100,000 people, China continued humanitarian aid, including support for infrastructure, education, and the building of a malaria research center (Newcomb, 2020).

Today, China is Kenya and Africa's largest trading partner, accounting for 17.2 percent of Kenya's total trade (Kimutai, 2018), with exports to China amounting to approximately US$139 million post-Covid, according to the 2022 updated United Nations COMTRADE database; Kenya's exports include mineral ore slag and ash, fuels, animal skins, agricultural products, and copper. Meanwhile, China's imports to Kenya total US$3.39 billion (Trading Economics, 2022). This trade imbalance continues to rankle Kenyan citizens, who complain that Chinese imports have continuously displaced local producers, causing job loss, especially among women producing or selling textiles, *mitumba* (bags of clothing donated for resale), and other consumer goods (Newcomb, 2020). Kenya's attempts to rectify the trade imbalance through expanded agricultural export agreements with Beijing, mostly for tea, sugar, coffee, and avocados, improved the balance sheet in 2019 but did not substantially alter it (Olander, 2021).

METHODOLOGY

My investigations of the Chinese in Kenya began in January 2017 when I was commissioned to teach research and legal writing at Strathmore University Law School in Nairobi. At that time, I was piqued by the presence of the Chinese – 118 companies operating in the city – building skyscrapers, apartments, roads, dams, bridges, and railroads. I wondered how Kenyan laborers, including women and children, experienced their interactions with Chinese managers, and having read several negative reports of worker abuse on Chinese projects, particularly on the SGR, I wanted to investigate.

The second time, when I returned to Kenya on a ten-month Fulbright Scholar Research grant (2018–2019), I conducted more than four dozen in-person interviews, focusing on Chinese and Kenyan attitudes toward the most controversial infrastructure projects, particularly the SGR first phase (Mombasa to Nairobi) and the nascent LAPSSET project. Those interviews were conducted principally in the cities of Nairobi and Mombasa, the Rift Valley, and the south-eastern seaport of Lamu (seat of the LAPSSET project). Early on I rode the SGR railway, interviewing Chinese maintenance men and Kenyan wildlife security officers, along with the Chinese Commercial Counselor of Kenya, Dr. Guo Ce,[5] and two Kenya Port

---

[5] China's lending and construction presence in East Africa is now regarded as another example of "soft power," a paradigm shift, i.e., an attempt to challenge the global order with "few strings attached" models of bilateral and multilateral cooperation (Levtov, 2018). By contrast, the World Bank and the International Monetary Fund have imposed "good governance" restrictions on loans emphasizing human

Authority officers. Through networking I met and interviewed leading Kenyan economist David Ndii, along with Joe Mutugu, a special advisor to Secretary James Macharia of the Ministry of Transport, Infrastructure, Housing, Urban Development and Public Works. In addition, Sylvester Kasuku, former chief executive officer/director of LAPSSET, spent hours with me discussing the LAPSSET rationale and long-term plans. Included in the mix were railroad and port employees, cleaning women, security officers at SGR, construction workers, union leaders, Chinese business people, attorneys, taxi drivers, and independent researchers and journalists.

Some key research questions were as follows:

- RQ1: Do you think the Chinese involvement in the SGR/LAPSSET projects has been successful? Describe the advantages and shortcomings of these projects. Will they stimulate the Kenyan economy and provide more local jobs?
- RQ2: Does a difference in time perspective affect Chinese versus Kenyan assessments of these projects and their prospects for Kenyan economic improvement?
- RQ3: Does severe economic disparity, poor wages, and lack of government transparency produce negative perceptions of the major Chinese-financed projects?

For this chapter I will focus first on a conceptual framework and literature review of divergent cultural perceptions of time, both Chinese and Kenyan, followed by an in-depth discussion of the first research question. Findings on disparate time perspectives, both Chinese and Kenyan, emerged from my interviews and will be covered throughout this chapter. I'll summarize general findings for the last two questions.

FRAMEWORK AND LITERATURE REVIEW

A cultural view of time, or specifically time *now* – a "show me the money" insistence on economic/social reward and fast repayment – may partially account for Kenyans' response to the Chinese and their leapfrogging projects. Medeiros (2019) proposes in his provocative thesis that cultural time perception is directly related to economic performance. Citing the original work of Max Weber, Medeiros defines cultural time perception as a "socially transmitted code," an institution of shared perception that molds human behavior within a culture. Every culture assigns significance to hours and days passing, setting up expectations on how to use time to advantage (2019, p. 8).

Lévesque and Stephan (2020) reference technologically sophisticated business projects, describing time and time-sensitive processes as playing a key role in entrepreneurial ventures – from the timing of decisions for start-up, plans for growth and market launch, to the management of entrepreneurs' time. Arguing that the "time perspective has elements of a trait of individuals, firms and societies that impact the way they typically make decisions related to time and experience emotions related to time" (2020, p. 165), the authors draw on the work of Zimbardo and Boyd (1999, 2008, as cited in Medeiros, 2019) by differentiating five distinct time perspectives affecting work and productivity. These include (1) *"future time perspective,"* a focus/willingness to delay gratification to achieve long-term goals; (2) a *"hedonistic time*

---

rights protections and poverty reduction. Kenyan officials now describe these restrictions as development "roadblocks" which, given the Chinese lending alternative, Kenya can now reject.

perspective," an enjoyment of the "here and now"; (3) a "*present-fatalistic time perspective*," enduring the present without being able to influence it; (4) a "*past-positive time perspective*," drawing strength from past experience; and (5) a "*past-negative time perspective*," regretting opportunities passed up (Lévesque & Stephan, 2020, p. 165). The authors found that three perspectives – *future focus*, *present/hedonistic time perspective*, and *positive past time perspective* – impact individual productivity and achievement, health and well-being, and environmental stewardship in positive ways. The other two perspectives – *present fatalistic* and *past negative time perspective* – did just the opposite, hindering productivity, health and environmental care. The authors stated, though, that most research in this area has concentrated on individuals, not firms, societies, or cultures writ large. Views of time and time management across cultures – say, the difference between Chinese time orientation in the workplace versus that of present-day East Africans working for the Chinese – is historically much less explored.[6]

Ironically, time perception by culture, both pre- and post-industrial, has shown surprising reversals in recent years. The classic case is modern Communist China, where an emphasis on the wisdom and guidance of the past has been subsumed by industrial time clocks and state emphasis on arduous work schedules and increasing productivity to guarantee prosperous futures (Tang & Eom, 2019). China experienced major disorientation in its view of time and traditions from the 1930s to the Second World War and beyond. The country not only endured Japanese invasion but the "seepage of modern ideas and gadgets into the village, the breaking of family bonds, the decline of old authorities, [and] the collapse of peasant livelihoods," according to John K. Fairbank (Peck, 1967, p. 1). American journalist Graham Peck further elaborated on China's traditional time sense:

> By one Chinese view of time, the future is behind you, above you, where you cannot see it. The past is before you, below you, where you can examine it. Man's position in time is that of a person sitting beside a river, facing always downstream as he watches the river flow past. (Peck, 1967, p. 7)

But Peck also argued that the Chinese Nationalist–Communist civil war, the dropping of the Hiroshima bomb, and the Maoist revolution produced a dramatic reversal of time perception:
"It began to seem that everyone alive was locked in a sort of plane or rocket, embarked on a swift trajectory into the future" (Peck, 1967, p. 9).

In contrast, African tribal culture has remained firmly rooted in the past. In 1969 scholar John Mbiti described the tribal sense of future time, its risks and rewards, to be mostly amorphous, not "real" because the future hasn't happened yet (Mbiti, 1969). "The linear concept of time in western thought, with an indefinite past, present, and infinite future, is practically foreign to African thinking," Mbiti claimed. "The future is virtually absent because events which lie in it have not taken place, they have not been realized and cannot, therefore, constitute time" (1969, pp. 16–17).

---

6   In my research it was apparent that many of the Kenyan construction workers who expressed a "present-fatalistic time perspective" when speaking about their jobs believed their own government had "sold out" to the Chinese, ensuring that working conditions, wages, and opportunities for education or job advancement would not substantially improve.

Mbiti, however, may have discounted a key element of African time sense, i.e., the assurance of a *future* through property ownership passed down from one generation to the next, according to Grace Diida, a Kenyan attorney-scholar specializing in technology law:

> The individual family's view of time is very continuous. [For example], just looking at it from a cultural perspective, we view death as a *continuation*. That's why we take seriously [the practice of] naming. For example, my father's name is Diida, and his grandchild is Diida. The idea that life continues past him to his grandchild is very present in him. (Personal communication, June 24, 2021)

The future, she argues, is real, tangible, and achievable for African homes as long as property – principally land and housing – can be passed down to future generations:

> For obvious reasons, we view land as having ancestral links, ancestral ties. Land is also viewed from our colonial background – they [the British] took the land from us, so the issue of land is a very touchy subject. It's also one of the focal points of the 2010 Kenyan Constitution. We wanted lands to be protected; we want Kenyans to own the land and not foreigners. (Personal communication, June 24, 2021)

But rapid modernization coming from a foreign source like China has introduced new challenges. For example, prices for land in major cities like Nairobi undergoing rapid development have skyrocketed, making private property purchases unattainable for many. The common presence of Chinese contractors, managers, and laborers, along with the assumed compliance of Kenya's governing elite, accentuates socio-economic inequalities in the present tense (Schifrin, 2016). Consequently, while Chinese and Kenyans may have started out with a similar time orientation – a knowable past, tangible present, and an unknowable future – China's rapid transformation into the world's fastest growing market economy has accentuated its future time perspective, its impulse toward five-year plans, global investment, and aggressive BRI expansion.

By contrast, Kenya today is experiencing a neo-colonial *deja vu*, exacerbated by ubiquitous government and private-contractor corruption, a lack of coherent policies addressing income inequality, and also government failures to disclose transparently the content of Chinese infrastructure contracts, labor agreements, and the ecological damage caused (Ndii, 2018b). This latter problem was underscored when Kenyan officials ignored several feasibility studies arguing against the SGR because it would never pay for itself (Taylor, 2020).[7] Conservationists also warned that plans for the railway running through Kenya's giant Tsavo and Nairobi National Parks would impact wildlife migration and decrease already declining animal populations. Their objections were dismissed.[8]

---

[7]   Researcher Ian Taylor cites numerous feasibility studies on SGR, including a World Bank Africa Transport Unit report comparing investment costs per km to anticipated freight volumes. "The report stated that freight traffic within the entire East African Community (EAC) rail network could, by 2030, reach 14.4 million tons annually but that to be viable, the SGR would necessitate a volume of 55.2 million tons annually … There is no economic or financial case for standard gauge in East African Community area at this time. A refurbished meter gauge would appear to be the most appropriate option in economic and financial terms."

[8]   In a second phase, the Chinese and Kenyans extended the rail line through Nairobi National Park – a choice that the Conservation Alliance of Kenya has decried as another government sham job sacri-

RESEARCH FINDINGS

My interviews suggest that Chinese and Kenyans viewed both projects through an altered, and frequently divergent, time-sensitive lens, which directly colored their perceptions of project successes and failures.

For example, Chinese officials and researchers appeared to be operating in the "ten thousand-foot" view, arguing that investment payback, including plans for improving the trade, transport, and livelihoods of average Kenyan citizens, would be realized in a decade or more. This viewpoint is much in keeping with President Uhuru Kenyatta's 2008 policy blueprint "Kenya Vision 2030," aimed at making his nation a "newly industrializing middle-income country providing high quality life for all its citizens by the year 2030" (Kenya Vision 2030, n.d., para. 1).[9] The Chinese view, in concert, is future focused, stressing hard work and local sacrifice now, but long-term investment and social payback later. Chinese scholar Zhengli Huang also expressed a past-positive time perspective, citing China's own debt crisis in the 1970s and 1980s, which eventually resolved when the country became a manufacturing powerhouse and accumulated huge capital reserves (personal communication, April 24, 2020).

In turn, many of the Kenyans I spoke with, though admiring the Chinese ethos of "get it done" and hard work, voiced suspicions and genuine disappointment about the influx of Chinese into their country, some of whom they characterized as insular and disinterested in learning about or interacting with Kenyans and Kenyan culture. Locals repeatedly questioned the murky nature of Kenyatta's infrastructure contracts negotiated with Beijing, expressing worry about financing terms and an escalating national "debt trap." Their view of Chinese success has been dimmed by media reports of Chinese–Kenyan labor conflicts at the construction site, fears of escalating Chinese take-overs of national assets, including the Mombasa port, and tensions regarding alleged Chinese mistreatment and "racism" against Kenyans both in Kenya and in China (Goldstein, 2018). Kenyans argue that contract opacity has allowed the Chinese too much leeway in determining financial agreements and interest rates (too high), local wages (too low), working hours (too long), and importing their own skilled labor to job sites instead of focusing on providing Kenyans with skills training and advancement. In Lévesque and Stephan's view (2020), these lower-skilled workers displayed a "present-fatalistic time perspective" and distrust based on negative past experience ("past-negative time perspective").

On LAPSSET, which is in an early stage of completion, its future uncertain given recent terrorist attacks on Chinese contractors and budget concerns, interviewees were more optimistic overall. But they consistently described the impact of Kenyan government corruption and China's apparent disregard for the environment and Kenyan social welfare. Activists also argue that runaway borrowing both from Chinese and Western sources is taking an enormous toll on Kenya's development timetable. Further, lack of contract transparency and fear of loan default and loss of sovereignty continue as themes showing erosion of confidence in Chinese projects, the Kenyan elite, and public hopes for the future.

---

ficing environmental stewardship and due process of law for get-rich-quick special interests. See http://arielleemmett.com/the-great-nairobi-chinese-railway-bazaar/.

⁹ Kenyatta outlined a "Big Four" strategy of improvements and technological leapfrogging in food security, affordable housing, manufacturing, and health care for all citizens (Kenya Vision 2030, n.d.).

RQ1: CRITIQUES OF THE STANDARD GAUGE RAILWAY

The Kenyans conducted feasibility studies for a new SGR during the Mwai Kibaki administration (1978–1988). The object was to offload cargo traffic from highways and facilitate pan-African trade and transport. Understanding his budget constraints, Kibaki originally intended for the Chinese to self-finance, build, and operate the railway themselves. The original plan was that after a decade of operation, the Chinese would recoup their investment and transfer the railway to Kenyan administration. Such a scheme is known as BOT (build, operate, transfer) (Paul Wafula, personal communication, October 28, 2018).

Nothing went as planned. Kibaki's first feasibility study indicated that the 478 km Mombasa–Nairobi route for SGR couldn't sustain sufficient two-way freight traffic to turn a profit, a projection which turned out to be true.[10] A second feasibility study undertaken by China Road and Bridge Corp (CRBC) in 2009 forecast "high profitability" and "financial accumulation capability" with no cash projections to back it up (Taylor, 2020). Moreover, there were questions regarding the Chinese–Kenyan plan to "leapfrog" to a national rail system based on the costly "standard gauge" railway infrastructure (1435 mm between rails), a move that would require massive land purchases throughout Kenya and a new right of way rather than upgrading the existing British meter railway (1000 mm between rails).

In effect, a SGR offers high speeds, much faster passenger service, and capacity for frequent freight traffic with heavier cargo loads. The new SGR was expected to carry 60 kg per meter of rail at maximum speeds of 130 km/hour. This equates to a capacity maximum of 60 million tons of freight per year (African City Planner, 2015).[11] By contrast, the old British meter rail sustained at best 47.5 kg load per meter of rail and operated at maximum speeds of 80 km/hour, accommodating 5.5 million tons of cargo per year. Much of the meter rail system had already been abandoned or fallen into disrepair, and passenger trips from Nairobi to Mombasa could take as long as 22 hours (SGR's schedule is 6 hours for the same route). Kenyan and Chinese planners argued that the narrow railway was too inefficient to repair or upgrade, its tracks coming too close to existing towns and slums (Huang, personal communication, April 24, 2020).[12]

In short, the Chinese were intent on building SGR. According to University of St. Andrews international relations professor Ian Taylor:

> In May 2014 … during a trip to Kenya Premier Li Keqiang oversaw a $3.8 billion contract for the SGR between CRBC and Nairobi. Of this sum, 85 percent of the capital came from the Exim [Export–Import] Bank, with the Kenyan government providing the balance. The loan, whose interest

---

[10]　As journalist Paul Wafula, a reporter for Kenya's *Standard* newspaper, described the feasibility study: "It said the [SGR] railroad [couldn't] be profitable because of one-way traffic from Mombasa, of which 70% of that traffic terminates in Nairobi. The SGR train was planned to go all the way to Kampala, Uganda, but it would come back empty because there are not enough East African exports" (personal communication, October 28, 2018).

[11]　The original Kenyan meter gauge railway ("meter" is defined as 1000 mm distance between rails) fell into disrepair in the 1980s and 1990s, leaving half of the existing 2778 km lines out of service or abandoned (Taylor, 2020).

[12]　A World Bank feasibility study argued that the meter rail could be upgraded with advanced materials to operate at speeds of up to 120 km and with cargo loads comparable to SGR, at lower cost, but Kenyan officials rejected the findings (African City Planner, 2015).

is 3.6 percentage points above the six-month London Inter-Bank Offered Rate (Libor) average, is to be repaid in fifteen years. Kenya's Transport Cabinet Secretary, Michael Kamau, later admitted to the Parliamentary Public Investment Committee that procurement laws were ignored in negotiations with the Chinese and that Kenya had had to work under the conditions set by the Chinese. (Taylor, 2020)

The train represented a milestone in Xi Jinping's BRI master plan to bolster trade to East African markets. A follow-on phase of SGR was planned to extend the railway from Nairobi to the Kenyan cities of Naivasha, Kisumu, and Malaba, followed by Uganda (Kampala), South Sudan (Juba), and Rwanda (Kigali) (Figure 7.1). However, in early 2019 the Chinese Export–Import Bank withheld the billions needed to fund third-phase completion (Olingo, 2019). The decision seems to have been made, at least in part, because of a global perception that China was loading developing countries with unsustainable debt (Ndii, 2018a).

In fact, the completed SGR in Kenya costs three times the international standard and four times the original estimate (Kacungira, 2017).[13] The price tag has prompted Kenyan economists to wonder how the country will ever pay back its US$4.7 billion railway debt to China without forfeiting the railway itself (Mureithi, 2020).[14]

Journalist Paul Wafula argued that Kibaki and Moi's successor, Uhuru Kenyatta, didn't understand the ramifications of the Chinese decision to loan Kenya with the money rather than following Mwai Kibaki's BOT plan:

> The Chinese knew these guys [the Kenyatta Jubilee Administration] wanted the railway, so they said, "We'll build the railway free of charge, and we'll get you financing for the project. Just sign the dotted line." Uhuru went to China, came back and signed the commercial project, and the Chinese started building. (Wafula, personal communication, October 18, 2018)

Kenya's leading economist and public intellectual David Ndii wrote a scathing analysis of SGR in *The Elephant* (2018b), accusing both the Chinese and Kenyan governments of fabricating freight numbers to wow the public:

> In the beginning was a fiction – that the Chinese railway would freight 22 million tons a year, and in so doing, replace the trucking business. Turns out – and this from the government's own internal assessments – that the maximum amount of annual freight on the SGR is 8.76 million tons, almost a third of what was promised. Interest alone on the $3 billion debt is in US$200 million (KSh20 billion) per year, which works out to KSh45,000 – KSh60,000 per container. Contrary to official assurances, the railway will require both State coercion and a massive public subsidy to stay in business. (Ndii, 2018b)

---

[13] Diesel-powered SGR now costs US$5.6 million per km for the track alone, more than triple the international standard and four times the original estimate. By contrast, the Chinese-financed 756 km Addis Ababa–Djibouti line launched in 2018 as an all-electric project cost just about the same as Kenya's line – US$3.4 billion, but was also 250 km longer (Kacungira, 2017). The Kenyan government argued that SGR cost more because of the challenging terrain, the need for additional bridges and tunnels, along with land purchases and materials to support heavy cargo loads.

[14] Both Kenyan and Ugandan governments are now reported to be planning to interconnect SGR with a refurbished colonial meter railway at Naivasha. But this will require freight transfer between incompatible railways (Gorecki, 2020).

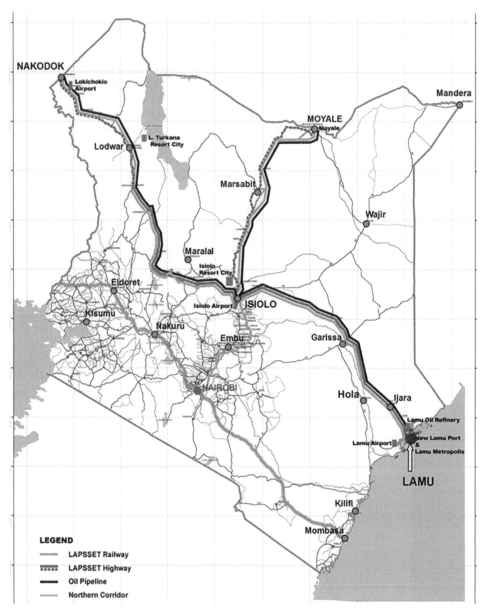

Note: The Chinese declined to finance third-phase SGR beyond Naivasha, forcing Kenyan planners to consider upgrading the more than a century old British meter rail.
Source: ALG Newsletter.

Figure 7.1   Original plan for SGR interconnecting Kenya's Malaba to Juba, Kampala, and Kilgali

The Chinese still claim success in the long term. Dr. Guo Ce, the commercial counselor at the Chinese Embassy, told me that SGR is absolutely necessary for Kenya's future economic growth and China's market expansion throughout East Africa. He challenged my perception that SGR's 12 back-and-forth trips a day along the Mombasa–Nairobi route would prove insufficient to support the train's profitability (Ndii, 2018b). Guo picked up his phone during our talk and called an SGR scheduler who told him that 22 daily back-and-forth trips (both passenger and freight) were planned (Guo Ce, personal communication, December 24, 2018). These numbers have since been contested (Ndii, 2018b). Guo stated: "Africa borrows from everyone, including America and Europe. So why is everyone worried about Chinese debt? If the economy in Kenya grows, China will profit. We'll see an impressive expansion of the economy here," he predicts. "We'll see it within ten years" (Guo Ce, personal communication, October 10, 2018).

Admittedly, certain benefits of first-phase SGR are demonstrable. The rail has increased Kenya's freight traffic, decongesting port operations and speeding freight delivery along with cargo security operations. According to a report by the China Communications Construction Company, the parent of CRBC, which built SGR, 46,000 local jobs were created during first-phase construction (Ndegwa, 2019). Bernard Osero, a senior communications officer with the Kenyan Port Authority in Mombasa, where SGR terminates, claims the new rail is a linchpin for expanding both the Mombasa and coming LAPSSET port traffic (B. Osero, personal communication, December 12, 2018). In the same breath, though, he wondered whether Mombasa, put up as collateral for SGR, could be seized by the Chinese if Kenya defaulted on its loans.

> The best port in the world with a big hinterland in Kenya is hinged on a competitive rail and road system. For the last 20 years Kenya was disadvantaged because our rail system wasn't efficient. The British meter rail system [supported] less than 5% of the cargo from Mombasa [with] 95% going by road, which meant the road was heavily congested and wear and tear on the road was very expensive for the country. [But] with a new railroad, best practices indicate cargo rail is 40% in any country.[15] (Osero, personal communication, December 12, 2018)

LAND OWNERSHIP BLUNDERS

One of the major traps China fell into by loaning billions for SGR was assuming a Chinese model of state land ownership. In Kenya, a democracy, there are patchworks of land claims and rights. Land is owned by federal ministries, local municipalities, tribes, and private citizens, not by a single government entity, as it is in China. An independent researcher in Nairobi, Zhengli Huang, explains:

> The land ownership problem in Kenya has caused these infrastructure projects to fail – or at least not to realize the level of economic growth originally projected. We took the system for granted … land ownership in China is a very specific one, very unique, it's one of the most important factors [why]

---

[15] At the time Osero spoke, the rail was handling roughly 20 percent of the available cargo. He and chief engineer David Arika seemed concerned about the reported Mombasa Port collateral clause, asking me whether the Chinese could actually seize and run the port if Kenya ultimately defaults on its loans. I couldn't reply yay or nay; Dr. Guo Ce informed me the Chinese would likely renegotiate loan repayment terms and time lines as necessary.

the infrastructure formula in China's development worked. We tend to dismiss the importance of that … we tend to export the same formula to a new continent and take it for granted that all the elements are there, which is not true. (Huang, personal communication, April 18, 2019)

I asked Dr. Huang to elaborate on the Chinese and Kenyan land ownership systems. "In China we have urban–rural binary land ownership system, meaning that the urban government has complete ownership and rights to use of the land, and that's not the case in Kenya, which is why there is no way to bring that scale of development in China to a new country," she said (personal communication, April 18, 2019).

Land ownership negotiations for the new railway produced costly delays, complaints, and unsettled lawsuits. Private owners in Kenya have claimed that the Kenyan government is grabbing land for projects without adequate compensation (R. Kibugi, personal communication, June 22, 2019). Government promises of short-term reward have not as yet resulted in overall gross domestic product (GDP) growth (Gorecki, 2020).

RQ1: THE LAPSSET PROJECT

The LAPSSET Project in Lamu, on the south-east coast of Kenya, is a different infrastructure phenomenon – not financed by the Chinese, but built by them. Kenyan intelligentsia lauded the project for its long-term plan to interconnect and modernize Kenyan cities and rural areas (e.g., Marsabit, Turkana). However, local environmentalists, land rights activists, and some Lamu fishermen and land owners have voiced objections. A consistent argument is that the port, originally intended as a trans-shipment hub, will become another white elephant if the long-term plan to build roads and rails to integrate economically marginalized northern Kenya fails to materialize.[16]

LAPSSET has a US$24.5 billion price tag which includes plans to build 32 berths for incoming ships in Lamu off the Indian Ocean and seven separate projects that include oil pipelines, railroads, airports, and roads from south-east Kenya to the hinterlands of northern Kenya and surrounding countries, including Ethiopia, South Sudan, and Uganda. Construction of the US$354 million first phase of the port has been completed thus far, including construction of three berths by December 2021. Kenya is floating tenders for 20 more berths under a public–private partnership plan. But in January 2022 suspected al-Shabaab militants torched eight contractor vehicles on a LAPSSET access road and were also reported to have attacked local residents. Project contractor China Communications Construction Company withdrew its workers from the LAPSSET construction sites, citing security concerns that as yet remain unsolved (Kitimo, 2022).

LAPSSET has also raised environmental concerns. Critics argue that water shunted away from the farmlands surrounding the Tana River delta and the killing of mangrove forests and fishing populations in Lamu's protected waters constitute irreversible damage (Lamu was designated a UNESCO World Heritage Site in 2001). Citizen resistance to the project in the form

---

[16]   LAPSSET is intended to include a "corridor" to northern Kenya which will include a pipeline, railway, and road network connecting Lamu, Garissa, Isiolo, Moyale, and Turkana in the north, along with a dam along the Tana River and airports and resorts. Thus far, a 500 km Isiolo–Moyale road has been completed. The China Communication Construction Company is contracted to build the first three of 32 planned port berths (J. Nyabiage, April 26, 2021).

of SAVE LAMU, an association of locals, went to court in 2012, alleging government land grabs without compensation and lack of local participation in planning the LAPSSET project. The Kenyan government eventually disbursed US$8.8 billion to 154 land-owning families who were displaced during the initial port construction. However, Human Rights Watch in 2017 reported that many displaced LAMU land owners haven't been compensated at all.

LAPSSET nonetheless is dubbed Africa's most ambitious infrastructure project. The China Communications Construction Company won the US$478 million contract in 2013 to complete the first three berths by 2019.[17] A parallel Chinese project to build a 1 gigawatt coal-fired plant in Lamu County met with fierce community opposition. Activists filed a lawsuit in 2019 to stop construction of the plant near mangrove forests, and the Industrial and Community Bank of China, a major financier, pulled out. In November 2020, the Kenyan government cancelled the project entirely (Shi Yi, 2021).

Despite its promise, LAPSSET has lost financial support in recent years. A project originally conceived in 1972 and revived by the Mwai Kibaki administration in 2008, the corridor initially attracted commitments from multiple foreign private investors. However, Brazil, China, the European Union, India, Japan, Qatar, and South Korea, though promising to fund the project, failed to follow through. This forced Ethiopia, Kenya, and South Sudan to agree to use domestic resources to finance their respective parts of the project (Kabukuru, 2016). Construction delays have been considerable. Further, project planners discounted less expensive projects emphasizing local community development and participation. According to Paul Goldsmith, a researcher living in Kenya:

Kenya was left holding the baby. In 2016, the Ugandan government announced plans to build a railroad that would connect Juba to another planned rail line from Kampala to the port of Tanga in Tanzania. Kampala explained that although the Tanzanian route was longer, the lower cost of construction justified the decision to withdraw from the planned link-up with the LAPSSET route through Kenya. In September, Ethiopia set in motion plans to build a 1500-kilometre railway to Khartoum and Port Sudan. The planned rail line effectively removing Ethiopia from the LAPSSET equation added another nail in the project's coffin. (Goldsmith, 2020)

According to United Nations sources, LAPSSET will survive in some form. In May 2016, a Sustainable Development Investment Partnership was announced on the first day of the World Economic Forum, reportedly to mobilize US$20 billion for cross-border infrastructure projects.[18] But exactly how that financing materializes remains to be seen. Independent

---

[17]   If and when LAPSSET in its entirety is completed, the project will consist of inter-regional highways and concurrent SGR train links from the port of Lamu to Isolo and Juba, South Sudan, Addis Ababa, Ethiopia, and Garsen, East Kenya. The project also plans an oil pipeline from Lamu to Isiolo and Isolo to Addis Ababa – in part to offer South Sudan oil producers a cheaper route to pipe their oil to the Indian Ocean. The project calls for the building of three international airports and resort cities (in Lamu, Isiolo, and Lake Turkana), an oil refinery, and a multipurpose High Grand Falls Dam along the Tana River, Kenya's longest and possibly most ecologically fragile river delta extending from the Aberdare Mountains in central Kenya to Garsen (a town north of Lamu), before entering the Indian Ocean.
[18]   The Sustainable Development Investment Partnership Africa Hub will mobilize blended finance, a combination of funding from private investors and lenders, governments, and philanthropic funds. Sustainable Development Investment Partnership members include the Bill & Melinda Gates Foundation, Citi, Denmark, the Netherlands, Norway, Sweden, the United Kingdom, and the United States. Others are the Development Bank of Southern Africa, Deutsche Bank, East Capital, the European Bank for

scholar Goldsmith suggests that a failure of Kenya's central planning oligarchy and a lack of critical thinking has thrown Kenya into "passive acceptance" of the Chinese model of techno-infrastructural development with little regard for community or ecological welfare.

> The Infrastructural Master Plan for the LAPSSET Corridor and Lamu Port ... does not mention the regional population and communities affected. [And] the attempt to build a technologically obsolete pollution-belching coal plant next to one of the planet's most unique near zero-carbon urban settlements and a UNESCO World Heritage Site is proof of what can happen in the absence of a countervailing developmental narrative. (Goldsmith, 2020)

Stakeholders in the LAPSSET project think differently, of course. Former LAPSSET director general/chief executive officer Silvester Kasuku spoke with me in 2019 about the project's long-term benefits and the care with which environmental and training issues were addressed. Kasuku, whose two-term directorship expired in January 2021, not only defended the infrastructure program but also Chinese participation in it. He outlined Kenya's bid for a "knowledge economy" outside of Chinese influence. In the LAPSSET case, he pointed to a home-grown training and scholarship program supporting 1000 Lamu students in maritime engineering degree and certificate programs. As many as 2000 local jobs had already been created in the first phase of port construction, Kasuku said, although many Lamu locals are untrained and have no education, so Chinese managers and technical people fill the top construction roles:

> The whole issue that goes with China gets to be exaggerated in Africa; even the current propaganda is extremely hyped. African countries are looking for infrastructure ... a lot of development issues have come from *lack of* infrastructure. So now that the Chinese have come, they've gotten themselves a fair share of the blame, and sometimes they are not even involved in areas being blamed. They've come with cheap labor and cheap money with less stringent conditions for accessing the money than the World Bank ... whose loans are pegged with so many conditionalities that many times the loans are suspended. This has created a huge development infrastructure bottleneck. (S. Kasuku, personal communication, March 11, 2019)

DISCUSSION

Public suspicion regarding China's relationship with the Kenyatta government has increased since *The Daily Nation* newspaper in January 2021 published excerpts from an original SGR contract showing China's Export–Import Bank's conditions for debt repayment. According to one excerpt, "Neither the borrower (Kenya) nor any of its assets is entitled to any right of immunity on the grounds of sovereignty" (Niba, 2019). The statement suggests that Kenya put up its new railway as collateral for the Chinese loan. As economist David Ndii reflected:

> The question that is frequently asked now is whether, if Kenya cannot pay, the Chinese will take over the port of Mombasa ... In a manner of speaking, they already have. The Chinese have a concession to run the railway until 2027. That includes a take-or-pay freight assignment contract, which is to say, the Kenya Ports Authority, the port operator, has to meet the railway's freight target or pay the railway for the unused capacity. In effect, the port is working for the railway. (Ndii, 2018a)

Reconstruction and Development, and the European Investment Bank. See www.un.org/africarenewal/magazine/august-2016/megaproject-rises-east-africa.

Although China's Commercial Counselor Dr. Guo Ce dismisses this notion of collateral (he also disputed the *New York Times* representation of China's reappropriation of Sri Lanka's Hambantota port when the country failed to repay its loans (Abi-Habib, 2018)), he did confirm that China has the flexibility to renegotiate the timetable of loan repayment and to forgive certain debts entirely (Guo Ce, personal communication, January 23, 2019). The term "take or pay" is a contract scheme the Chinese favor in connection with loans to developing countries. "Take or pay" means that borrowing governments guarantee to China the *operating income* from infrastructure projects that can be used as a means of debt repayment. In effect, China can recover its loans *de facto* by commandeering the operation of SGR or other projects it finances, demanding that Kenya produces a certain level of freight traffic in which the Chinese take the profits until the debt is paid off (Huang, personal communication, June 19, 2019).

Since its inception, though, the SGR gambit has drastically altered China's relationship with Kenya. Not only has Kenyatta borrowed billions from the Chinese, he has also authorized tenders and signed restrictive contracts (without normal competitive bids) in which the Kenyans are obligated to use Chinese state-owned contractors exclusively for megaprojects like SGR and LAPSSET. The presence of the Chinese – an estimated 40,000 or more in Kenya – has raised new questions about China's alleged "debt imperialism," the secrecy of Kenyan elites collaborating on megaprojects, and the inability of the country to account for its own budget deficits. "Public debt has tripled in five years," said economist David Ndii, who completed an audit of the Kenyatta administration budgets between 2013 and 2018. He continued:

This government has borrowed 2.5 trillion KSh in last five years, not only from domestic sources but from Eurobonds (sovereign bonds) purchased in London. When Uhura Kenyatta took over we had no external commercial debt. Zero. Though the Chinese railroad accounted for less than $4 billion, the rest has been taken up in public projects and deposits in overseas banks that can't be accounted for. How much of the 2.5 trillion KSh can we see on the ground? It can't be more than half. (Ndii, personal communication, January 25, 2019)

Ndii cites government projects like missing dams (designated but never built because the funds were stolen) along with a national budget allocation to build 6000 km of new electric transmission lines throughout the country, of which only 2800 km were built. "Where is the money going? It's a big mystery. This has been a very corrupt country from the beginning, but this Kenyatta stuff is completely off the charts" (personal communication, January 25, 2019).

The fascinating wrinkle here is that China's long-term perspective in Kenya may be its greatest vulnerability. It comes in direct conflict with the Kenyan government's short-term grandiosity and borrowing spree for megaprojects without a feasible way to pay for them. As of July 2021, Kenya resumed servicing its loans owed to China for SGR and LAPSSET after Beijing's six-month Covid-19-related debt repayment suspension expired in June 2021. "Kenya's debt-servicing costs are poised to surge 35% [from June 2021 to June 2022] to a record 1.17 trillion shillings (US$10,187,200,647)," according to Bloomberg's David Herbling (2021, para. 3). "That exceeds the [Kenyan] administration's 669 billion shillings (US$5.825 billion) budget for development projects during the period."

CONCLUSION

Today, time sense and expectations for socio-economic improvement in Kenya are muddled, especially with the pressures of the Covid-19 pandemic. Chinese and sovereign bond "debt traps" have skewed public opinion on how Kenya will dig itself out. Today China is Kenya's biggest foreign creditor after the World Bank (Herbling, 2021). China holds more than 70 percent of Kenya's bilateral debt, yet the Chinese portion is only 21 percent of Kenya's total external debt. The Kenyan Treasury now reports its budget deficit has risen to nearly 9 percent of GDP (Herbling, 2021). By 2018 Kenya was also spending KSh459.4 billion servicing debt, the largest item in the nation's expenditure, exceeding everything the government spent on transportation (KSh225 billion), healthcare (KSh65.5 billion), or education (KSh415.3 billion) (Marete, 2019).

How does corruption reinforce time perception mirroring past colonial domination? What role does China now play in the liberation or corruption of Kenyan society? Is China the new villain in Kenya's history, its angel, or just the most recent grifter bumbling by when the real debt trap – Kenya's corruption mindset – goes unresolved?

If Kenya is to proceed on a path toward modernization and social justice, it will likely do so by strengthening its private sector. In fact, native Kenyan entrepreneurs have developed a number of successful technological projects without significant help or investment either from the Chinese or Kenyan governments. An example of a socially "disruptive" tech innovation isn't SGR, but M-Pesa, a system of electronic payments developed by Safaricom inventor Michael Joseph in 2007. By 2017, the volume of M-Pesa transactions on Kenyan cell phones amounted to nearly half of Kenya's total GDP. A group of MIT researchers who studied the social impact of the invention found that it increased the efficiency of purchasing and consuming, and even boosted savings and changed labor market outcomes, moving more women out of agriculture into business and hence lifting 194,000 households, or 2 percent of Kenyan households, out of poverty (Suri & Jack, 2016).

Regional development, investment in private start-ups and a promotion of health, environment, and education among neglected communities need present-tense strategies to create a brighter Kenyan future. While the Chinese may be part of infrastructure development, neither the Chinese nor the Kenyan government can facilitate social justice and economic parity by loaning or borrowing prodigiously, or by building megaprojects alone to the exclusion of citizen welfare in the present. Kenya needs responsible financing and investing, a clean sweep of highly corrupt elite actors, and a long-term vision of self-strengthening most of all.

REFERENCES

Abi-Habib, M. (2018, June 25). How China got Sri Lanka to cough up a port. *New York Times*. www.nytimes.com/2018/06/25/world/asia/china-sri-lanka-port.html

African City Planner. (2015, July 15). Kenya: Two railway lines running parallel on different gauges. http://africancityplanner.com/kenya-2-parallel-railway-lines-running-on-different-gauges/

Chome, N. (2020, March 17). Land, livelihoods and belonging: Negotiating change and anticipating LAPSSET in Kenya's Lamu county. *Journal of East African Studies*, 14:2, 310–331.

Dickson, W. (2021, July 9). A snapshot of Kenya's debt profile. University of Nairobi. www.uonbi.ac.ke/news/snapshot-kenya%E2%80%99s-debt-profile-and-dealing-debt

Goldsmith, P. (2020, November 6). Ideas: The death of LAPSSET and Kenya's poverty of imagination. *The Elephant.* www.theelephant.info/ideas/2020/11/06/the-death-of-lapsset-and-kenyas-poverty-of -imagination/

Goldstein, J. (2018, October 15). Kenyans say Chinese investment brings racism and discrimination. *New York Times.* www.nytimes.com/2018/10/15/world/africa/kenya-china-racism.html

Gorecki, I. (2020, September 24). Kenya's Standard Gauge Railway: The promise and risks of rail meg-aprojects. *Africa Up Close.* https://africaupclose.wilsoncenter.org/kenyas-standard-gauge-railway-the -promise-and-risks-of-rail-megaprojects/

Herbling, D. (2021, July 31). Kenya resumes China debt repayment with $761 million. Bloomberg. www .bloomberg.com/news/articles/2021-07-31/kenya-resumes-china-debt-repayment-with-761-million -remittance

Human Rights Watch. (2018, December). They just want to silence us: Abuses against environmental activists in Kenya's Coast Region. www.hrw.org/report/2018/12/17/they-just-want-silence-us/abuses -against-environmental-activists-kenyas-coast

Kabukuru, W. (2016, August–November). A megaproject arises in East Africa. *Africa Renewal.* www.un .org/africarenewal/magazine/august-2016/megaproject-rises-east-africa

Kacungira, N. (2017, June 8). Will Kenya get value for money from its new railway? BBC. www.bbc .com/news/world-africa-40171095

Kenya Vision 2030. (n.d.) https://vision2030.go.ke/

Kimutai, C. (2018, December 4). Yes, China is Kenya's biggest trading partner – but it's not a balanced trade. *Africa Check.* https://africacheck.org/fact-checks/reports/yes-china-kenyas-biggest-trading -partner-its-not-balanced-trade

Kitimo, A. (2022, February 9). Why LAPSSET is stuck on the starting blocks. *The East African.* www .theeastafrican.co.ke/tea/business/why-lapsset-is-stuck-on-the-starting-blocks-3709384

LAPSSET Corridor Development Authority. (n.d.). A seamless connected Africa. www.lapsset.go.ke/

Lévesque, M. & Stephan, U. (2020). It's time we talk about time in entrepreneurship. *Entrepreneurship Theory and Practice*, 44:2, 163–184.

Levtov, M. (2018). African venture of China: Déjà vu? or the soft power of words. *The African Review*, 45:2, 1–25.

Marete, S. (2019, April 25). Winter Is coming: Why our national debt is illegitimate, unjust and unsus-tainable … and why we should be worried. *The Elephant.* www.theelephant.info/features/2019/04/25/ winter-is-coming-why-our-national-debt-is-illegitimate-unjust-and-unsustainableland-why-we-should -be-worried/

Mbiti, J.S. (1969). *African religions and philosophy.* Heinemann.

Medeiros. R.P.R. de (2019). The impact of cultural time perception in economic behavior: Our enforce-ment of Max Weber's thesis. Dissertation, Iscte-Instituto Universitário de Lisboa. http://hdl.handle .net/10071/19318

Mohammed, O. (2019, February 19). Kenya says crude oil capacity insufficient for refinery. Reuters. www.reuters.com/article/us-kenya-oil/kenya-says-crude-oil-capacity-insufficient-for-refinery -idUSKCN1Q80JZ

Mureithi, C. (2020, October 9). Kenya's expensive Chinese-built railway is racking up losses even as loans come due. *Quartz Africa.* https://qz.com/africa/1915399/kenyas-chinese-built-sgr-railway-racks -up-losses-as-loans-due/

Ndegwa, S. (2019, August 2). China's Standard Gauge Railway makes strong impact on Kenya's economy. CGTN. https://news.cgtn.com/news/2019-08-02/China-s-standard-gauge-railway-makes -strong-impact-on-Kenya-s-economy-IPds2CE4zm/index.html

Ndii, D. (2018, July 21). SGR by the numbers: Some unpleasant arithmetic. *The Elephant.* www .theelephant.info/op-eds/2018/07/21/sgr-by-the-numbers-some-unpleasant-arithmetic/

Ndii, D. (2018, August 18). China's debt imperialism: The art of war by other means? *The Elephant.* www.theelephant.info/op-eds/2018/08/18/chinas-debt-imperialism-the-art-of-war-by-other-means/

Newcomb, C. (2020). The impact of Chinese investments on the Kenyan economy. Master's thesis, Chapman University. DOI:10.36837/chapman.000190

Niba, W. (2019, January 15). Will Kenya's Mombasa port be taken over by the Chinese? *Rfi.* www.rfi.fr/ en/africa/20190114-kenya-mombasa-port-china-debt-default

Nyabiage, J. (2021, April 26). Why Chinese construction firms remain big builders in Africa. *South China Morning Post*. www.scmp.com/news/china/diplomacy/article/3130988/why-chinese-construction-firms-will-remain-big-builders-africa

Nyabiage, J. & Elmer, K. (2020, December 19). African railways feel pinch of China's Belt and Road. *South China Morning Post*. www.scmp.com/news/china/ diplomacy/article/3114551/african-railways-feel-pinch-chinas-belt-and-road-funding

Olander, E. (2021, January 22). China and Kenya in talks about debt challenges. *The Africa Report*. www.theafricareport.com/60569/china-and-kenya-in-talks-about-debt-challenges/

Olingo, A. (2019, April 27). Kenya fails to secure $3.6b from China for third phase of SGR line to Kisumu. *The East African*. www.theeastafrican.co.ke/tea/business/kenya-fails-to-secure-3-6b-from-china-for-third-phase-of-sgr-line-to-kisumu-1416820

Peck, G. (1967). *Two kinds of time* (2nd ed.). Houghton Mifflin.

People's Daily Online. (2009, August 22). Kenya launches Chinese-funded road construction work. http://en.people.cn/90001/90776/90883/6736267.html

Praxides, C. (2015, April 14). New port bad news for Aweer, Lamu's last forest community. *Star*. www.the-star.co.ke/sasa/2015-04-14-new-port-bad-news-for-aweer-lamus-last-forest-community/

Schifrin, N. (2016, April 11). How widespread corruption is hurting Kenya. *PBS News Hour*. www.pbs.org/newshour/show/how-widespread-corruption-is-hurting-kenya

Shi Yi (2021, March 9). Kenyan coal project shows why Chinese investors need to take environmental risks seriously. *China Dialogue*. https://chinadialogue.net/en/energy/lamu-kenyan-coal-project-chinese-investors-take-environmental-risks-seriously/

Skidmore, D. (2022, March 5). How China's ambitious Belt and Road plans for East Africa came apart. https://thediplomat.com/2022/03/how-chinas-ambitious-belt-and-road-plans-for-east-africa-came-apart/

Suri, T. & Jack, W. (2016, December 9). The long-run poverty and gender impacts of mobile money. *Science*, 354:6317, 1288–1292.

Tang X.Y. & Eom, J. (2019, June). Time perception and industrialization: Divergence and convergence of work ethics in Chinese enterprises in Africa. *The China Quarterly*, 238, 461–481.

Taylor, I. (2020). Kenya's new lunatic express: The Standard Gauge Railway. *African Studies Quarterly*, 19:3–4, 29–52.

Trading Economics. (2022, March). Kenya imports from China. https://tradingeconomics.com/kenya/imports/china

World Bank (2018, April 10). Poverty incidence in Kenya declined significantly, but unlikely to be eradicated by 2030. www.worldbank.org/ /en/country/kenya/publication/kenya-economic-update-poverty-incidence-in-kenya-declined-significantly-but-unlikely-to-be-eradicated-by-2030

8. Ongoing technological innovation in the home: a blessing or a curse?

Alet C. Erasmus

INTRODUCTION

In an era where technology is changing rapidly and significantly influences the way people live, changes in household technology – even on a basic level – have certainly not taken a back seat. This chapter provides an overview of the relevance of changes in household technology, particularly in Africa, of how people perceive, appreciate, distrust, or even reject novel technologies designed to improve households' quality of life. Indications are that although technologies such as home appliances and electricity may cause excitement and can be a blessing in some households, they may, unfortunately, also cause grave concerns among those who are ill-equipped to appreciate unfamiliar commodities in their homes and workplaces. Essentially, leapfrogging encompasses change fueled by innovation, and although technological innovation mostly precedes leapfrogging, it is not the only determinant of its success (Gallagher, 2006; Tigabu et al., 2015). Equally important is the social impact of radical change, as a society needs to understand how it will benefit from any innovation relative to more familiar alternatives (Hackett, 2012; Tukker, 2005) so that they can embrace change rather than feel intimidated. In this chapter, we adopt a positive stance and indicate how access to electricity and other technological resources can improve people's living conditions and provide opportunities for African societies that are desperately seeking to advance. The concept of leapfrogging is introduced to indicate that technological change often occurs at a fast pace, even unexpectedly, with diverse consequences. We frame the discussions on technological leapfrogging on the assumptions of Resource Advantage Theory (RAT).

TECHNOLOGICAL LEAPFROGGING EXPLAINED

Technological leapfrogging, as a phenomenon, is grounded in the assumption that some countries – even emerging countries – can acquire and develop the technical and managerial know-how to leapfrog older vintages of technology. Thereby, communities could skip investments in older, less efficient technologies, and rather invest in future technologies from the start (Amankwah-Amoah, 2015; Gallagher, 2006; Hughes & Larmour, 2021). Countries could, therefore, skip resource-intensive, expensive forms of economic development to adopt the most advanced technologies that are available, rather than follow the conventional path of energy development pursued by highly industrialized countries (Amankwah-Amoah, 2015;

Gallagher, 2006). In some instances, technological leapfrogging could even advance a country or community to become a leader in a specific field of technology (Amankwah-Amoah, 2015).

Concerning leapfrogging in the context of lifestyle changes, it is important to understand how the phenomenon can influence people's everyday lives. Three paradigms of leapfrogging are distinguished in the context of technology, based on differences in the pace and magnitude of change in technology, namely *revolutionary, scattered, and coned leapfrogging*. Steinbuks and Foster (2010) explain that "revolutionary leapfrogging" occurs when the transition to a novel technology is rapid and takes place on a large scale, for example, the adoption of online teaching in South Africa during the COVID-19 pandemic. Although online teaching and learning was not a novel phenomenon, the need for an entire switch to remote education took the world by storm during the enforced lockdown periods that were introduced in 2020 (Hoeffner-Shah, 2020). With "scattered leapfrogging," the magnitude of change is smaller. An example is the introduction of solar heating during the development of new housing projects in parts of South Africa in recent years. "Coned leapfrogging" occurs when the transition to a novel technology requires a major, large-scale change in infrastructure with considerable economic implications. It generally occurs at a slower pace, for example, fiber installation to enhance internet connectivity across South Africa. Conventional technology transitions, such as progress from analogue to digitally controlled household appliances, do not constitute "leapfrogging," although the accumulated effect of the change may be large. These status quo changes occur over a longer period, for various reasons, including ongoing advancements in technology (Steinbuk & Foster, 2010). The introduction of smartphone technology is another good example of a "conventional" technology transition which does not constitute leapfrogging. In the next section, we present the theoretical anchor that frames the discussion, followed by examples of leapfrogging in Africa.

RESOURCE ADVANTAGE THEORY

The theoretical anchor used to frame the conversation in this chapter is RAT, which is an evolution and integration of Resource-Based Theory (Conner, 1991) and Competitiveness Theory (Alderson, 1957, 1965). Initially, Resource-Based Theory was meant to explain factors that constrain business operations, admitting reasons for constraints while acknowledging diverse demands and the reality that resources change continually. Competitiveness Theory, on the other hand, focuses on competitiveness, elevating an organization's aim to gain a differential advantage, which is evident when examining the assumptions of RAT (Alderson, 1957, 1965). In combination, RAT serves to explain the strategies used by organizations to produce the best outcomes in a specific context (Hunt & Madhavaram, 2006, 2012). An example would be when households' energy needs in a specific geographic area are addressed while acknowledging available resources that may be tangible (such as existing infrastructure and finances) and intangible (such as communities' understanding of the technologies that are proposed or introduced).

The following assumptions of RAT are relevant in this chapter (Hunt & Madhavaram, 2006, 2012):[1]

- Because the demands of industries and consumers are not fixed, they are difficult to predict.
- Consumers' demands are continually shifting, depending on their circumstances and exposure, which complicates initiatives to address their needs in an appropriate manner.
- Information about products and services dispensed to consumers is mostly incomplete as parts may be too technical and too difficult to assimilate in a way that everybody will understand. This condition affects communities with lower education levels, making assimilation and acceptance of novel technologies more challenging.
- Motivation drives consumers' needs, for example, to acquire novel technology and services to improve their way of living. On the contrary, organizations' goals are fundamentally to maximize profit. The difference in role players' goals influences the speed, effectiveness, and completion of the dissemination of a new commodity or service, such as energy supply.
- Resources held by a business organization to accomplish specific goals, such as supplying electricity to communities, are diverse and continually changing and evolving. In the end, change and resource availability affect the outcome of organizations' plans. A salient example is the onset of the COVID-19 pandemic, spurring consumer frustration and discontent due to supply-chain delays and price hikes.

Concerning consumers' use of novel innovations, Strengers (2014) introduced the notion of the so-called "Resource Man," a rational person who is knowledgeable and motivated and who optimizes innovations in a sustainable, affordable, and positive way. Verkade and Höffken (2017) adopted a different stance, cautioning that a consumer needs to display an understanding of how a novel technology will change existing habits and practices. Often, households have established culturally ingrained ways of doing things (and by whom), with established routines. For example, in rural Africa, several families generally socialize together while cooking meals on an open fire outside their homes. Standards offered by novel technology, such as electric or gas ranges and cooktops, might violate these practices. Moreover, attributes of modern technology, such as pre-programming that allows certain appliances to operate while a family is away from home, might seem superfluous to them. Subsequently, when purchasing certain appliances, consumers might be introduced to, and even be paying for, technological ideas and functionality that they will not continue to use once the novelty has worn off. Similarly, purchasing a sewing machine with an extensive array of embroidery stitches may be superfluous if the seamstress uses at most four different stitches for basic sewing and repairs.

In summary, therefore, it is difficult to align consumers' needs and service providers' execution of plans. Accordingly, in the domain of health practices, the World Health Organization

---

[1] Due to prevailing social and economic circumstances, organizations often have to adjust their plans for reform and uplift, which may spur extreme frustration and discontent within communities – as was the case with the onset of the COVID-19 pandemic. Similarly, price hikes due to unstable monetary exchange rates may severely influence the budget allocated to execute certain projects. Due to external circumstances, therefore, governing bodies' available financial resources may be affected from time to time, negatively impacting initiatives for sought-after social reconstruction and uplift.

(Hackett, 2012) views social sustainability (acceptance) as vital in the adoption of any technology and considers technical performance as inextricably linked to the impact of a new initiative (Hackett, 2012). We use examples to further the fundamentals of RAT throughout this chapter. The following section is devoted to the importance of energy supply – particularly clean energy – to communities, to improve their lifestyles and to enable access to modern technologies.

ENERGY SUPPLY: THE BRIDGE TO IMPROVED SOCIO-ECONOMIC WELL-BEING

Households' access to particular energy sources is an important indication of communities' socio-economic well-being and lifestyles, thus the way they live (Dziechciarz et al., 2010; Walker & Li, 2007). Households' self-identity is an important factor in accepting or rejecting change (Axsen et al., 2012). Lifestyle theory suggests that someone is more likely to adopt and purchase new technology if it fits their current lifestyle or will facilitate their desired lifestyle (Axsen et al., 2012, 2015). While many definitions for "lifestyle" exist, it is noteworthy that the operationalization of the construct generally acknowledges demographic characteristics, including income, accessibility to commodities, and housing types (Axsen et al., 2012). Earlier lifestyle research by Giddens (2013) proposed that in a modern world that lacks definite expectations – contrary to the more rigid guidance provided by tradition – consumers tend to intentionally create their identity through their everyday way of life. Of particular importance in this chapter is the explanation of Giddens (2013) that lifestyle construction is an ongoing process, during which new lifestyles and dimensions of self-identify are constructed as people's circumstances change (for example, gaining access to electricity and related commodities) or as they engage with new social groups (for example, through urbanization).

In Africa, consumers' use of energy sources deserves specific attention because access to energy signifies communities' level of poverty (or affluence) and the challenges encountered in daily existence (Kwac et al., 2018; Taale & Kyeremeh, 2015). Having no access to electricity signifies poverty, as does the use of elementary cooking fuels such as wood, charcoal, or animal dung (Kachale et al., 2019). Globally, nearly 3 billion people, mostly concentrated in rural areas in Sub-Saharan Africa and South Asia, rely on wood, coal, charcoal, or animal waste for cooking and heating (World Bank, 2018).[2] Furthermore, lack of electricity prevents communities' access to the technological fortunes of the twenty-first-century digital era – a paradox considering evidence of notable progress and leapfrogging in wealthier parts of the world. The dilemma is best explained by using the concept of the "ladder of energy sources" that distinguishes households' financial well-being and prevailing lifestyle. This frame places fuelwood or dung at the bottom of that so-called ladder because it can be accessed for free; followed by charcoal used for lighting and cooking for those who can afford it; to kerosene and gas; and finally to electricity at the top, as the ultimate energy source (Behera & Ali, 2016; Bervoets et al., 2016). It is only when households have access to, and can afford, gas and electricity that opportunities for the adoption of more sophisticated technologies present themselves.

---

[2]   This has a disproportionate effect on women and girls, who are primarily responsible to gather, manage, and provide the energy for everyday household tasks (Oparaocha & Dutta, 2011).

More recently, reference is made to the so-called "energy lifestyle" of a person or household (Schwarzinger et al., 2019), which involves all the activities that people are involved in as part of their daily lives that have an impact on their energy demand and consumption of privately consumed products and services. This includes the lifespan of products and climate impact and affirms how important energy provision and consumption have become in societies today.

Accordingly, the United Nations explicitly captures access to reliable and affordable energy sources and relief from energy poverty as part of their Sustainable Development Goals (Sovacool et al., 2016; UNDP, 2019). Conventional electricity or another appropriate, modern energy source has the potential to change households' lifestyles in a significant way. For example, when people migrate to urban communities, they are unavoidably exposed to commodities such as electricity and all the related advantages such as time- and labor-saving household appliances. The subsequent feedback of others in their social circle about their new lifestyle inevitably changes (boosts) how they perceive themselves. Lutzenhiser and Gossard (2000) explain that lifestyles are the fundamental building blocks of complex societies, and are meaningful to "place" people and households within a social landscape. Therefore, households' access to electricity and their possession of household technologies can position them in an admirable higher social hierarchy.

Despite an awareness of the crucial role of electricity in terms of technological progress, Sub-Saharan Africa is still the most electricity-deprived region on earth. The United Nations has therefore identified universal access to modern energy by 2030 as one of the most important Sustainable Development Goals (UNDP, 2019). Of particular interest to industries and scholars alike is the transition to renewable energy as a conduit to provide worldwide energy access for all. In other words, leapfrogging from very basic elementary sources of energy to renewables can potentially make energy security a reality for the majority (Burlamaqui & Kattel, 2016; Goldemberg, 2011; Tigabu et al., 2015; Zerriffi & Wilson, 2010), elevating the importance of renewable energy for the future. It can reduce man's destruction of natural resources (such as the destruction of forests to gain access to fuelwood), while also curtailing people's carbon footprint on earth (Kachale et al., 2019). Technological progress could therefore promote much-needed economic and social development in Sub-Saharan countries (Rahut et al., 2017). Alternative energy sources such as elementary solar energy can, for example, be optimized for cooking and water heating.

LEAPFROGGING: AN ATTAINABLE IDEAL?

Unfortunately, countries in Eastern and Southern Africa, despite having an abundance of renewable energy resources such as solar, wind, geothermal, and hydropower, have not yet been able to harness these clean energy resources to leapfrog their existing energy practices. This predicament is best explained within the fundamental assumptions of RAT: communities are likely to distrust novel technologies unless they are aptly introduced. Moreover, the lack of leadership to address issues related to poor infrastructure, and problems related to affordability amid service providers' goal to maximize profit, are indeed counterproductive. Although certain societies may be unfamiliar with the idea of renewable energy, proper guidance and transition management can facilitate opportunities to leapfrog their consumption practices in ways that exceed conventional practices among upper-income households (Hughes & Larmour, 2021).

Essentially, leapfrogging refers to a change that is fueled by innovation. Although technological innovation mostly precedes leapfrogging, it is not the only determinant of its success (Gallagher, 2006; Tigabu et al., 2015). The social impact of radical change is equally relevant, as a society needs to understand how it will benefit from any innovation relative to more familiar alternatives (Hackett, 2012; Tukker, 2005). For example, while electricity in Africa may be a highly sought-after commodity, it is often not affordable, explaining why households continue to cook on paraffin/kerosene stoves, or rather use firewood to meet their energy requirements (Kachale et al., 2019). In these circumstances, the installation of solar systems can address communities' energy needs without the burden of additional costs to households. A study conducted in rural China found that to succeed, the appropriation of new technology or technical products needs to be strongly integrated into the habitus of society, thus households' conventional thought and behavior patterns (Wu, 2008).

Transition management, which implies a well-organized drive within communities to explicate envisaged options such as solar power that may differ from what communities anticipate, is hence crucial when introducing novel technologies. Transition management constitutes a break with approaches where communities are excluded from decisions that concern them (Ackom et al., 2016; Loorbach, 2010). RAT explains that transition management is particularly important for "supply push" technology where communities have limited experience and say. In terms of energy supply, for example, the reality is that renewable sources will become more strongly promoted in the future to reduce carbon footprint, as well as to promote environmentally sustainable consumption (Calitz & Wright, 2021).[3]

TECHNOLOGICAL LEAPFROGGING: THE PARADOX OF PROGRESS

While access to electricity is a way to fast-forward previously disadvantaged households to new lifestyles and levels of prosperity, the outcomes are not necessarily rosy.

One study on the service life of household appliances involving 638 heads of households in Tshwane, South Africa, suggested that lack of consumer knowledge while purchasing and using appliances directly impacted product performance, expectations for maintenance, and even appliances' service life (Erasmus et al., 2005). Study subjects who came from previously disadvantaged backgrounds had migrated to the city within the preceding five-year period. Researchers tested respondents' knowledge of the appliances they owned at the time and the indicators they relied on during the pre-purchase evaluation (Erasmus et al., 2005). Although conducted more than two decades ago, the findings depict the typical predicament consumers face if a leapfrogging transition is not managed well. For example, the majority of the respondents in the Erasmus study relied on the brand name as the most important quality indicator, although most could only list two different brand names. A significant reliance was also reported on surrogate indicators of quality, such as price and advertising, while friends and family generally guided their product decisions rather than consulting salespeople in the stores. Similar outcomes were reported in a study conducted in rural China (Wu, 2008),

---

[3]   Details summarized in the Council for Scientific and Industrial Research report on South Africa's energy needs and consumption are updated regularly. The following link can be consulted to remain informed: www.csir.co.za/media-release.

where men generally exercised the appliance type and brand choices for their households after gaining access to electricity, arguing that they earned the money to run their households. In the Erasmus study, respondents' poor performance in the product knowledge test about energy consumption, electricity costs, product installation, maintenance, and care confirmed respondents' inexperience and vulnerability. The majority admitted that they were treading in the dark, having no frame of reference to evaluate purchase quality or product performance. Respondents' expectations about the service life of household appliances were as low as five years, mostly displaying a willingness to replace appliances that were supposed to function for ten years or more prematurely, and the short service life posed no problem to them.

Accordingly, Burger and fellow researchers (2014) reported that assets where major innovations occur frequently, such as television sets and major household appliances, are often replaced prematurely by less experienced households to signal social status and to benefit from new luxury features. They upgrade frequently, even opting for more advanced technologies to proudly indicate their ability to do so. A study by Craviotoa et al. (2017) summarizing the actual service life information of six product categories across different developed countries reported that household income level and the penetration rate of appliances in a particular community influenced service life before replacement. Generally, lower-income households tend to replace appliances sooner, and often, appliances considered more essential for living, including washing machines, television sets, and refrigerators, are replaced prematurely out of fear that they might break down. Wu (2008) reported similar findings in a study that involved lower-income Chinese households, explaining that after the electrification of their villages, television sets provided an opportunity for relatives, friends, and neighbors to arrange shared family gatherings in the evening while previously men used to socialize on their own. Therefore, households' adoption of the latest technologies and preference for certain commodities is not an unfamiliar phenomenon, even when consumers are not yet equipped to deal with and optimize the latest technology (Hughes & Larmour, 2021).

Following several surveys, Nieftagodien and van der Berg (2007) concluded that previously disadvantaged consumers' consumption patterns are driven by an asset deficit and a strong preference for middle-class goods. These consumers prioritized electrical goods, ranking refrigerators, washing machines, and microwave ovens first. Their research concluded that once an asset deficit is erased, the consumption patterns of household appliances of different cultural groups are alike. Burger et al. (2014) explained that for first-generation middle-class households, an asset accumulation process may be a proxy for an equally important process of socio-economic orientation and consolidation. This is important to strengthen social networks and acquire tacit knowledge concerning social conventions, enhance feelings of security and belonging, and reduce vulnerability (Burger et al., 2014). Usually, conspicuous consumption is rife among lower-income groups to reflect progress in life. However, as households' asset ownership increases, conspicuous consumption declines because consumers have become more comfortable in their new social surroundings (Rao & Ummel, 2017).

ENERGY PROVISION IN AFRICA: THE PREDICAMENT

Research indicates notable changes in consumer households' behavior following their exposure to the fortunes related to electricity supply and related technologies. Unfortunately, affordability, which is a typical constraint according to RAT, remains a primary issue of concern and dissatisfaction (Alderson, 1957, 1965; Kachale et al., 2019). Minnaar (2021) explains that, in South Africa specifically, Eskom's continuous plea to increase electricity tariffs remains a contentious issue that is threatening households' financial well-being in the current economically constrained environment where unemployment is rife. Households have had to bear with electricity tariff increases that significantly exceed inflation levels since 2008, being 25 percent above inflation from 2012 to 2016. Contrary arguments, however, are that South Africa's electricity prices (benchmarked at 0.07 in 2021) are low compared to both developed countries (e.g. the Netherlands, the United Kingdom, and Germany, benchmarked at 0.18, 0.22, and 0.33, respectively), as well as major developing countries such as China, India, Indonesia, Brazil, and Turkey (benchmarked 0.08, 0.08, 0.10, 0.13, and 0.15, respectively). Notwithstanding, the benefits derived from electricity supply to larger parts of South Africa are overshadowed by constant power outages amid the surge in electricity prices (Minnaar, 2021).

It is unfortunate that the electricity provision in many parts of Africa is still critically low. In countries such as Malawi, structural challenges such as insufficient generation capacity, unreliable supply, and high unit costs have thus far jeopardized progress in disseminating electrical service to large parts of the population, particularly in rural areas (Oseni, 2019; Ouedraogo, 2017). According to a 2017 International Energy Agency report, 1.3 billion people in the world lacked electricity at the time, of which nearly 95 percent live in Sub-Saharan Africa and Asian developing countries. Indications are that this figure is growing annually, rather than declining (Dagnachen et al., 2017, 2018). In Malawi, for example, only 8 percent of households are connected to the grid due to prevailing logistical issues, and because households simply cannot afford the luxury (Chirambo, 2016; Seim & Robinson, 2019; Taulo et al., 2015). In Mozambique, Malawi, Tanzania, and Zambia, it is predominantly the wealthier households that use electricity and liquid petroleum gas. In rapidly growing poor urban and peri-urban areas in South Africa, the problem for the majority of households is often an affordability issue, and with rapid increases in electricity prices, the situation is not expected to improve any time soon (Ye et al., 2018). In the decade up to 2018, Eskom, the South African power utility, more than doubled the average domestic electricity price, increasing the financial burden on households and negatively impacting energy demand (Ye et al., 2018). The 2021 mid-year Council for Scientific and Industrial Research report supports this notion, in that the annual increase in demand for electricity in South Africa was only 5 percent in the year up to mid-2021 (Calitz & Wright, 2021). Ultimately, leapfrogging to renewable energy deserves more attention and should play a more significant role in endeavors aimed at the social and economic uplift of societies across the world. The following section introduces the South African scenario to highlight context-specific challenges and opportunities.

THE SOUTH AFRICAN SCENARIO

Despite price increases, South Africa is still more fortunate than other African countries. With the introduction of a new socio-political dispensation in 1994, South Africa's new government announced electricity provision for all as a priority for the country's economic growth and development. A national electrification program was hence prioritized (Essex & de Groot, 2019), reaching an electrification rate of 90 percent in 2018, reflecting an improvement from 58 percent in 1996. Researchers predict that by 2040 95.6 percent of South African households will have access to electricity (Hughes & Larmour, 2021). In rural areas, the percentage of the population with access to electricity has increased from 24 percent to more than 90 percent to date, hence leapfrogging the lifestyles of millions, including their ownership of commodities such as stoves, washing machines, microwave ovens, and television sets (Hughes & Larmour, 2021). Simultaneously, a steady increase in the household incomes of previously disadvantaged households since 1994 in South Africa has contributed to increased urbanization, as well as home ownership, resulting in soaring demand for household technologies. Electrical appliances, for example, became highly sought-after commodities, particularly among households that did not have access to such luxuries before (Nieftagodien & van der Berg, 2007). For many South Africans, this meant a choice explosion with an abundance of information, products, and ideas, thus leapfrogging households from a vintage form of technology such as cooking on wood-burning stoves, even skipping the current dominant technology forms, to the adoption of the most recent advanced technologies, such as induction cooking. Similarly, households that previously did washing by hand, collecting water in buckets from remote taps or streams, can now purchase a fully automatic, electronically programmed washing machine rather than a basic single- or twin-tub model. Table 8.1 indicates the appliance ownership of South African households, according to a survey conducted in 2021 (Hughes & Larmour, 2021). Evidence is undeniable of leapfrogging among low-income households whose ownership of induction stoves (14.4 percent) was slightly higher than the figures for middle-income households (10.9 percent) and almost on par with its adoption rate among high-income households (13.7 percent). Based on the complexity of induction cooking and the need to use specific cookware, one would not expect first-time users of electricity to adopt this technology first. However, compact induction hobs (cooktops) that users purchase separately are popular because they are smaller, cheaper to operate, and use less energy than conventional stove plates (Hughes & Larmour, 2021). Another common example of leapfrogging technology is the adoption of mobile cellphones without ever adopting a landline telephone system (Mu & Lee, 2005).

Table 8.1   Household appliance ownership (%)

Appliance	Tumble dryer	Washing machine	Dishwasher	Television	Fridge	Freezer
All households	19.1	76.1	14.3	92.1	98.0	35.5
Low income	10.6	51.7	5.3	84.4	94.2	20.9
Middle income	18.4	76.4	10.0	93.0	98.7	35.8
High income	26.6	90.6	25.6	95.0	99.8	45.3

Source: Adapted from Hughes and Larmour (2021).

While figures for appliance ownership in labor-saving categories, such as washing machines and dishwashers, are notably lower for low-income households compared to higher-income households, ownership of recreational equipment (television sets) and more essential appliances such as refrigerators differ only slightly. While almost twice as many high-income households possessed a separate freezer, it should be noted that many of these appliances are combination fridge-freezers, and therefore many low-income households in South Africa do indeed possess freezing facilities. Equally interesting is households' ownership of microwave ovens, where the possession almost doubled from 34.6 to 69.9 percent in low-income households between 2015 and 2021, with a smaller percentage increase for middle-income households (66.6 to 89.9 percent) and a slight decrease for high-income households (96.9 to 94.7 percent) during the same period (Hughes & Larmour, 2021). Low-income households, therefore, seem very susceptible to the benefits to be gained from modern, environmentally friendly technology. The unique situation in South Africa, compared to developed countries, is that many low-literate females work as domestic help in South African households, where they see and use modern technologies, while not owning these appliances themselves. In a typical upper-income household, a domestic helper would be expected to prepare household meals using a sophisticated stove (De Villiers & Taylor, 2019). Thereby, they become acquainted with the technology, even surpassing the employer's confidence levels, and are "groomed" to adopt novel technologies in their own homes. Some of the biggest advantages of technological leapfrogging for disadvantaged communities is that it provides a sense of empowerment as it expands their ability to make choices due to access to information and resources and their participation in change. It provides them a voice, as well as self-efficacy, and the belief that they can accomplish the things they want to do (Shankar et al., 2019). Alternative energy sources, and their application across all levels of society as a way to address shortcomings in energy supply as well as to leapfrog novel technologies, are discussed next.

ALTERNATIVE ENERGY SOURCES: NEW TRENDS

World Trends

Worldwide, attention to electrification programs has intensified the need to explore cleaner energy sources, of which solar and wind energy are the most accessible and affordable in South Africa. Because the generation of electricity from renewable sources confers many benefits, several developed countries are already optimizing these new sources. In Norway, for example, hydropower is used to produce more than 95 percent of the country's electricity (García-Gusano et al., 2016), Denmark is a leader in the production of wind-generated power, and Germany is significantly investing in solar power, despite limited solar sources (Schroeder & Chapman, 2014). In comparison, harnessing renewable energy resources (solar, hydro, wind, geothermal energy, and biomass) in Sub-Saharan Africa should produce cost savings and wider penetration of electricity. Unfortunately, these countries are still struggling to supply clean energy to poor households on a large scale. South Africa's strong reliance on coal for electricity production, for example, is severely criticized (TWI, n.d.). Wind farms are, however, very familiar in the Eastern Cape and parts of the Western Cape province in South Africa.

According to RAT (Hunt & Madhavaram, 2006, 2012), the supply of clean energy to poorer communities should entail strong initiatives from governing bodies and industry to avail the resources that are required to execute their plans, as well-organized interaction with communities will facilitate their understanding of the associated benefits of novel technologies.

Several examples of the successful application of alternative forms of energy in Africa exist, including interesting examples of leapfrogging (Lee, 2019). In Kenya, the so-called M-Pesa system has transformed the country's banking system into an efficient and convenient mobile banking and payment system. It provides financial services to millions of mobile phone owners with limited access to banking services. When linked to M-Kopa, a consumer can charge a cellphone to conduct business. M-Kopa generates electricity using a solar panel, a control unit, and a rechargeable radio, and has a USB port to charge cell phones as well as low-energy LED light bulbs that function perfectly in regions where infrastructure is underdeveloped and electricity supply is erratic. The technology uses SIM cards to provide solar energy products at affordable prices. M-Kopa makes it possible for children in rural areas to study and relieves households from the burden of fetching firewood for household energy purposes (Shapshak, 2016). M-Kopa has thus leapfrogged paraffin/kerosene-based lighting, bypassing grid-based electricity, and has advanced into off-grid renewable energies adapted to African conditions. In Jigawa, Nigeria, which is a semi-desert area with no water supply, water was generally lifted from open wells with ropes and buckets, hand pumps, or government-supplied diesel-powered pumps that frequently broke down. Solar-powered pumps, by contrast, are designed to run maintenance-free for up to ten years (Lee & Mathews, 2013). In Namibia, the O&L Group started to trade in retail and brewery, and later on diversified into dairy and solar energy, expanding quickly with government support to reach sales of approximately 4 percent of Namibia's GDP. The company intends to expand the wind power industry to counteract imports of electricity from South Africa and Angola (Lee et al., 2014).

Although the implementation of solar energy as a renewable energy source is cheaper compared to electricity, its penetration into rural African communities on a larger scale is often impractical due to a lack of proper maintenance and theft (Eales et al., 2017). RAT (Hunt & Madhavaram, 2006 2012) provides a relevant explanation for the failure of energy supply initiatives, in that conditions from the perspective of the consumer and the supplier need to be properly aligned. In rural Africa, this goal has not yet been realized.

Technology Transfer

An emerging concept when discussing alternative energy sources is "technology transfer," which involves the exchange of trademarked knowledge, tacit know-how, organizational practices, and technical equipment (Ogunlade et al., 2000). Accordingly, technology can be *transferred* fast (for example, when installing solar water heating systems (SWH) in areas that do not have electricity, leapfrogging them into the use and optimization of a novel technology), or can be introduced through *diffusion*, for example, within more fortunate communities to introduce novel technologies such as SWH more gradually to a community that wants to promote environmentally friendly energy sources so that it becomes increasingly familiar. The gradual introduction is a principle that is supported by RAT and proposes that strategies used by organizations should be introduced in a way that produces the best outcomes in a specific context (Hunt & Madhavaram, 2006, 2012).

In South Africa, solar energy has drastically improved the living conditions of millions of poorer households, reducing the strain on existing electricity resources, mitigating greenhouse gas emissions, and creating employment opportunities (Haselip et al., 2011). SWH supply to poor communities in South Africa is an example of revolutionary (strong) leapfrogging as the transition from the practice of water heating on open, wood-burning fires to the adoption of novel technology occurred fast and on a large scale across the country among new home-owners with the capabilities to benefit from it seamlessly. In this regard, leapfrogging is an effective way to shift to an environmentally friendly, sustainable mode of development (Lee, 2019; Wlokas, 2011).

SWH is also installed, however, in upmarket areas, nationwide, indicating the diffusion from electric geysers (household water heaters) that consume a lot of electrical energy to solar power. SWH installations have increased from 1 million in 2014 to around 5 million in 2020, equaling a 50 percent share of residential water heating in the country. Residential electricity consumption figures for South Africa, as reported on May 31, 2021, revealed that 13 percent of South African households owned SWH, while 10 percent had installed heat pumps to replace electric geysers. While overall 66 percent of households possessed electric geysers, the respective figures for low-income households were 33 percent, with 65 percent and 87 percent for middle- and upper-income households, respectively (Hughes & Larmour, 2021). Conversely, the introduction of solar systems into the households of wealthier, urban residents that already have electricity is often met with resistance because it is perceived to disrupt the lifestyles they are accustomed to due to problems encountered during periods of rainy weather causing resistance. To the contrary, underdeveloped communities do not have similar complaints, making them more receptive towards alternative energy systems (Lee, 2019).

The half-year updated report for 2021 of the Council for Scientific and Industrial Research revealed that energy demand in the country had increased by only 5 percent relative to the previous year, indicating good progress with South Africa's electrification program. Unfortunately, coal as a source of energy still dominates the country's energy mix (81.8 percent), with renewable energy sources contributing around 11 percent (Calitz & Wright, 2021).

THE FOURTH INDUSTRIAL REVOLUTION: A WINDOW OF OPPORTUNITY

Countries capable of developing and implementing innovations can optimize the Fourth Industrial Revolution as a new window of opportunity (Lee, 2013, 2019). At present, the majority of Fourth Industrial Revolution technologies tend to be initiated by advanced economies, and the response of latecomer economies has been slow or has taken place on a smaller scale, jeopardizing their eventual economic fortune. Countries that fail to grasp new opportunities – as proposed by RAT that emphasizes the best outcomes in a specific context should always take precedence (Hunt & Madhavaram, 2006, 2012) – will, unfortunately, fall behind, leaving poorer communities stuck in the low-income or middle-income trap (Lee, 2013). As far as African countries are concerned, time seems to be their worst enemy as change is not happening as fast as it should, due to multiple reasons that include corruption, elite stealing, and the draining of foreign aid, jeopardizing countries' social and economic development (Hogg, 2019). Hopefully, with foreign assistance, and per the principles of RAT, access to knowledge and funding will make it possible to leapfrog into newly emerging industries, such as renewable energy and the spectrum of technologies that are associated with the Fourth Industrial Revolution to decrease the gap between the rich and the poor (Lee, 2019).

THE WAY FORWARD

Concluding their energy consumption study that was conducted in the Netherlands, Verkade and Höffken (2017) explained that the introduction of novel technologies demonstrates the predicament of a "messy" reality where individual preferences, dependencies, and responsibilities are not always aptly aligned. While technological leapfrogging implies a multitude of exciting benefits, particularly in poorer countries, it mostly relies on the acceleration of industrialization and awareness of sustainable energy solutions in the more developed countries. Although access to solar heating, sophisticated cell phone technology, and electronic, pre-programmed household appliances sounds inviting, the diffusion of these technologies requires an understanding of the target population. Appliance manufacturers in Africa are often inundated with complaints arising from incorrect use and improper maintenance of appliances. Because repair costs are high, inexperienced consumers often replace appliances rather than have them fixed as they can pay for a new appliance over an extended period, while repair costs have to be settled immediately (Erasmus & Gothan, 2008). Consumers can become extremely frustrated, blaming the technology rather than the service provider when newly installed solar systems in rural communities lack the backing of a reputable service company. This has negative implications for new initiatives in the community.

More than three decades ago, Elias (1987) discussed changes in household technology, projecting that consumer facilitation would shift from "helping people to use technology" to "solving problems that are created by technology." Both conditions apply to consumers and technology suppliers in Sub-Saharan Africa. Transition management to convert from the traditional sources of energy and technology that people have become accustomed to over time and basic consumer education are essential to make technological leapfrogging a success. Without increased attention to education and transition management, this burden falls on innovators and suppliers, and leapfrogging in Africa is likely to take a slower and much more precarious path. To achieve success, it is crucial that every citizen understands how important it is to review our energy choices and to embrace environmentally friendly, more sustainable options such as solar energy and technologically advanced commodities that consume less electricity and water, and produce less waste, to preserve existing resources for future generations.

REFERENCES

Ackom, E.K., Larsen, T.H., & Mackenzie, G.A. (2016). Sustaining energy access: Lessons from energy plus approach and productive use in developing countries. Global Network on Energy for Sustainable Development. Summary for Policymakers. GNESD-SPM-E-Plus-12/2015.

Alderson, W. (1957). *Marketing behavior and executive action: A functionalist approach to marketing theory*. Home-wood, IL: Richard D. Irwin.

Alderson, W. (1965). *Dynamic marketing behavior: A functionalist theory of marketing*. Homewood, IL: Richard D. Irwin.

Amankwah-Amoah, J. (2015). Solar energy in Sub-Saharan Africa: The challenges and opportunities of technological leapfrogging. *Thunderbird International Business Review*, 57(1), 15–31.

Axsen, J., Tyree Hageman, J., & Lentz, A. (2012). Lifestyle practices and pro-environmental technology. *Ecology Economics*, 82, 64–74.

Axsen, J., Bailey, J., & Castro, M.A. (2015). Preference and lifestyle heterogeneity among potential plug-in electric vehicle buyers. *Energy Economics*, 50, 190–201.

Behera, B., & Ali, A. (2016). Factors determining household use of clean and renewable energy sources for lighting in Sub-Saharan Africa. *Renewable and Sustainable Energy Reviews*, 72, 661–672.

Bervoets, J., Boerstler, F., Dumas-Johansen, M., Thulstrup, A., & Xia, Z. (2016). Forests and access to energy in the context of climate change: The role of the woodfuel sector in selected INDCs in Sub-Saharan Africa. *Unasylva*, 67(246), 53–60.

Burger, R., Louw, M., De Oliveira Pegado, B.B.I., & Van Der Berg, S. (2014). Understanding consumption patterns of the established and emerging South African black middle class. *Stellenbosch Economic Working Papers*, 14(14). https://www.ekon.sun.ac.za/wpapers

Burlamaqui, L., & Kattel, R. (2016). Development as leapfrogging, not convergence, not catch-up: Towards Schumpeterian theories of finance and development. *Review of Political Economy*, 28(2), 270–288.

Calitz, J., & Wright, J.G. (2021). Statistics of utility-scale power generation in South Africa. H1-2021. http://hdl.handle.net/10204/12067

Chirambo, D. (2016). Addressing the renewable energy-financing gap in Africa to promote universal energy access: Integrated renewable energy financing in Malawi. *Renewable and Sustainable Energy Reviews*, 62, 793–803.

Conner, K.R. (1991). A historical comparison of resource based theory and five schools of thought within industrial organization economics: Do we have a new theory of the firm? *Journal of Management*, 17(1), 121–154.

Craviotoa, J., Yasunagab, R., & Yamasuea. E. (2017). Comparative analysis of average time of use of home appliances. 24th CIRP Conference on Life Cycle Engineering. *Procedia.* doi: 10.1016/j.procir.2016.11.248

Dagnachen, A.G., Lucas, P.L., Hof, A.F., & Vuuren, D.P. (2017). The role of decentralized systems in providing universal electricity access in Sub-Saharan Africa: A model-based approach. *Energy*, 139, 184–195.

Dagnachen, A.G., Lucas, P.L., Hof, A.F., & Vuuren, D.P. (2018). Trade-offs and synergies between universal electricity access and climate change mitigation in Sub-Saharan Africa. *Energy Policy*, 114, 355–366.

De Villiers, B., & Taylor, M. (2019). Promoting a positive work experience for South African domestic workers. *SA Journal of Human Resource Management/SA Tydskrif vir Menslikehulpbronbestuur*, 17, a1206.

Dziechciarz, J., Dziechciarz, M., & Przybysz, K. (2010). Household possession of consumer durables on background of some poverty lines: Classification as a tool for research, studies in classification, data analysis, and knowledge organization. Wroclaw: Wroclaw University of Economics and Business Publications.

Eales, A., Frame, D., Dauenhauer, P., Kambombo, B., & Kamanga, P. (2017). Electricity access options appraisal in Malawi: Dedza district case study. Paper presented at the 2017 IEEE PES Power Africa Conference: Harnessing Energy, Information and Communications Technology for Affordable Electrification of Africa, Accra, Ghana. http://sites.ieee.org/powerafrica/

Elias, J.G. (1987). Home economics and the growth of household technology. *Home Economics Forum*, Spring, 6–8.

Erasmus, A.C., & Gothan, A. (2008). Customers' judgment of the customer service in appliance sales departments in an emerging economy. *International Journal of Consumer Studies*, 32(6), 639–647.

Erasmus, A.C., Makgopa, M., & Kachale, M.G. (2005). The paradox of progress: Inexperienced consumers' choice of major household appliances. *European Advances in Consumer Research*, 7, 648–658.

Essex, S., & de Groot, J. (2019). Understanding energy transitions: The changing versions of the modern infrastructure ideal and the "energy underclass" in South Africa, 1860–2019. *Energy Policy*, 133, 110937.

Gallagher, K.S. (2006). Limits to leapfrogging in energy technologies? Evidence from the Chinese automobile industry. *Energy Policy*, 34, 383–394.

García-Gusano, D., Iribarren, D., Martín-Gamboa, M., Dufour, J., Espegren, K., & Lind, A. (2016). Integration of life-cycle indicators into energy optimisation models: The case study of power generation in Norway. *Journal of Cleaner Production*, 112, 2693–2696.

Giddens, A. (2013). *Modernity and self-identity: Self and society in the late modern age.* Chichester: Wiley.

Goldemberg, J. (2011). Technological leapfrogging in the developing world. *Georgetown Journal of International Affairs*, 12, 135–141.

Hackett, M.T. (2012). The everyday political economy of social enterprise: Lessons from Grameen Skakti in Bangladesh. PhD thesis, University of Adelaide. https://digital.library.adelaide.edu.au/dspace/bitstream/2440/83217/8/02whole.pdf

Haselip, J.A., Nygaard, I., Hansen, U.E., & Ackom, E. (2011). *Diffusion of renewable energy technologies: Case studies of enabling frameworks in developing countries.* Kongens Lyngby: Danmarks Tekniske Universitet, Risø Nationallaboratoriet for Bæredygtig Energi.

Hoeffner-Shah, K. (2020, March 17). Professors need to be flexible to successfully transition to online class. *The GW Hatchet.* www.gwhatchet.com/2020/03/17/professors-need-to-be-flexibleto -successfully-transition-to-online-class/

Hogg, A. (2019). Corruption is embedded in black elite circles, warns SA politics expert. www.biznews .com/thought-leaders/2019/03/12/corruption-embedded-black-elite-circles

Hughes, A., & Larmour, R. (2021, May 31). Residential electricity consumption in South Africa research project report, University of Cape Town. www.sanedi.org.za/

Hunt, S.D., & Madhavaram, S. (2006). The explanatory foundations of relationship marketing theory. *Journal of Business and Industrial Marketing*, 21(2), 72–87.

Hunt, S.D., & Madhavaram, S (2012). Managerial action and resource advantage theory: Conceptual frameworks emanating from a positive theory of competition. *Journal of Business & Industrial Marketing*, 27(7), 582–591.

International Energy Agency. (2017). World energy outlook. www.iea.org/reports/world-energy-outlook -2017

Kachale, M.G., Erasmus, A.C., & Sonnenberg, N.C. (2019). The sustainability of rural Malawi households' energy consumption practices amidst prevailing socio-economic conditions. UP Space Institutional Repository. https://repository.up.ac.za/handle/2263/73179

Kwac, J., Flora, J., & Rajagopal, R. (2018). Lifestyle segmentation based on energy consumption data. IEEE Transactions on Smart Grid, 9(4), 2409–2418.

Lee, J.W. (2013). The contribution of foreign direct investment to clean energy use, carbon emissions and economic growth. *Energy Policy*, 55, 483–489.

Lee, K. (2019). Economics of technological leapfrogging. Working paper 17/2019. Vienna: Department of Policy, Research and Statistics, Seoul National University and CIFAR Program on Innovation, Equity, & Prosperity, and United Nations Industrial Development. www.unido.org/api/opentext/ documents/download/16414872/unido-file-16414872

Lee, K., Juma, C., & Mathews, J. (2014). Innovation capabilities for sustainable development in Africa. In C.I. Monga & J.Y. Lin (Eds), *Handbook of Africa and economics.* Oxford: Oxford University Press.

Loorbach, D. (2010). Transition management for sustainable development: A prescriptive, complexity-based governance framework. *Governance: An International Journal of Policy, Administration, and Institutions*, 23(1), 161–183.

Lutzenhiser, L., & Gossard, M.H. (2000). Lifestyle, status and energy consumption. In *ACEEE summer study on energy efficiency in buildings.* Washington, DC: American Council for an Energy Efficient Economy. www.eceee.org/static/media/uploads/site-2/library/conference_proceedings/ACEEE_build ings/2000/Panel_8/p8_17/paper.pdf

Minnaar, U. (2021, September 27). A brief perspective on Eskom's electricity tariffs. www.energize.co .za/article/brief-perspective-eskoms-electricity-tariffs

Mu, Q., & Lee, K. (2005). Knowledge diffusion, market segmentation and technological catch-up: The case of the telecommunication industry in China. *Research Policy*, 34, 759–783.

Nieftagodien, S., & van der Berg, S. (2007). Consumption patterns and the black middle class: The role of assets. *Stellenbosch Economic Working Papers*, 02/07.

Ogunlade, B.M., Davidson, R., Martens, J., van Rooijen, S.N.M., & Van Wie, M.L. (2000). Methodological and technical issues in technology transfer. IPCC and UNFCCC. http://documentacion.ideam.gov.co/ openbiblio/bvirtual/005133/ipcc/tectran/IPCC_SRTT.pdf

Oparaocha, S. & Dutta, S. (2011). Gender and energy for sustainable development. *Current Opinion in Environmental Sustainability*, 3(4), 265–271.

Oseni, M. (2019). Cost of unreliable electricity to African firms: Energy for growth hub. www .energyforgrowth.org/memo/costs-of-unreliable-electricity-to-african-firms/

Ouedraogo, N.S. (2017). Africa energy future: Alternative scenarios and their implications for sustainable development strategies. *Energy Policy*, 106, 457–471.

Rahut, D.B., Behera, B., & Ali, A. (2017). Patterns and determinants of household use of fuels for cooking: Empirical evidence from Sub-Saharan Africa. *Energy*, 117(1), 93–104.

Rao, N.D., & Ummel. K. (2017). White goods for white people? Drivers of electric appliance growth in emerging economies. *Energy Research & Social Science*, 27, 106–116.

Schroeder, P.M., & Chapman, R.B. (2014). Renewable energy leapfrogging in China's urban development? Current status and outlook. *Sustainable Cities and Society*, 11, 31–39.

Schwarzinger, S., Bird, D.N., & Skjølsvold, T.M. (2019). Identifying consumer lifestyles through their energy impacts: Transforming social science data into policy-relevant group-level knowledge. *Sustainability*, 11, 6162.

Seim, B., & Robinson, A.L. (2019). Coethnicity and corruption: Field experimental evidence from public officials in Malawi. *Journal of Experimental Political Science*, 1–6.

Shankar, A., Elam, A., & Glinski, A. (2019). Women's energy entrepreneurship: A guiding framework and systematic literature review. *Energia International Network On Gender & Sustainable Energy*. www.energia.org/assets/2020/02/RA7-Womens-Energy-Entrepreneurship-Evidence-Report-Final .pdf

Shapshak, T. (2016). How Kenya's M-Kopa brings prepaid solar power to rural Africa. Enterprise Tech. www.forbes.com/sites/tobyshapshak/2016/01/28/how-kenyas-m-kopa-brings-prepaid-solar-power-to -rural-africa/?sh=7f82d58f2dbf

Sovacool, B.K., Bazilian, M., & Toman, M. (2016). Paradigms and poverty in global energy policy: Research needs for achieving universal energy access. *Environmental Research Letters*, 11, 064014.

Steinbuks, J., & Foster, V. (2010). When do firms generate? Evidence on in-house electricity supply in Africa. *Energy Economics*, 32, 505–514.

Strengers, Y. (2014). Smart energy in everyday life: Are you designing for resource man? *Interactions*, 21(4), 24–31.

Taale, F., & Kyeremeh, C. (2015). Households' willingness to pay for reliable electricity services in Ghana. *Munich Personal RPEc Archive*. Department of Economics, University of Cape Coast. https:// mpra.ub.uni-muenchen.de/65780/

Taulo, J.L., Gondwe, K.J., & Sebitosi, A.B. (2015). Energy supply in Malawi: Options and issues. *Journal of Energy in Southern Africa*, 26(2), 19–32.

Tigabu, A.D., Berkhout, F., & van Beukering, P. (2015). The diffusion of a renewable energy technology and innovation system functioning: Comparing bio-digestion in Kenya and Rwanda. *Technological Forecasting and Social Change*, 90, 331–345.

Tukker, A. (2005). Leapfrogging into the future: Developing for sustainability. *International Journal of Innovation and Sustainable Development*, 1, 65–84.

TWI. (n.d.). What is clean energy? How does it work? Why is it so important? www.twi-global.com/ technical-knowledge/faqs/clean-energy

UNDP. (2019). Beyond income, beyond averages, beyond today: Inequalities in human development in the 21st century. www.un-ilibrary.org/economic-and-social-development/human-development-report -2019_838f78fd-en

Verkade, N., & Höffken, J. (2017). Is the resource man coming home? Engaging with an energy monitoring platform to foster flexible energy consumption in the Netherlands. *Energy Research & Social Science*, 27, 36–44.

Walker, J.L., & Li, J. (2007). Latent lifestyle preferences and household location decisions. *Journal of Geographic Systems*, 9, 77–101.

Wlokas, H.L. (2011). What contribution does the installation of solar water heaters make towards the alleviation of energy poverty in South Africa? *Journal of Energy in Southern Africa*, 22(2), 27–39.

World Bank. (2018). Tracking SDG7. The energy progress report 2018. https://openknowledge .worldbank.org/handle/10986/29812

Wu, X. (2008). men purchase, women use: Coping with domestic electrical appliances in rural China. *East Asian Science, Technology and Society: An International Journal*, 2(2), 211–234.

Ye, Y., Koch, S.F., & Zhang, J. (2018). Determinants of household electricity consumption in South Africa. *Energy Economics*, 75, 120–133.

Zerriffi, H., & Wilson, E. (2010). Leapfrogging over development? Promoting rural renewables for climate change mitigation. *Energy Policy*, 38(4), 1689–1700.

9.   Can digital technologies help Africa to leapfrog its massive education gap?

Ali Parry and Wilma Viviers

INTRODUCTION

'Education is the great equaliser of the conditions of men,' said Horace Mann in the nineteenth century (Duncan, 2021). Indeed, education is widely regarded as both the bedrock of society and the springboard to professional and personal development. With a good education, many people – both younger and older – are able to recognise and exploit economic opportunities and find fulfilment in various forms of work and leisure activities. There is also a strong link between a country's level of economic development and the quality and equity of its education system.

Thus, education and economic well-being tend to go hand in hand. Many would say that the key distinction between developed and developing countries is their level of educational development and achievement. Investing in people's education pays dividends in the form of well-informed and productive societies as well as growing and sustainable economies. Yet while school attendance in developing countries has risen steadily over the years, there is a significant educational gap between developed and developing countries. A marked educational divide is also evident within most developing countries (Winthrop & McGivney, 2017).

Of all the regions in the world, Africa is the furthest behind in terms of educational achievement, with Sub-Saharan Africa's performance being the most disappointing. Of the roughly 60 million children of primary school-going age in the world who for various reasons do not go to school, 54 per cent live in Sub-Saharan Africa (UNESCO, 2018). Moreover, only about 29 per cent of students in Sub-Saharan Africa complete secondary school, compared with 41 per cent in South Asia, 63 per cent in Latin America, 64 per cent in the Middle East and North Africa and 73 per cent in East and South-East Asia (Cilliers, 2020). Another alarming statistic is that only four out of every 100 children in Africa are likely to enrol for postgraduate studies as young adults (United Nations, 2018). Girls and women are often discriminated against when it comes to educational opportunities on the continent.

Among the factors contributing to the parlous state of education in many African countries is a shortage of qualified and competent teachers and poor or non-existent infrastructure, which makes the process of teaching and learning very difficult. The debilitating effects of poverty on educational progress is a recurring theme. So, too, is the mismatch between school and university curricula and the knowledge and skills required by business. According to Winthrop and McGivney (2015), if current norms persist, it will take the average student in Sub-Saharan Africa almost 100 years to catch up with the average student in high-income countries in terms of years spent at school and level of knowledge attained. Building and equipping enough schools, educating enough teachers and investing enough money in the necessary infrastructure for Sub-Saharan Africans to catch up with their peers in other parts of the world will be enormously challenging and costly, as will be the task of overhauling academic curricula to make them more responsive to the changing world of work.

Clearly, conventional approaches to education on the continent need to undergo a paradigm shift – from the large-scale, government-funded education model to more focused initiatives aimed at producing cohorts of knowledgeable, skilled individuals capable of moving into in-demand jobs across all economic sectors. If Africa is lagging so far behind the rest of the world, should it be exploiting the technological leapfrogging phenomenon to catch up?

To many observers, Africa's mobile revolution in recent years is one of the clearest examples of leapfrogging in action. With the advent of mobile telephony, millions of Africans – long denied access to traditional landline services – have rapidly embraced mobile services and smartphones, enabling them to connect with others, communicate over long distances and transact in ways that were previously impossible. Leapfrogging in Africa is often associated with mobile money services, which allow individuals (many of whom are 'unbanked' in a formal sense) to use their mobile phones to transfer money, secure loans and receive payment for services rendered. The bridging of the gap in the financial services arena has broadened economic activity and helped to accelerate development in several African countries. Leapfrogging is also evident in sectors such as energy, health and agriculture, where the use of data analytics and artificial intelligence is helping businesses to become more productive and to satisfy market demand more cost-effectively (World Bank, 2017; Pilling, 2018).

There is no clear consensus, however, on whether education lends itself well to leapfrogging – particularly in Africa. After all, education is traditionally long term in nature, with knowledge acquired in a progressive, linear fashion – at least at the primary and secondary school levels. Moreover, many African countries still lack the basic requirements for productive, online learning experiences: a reliable electricity supply, appropriate telecommunications infrastructure and accessible (including affordable) digital devices and internet services. The question can therefore be asked:

> Can digital technologies help Africa to leapfrog its massive education gap, connect more people to quality jobs and create more inclusive societies?

That is the question we ponder in this chapter. To this end, we present a cross-section of views on the plausibility of leapfrogging in an educational context, and the implications for Africa, given its specific needs and circumstances. We also provide selected examples of leapfrogging in the educational sphere and conclude with some policy recommendations.

EDUCATION IN THE DIGITAL AGE

Traditionally, education was seen as the preserve of schools, universities and other tertiary institutions. However, in recent years – with the quickening pace of digital adoption, especially in the wake of the COVID-19 pandemic – education has become a more fluid concept, referring to a wide range of intellectual achievements attained through different means. Education covers formal academic programmes as well as vocational courses, on-the-job training, mentoring, self-paced learning and other interventions aimed at building knowledge and skills in a non-linear fashion.

Furthermore, successful countries embrace the concept of lifelong learning; they do not see education as being focused only on the youth (although in Africa's case, putting the youth dividend to good use must be a key policy objective). Continuing professional development helps people, younger and older, to continuously adapt to change, which is often driven by technology. With the digital era having made information much more freely available, self-learning has become a core feature of education today and has helped to fuel entrepreneurial activity in many countries and boost the 'gig' economy.

The Fourth Industrial Revolution is no longer a new phenomenon, but it continues to evolve and has changed the economic landscape irrevocably, bringing in its wake untold new opportunities but also critical challenges. As the digital age gains momentum, educational content (the what) and educational delivery methods (the how) are becoming more and more interdependent. This means that people need to acquire the necessary knowledge and competencies to cope in fields that are increasingly technology driven. At the same time, teaching and learning opportunities need to be accessible. COVID-19 has been devastating for many, but it has shown the world how it is possible – and indeed desirable – to embrace virtual communication and online learning as substitutes for, or supplements to, traditional face-to-face interventions.

Technology on its own, however, will not transform the education landscape in Africa. Strong educational outcomes are dependent on a wide range of factors, from the calibre of teachers and the allure of the teaching profession in general to the ease with which individuals can engage in learning pursuits (either physically or virtually). Ultimately, good governance – which broadly refers to structures and processes that ensure transparency, inclusiveness and accountability (UNESCO, 2022) – influences the effectiveness of education policies and outcomes in a country.

The fact that Africa trails the rest of the world in its educational standards and performance, which has in turn exacerbated its 'digital divide', has been attributed to poor policies, poor governance and insufficient investment in education, among other factors (Cilliers, 2020). According to the African Development Bank (2020), many African countries spend a considerable amount on education but, compared with other regions, this expenditure is low relative to the size of their populations. In fact, the amount that African governments spend on education per student is the lowest in the world, which is exacerbated by generally low economic growth rates and large numbers of children of school-going age. Moreover, Africa is widely regarded as the least efficient region for education spending, which suggests that governments have prioritised quantity over quality of education (African Development Bank, 2020).

Clearly, simply spending more money on education, including that aimed at building digital knowledge and skills, will not necessarily improve a country's economic circumstances. According to Harvard economist Ricardo Hausmann, 'rich countries are rich not just because of education, and conversely, investing in education alone won't make you rich' (Centre for Enterprise Development, 2017, p. 3).

The internet is a practically limitless source of knowledge on every conceivable topic, which means that internet connectivity should be at the core of African countries' education strategies. Yet most African countries were late starters in terms of internet adoption, resulting in an initial lag in the widespread application of digital platforms and devices for education purposes. It is interesting to note the growth in the share of the population using the internet in a range of African countries between 2000 and 2017/2018: Tunisia (2.75–66 per cent), Seychelles (7.4–58 per cent), Egypt (0.6–57 per cent), South Africa (5.35–56 per cent), Ghana (0.15–37 per cent), Kenya (0.32–23 per cent), Rwanda (0.06–22 per cent) and Ethiopia (0.02–18 per cent) (Ritchie, 2019). While some of these growth rates seem impressive, they come off a very low base and do not necessarily signal rising internet usage for educational or professional purposes.

Notwithstanding the critical role played by the internet in modern life, even in the digital age internet connectivity is not enough. Hausmann (Centre for Enterprise Development, 2017) largely attributes the differences in education levels between developed and developing countries to how they *apply* knowledge. It is the quality of education, and not the quantity, that counts (Centre for Enterprise Development, 2017).

LEAPFROGGING IN AN EDUCATIONAL CONTEXT

Whether or not leapfrogging can be successfully applied to education has prompted a fair amount of debate in the literature. However, authors appear to focus primarily on education at the secondary school and tertiary levels and not education in the broadest sense of the word, which caters for different age groups and stages in life (Carbone, 2018; Istance & Paniagua, 2019; Winthrop & Ziegler, 2019; Ezumah, 2020).

In Africa's case, where the traditional (government-funded), linear approach to education has steadily deteriorated and is now too costly to repair, the idea of harnessing and applying innovative technologies in non-linear ways to expand educational delivery and enhance out-comes is very appealing (Winthrop & Ziegler, 2019). Yet there are few short cuts to finding sustainable employment and making a meaningful economic contribution – particularly if people lack basic literacy, numeracy and life skills.

Put simply, leapfrogging in an educational context involves the use of technological inno-vation to create better, more holistic learning experiences which in turn help to fast-track people's entry into the job market or, if already there, to enhance their professional status and mobility (Winthrop & Ziegler, 2019). It does not mean that the fundamentals – at a personal level and a societal level – can be overlooked. This is important to remember given the con-tinent's well-publicised shortcomings in basic education and skills (including digital skills) development, internet connectivity and business- and investor-friendly policies and laws (World Bank, 2017; Ezumah, 2020). In other words, leapfrogging does not enable a country to side-step crucial stages in its development or compensate for past developmental failures.

The fact that the mobile phone has become ubiquitous in Africa and the continent has undergone (what many people refer to as) a mobile revolution in recent years, does not mean that the majority of African countries are destined to become e-commerce or fintech hubs. Nevertheless, certain countries have developed considerable appeal as regional digital hubs. For example, both Twitter (African News, 2021) and Google (Asemota, 2018) have established their African headquarters in Accra, Ghana, while the e-commerce giant Jumia (operating from Lagos in Nigeria) has extended its reach to about 13 other African countries, including South Africa, Egypt and Kenya (Oyesola, 2021).

Ultimately, leapfrogging is less about skipping key stages on a country's developmental journey (such as transitioning from an agriculture-based economy to a service-based one, and bypassing manufacturing) and more about using technology to acquire – comparatively rapidly – a new competitive edge within one or more sectors. This might involve, for example, adding value to agricultural output through agro-processing or using online teaching to reach a wider audience of students, thereby making education more equitable (World Bank, 2017).

Several authors assert that technological leapfrogging has a role to play in education, and that it is becoming increasingly urgent in the face of the widening education and skills gaps in societies around the world. Istance and Paniagua (2019) make a strong case for the process to start at the foundational (school) level, where inequality in teaching and learning is often painfully apparent. They maintain that innovative approaches to education must 'take place in the mainstream of schooling, and not be confined to tinkering around the experimental margins' (p. 11). Such innovative approaches might include helping students, using various pedagogies and assessment techniques, to acquire deep understanding (as opposed to superficial knowledge), to creatively adapt conventional learning methods to new challenges and to solve unfamiliar problems.

Istance and Paniagua (2019) therefore advocate that innovation in education should focus on making young people flexible and adaptable so that they can cope with (and even thrive in the face of) turbulence and uncertainty, but not at the expense of acquiring an in-depth understanding of important subjects and disciplines. To them, it is the traditions, policies and teaching and learning practices that stoke inequality in education systems around the world that need to be leapfrogged. Much of the problem with education in different parts of the world, particularly in Africa, originates in the limitations of educators themselves who are ill equipped to teach the basics, let alone prepare students for unfolding twenty-first-century challenges (Winthrop & Ziegler, 2019). Poor educational infrastructure is another major drawback in many parts of Africa (World Economic Forum, 2015).

Winthrop and McGivney (2017) see leapfrogging as any means of accelerating the bridging of skills inequality, although they do not narrowly subscribe to the view that leapfrogging allows one to skip steps to make more rapid progress. Rather, innovative approaches should enable people to follow different, quicker (yet still well-considered) paths. They go on to argue that leapfrogging in education is made complicated by the fact that it does not merely involve adding new skill sets to an existing system; instead, it involves rethinking education systems altogether.

Sarabhai and Vyas (2017) present a number of case studies where technological leapfrogging has had a positive impact on climate change mitigation and inclusive development efforts in the countries concerned. We will mention two of these.

In the 1970s, Brazil pioneered the bus rapid transport system, comprising a dedicated corridor for buses on busy roads and separate bus stations, which offered the advantages of a light rail system but at a lower cost. This model has since been replicated in more than 200 countries, providing a convenient and cost-effective transport solution to millions of commuters.

In the 1980s, Barefoot College, an Indian non-governmental organisation, and Solar Sister, a social development agency operating in several African countries, launched an initiative to integrate women into the solar energy sector. While Barefoot College trains largely uneducated women from rural areas in the installation, use and maintenance of solar-powered equipment (including lanterns, cookers and water desalination systems), Solar Sister provides entrepreneurial training, equipping African women with the skills to market the products in their communities. This has gone a long way towards making remote villages, which would otherwise be energy-deprived, more self-sufficient.

In each of these case studies, education has played a significant role, evidenced in extensive knowledge sharing among stakeholders and efficient project execution. The technological leapfrogging effort has been broad-based, with local governments, private-sector contractors and communities all thrown into the mix. Among the key lessons that can be drawn from these studies are that educational leapfrogging needs to focus on capacity-building, both at the individual and institutional level, and that public awareness and acceptance of the transformation process are paramount.

However, some authors are less sanguine about the merits of leapfrogging, suggesting that it may even be missing the point. As Alzouma (2005, p. 351) remarks: 'ICTs [information and communication technologies] cannot leapfrog beyond the ordinary development problems Africans are faced with. Introducing computers in rural areas, for example, does not automatically solve the problem of illiteracy, health-related problems or poverty. The solutions to these problems reside outside of the realm of technology.' Pilling (2018) is critical of those leapfrogging proponents who view technology as the answer to many of Africa's most intractable problems, choosing to downplay the harsh reality of infrastructural and governance failings.

Unwin (2018), in turn, expresses concerns about the image that leapfrogging conveys – that is, using someone else's back to gain an advantage over them. He even goes so far as to suggest that rich countries are in fact leapfrogging over the poor countries by unfairly benefiting from access to their large markets and lower labour costs, which has exacerbated (and not bridged) their economic and digital divides. The fact that poor countries lack the resources to develop homegrown ICT sectors and have to rely heavily on ICT imports and international service providers such as Apple, Google and Amazon is a case in point (Unwin, 2018).

In their study on the rate of adoption of learning management system technology to support blended and online e-learning in Sub-Saharan Africa, Bervell and Umar (2017) found that a positive attitude towards such technology on the part of educators and students had a major impact on the adoption thereof. This in turn hinged on the availability of ICT facilities and training. For example, South Africa, Ghana and Nigeria, which have invested quite heavily in ICT solutions for the education sector in recent years, emerged as stronger proponents of learning management system technology than many other countries in the region, which lagged behind on the ICT infrastructure and literacy fronts.

South Africa, in particular, is home to a growing number of companies that are leveraging digital technologies to facilitate learning and self-improvement in a number of spheres. For example, Obami (www.obami.com), a technology company based in Johannesburg but with a global reach, offers a range of services in the digital teaching and learning space – from online courses to entrepreneurship and productivity improvement programmes.

It is true that technology and innovation, used in a leapfrogging sense, are not an antidote to poor policy decisions and a long legacy of developmental or market failures. However, they can provide some novel solutions to old problems and help to scale up access to economic opportunities (Istance & Paniagua, 2019).

LEAPFROGGING: THE SOLUTION TO AFRICA'S EDUCATION SHORTCOMINGS?

Labour markets are constantly changing, with COVID-19 having compounded the situation by creating the need for very different skill sets and working styles. Education naturally needs to follow suit. While stories of technological breakthroughs in Africa abound, from innovative drone applications to solar energy solutions, these successes need to be replicated on a massive scale, supported by appropriate policy and regulatory frameworks. Moreover, existing educational or technological bottlenecks need to be cleared.

As digital transformation surges ahead and technologies like robotics, artificial intelligence, 3D printing and cloud computing become more pervasive, critical thinking and analytical skills will be ever more in demand as many traditional jobs fall away and people are forced to move into different occupations that may require more complex and cognitively demanding work. African countries cannot afford to waste any time in rethinking their traditional approaches to education. Looking ahead, the extent to which technology is used both as a medium of instruction and as a way to develop skills and encourage mobility in the job market will be a strong determinant of a country's success.

In offering their views on whether Africa is capable of transforming so that it becomes part of the global knowledge society, Holmner and Britz (2013) reference two significant challenges that the continent faces: the 'last mile problem' and the 'longest mile problem'. The former relates to how Africa can connect people to the global body of knowledge through digital means. The latter relates to how Africa can ensure that people use information in optimal ways while also creating new knowledge, which includes generating useful research outputs that complement the existing body of knowledge.

We are of the view that whereas African countries have made strides in tackling the last mile problem in recent years – evidenced in the rapid spread of mobile technologies on the continent and a marked increase in the rollout of broadband connectivity – the longest mile problem has proved more difficult to address. As a result, human capacity development in Africa has fallen behind that of many other regions. Not only has this produced a largely unskilled workforce, but African countries are generally importers of knowledge – often from developed countries, whose histories and circumstances stand in stark contrast to the realities in Africa.

From an educational standpoint, addressing Africa's last mile and longest mile problems require both technical and human-centred solutions.

Technology and Innovation Initiatives

There are encouraging signs that several African countries are taking technology training and development seriously. For example, a growing number of technology/innovation hubs are springing up for the purposes of launching technology initiatives in different sectors and/or giving support to start-ups to help them gain traction in the marketplace. Such hubs (largely concentrated in South Africa, Kenya, Rwanda, Nigeria and Egypt) provide a foundation for accelerated and highly focused learning, which is a hallmark of the leapfrogging phenomenon. These five countries are regarded as the leaders in digital adoption in Africa, according to Mastercard's African Leapfrog Index (Mastercard Center for Inclusive Growth, 2019).

There were more than 600 technology hubs across Africa at the end of 2019, covering institutional categories like incubators, accelerators, innovation centres and technology parks (GSMA, 2019). For example, FabLabs (an initiative of the Massachusetts Institute of Technology in the United States, with one of the labs situated in South Africa) manage a platform that enables local entrepreneurs to test their technology prototypes (Chandler, 2016; Kühn, 2021).

Another internationally backed programme that has been introduced in Africa – designed to promote greater collaboration in education ecosystems – is the Broadband Commission for Sustainable Development. This is a joint venture between the International Telecommunication Union and UNESCO, the World Bank's Digital Economy for Africa initiative (World Bank, 2020) and the African Development Bank–Microsoft Coding for Employment initiative, which forms part of its Jobs for Youth in Africa strategy (African Development Bank, 2016). According to the World Bank, the success to date of several technology/innovation hubs in Africa is due to their enjoying the support of multi-party ecosystems instead of being backed only by the government or the private sector (Liu, 2019).

Admittedly, these sorts of programmes and initiatives need to be rolled out much more extensively, in many more African countries, if they are to make a real difference on the ground. Importantly, too, they cannot take the place of broad-based education at the foundational (school) level, which is where the seeds of technological appreciation and entrepreneurship should be sown. Governments therefore have a crucial role to play – creating an enabling environment that supports innovation, sets appropriate standards and attracts investment (including cross-border investment) to develop high-potential sectors, enhance infrastructure and improve skills development (Travaly & Muvunyi, 2020). If governments are remiss in this regard, African countries will see the departure of high-end, skilled jobs and capable people to other parts of the world where they are in demand (Naudé, 2017).

Education Ecosystems

The fact that leapfrogging is powered by technology means that educational transformation on the continent must be the responsibility of an extended 'education ecosystem'. An education ecosystem as depicted in Figure 9.1 can be described as a collection of stakeholders participating in the education process (either as practitioners or as facilitators) who have a vested interest in the quality of outputs (Naudé, 2017). It comprises elements that are internal and external to an educational institution, which in turn fall within the broader technological, political/economic, business/investment and policy/regulatory environments. Internal elements include educators, management, technical and administrative staff, buildings and equipment. External elements include policymakers and regulators, funders and investors, technology service providers, industry associations, commercial enterprises, students and participants, laws, policies and regulations, infrastructure, digital platforms and devices, intellectual property and research outputs (Campbell & Rozsnyai, 2002; Mueller & Toutain, 2015; Naudé, 2017).

For educational leapfrogging to be effective, therefore, the various stakeholders in the education ecosystem (particularly government, private-sector employers and the education community) need to work together, ensuring that their respective strategies and technological tools are well integrated and geared to a common purpose. Having sound and responsive education policies and regulations – which are harmonised with other policy and regulatory frameworks (energy, telecommunications, trade, investment and others) – is paramount. Moreover, getting the basics right in various spheres – electricity generation, internet connectivity, infrastructure development, rural development, financial inclusion and so on – is non-negotiable if African countries wish to catch up with more technologically agile countries elsewhere in the world.

Technological environment

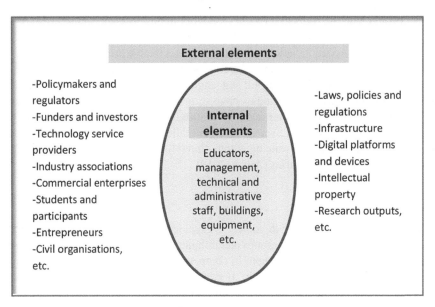

Source: Adapted from Kühn (2021, p. 277).

Figure 9.1   An education ecosystem

Ideological Compatibility

The new educational paradigm in Africa also needs to be one in which governments and private-sector actors cooperate more effectively in bringing technology to formal education and training institutions, as well as to businesses and individuals. Leapfrogging involves a collective effort, but responsibilities and accountability nevertheless need to be apportioned in line with different entities' mandates and areas of expertise. Where digital technologies are concerned, it is natural to assume that this will mainly be the domain of the private sector. However, technological developments in the education arena need to be guided by and should also help to inform a country's economic and trade policy, digitalisation policy, competition policy, small business development policy and so on.

At the core of the collaborative partnerships that fuel an education ecosystem there should be compatible ideologies. For example, whether and how the adoption of digital technologies, such as automation, may threaten different types of jobs is a significant concern to government and private-sector stakeholders alike. However, governments' attempts to delay inevitable job losses (which have socio-political consequences) by deterring investment in and development of at-risk sectors will only worsen the situation in the long run and leave a sector (or country) further behind.

Education can and must be a powerful lever to prepare society for the 'inevitable' by equipping people with the skills to do traditional work in new, more effective ways or to move into entirely new professions. According to the World Economic Forum (2017), jobs that are currently trending in Africa include food technologists, creative artists, data centre personnel, health-care workers, 3D designers and educators. Furthermore, sectors poised for job-related growth include ICT (especially design and engineering), infrastructure development and the green economy. Interestingly, studies have shown that Africa is at less risk of job losses through automation than many other regions because its level of industrialisation is comparatively low. As a result, there are fewer so-called 'middle-segment' job holders who risk being made redundant in the face of advancing automation (Hjort & Poulsen, 2019; Strydom, 2021), as is the case in developed countries (Autor, 2019).

Inclusivity

Education should act as a unifier in society – capable of taking people from disparate geographical, socio-economic and age groups and imbuing them with facts, insights and analytical and practical skills that will enable them to compete on a more level playing field and make inroads into diverse fields of endeavour. If education is not inclusive and remains largely reserved for, say, the urban elite, it will accentuate existing divisions in society.

Given the serious economic fissures that characterise most African countries, the ability of leapfrogging to re-energise and expand education on the continent needs to be considered in terms of its potential to speed up the process of making education job-relevant and inclusive. This is an important call to action which is echoed in United Nations Sustainable Development Goal 4 which states: 'Ensure inclusive and equitable quality education and promote lifelong learning opportunities for all' (UNESCO, 2018; United Nations Division for Sustainable Growth, 2020).

A Knowledge Society

'Human capital development forms the cornerstone of a knowledge society and is essential for sustainable development and economic growth' (Holmner & Britz, 2013, p. 122). This is a simple yet profound acknowledgement that knowledge – how people internalise and use the information at their disposal – is the foundation of a well-functioning and sustainable economy. This applies just as much to policymakers, business leaders, educators, skills development specialists and facilitators as it does to students and programme participants. Building human capital is a long-term endeavour, which coincides with the philosophy of lifelong learning.

While the digital age tends to evoke images of electronic devices, robots and other machines displacing humans, it is at the same time giving humans new opportunities and new roles. Far from making people redundant, the digital age needs people more than ever. Certainly, leapfrogging is dependent on the successful coexistence of human-centred knowledge and foresight, on the one hand, and appropriate technologies, on the other. Technology can augment the education process, but humans must drive it.

Therefore, governments and other economic stakeholders need to be able to create conditions in which people can become part of the knowledge economy, failing which the transformational power of the digital age will be lost. The most severely affected will unfortunately be marginalised groups in Africa (such as women, youth and rural inhabitants – especially if unemployed) who need to make the most profound leap in accessing economic opportunities and a more promising future.

IN CLOSING

Finding ways for African countries to bridge the gap between the educational shortcomings of the past and the knowledge, skills and technology requirements of the future will be a major challenge. Even the best practices from around the world may not fit Africa's historical circumstances and future aspirations. A delicate balance is required to accommodate a wide range of vested interests.

What is interesting is that private education (at the primary, secondary and tertiary levels) is showing strong growth in Africa. With most African governments facing severe financial constraints, private education could be a game changer when it comes to tackling the huge skills deficit on the continent, with time- and cost-efficient technologies playing a major role in this regard. One in five students in Africa already receives private-sector education (Caerus Capital, 2017). To meet the enormous demand for knowledge and skills in the years ahead, African governments must engage more fully with the private sector in their thinking, planning and execution. There are encouraging signs, but successful initiatives need to be replicated on a much grander scale in Africa and become the rule rather than the exception.

The digital age presents an unprecedented opportunity to proactively design the future. Yet education stakeholders in Africa need to remember that while digital technologies can make things possible, *people* are still required to make things happen.

REFERENCES

African Development Bank. (2016). *Jobs for youth in Africa strategy 2016–2025*. www.afdb.org/fileadmin/uploads/afdb/Documents/Boards-Documents/Bank_Group_Strategy_for_Jobs_for_Youth_in_Africa_2016-2025_Rev_2.pdf

African Development Bank. (2020). *African economic outlook 2020*. https://afdb.org/en/documents/african-economic-outlook-2020

African News. (2021). *Ghana to host Twitter's first Africa office*. 24 April. www.africanews.com/2021/04/12/ghana-to-host-twitter-s-first-africa-office//

Alzouma, G. (2005). *Myths of digital technology in Africa*. December. www.researchgate.net/publication/239551594_Myths_of_Digital_Technology_in_Africa_Leapfrogging_Development

Asemota, V. (2018). *'Ghana is the future of Africa': Why Google built an AI lab in Accra*. Marketplace Africa, 15 July. https://edition.cnn.com/2018/07/14/africa/google-ghana-ai/index.html

Autor, D. H. (2019). Work of the past, work of the future. *American Economic Review*, 109, 1–32.

Bervell, B., & Umar, I. (2017). A decade of LMS acceptance and adoption research in Sub-Saharan African higher education: A systematic review of models, methodologies, milestones and main challenges. *Eurasia Journal of Mathematics, Science and Technology Education*, 13(11).

Caerus Capital. (2017). *The business of education in Africa*. Report. https://edafricareport.caeruscapital.co/thebusinessofeducationinafrica.pdf

Campbell, C., & Rozsnyai, C. (2002). *Quality assurance and the development of course programmes*. UNESCO European Centre for Higher Education Papers on Higher Education. www.researchgate.net/publication/44829801_Quality_Assurance_and_the_Development_of_Course_Programmes

Carbone, G. (2018). *A vision of Africa's future: Mapping change, transformations and trajectories towards 2030.* www.amazon.com/Vision-Africas-Future-Transformations-Trajectories/dp/8867058266

Centre for Enterprise Development. (2017). *Is South Africa about to make an historic mistake?* Presentation by Ricardo Hausmann, June. www.cde.org.za/wp-content/uploads/2018/06/CDE-Insight-Professor-Ricardo-Hausmann-Is-South-Africa-about-to-make-a-historic-mistake.pdf

Chandler, D. (2016). *3 questions: Neil Gershenfeld and the spread of FabLabs.* Massachusetts Institute of Technology. https://news.mit.edu/2016/3-questions-neil-gershenfeld-fab-labs-0104

Cilliers, J. (2020). *Africa first! Igniting a growth revolution.* Jonathan Ball.

Duncan, A. (2021). *Education: The great equalizer.* www.britannica.com/topic/Education-The-Great-Equalizer-2119678

Ezumah, B. (2020). *Critical perspectives of educational technology in Africa: Design, implementation and evaluation.* Palgrave Macmillan.

GSMA. (2019). *618 active tech hubs: The backbone of Africa's tech ecosystem.* www.gsma.com/mobilefordevelopment/blog/618-active-tech-hubs-the-backbone-of-africas-tech-ecosystem/

Hjort, J., & Poulsen, J. (2019). The arrival of fast internet and employment in Africa. *American Economic Review, 109*(3), 1032–1079.

Holmner, M., & Britz, J. J. (2013). *When the last mile becomes the longest mile: A critical reflection on Africa's ability to transform itself to become part of the global knowledge society.* https://repository.up.ac.za/handle/2263/40389

Istance, D., & Paniagua, A. (2019). *Learning to leapfrog: Innovative pedagogies to transform education.* Center for Universal Education at Brookings, September. www.brookings.edu/wp-content/uploads/2019/09/Learning-to-Leapfrog-InnovativePedagogiestoTransformEducation-Web.pdf

Kühn, M.-L. (2021). Rethinking Africa's education ecosystem: Why all economic sectors need to be digitally responsive. In W. Viviers, A. Parry & S. Jansen van Rensburg (Eds), *Africa's digital future: From theory to action* (pp. 271–302). AOSIS.

Liu, A. (2019). *Africa's future is innovation rather than industrialisation.* World Economic Forum on Africa, September. www.palgrave.com/gp/book/9783030537272

Mastercard Center for Inclusive Growth. (2019). *Getting lions to leapfrog: Understanding the role of technology in promoting inclusive growth in Africa.* 6 September. www.mastercardcenter.org/press-releases/african-leapfrog-index

Mueller, S., & Toutain, O. (2015). *The outward looking school and its ecosystem.* www.researchgate.net/publication/295402886_The_Outward_Looking_School_and_its_Ecosystem

Naudé, W. (2017). *Entrepreneurship, education and the Fourth Industrial Revolution.* IZA Institute of Labor Economics discussion paper 10855, June. www.iza.org/publications/dp/10855/entrepreneurship-education-and-the-fourth-industrial-revolution-in-africa

Oyesola, B. (2021). *Africa's Amazon.* D & C Development Cooperation, 24 September. www.dandc.eu/en/article/nigerian-e-commerce-platform-jumia-has-been-making-difference-consumers-lives-nine-years

Pilling, D. (2018). African economy: The limits of 'leapfrogging'. *Financial Times,* 13 August. www.ft.com/content/052b0a34-9b1b-11e8-9702-5946bae86e6d

Ritchie, H. (2019). *How many internet users does each country have?* Our World in Data, 22 January. https://ourworldindata.org/how-many-internet-users-does-each-country-have

Sarabhai, K., & Vyas, P. (2017). The leapfrogging opportunity: The role of education in sustainable development and climate change mitigation. *European Journal of Education Research, Development and Policy, 52*(4), 427–436.

Strydom, P. D. F. (2021). Digital technologies, employment and labour-market polarisation in Africa. In W. Viviers, A. Parry & S. Jansen van Rensburg (Eds), *Africa's digital future: From theory to action* (pp. 101–127). AOSIS.

Travaly, Y., & Muvunyi, K. (2020). *The future is intelligent: Harnessing the potential of artificial intelligence in Africa.* Brookings Foresight Africa 2020 series. www.brookings.edu/blog/africa-in-focus/2020/01/13/the-future-is-intelligent-harnessing-the-potential-of-artificial-intelligence-in-africa/

UNESCO (United Nations Educational, Scientific and Cultural Organization). (2018). *Accountability in education: Meeting our commitments: Global education monitoring report summary 2017/8.* https://

reliefweb.int/report/world/global-education-monitoring-report-20178-accountability-education-meeting-our

UNESCO (United Nations Educational, Scientific and Cultural Organization). (2022). *Concept of governance*. International Bureau of Education. www.ibe.unesco.orgen/geqaf/tecnical-notes/concept-governance

United Nations. (2018). *Africa grapples with huge disparities in education: Higher enrolment numbers mask exclusion and inefficiencies*. www.un.org/africarenewal/magazine/december-2017-march-2018/africa-grapples-huge-disparities-education

United Nations Division for Sustainable Growth. (2020). *Sustainable Development Goals knowledge platform*. https://sustainabledevelopment.un.org/index.html

Unwin, T. (2018). *Why we shouldn't use terms such as 'bridging the digital divide' or 'digital leapfrogging'*. 3 October. https://unwin.wordpress.com/2018/10/03/why-we-shouldnt-use-terms-such-as-bridging-the-digital-divide-or-digital-leapfrogging/

Winthrop, R., & McGivney, E. (2015). *Why wait 100 years? Bridging the gap in global education*. Brookings. www.brookings.edu/research/why-wait-100-years-bridging-the-gap-in-global-education/ Brookings

Winthrop, R., & McGivney, E. (2017). *Can we leapfrog? The potential of education innovations to rapidly accelerate progress*. Brookings. https://files.eric.ed.gov/fulltext/ED583015.pdf

Winthrop, R., & Ziegler, L. (2019). Leapfrogging to ensure no child is left without access to a twenty-first century education. In H. Kharas, J. W. McArthur & I. Ohno (Eds), *Leave no one behind: Time for specifics on the Sustainable Development Goals*. Brookings. www.jstor.org/stable/10.7864/j.ctvkjb38h

World Bank. (2017). *Leapfrogging: The key to Africa's development? From constraints to investment opportunities*. http://documents1.worldbank.org/curated/en/121581505973379739/pdf/Leapfrogging-the-key-to-Africas-development-from-constraints-to-investment-opportunities.pdf

World Bank. (2020). *Digital economy for Africa*. Newsletter, Spring. https://thedocs.worldbank.org/en/doc/b618f9ef700dde6e605c994f2170b704-0360022021/original/DE4A-newsletter-Spring-2021-spread-Final.pdf

World Economic Forum. (2015). *3 steps that can fix education problems in Africa*. 8 June. https://weforum.org/agenda/2015/06/3-steps-to-fix-education-in-Africa

World Economic Forum. (2017). *The future of jobs and skills in Africa: Preparing the region for the Fourth Industrial Revolution*. 3 May. www.weforum.org/reports/the-future-of-jobs-and-skills-in-africa-preparing-the-region-for-the-fourth-industrial-revolution

10. Digital leadership skills that South African leaders require for successful digital transformation

Asmitha Tiekam[1] and Hugh Myres

INTRODUCTION

The impact of technology and disruptive innovation has grown enormously over the years (Bughin & Van Zeebroeck, 2017). Organisations have to implement the relevant technologies and ensure successful digital transformation or they face being displaced by their competitors (Fitzgerald et al., 2013; Bughin & Van Zeebroeck, 2017; Jardim, 2020). As organisations now compete in a volatile and disruptive digital world, many struggle to achieve the core benefits of these technologies for their businesses (Fitzgerald et al., 2013).

However, digital transformation is not about the technologies alone. Rather, a key component is the leadership and digital leadership skills required to drive successful digital transformation of an organisation (Kane, 2019). Leaders are finding that their traditional leadership skills are no longer sufficient and that they have to become digital leaders and acquire the necessary skills to take their organisations forward and ensure their survival (Uhl-Bien et al., 2007). Digital transformation in Africa can help leapfrog the current legacy system challenges and leadership competencies through gaining the skills needed to accelerate digital transformation (African Union, 2020; Digital Economy for Africa Initiative, n.d.). In this chapter, we explore what digital leadership skills South African leaders require to carry out successful digital transformation.

According to Uhl-Bien et al. (2007, p. 298), 'We're in a knowledge economy, but our managerial and governance systems are stuck in the Industrial Era'. Many leaders want to achieve

[1]   A special acknowledgment is made to Professor Ethné Swartz, from the Feliciano School of Business, Montclair State University in New Jersey, and Professor Caren Brenda Scheepers from the Gordon Institute of Business Science (GIBS) under the University of Pretoria in Johannesburg, for recognising my research as a valuable addition to this book, and for all their invaluable guidance, support and help in drafting this chapter. This opportunity would not have been possible without both your recognition, and I am grateful for this opportunity.

To Hugh Myres from GIBS, my supervisor, thank you for your positivity, guidance, support and help in writing up this chapter.

Finally, a HUGE thank you to my Maker, The Almighty, and my family, my Mum and my Boys (Dad, Dipesh, Pranay and Aariv), for being my inspiration, strength and motivators on this journey! This is for you all, especially you, Mum!

transformation of their organisation through the new technologies, but not all leaders know how to bring about this transformation (Iordanaglou, 2018). This is because the innovative digital technologies such as mobile technologies, social media, implanted devices and cloud services demand more diverse mindsets (growth mindsets) and skillsets than previous generations of technology (Fitzgerald et al., 2013).

South Africa, as elsewhere, has only a small percentage of digital leaders (BusinessTech, 2018). Many South African CEOs, according to a report by audit firm PricewaterhouseCoopers (PWC) in 2018, have expressed their concern about the inadequate level of digital skills among managers in their organisations that hampers digital transformation (see also ITWeb, 2018). High-performing leaders need more diverse skills and competencies than before. However, most organisations have not progressed fast enough to encourage leadership growth and development of existing and future digital skills for leaders (Deloitte, 2017).

Africa is a continent of economic opportunity due to its large youth population. Many believe this cohort can help drive digital transformation and assist in eliminating poverty, create more job opportunities and use technology to transform its socio-economic sectors (African Union, 2020; Digital Economy for Africa Initiative, n.d.). Some successful African companies such as Flutterwave.com, the Nigerian financial technology company, and MTN, the South African telecommunications giant, are examples of companies that have embraced digital transformation. These companies have utilised their understanding of the African market and combined this with their technological skills and leadership mindset to make huge strides.

This chapter explores the literature around digital transformation in Africa and South Africa, and the various forms of leadership and digital leadership skills. We then discuss the research approach that guided our research with 17 South African leaders who have carried out digital transformation successfully in their organisations and who have embraced the opportunity to leapfrog industrial-era management and thinking. Those data inform the findings on the type of leader and digital leadership skills required for successful digital transformation. Complexity Leadership Theory (CLT) undergirds our theoretical approach, and we explore whether adaptive leadership is relevant for the disruptive environment of digital transformation. The Skills Strataplex by Mumford et al. (2007), which is a study of leadership skills over the decades, is used as a foundation to understand if traditional leadership skills still apply.

The chapter concludes with a discussion of the Adaptive Digital Leadership Skills Model that we developed based on what South African digital leaders believe is the ideal that a leader should possess to carry out successful digital transformation.

LITERATURE REVIEW

Digital Transformation

Digital transformation, with all its rapid new technological advances in disruptive technologies, such as mobile computing, virtual reality, sensory embedded devices and robotics, impact the way we work and how leadership is executed in the workplace. Leaders have realised they now need new skills and new ways of leading (Schwarzmüller et al., 2018). However, digital transformation is not only about the technology. It involves many other factors such as having a good strategy that drives better operational performance (Hess et al., 2016; Kane et al., 2015a) and leadership is critical for running successful digital transformation (Kane, 2018). Additionally, a forward-looking perspective and a change-orientated mindset is key (Kane et al., 2015a), developing the talent of the people so that they may become the next digital leaders, encouraging them to develop the right skillset and empowering them to think differently (Kane, 2018).

Furthermore, leadership needs to leverage their organisations' components, including processes, structure and culture, to create safe environments for experimentation (Kane, 2018; Kane et al., 2016). In this regard, Kane et al. (2018) advised that experimentation plays a vital role in ensuring successful digital transformation. In essence, 'digital transformation isn't a single effort but rather a portfolio of initiatives that work together to scale the change' (Kohnke, 2018, p. 70). This therefore illustrates that digital transformation is not a once-off effort, but happens continually.

We have now explored the factors of digital transformation. In the next section we will explore the African and South African contexts of digital transformation which determine leapfrogging into the digital era.

Digital transformation in Africa

It is critical that African organisations learn to digitally transform themselves, and do so successfully, in order to be able to compete on the global stage, or they risk being left behind or becoming obsolete. Such an eventuality would increase the digital divide between Africa and the rest of the world (Christensen, 2006; Jansen van Rensburg et al., 2021; Weiling & Wei, 2004). There are African companies that have upstaged multinational corporations in Africa in their field. These African companies have understood the African context better, made good management decisions and strategies and, in some cases, utilised their digital and collaboration skills to compete (Dupoux et al., 2015).

MTN is one such example. Its strategic intent is 'Leading digital solutions for Africa's progress'. During its expansion into Nigeria, it gained an additional 50 million customers on the continent (Dupoux et al., 2015), making the customer base in Africa 272 million customers in 20 markets in Africa as of the end of September 2021 (MTN, 2021). In contrast, its competitors focused more on risks than opportunities presented by the continent that held them back from achieving that market share (Dupoux et al., 2015).

Digital transformation is therefore a key opportunity for Africa to drive innovation, sustainable growth and reduce poverty and create jobs in Africa. The use of digital technologies and gaining the right skills has the potential to unlock many opportunities, create jobs and allow access to services and innovation which was not possible in the past, and give Africa an opportunity to leapfrog into the knowledge era (African Union, 2020; Digital Economy for Africa Initiative, n.d.).

There has been much progress in Africa in terms of internet access where, as recently as the year 2000, Africa had less internet bandwidth than Luxembourg, a very tiny country in Europe (Arderne et al., 2019). In 2010 only 9.3 percent of Africa was using the internet, in 2017 only 22 percent of the African continent had access to internet and in 2020 an average of 31.7 percent had internet penetration, with only seven countries having under 10 percent internet penetration. This is quite significant if compared to South Asia that has about 35.3 percent internet penetration (Armstrong, 2022; Ndemo & Weiss, 2017). Overall this constitutes an

8500 percent increase in internet penetration from the end of 2000 to mid-2017 for Africa (Ndemo & Weiss, 2017).

This suggests that Africa is well on its way to solving at least some problems of access to the internet, without which the African Union's strategy for digital transformation[2] is impossible to implement. Lack of connectivity also threatens the achievement of Agenda 2063 and the Sustainable Development Goals[3] (African Union, 2020; Digital Economy for Africa Initiative, n.d.).

However, in order to achieve the African Union's goals of digital transformation, countries and companies must ensure that people have the right digital skills. Africa's population comprises 60 percent youth, of whom about 375 million will be entering the work force by 2030. By harnessing digital skills, businesses and the people of Africa will benefit in the future. This will also be Africa's leap frogging opportunity, as the continent does not have many legacy challenges to overcome compared to other more technologically advanced countries (African Union, 2020; Digital Economy for Africa Initiative, n.d.).

Digital transformation in South Africa
South African businesses are slow at adopting digitalisation (ITWeb, 2018). This has been attributed to the rapid change of the business landscape and pressure to innovate, thereby resulting in organisations hesitating to react to the change (Kohnke, 2018; Vey et al., 2017). This hesitance to adapt is confirmed by research conducted by Fitzgerald et al. (2013), which showed that the main reasons for many organisations not adopting digital transformation, or failing to implement it correctly, is the absence of a vision, roles and responsibilities not being clear, and a lack of leadership skills. There is also no sense of urgency by leadership to achieve digital transformation (Fitzgerald et al., 2013).

Wright (2019) states that South African organisations are trying to deal with their huge legacy system issues or are struggling to figure out how to get onto the digital transformation path, while there are other companies that are leading the race due to creativity or competition, like MTN and Vodacom, the mobile telecommunications giants. Most organisations are aware of the need to digitally transform, but many are held back due to legacy systems, lack of leadership and digital foresight and shortage of skills (Deloitte, 2017; ITWeb, 2018; Wright, 2019). This affects the consumer as they are losing out from cost and product perspectives, particularly in the financial services and telecommunications sectors.

In the 2018 Global Competitive Index 4.0 rankings, South Africa dropped five places from 2017 and was ranked 67th out of 140 countries in terms of its global competitiveness, with Sub-Saharan countries still ranked the lowest when it comes to competitiveness, innovation and technology transformation (Schwab, 2018).

Many leaders want to achieve transformation of their organisation through new technologies, but only some leaders know *how* to bring about this transformation (Iordanaglou,

---

[2]   This is Africa's Digital Transformation Strategy to be achieved between 2020 and 2030. See document at https://au.int/en/documents/20200518/digital-transformation-strategy-africa-2020-2030.

[3]   Agenda 2063 and the Sustainable Development Goals relate to the goals that the United Nations adopted for the world as a universal call to action to end poverty, protect the planet and ensure that by 2030 all people enjoy peace and prosperity. The African Union has incorporated part of this in their Digital Transformation Strategy 2020–2030. See https://www.undp.org/ and https://au.int/en/documents/20200518/digital-transformation-strategy-africa-2020-2030.

2018). This is because innovative digital technologies such as mobile technologies, social media, implanted devices and cloud services demand mindsets that are more diverse (growth mindsets, learner mindsets, challenger mindset) and different skillsets compared to previous generations of technology (Fitzgerald et al., 2013). Companies like Apple, Google, Amazon and Starbucks illustrate where leaders execute digital transformation well. In Africa and South Africa, companies like MTN, Vodacom, Nigeria's Dangote Cement, the Moroccan diary company, Copaq, Bidco and others have embraced forward thinking, growth mindsets, skillsets and strategies in their industries. Additionally, they use technology and data to advance their businesses in Africa and compete effectively against multinational competitors (Dupoux et al., 2015). However, Wright (2019) argues that transformation varies widely among industries.

Therefore, in order to leapfrog into this knowledge era and compete on the global stage, it is important that African leaders allow this learning to take place by acquiring the correct digital leadership skills, and understanding the kind of leader they need to be, to carry out successful digital transformation and maintain these skills. In so doing the people of their organisations will think and behave according to the actions of their leaders, thus creating a new digital-ready organisational culture (Christensen, 2006; Weiling & Wei, 2004).

Digital Leadership

As time has passed and technology has evolved, so have the roles and capabilities of leadership. Leaders have realised that they cannot lead and manage organisations as they did in the past. Their skills and competencies also need to adapt and change with the times to ensure successful organisations and a competitive advantage. In the past traditional leadership was designed to lead for efficiency and effectiveness, and organisations were led to operate as complicated and siloed units in predictable commercial environments (Deloitte, 2017). In today's digital age, the environment is much more unpredictable and disruptive. Leadership has to adapt to these environments based on the context of the situation (Uhl-Bien, 2021). Effective leaders drive all activities in an organisation. Therefore, according to Uhl-Bien et al. (2007; see also Uhl-Bien, 2021), knowledge development, adaptability and innovation are relevant in organisations.

The sections below expand on the various types of leadership suitable for digital transformation and the leadership required for the digital age.

Adaptive leadership

Adaptive leadership was developed so that people could learn how to resolve their own problems and challenging situations (Böck & Lange, 2018). Leaders use adaptive leadership styles to bring about change at the organisational, societal or individual level (Northouse, 2006).

Adaptive leadership, also known as effective leadership (Uhl-Bien et al., 2007) or flexible leadership (Yukl & Mahsud, 2010), has been defined as a change in behaviour that emerges when individuals face various interactions, networks, interdependence and complex, constantly changing environments (Uhl-Bien et al., 2007). In a continuously changing environment, leaders are expected to deal with new challenges, and need to adapt their leadership style and their organisation to this new environment (Kane, 2018). To meet this complexity in their work environments knowledge-era leaders need 'a change in thinking away from individual, controlling views, and toward views of organizations as complex adaptive systems that enable continuous creation and capture of knowledge' (Uhl-Bien et al., 2007, p. 301). Lichtenstein and Uhl-Bien (2006) build on this notion of complexity theory and illustrate that leadership is more than a competency, but rather emerges through continuous interactions in various environments.

CLT frames how leadership enables the learning, creative and adaptive capacity of complex adaptive systems, where adaptive leadership is key. CLT offers a new approach to understanding leadership that has moved from the industrial era to new ways of leading in the knowledge era (Uhl-Bien et al., 2007). There are three types of leadership that CLT recognises: (1) administrative leadership that relates to the administrative activities creating a plan, building a vision, finding resources and managing the strategy; (2) adaptive leadership that relates to being adaptable, being a creative problem solver and learning from complex adaptive systems; and (3) enabling leadership which enables parts of adaptive leadership and creativity (Uhl-Bien et al., 2007). According to CLT, these three leaderships are intertwined.

Digital leadership

Digital leadership is defined as what leaders do right strategically to ensure the success of digitalisation for the organisation and its business environment (El Sawy et al., 2016). Digital leaders stand out from other leaders as they require a combination of new skills, attitudes, knowledge and different experiences. These leaders need a vision for what they want to achieve, must be searching locally and globally for solutions, must have a passion for what they do and must possess a hunger for constant learning from both their competitors and their peers (Goethals et al., 2003).

Additionally, a digital leader must be competent in using modern communications technology, be able to guide the people in their organisations and in society to use it correctly to communicate and make proper use of the information they gather (Van Outvorst et al., 2017). Digital leaders need to be more open and transparent in their communication due to the nature of the rapidly changing information and their ability to assess the quality, reliability and validity of the information they are receiving (Van Outvorst et al., 2017).

Digital leadership is therefore an amalgamation of digital culture and digital competence, and can be grouped into five areas:

> i) Thought leader, having the ability to be tough in facing market and competition change; ii) Creative leader, having the creativity and innovation mindset to formulate the idea into reality; iii) Global visionary leader, being able to provide direction and become an orchestra in transforming the digital business transformation; iv) Inquisitive leader, having the learning capability to face complex and dynamic ecosystems due to volatility, uncertainty, complexity, and ambiguity (VUCA) factors; v) Profound leader, having in-depth knowledge and comprehension to make interpretations and assumptions, and synthesising of information in making decision. (Mihardjo et al., 2019, p. 1750)

In this knowledge era digital leaders need these new digital competencies to lead their organisations effectively (Deloitte, 2017), but most organisations have not progressed fast enough to develop and encourage digital leaders to build new ways of leading. Strong digital leadership is very much in demand (Kane et al., 2018).

Leadership Competencies

Leadership skills Strataplex

Leadership skills are described by Mumford et al. (2007, p. 155) as 'stratified by organisational level, and a complex of multiple categories called a Strataplex, which captures the stratified and complex nature of leadership skill requirements and their relationship with the level in the organization'. The Skills Strataplex can be divided into four different categories, namely: cognitive skills, interpersonal skills, business skills and strategic skills:

1. *Cognitive Skills* are a leader's most important skill (Mumford et al., 2007, 2017). This entails basic skills that relate to cognitive capabilities such as gathering, understanding and distributing information and learning. These skills entail speaking so as to communicate appropriately, listening skills to understand the context, written communication and learning skills and critical thinking skills, which entails using logic to analyse various situations (Mumford et al., 2007).
2. *Interpersonal skills* are the social skills of interacting and influencing others with negotiation skills, persuasion skills and co-ordinating oneself and others (Mumford et al., 2007). Interpersonal skills also include the emotional intelligence aspect of connecting with others at an emotional level such as being self-aware, self-managing oneself by being adaptable, social awareness and empathy of all around and social skills of managing conflict, collaborating and people skills (Goleman, 2000; Riggio & Lee, 2007).
3. *Business Skills* relate to the area of the leader's work that involves management decisions such as managing personal resources as well as financial resources (Mumford et al., 2007). Business and business networking skills are highly important.
4. *Strategic skills* relate to conceptual skills needed to understand complexity by taking a systems perspective. This entails looking at alternative options for solving problems (Mumford et al., 2007). Digital leadership needs to provide a vision and purpose so their people know what to follow (Kane, 2019). However, having a strong vision alone is not sufficient – leaders must be able to execute this vision and have good governance in place. Leaders therefore do not need to be technically savvy, but must have good digital literacy and understanding in order to set the vision (Kane, 2016).

These skills are the foundation of traditional leadership and possibly the foundation of developing as a digital leader.

Adaptive leadership skills

According to complexity theory, organisational learning and leadership development theory, adaptive leadership comprises the following knowledge and competencies: organisational knowledge and interdependencies; strategic thinking; ability to control personal feelings; comfort during uncertainty and ambiguity; listening and communication skills; and conflict resolution (Doyle, 2016). Much of these competencies are similar to and overlap with the Skills Strataplex in terms of cognitive, interpersonal and strategic skills.

However, adaptive leaders need additional competencies that involve understanding different situations (cognitive complexity and systems thinking) and being flexible when faced with instances that require a change in strategy or behaviour (Yukl & Mahsud, 2010). This entails social intelligence skills to understand the leadership situation, openness to learn and grow from feedback to better oneself and always be open to learning to grow themselves. Interpersonal skills, conceptual skills and technical skills are necessary for most leadership roles, however, the importance of these skills varies depending on the situation to which the leader needs to adjust (Yukl, 1989).

Digital leadership competencies
There are multiple digital leadership competencies required for successful digital transformation. Many of these competencies align to the four core skills of the Skills Strataplex again in terms of strong business skills, excellent communication skills, good strategic thinking skills and a strong business acumen (Kappelman et al., 2016).

Additionally, digital leaders need to be flexible and adaptable to their circumstances and comfortable with constant change and unpredictability. They must also listen to their surroundings and understand their environment, and be able to influence (Goethals et al., 2003; Kane et al., 2015a). This illustrates that digital leaders align to CLT and that the adaptive leadership skills of leaders adjusting their behaviours in response to changes in their environment is also critical.

However, as per Goethals et al. (2003), digital leaders are more open and result-orientated than earlier leaders, which entails competencies such as being able to see things from various angles, being truly passionate about what they do, being more collaborative, focused on their own priorities while seeking common ground with other leaders in other areas and learning about things unknown to them. Digital leaders therefore need a combination of new knowledge, skills and attitudes that allow them to work across silos and cross-collaborate, but still remain morally and ethically grounded in their ways (Goethals et al., 2003).

Additionally, Kane et al. (2018) suggest that an organisation's culture is critically important to leverage digital technologies in the workplace. However, a characteristic that most organisations lack, and which is needed to do the aforementioned, is that of 'willingness to experiment and take risk' (Kane et al., 2015b, p. 40). This relationship between digital technologies and organisational culture requires a certain mindset, and leveraging these digital technologies successfully, as digital transformation is not a once off, requires a mindset shift. Digital leaders do not therefore have to be technically savvy, but must have good digital literacy, be curious and foster a different way of thinking (Kane et al., 2015a).

Overall, the similarities between digital leadership and adaptive leadership are clearly visible. The core foundational Strataplex skills are also required as per CLT. A leader's adaptability and ability to change their thinking based on changes in their environment, as well as how they respond, differentiate a digital leader from a traditional one. Additionally, a leader who creates a safe space to learn, experiment and most importantly drives a growth and learning mindset for themselves and their people to grow in is a key differentiator from traditional leadership to digital leadership.

METHODOLOGY

To understand the digital leadership skills required by South African leaders, and the kind of leader required, we adopted a qualitative, exploratory approach of in-depth, semi-structured, face-to-face interviews. The research strategy, design, sample selection and analysis reinforced the selected approach. The University of Pretoria's Gordon Institute of Business Science Ethical Clearance Committee approved the research before we conducted any interviews.

Population

The objective of the research was to target any organisation in any industry that had been directly involved in implementing successful digital transformation, so they could then provide an overview of leadership skills and competencies required for successful digitalisation, as limited literature existed in this field in a South African context. The population originated mainly from Johannesburg and the surrounding areas of Pretoria and Rustenburg, and from Cape Town. The objective of taking different companies from different industries was to ensure a broader perspective and gain wider insight, which allows a stronger foundation than only gathering content from a single organisation (Haffke & Benlian, 2016).

Unit of Analysis

The unit of analysis for this research was the perceptions and experiences of the leadership who were involved in digital transformation. Understanding their digital leadership skillsets, the kind of leader one has to be, was a critical factor for the research and theory contribution to understand and address the three constructs of digital transformation, leadership and skills needed.

The Sample

We used purposive sampling that allowed the researcher to collect data for a specific purpose from a specific type of sample that would be suitable for that research purpose only (Robinson, 2014; Saunders & Lewis, 2018).

One of the authors used networks and relationships with senior leaders to source initial interviews with individuals who had carried out successful digital transformation in their organisations. Recommendations of other acquaintances were also requested from the researcher's current network, and existing respondents interviewed. This then gave rise to the snowball effect of finding more contacts in the field (Robinson, 2014; Saunders & Lewis, 2018). The final sample consisted of 17 leaders who were the key leaders of digital transformation in their organisations. The leaders were of senior level and executive level and had been involved in successful digital transformation. The sample group included industries from several sectors, such as mining, manufacturing, fast-moving consumable goods, insurance and medical aid, the freight industry, investment houses and retail. The aim was to understand the general digital skills required by leadership across various industries. The banking industry was excluded as past research of a similar nature had been conducted by Duburu (2018).

The sample size included three women and 14 men. The individuals interviewed were chief information officers (CIOs), a chief operational officer (COO), chief digital officers (CDOs), managing directors (MDs) of companies, directors of digital transformation, heads of information technology (IT) or digital transformation officers and a head of human resources (HR). These individuals were chosen as they were responsible for, or drove, digital transformation in their respective organisations. All face-to-face interviews took place in a boardroom environment except one, which occurred at a coffee shop. The four interviews that were online video calls were also conducted in boardroom environments. Table 10.1 provides details of all respondents.

Table 10.1   List of interviewees and their industry

Interviewee	Position	Industry sector
P1 (Female)	CIO	Manufacturing
P2 (Female)	Head of Technology	Mining
P3 (Male)	MD of Technology Division	Investment
P4 (Female)	Head of IT and Business Process Management	Freight
P5 (Male)	Head of Information Management	Mining
P6 (Male)	CIO	Online legal contracts
P7 (Male)	Digital Transformation Officer	Retail
P8 (Male)	CIO	Investment
P9 (Male)	CDO	Retail
P10 (Male)	MD	Software/IT
P11 (Male)	Head of HR Business Partnering for South Africa	Mobile/ICT
P12 (Male)	COO of Organisation	Investment and health-care provider
P13 (Male)	CDO for Group IT	Investment and health-care provider
P14 (Male)	MD/Head of Digital Supply Chain	Software/IT
P15 (Male)	CIO	Soft drinks/beverages
P16 (Male)	Head of Digital Innovation	Retail
P17 (Female)	Digital Transformation Director	Alcoholic beverages

Sector	Number of companies	Gender	Job title
Investment	4	4 males	MD of Technology Division CIO, COO of Organisation, CDO for Group IT
Mining	2	1 female, 1 male	Head of Technology, Head of Information Management
Retail	3	3 males	Digital Transformation Officer, Head of Digital Innovation, CDO
Beverages	2	1 male, 1 female	CIO, Digital Transformation Director
Software/ICT	4	4 males	CIO, MD, Head of HR Business Partnering for South Africa, MD/Head of Digital Supply Chain
Logistics	1	1 female	Head of IT and Business Process Management
Manufacturing	1	1 female	CIO
Total	*17*	*3 females, 14 males*	

The Research Instrument

The research instrument was a set of 12 interview questions, which were based on research questions that participants answered as openly and exploratorily as possible, drawing on their current and past experiences of carrying out a successful digital transformation. The interview guide's main use was consistency. We asked the various leaders in each of the organisations the same questions, thus ensuring the content validity and reliability throughout the research approach (Saunders & Lewis, 2018). We conducted 17 semi-structured, in-depth, face-to-face interviews. Interviews were recorded and then transcribed. The interview time varied based on the individual interviewed. The longest interview took about 75 minutes and the shortest interview took 30 minutes. On average, interviews lasted approximately 45 minutes. In this research, saturation occurred by the 12th interview; however, we completed 17 interviews to reaffirm data saturation.

FINDINGS

What Is Leadership's Understanding of Digital Transformation?

This research question set the context of the interview. The aim of this question was to gauge South African leadership's understanding of digital transformation in line with the technologies that relate to it, and to gauge the relevance and importance of digital transformation to their organisations.

Overall, the respondents concurred that their understanding of digital transformation was about changing the way you worked, so that you serve the customer in the most interactive ways, reduce costs and increase revenue, because of new business models. Digital transformation is also a continuous process, and not a once-off implementation.

What Are the Factors That Contribute to a Leader Carrying Out Successful Digital Transformation?

The objective of this research question was to understand what were the key factors that contributed to the success of digital transformation in the respondent's organisation. This research question sought to understand examples of successful digital transformations carried out by the leaders of the relevant organisations and, based on that, what factors South African leaders regard as being key contributors to their organisations' successful digital transformations.

Organisation examples of digital transformation

One of the main reasons for choosing these particular leaders for this research was to learn from their experience of successful digital transformations that they had implemented, and then identify what contributed to this success. The details of the transformation for each leader's organisation varied; however, for most, it was a journey of implementing various technologies in the form of system automation and a change in business processes occurred. This entailed the use of mobile technologies, the use of robotics and implanted/sensory technologies, digitalisation of supply chain processes, big data analysis technology, social media implementations, systems automations that integrated with big data technologies and cloud upgrades, bringing about significant change.

Factors contributing to successful digital transformation
In light of the various digital transformation technologies that the various leaders implemented in their organisations, a plethora of factors that contributed to their success emerged. A frequency count could not be done as each factor varied based on each leader's context of successful digital transformation implemented. However, the most emphasised factors as per the respondents, in no particular order, are as follows:

* leadership buy-in;
* learning from failure;
* big data;
* employing the right people;
* culture; and
* collaboration across silos.

Nearly all of the respondents believed that no digital transformation is successful without the support and buy-in of senior leadership, as confirmed by the Head of IT at a freight company: 'The first is the leadership. For any change, as long as you don't have the buy-in of the leadership, you are in big trouble' (P4, Head of IT and Business Process Management, Freight, Female).

A few respondents mentioned that leadership that listens to people and understands the customer, user and the environment is paramount. Close to half of the respondents believed that the collaboration of teams across the once-siloed way of working brings about success in digital transformation. The majority of the respondents mentioned that they had to learn to fail, but had to learn from these failures. Leaders also have to think quickly and take opportunities when they arise or risk losing them: 'one has to take a risk sometimes to make something work' (P9, CDO, Retail, Male).

The Importance of Leadership and the Kind of Leader Required for Digital Transformation

This research question was asked to understand if South African organisations consider leadership to be important in digital transformation or if there are other factors. Based on this, the next objective was to understand what kind of leader is required for successful digital transformation to occur.

Respondents were unanimous in regarding leadership as a key driver in carrying out any change successfully. As one Head of IT mentions: 'So leadership is key to ensuring that any change is driven successfully' (P2, Head of Technology, Mining, Female).

Several descriptions emerged regarding the kind of leadership required for successful digital transformation. A unique mention was that a leader must be a unicorn, generous/servant leader. Figure 10.1 lists the top characteristics for the kind of leader that is ideal for carrying out successful digital transformation, based on a frequency count done on the mention of the kind of leaders by the respondents.

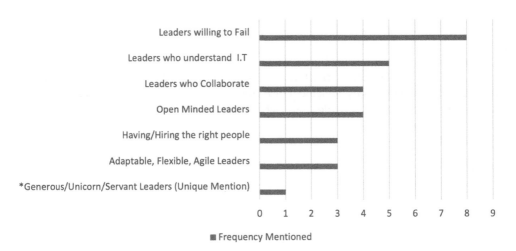

Figure 10.1   Kind of leadership required for successful digital transformation

To What Extent Does Adaptive Leadership Contribute to Digital Transformation?

Most respondents described adaptive leadership as the sort of leadership that adapts to the context of the situation, is situationally aware, is contextual, adapts to situations and understands the environment and acts accordingly. As confirmed by the Head of IT for a mining company: 'It's a leader basically that has context of the environment, that understands contextually what the environment is, assesses the environment and acts accordingly' (P2, Head of Technology, Mining, Female).

Each respondent's understanding of adaptive leadership varied; however, the common underlying notion was that adaptive leaders work with what comes their way, adapt to situations, are open minded and understand the different aspects of their business that change with time. Adaptive leadership was also defined as flexible and agile by many of the respondents. The concept of failing was mentioned by many of the leaders, with a leader needing to learn to fail quickly and cheaply coming up again for adaptive leadership.

Adaptive leadership relevance and skills

Adaptive leadership was considered relevant for digital transformations, but almost all of the respondents considered it critical. The key skills required for successful digital transformation through adaptive leadership are listed in Figure 10.2 according to their importance and the number of times they were mentioned. The main skills identified were a high tolerance and willingness to fail, understanding and accepting technology, having a learner mindset, being agile and being open minded/open to new ways of thinking and doing. Most of the respondents mentioned and ranked highly the need to have a growth, learner and open mindset.

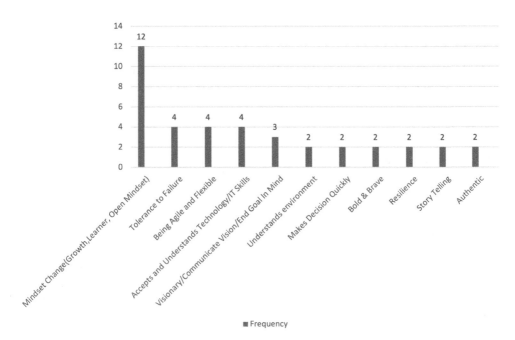

Figure 10.2   Adaptive leadership skills

What Is Leadership's Understanding of Digital Leadership, and What Digital Leadership Skills Are Needed for Successful Digital Transformation by South African Leaders?

This research question focuses on gaining an understanding of what digital leadership is, and attempts to gauge if this digital leader is seen differently from traditional leaders, which is addressed by interview question 7. The research question also aimed at understanding the various respondents' understanding of the four skills of the Skills Strataplex, namely cognitive, business, influencing and strategic, which relate to interview question 8. Gaining an understanding of the digital leadership skills that South African leaders should have, along with which skills are important and which were the key skills used in their organisation for carrying out successful digital transformation, is also addressed through interview questions 9, 10 and 11, respectively.

Respondents' understanding of digital leadership

The majority of respondents shared the perspective that digital leadership was being a leader who needed to adjust to the technologies they are leading and adapt to the digital times they are in. However, a few respondents believed that *digital leadership* is how leaders should be now and cannot be different from *leadership*. In the words of the CIO of a digital legal company: 'every company is an IT company now, so I don't think you can separate leadership from digital leadership' (P6, CIO, Legal, Male).

Another key theme that most respondents mentioned was that digital leadership is about the way that leaders think. A mindset shift is key to digital leadership and leaders have to adjust to the digital way of doing things. Therefore, most respondents regarded digital leadership as a leadership type that embraces digital change and technology, and which needs to change based on context.

Most respondents believed that digital leaders are different from traditional leadership. However, a few respondents did see digital leadership as being the way leaders need to be in this day and age, as all leaders need to be digital. A summary of the key digital leadership traits or characteristics mentioned by the respondents is as follows:

* collaborating across silos;
* think differently (mindset shift/mindset change);
* understanding digital technology; and
* having a vision.

The importance of the key Strataplex skills

This question was included to gain respondents' understanding of the various skills as per the Skills Strataplex, and getting leaders to think indirectly if these skills were relevant for digital transformation and what other skills they could consider apart from these. The question was very open ended and the outcome was that most of the leaders unconsciously related it to digital transformation and ranked the various skills in terms of importance on their own accord. Additional skills were also mentioned as being important over and above the four key Strataplex skills. Figure 10.3 lists the skills ranked by respondents in terms of importance (which they did of their own accord), as well as the additional skills that were mentioned by some of the respondents. The additional skills that respondents added as necessary were entrepreneurial skills/mindset, meta-cognition and a challenger mindset over and above the four key Strataplex skills.

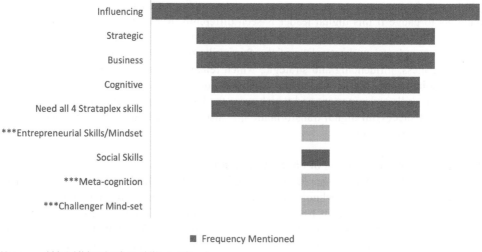

Note: *** Additional unique skills mentioned.

Figure 10.3   Key Strataplex skills

Digital leadership skills for South African leaders

The objective of this question was to understand the digital leadership skills that South African leaders require to ensure successful digital transformation in their organisations. These skills are those that the respondents, who have implemented digital transformation successfully, believe South African leaders need. Figure 10.4 lists the top ten skills mentioned most frequently, in order of frequency.

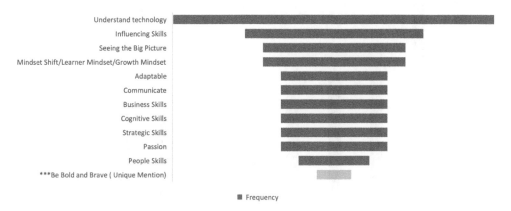

Figure 10.4   Digital leadership skills for South African leaders

The respondents then had to determine which of the digital leadership skills mentioned were most important for South African leaders. Most leaders felt that they could not keep to one skillset, but narrowed down their initial range to a few skills. Most of the skills mentioned above occurred again; however, there were a few new ones that some leaders realised were most important and missing in the previous list. The skills mentioned that are most important by the respondents were not always in line with the skills already mentioned that South African leaders need. Some respondents felt that all of the skills mentioned in the prior section were important and were not comfortable ranking them. Figure 10.5 lists the key skills mentioned by most of the respondents. Additional skills that emerged included being assertive/standing up for one's beliefs, being bold and brave, determination and resilience. Understanding technology, mindset shifts and learning from failure are skills that are also common from the previous list of skills for digital leaders.

Which digital leadership skills used in respondents' organisations were key for successful digital transformation?

The objective here was to understand the skills that the respondents used in their organisations when implementing digital transformation. The skillsets mentioned are similar to those in the previous questions, but the importance in this context is different as it relates to what the respondents actually used or considered important in their implementation of transformation. The respondents mentioned that to carry out successful digital transformation in their organisation they had to have a vision, use communication skills and influencing skills when working with key stakeholders and other parties and they needed problem-solving skills to resolve issues that came up in the implementation. Many respondents stressed the impor-

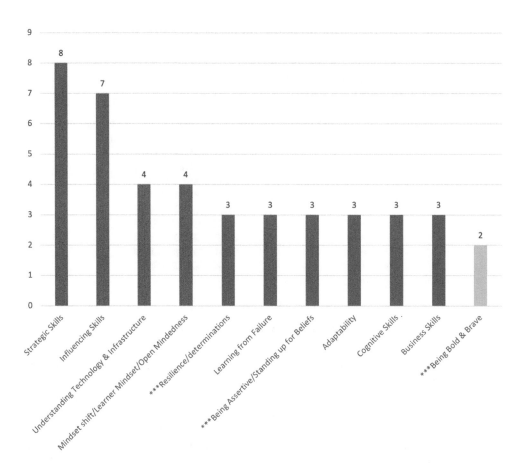

Note: *** Unique skills and those indicated from a South African context.

Figure 10.5   Most important skills listed for successful digital transformation

tance of having the right people and that people skills were important, along with project management skills to ensure the success of the project. The skills used in the respondents' organisations for digital transformation are similar to the skills that South African leaders need. However, many of the skills listed as the top skills that South African leaders need, or that the respondents regarded as being most important, did not feature in the top listings here. A unique note of skills that surfaced in the three variations of digital leadership skills asked are being resilient, being bold, being assertive/standing up for yourself and being determined. Learning from failure/tolerance from failure came up again as well. Refer to Figure 10.6 for the details.

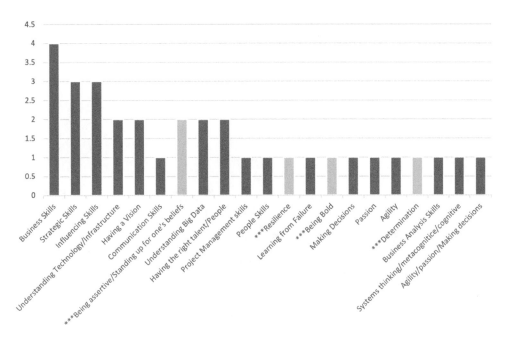

Figure 10.6   Digital leadership skills used in respondents' organisation

DISCUSSION AND ADAPTIVE DIGITAL SKILLS MODEL

The research findings illustrate that South African leaders understand digital transformation and digital leadership, and their views align with the literature on the factors that contribute to successful digital transformation. The vital importance of leadership in digital transformation was reaffirmed and our respondents confirmed the relevance of adaptive leadership in successful digital transformation as being crucial.

Most leaders see digital leadership as being different from traditional leadership as per our research and there is a strong suggestion that digital leadership should become the norm of leadership in this digital age. Digital leaders are also those who adjust according to the times and the context of the situation, conforming to adaptive leadership. The skills that we uncovered are in agreement with the literature, indicating that the respondents understand the key competencies that adaptive leaders need to carry out successful digital transformation.

The Adaptive Digital Leadership Skills Model

Based on our findings we created a new framework (Figure 10.7) for leadership suitable to digital transformation. The Adaptive Digital Leadership Skills Model was derived from the Digital Leadership Skills Model through the literature and the findings of the study on 'Digital leadership skills needed by South African leaders for successful digital transformation'

(Tiekam, 2019). Considering the environment of digital transformation being volatile, uncertain, complex, ambiguous and with constant disruption, leaders have to adapt and be flexible to the constant changing environment in which leaders do their work.

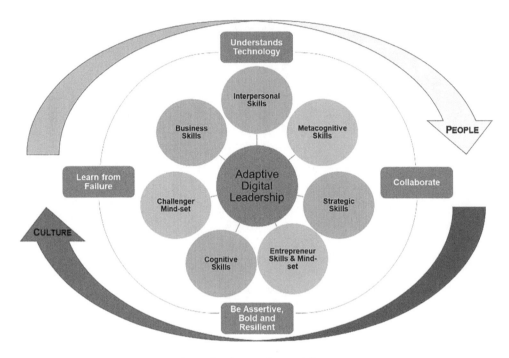

Figure 10.7   *Adaptive Digital Leadership Skills Model*

Adaptive leadership emerged as crucial to successful digital transformation, and the similarities between adaptive leadership characteristics and the characteristics of a leader for successful digital transformation indicate that digital leaders are adaptive leaders who need to adapt to the constant changing environment and adjust to the context of the situation in which they find themselves. The extant literature confirms this, but does not highlight adaptive leadership being the ideal leadership for digital transformation. However, according to CLT, adaptive leadership is key for operating in complex adaptive systems which is part of the volatile, fast-paced knowledge era (Uhl-Bien et al., 2007), and this flexible leadership has to adapt and change to the context of the situation. South African leaders have confirmed that they understand what an adaptive leader is, and consider it crucial to digital transformation. We therefore posit that digital leaders can also be called adaptive digital leaders, resulting in an adaptive digital leader being the core of the Adaptive Digital Leadership Skills Model.

When determining if the four traditional skills from the Skills Strataplex were relevant for successful digital transformation, an additional three skills were identified by the digital leaders during the research as being relevant to digital transformation. These are:

1. *Entrepreneurial skills and entrepreneurial mindset*, which relate to applying an entrepreneurial perspective to digitalisation to be more creative, think differently and look for opportunities.
2. *Challenger mentality*, which involves changing one's mindset to be more open minded, having a growth and learner mindset and ensuring there is a mindset shift to constantly grow, learn, innovate and challenge. Having a growth mindset was rated as the most important factor for adaptive leadership skills in the findings, indicating that the right mindset is vital to drive successful digital transformation.
3. *Metacognition skills*, which relate to self-reflection and self-development, requiring leaders to constantly self-reflect, learn and develop themselves. This ties in with digital leaders having to constantly keep their skills up to date to lead in the digital age.

These skills have been added to the four key skills to show the new skills required over and above the traditional Strataplex skills shown in the Adaptive Leadership Skills Model.

In addition to the key traditional skills needed by digital leaders as per the Skills Strataplex, the findings also indicated the digital leadership skills that *South African leaders* are required to have for successful digital transformation based on what was rated important to their organisations. These skills are:

1. *A leader who understands technology.* This is a leader who is not necessarily a technical guru, but who has a good understanding of the basics of the existing and new technologies.
2. *A leader who is not afraid to fail and who learns from failure.* These are leaders who create environments in which to experiment and fail.
3. *A leader who is bold and brave, resilient and assertive or stands up for him/herself.* This is a leader stands up for their beliefs and their vision to be delivered and endures all that comes their way.
4. There has also been much mention in understanding the digital leadership skills that *digital leaders need to collaborate across silo's*, cross-functionally, and who cannot work in verticals anymore. Hence, collaboration is seen as important for a leader to carry out successful digital transformation.
5. *A leader who has a mindset shift/learner mindset/growth mindset* to deal with constant disruption of digital transformation. Leaders having the right mindset has been a key finding of this research, as most respondents believed this was the key to ensuring successful digital transformation. Dweck (2012) confirms that companies which have succeeded in being continuously successful are those that have a growth mindset, as they constantly try to improve themselves and those around them, try to understand the skills needed in the future and surround themselves with the most able people.

The mindset aspects form part of the challenger mentality/mindset skills of the model. The findings also brought about two additional themes that were identified as important, namely the role of people/talent in the organisation, as leaders need the right people to help them with digital transformation (Kane et al., 2015a), and the fact that the behaviours of the leader have an impact on people and create the culture of the organisation (Kane et al., 2015a). Culture has been regarded as a key tool of a leader, as culture is dynamic and changes with situations and times (Christensen, 2006). On the model, this is illustrated by the people that impact culture and culture that impacts people, and that they are both affected by the behaviours and skills of the digital adaptive leader.

CONCLUSION

In this chapter, we discussed the impact of digital transformation in Africa and South Africa and the importance of leaders adjusting and changing their leadership style, while acquiring the relevant digital leadership skills to lead in the disruptive knowledge era. This resulted in the creation of the Adaptive Digital Leadership Skills Model, where the ideal type of leader and the core skills needed to ensure successful digital transformation are illustrated.

It is clear from the literature on Africa and South Africa (African Union, 2020; Deloitte, 2017); Digital Economy for Africa Initiative, n.d.; Dupoux et al., 2015; ITWeb, 2018; Fitzgerald et al., 2013; Wright, 2019 and the outcomes of this qualitative research that business leaders in South Africa are capable of leapfrogging into the new knowledge era and carrying out successful digital transformation. However, they need to acquire the right skillsets (Tiekam, 2019). Most importantly, such leaders need to develop the right mindset that allows leaders to change and persevere when things are tough. Such mindsets include growth, learner and challenger mindsets that enable one to thrive in the most challenging times, and to be open to learn and grow as a key underlying factor in what differentiates leaders from the industrial era to being an adaptive leader in the digital era.

African leaders are pivotal in being the role models of adaptive digital leaders who continuously work to improve themselves and keep themselves up to date. Role modelling such leadership creates a culture that transformation starts with the individual and a personal interest in self-development, growth and a vision to leapfrog the African continent and its people to successfully digitally transform.

REFERENCES

African Union (2020). *The Digital Transformation Strategy for Africa (2020–2030)*. https://au.int/sites/default/files/documents/38507-doc-dts-english.pdf

Arderne, C. J., Fikui, R., & Kelly, T. (2019, 7 November). *Africa's connectivity gap: Can a map tell the story?* World Bank Blogs. https://blogs.worldbank.org/digital-development/africas-connectivity-gap-can-map-tell-story

Armstrong, M. (2022, 4 February). *Internet in Africa: Progress and potential*. Statista. www.statista.com/chart/26781/internet-penetration-africa-progress/

Böck, V., & Lange, M. S. (2018). *Leadership in digitalisation employees' perception of effective leadership in* digitalisation. Thesis.

Bughin, J., & Van Zeebroeck, N. (2017). The best response to digital disruption. *MIT Sloan Management Review, 58*(4), 80–86.

BusinessTech. (2018). *South African CEOs are struggling to find digital skills*. https://businesstech.co.za/news/business/258889/south-african-ceos-are-struggling-to-find-digital-skills/

Christensen, C. M. (2006). What is an organization culture? *Harvard Business Review*. https://doi.org/10.1057/9780230250932_4

Deloitte. (2017). *Rewriting the rules for the digital age 2017 Deloitte Global Human Capital Trends*.

Digital Economy for Africa Initiative. (n.d.). www.worldbank.org/en/programs/all-africa-digital-transformation

Doyle, A. (2016). Adaptive challenges require adaptive leaders. *Performance Improvement*, 18–27. https://doi.org/10.1002/pfi

Dubru, R. (2018). *Critical competencies of leaders in the digital transformation of banking in South Africa*. MBA dissertation, University of Pretoria.

Dupoux, P., Ivers, L., Abouzied, A., Chraïti, A., Dia, F., Maher, H., & Niavas, S. (2015, 10 November). *Dueling with lions: Playing the new game of business success in Africa*. BCG. www.bcg.com/publications/2015/globalization-growth-dueling-with-lions-playing-new-game-business-success-africa

Dweck, C. (2012). *Mindset: Changing the way you think to fulfil your potential*. New York: Balantine Books.

El Sawy, O. A., Amsinck, H., Kraemmergaard, P., & Vinther, A. (2016). How LEGO built the foundations and enterprise capabilities for digital leadership. *MIS Quarterly Executive*, *15*(2).

Fitzgerald, M., Kruschwitz, N., Bonnet, D., & Welch, M. (2013). *Embracing digital technology: A new strategic imperative*. MIT Sloan Management Review and Capgemini Consulting.

Goethals, G. R., Sorenson, G., Burns, M., & Burns, J. M. (2003). Leadership in the digital age. *The Encyclopedia of Leadership*, 1–5.

Goleman, D. (2000). HBR's must-reads on managing people leadership that gets results: Leadership that gets results. *Harvard Business Review*, March–April.

Haffke, I., & Benlian, A. (2016). *The role of the CIO and the CDO in an organization's digital transformation*. www.researchgate.net/publication/311653140

Hess, T., Benlian, A., Matt, C., & Wiesböck, F. (2016). Options for formulating a digital transformation strategy. *MIS Quarterly Executive*, *15*(2), 123–139.

Iordanaglou, D. (2018). Future trends in leadership development practices and the crucial leadership skills. *Journal of Leadership, Accountability and Ethics*, *15*(2), 118–119.

ITWeb. (2018). *SA lags on digital transformation*. www.itweb.co.za/content/WnpNgq2ALWgMVrGd

Jardim, J. (2020). Leadership characteristics and digital transformation. *Journal of Business Research*. https://doi.org/10.1016/j.jbusres.2020.10.058

Kane, G. C. (2016). Do you have the will for digital transformation? *MIT Sloan Management Review*, 1–3.

Kane, G. C. (2018). Common traits of the best digital leaders. *MIT Sloan Management Review. Big Idea: Digital Leadership – Blog*, 1–5.

Kane, G. C. (2019). The technology fallacy: People are the real key to digital transformation. *Research Technology Management*, *62*(6), 44–49.

Kane, G. C., Palmer, D., Phillips, A. N., Kiron, D., & Buckley, N. (2015a). *Becoming a digitally mature enterprise*. https://kityna.ga/146142.pdf

Kane, G. C., Palmer, D., Phillips, A. N., Kiron, D., & Buckley, N. (2015b). Strategy, not technology, drives digital transformation. https://sloanreview.mit.edu/projects/strategy-drives-digital-transformation/

Kane, G. C., Palmer, D., Phillips, A. N., Kiron, D., & Buckley, N. (2016). Reframing the organization for a digital future. *Sloan Management review*.

Kane, G., Palmer, D., Phillips, A. N., Kiron, D., & Buckley, N. (2018). Coming of age digitally. *MIT Sloan Management Review*.

Kappelman, L., Jones, M. C., Johnson, V., Mclean, E. R., & Boonme, K. (2016). Skills for success at different stages of an IT professional's career. *Communication of the ACM*, *59*(8).

Kohnke, O. (2018). It's not just about technology: The people side of digitization. In G. Oswald & M. Kleinemeier (Eds), *Shaping the Digital Enterprise*. Cham: Springer, pp. 69–91.

Lichtenstein, B. B., & Uhl-bien, M. (2006). *Complexity Leadership Theory: An interactive perspective on leading in complex adaptive systems*. Lincoln, NE: University of Nebraska.

Mihardjo, L. W. W., Sasmoko, S., Alamsjah, F., & Elidjen, E. (2019). Digital leadership role in developing business model innovation and customer experience orientation in Industry 4.0. *Management Science Letters*, *9*, 1749–1762.

MTN. (2021). *JSE SENS announcement*. www.mtn.com/wp-content/uploads/2022/02/MTN-Group-Q3-2021-JSE-SENS-announcement.pdf

Mumford, T., Campion, M. A., & Morgeson, F. P. (2007). The Leadership Skills Strataplex: Leadership skill requirements across organizational levels. *Leadership Quarterly*, *18*(2), 154–166.

Mumford, M. D., Todd, E. M., Higgs, C., & Mcintosh, T. (2017). Cognitive skills and leadership   performance: The nine critical skills. *The Leadership Quarterly*, *28*(1), 24–39.

Ndemo, B., & Weiss, T. (2017). Making sense of Africa's emerging digital transformation and its many futures. *Africa Journal of Management*, *3*(3–4), 328–347.

Northouse, P. G. (2006). *Leadership: Theory and practice*. Thousand Oaks, CA: SAGE.

PWC. (2018). South Africa falling behind with digital transformation. www.pwc.co.za/en/press-room/south-africa-falling-behind-with-digital transformation.html

Riggio, R. E., & Lee, J. (2007). Emotional and interpersonal competencies and leader development. *Human Resource Management Review*, *17*, 418–426.

Robinson, O. (2014). Sampling in interview-based qualitative research: A theoretical and practical guide. *Qualitative Research in Psychology*, *11*(1), 25–41.

Saunders, M., & Lewis, P. (2018). *Doing research in business and management* (Second Edition). Harlow: Pearson.

Schwab, K. (2018). The global competitiveness report 2018. *World Economic Forum Reports 2018*.

Schwarzmüller, T., Brosi, P., Duman, D., & Welpe, I. M. (2018). How does the digital transformation affect organizations? *Management Review*, *29*(2), 114–138.

Tiekam, A. (2019). *Digital leadership skills that South African leaders need for successful digital transformation*. https://repository.up.ac.za/handle/2263/74033

Uhl-Bien, M. (2021). Complexity leadership and followership: Changed leadership in a changed world. *Journal of Change Management*, 21(2), 144–162.

Uhl-Bien, M., Marion, R., & McKelvey, B. (2007). Complexity Leadership Theory: Shifting leadership from the industrial age to the knowledge era. *Leadership Quarterly*, *18*(4), 298–318.

Van Outvorst, F., Visker, C., & De Waal, B. (2017). *Digital leadership: The consequences of organizing and working in a digital society*. Utrecht: University of Applied Sciences.

Vey, K., Fandel-Meyer, T., Zipp, J. S., & Schneider, C. (2017). Learning and development in times of digital transformation: Facilitating a culture of change and innovation. *International Journal of Advanced Corporate Learning*, *10*, 22–32.

Viviers, W., Parry, A., & Jansen van Rensburg, S. J. (2021). *Africa's digital future: From theory to action*. Cape Town: AOSIS Publishing.

Weiling, K., & Wei, K. K. (2004). Organizational culture and leadership in ERP implementation. *Decision Support Systems*, *45*(2), 208–218.

Wright, B. (2019). *Just what is the state of digital transformation in South Africa?* CIO Africa. www.cio.com/article/3431617/just-what-is-the-state-of-digital-transformation-in-south-africa.html

Yukl, G. (1989). Managerial leadership: A review of theory and research. *Journal of Management*. https://doi.org/10.1177/014920638901500207

Yukl, G., & Mahsud, R. (2010). Why flexible and adaptive leadership is essential. *Consulting Psychology Journal*, *62*(2), 81–93.

11. Legal leapfrogging? Legal system and rule of law effects on cross-listing to bond by emerging-market firms

Joel Malen, Paul M. Vaaler, and Ivy Zhang

INTRODUCTION

A common assumption underlying research on firm internationalization is that location choice is operationally defined. It is about where firms locate plant, property, equipment, and people around the world (e.g., Melin, 1992). But management research in the last decade broadened this focus to assess non-operational *legal* aspects of firm location (Hasan, Kobeissi, and Wang, 2011; Moore, Filatotchev, Bell, and Rasheed, 2012; Bell, Filatotchev, and Aguilera, 2014). It asked about determinants of firm choice regarding the country in which to file articles of incorporation, issue securities, or undertake some other transaction that activates substantive laws and legal procedures governing firm behavior even if the firm has little or no operational presence there. Moore and colleagues (2012) and Bell and colleagues (2014) highlight laws providing more protection of shareholder rights and decreasing regulatory compliance costs as significant factors influencing where firms chose to locate initial public offerings (IPOs) of shares abroad. According to Hasan and colleagues (2011), IPO location characteristics increase firm visibility with various financial stakeholders, such as analysts who provide expert assessments of firm strategy and corporate governance, i.e., the ways stakeholders assure themselves of an adequate return on resources they make available to firms. These studies and others suggest that where firms initially choose to locate legally follows from how firms prefer to engage shareholders and related financial players supplying capital and seeking assurances of an adequate return through effective corporate governance.

Understanding where firms initially establish their legal presence begs follow-on questions for management researchers, including why and how firms might shift an established legal presence to another international location—legal "leapfrogging." We answer these questions guided by a cross-level theoretical framework (Rousseau, 1985; Henisz and Macher, 2004; Martin, Cullen, Johnson, and Parboteeah, 2007), explaining legal leapfrogging as a function of two country-level legal factors firms compare between their current legal home and prospective legal host countries and one firm-level factor. The two comparative legal factors are the type of legal system—common or civil law systems—and the rule of law commitment—no matter the type of legal system—in each country. The firm-specific factor is growth opportunity, that is, the potential for profitable growth given better access to capital. Firms become increasingly likely to shift their legal presence as home-country weakness on these two legal dimensions complicates their ability to assure shareholders of an adequate return on supplied capital and as profitable growth opportunities for firms funded by that shareholder capital expand. As Doidge, Karolyi, and Stulz (2004) point out, such conditions most typically characterize emerging-market countries with basic, but often still-developing, legal institutions and faster-growing, but often capital-starved, firms. We have that same emerging-market institutional context generally in mind as we develop our cross-level theoretical framework. That context relates to many geographic regions but has particular relevance for Africa with a rich diversity of native and colonially transplanted legal systems historically as well as more recent trends strengthening and weakening rule of law.

We investigate empirical support for our legal leapfrogging framework by analyzing the likelihood that emerging-market firms will make secondary (to initial public) securities offerings to potential shareholders in the United States (US). Our empirical approach follows prior "law and finance" research (e.g., Reese and Weisbach, 2002), assuming that cross-listing shares in the US signals intent to adhere to more demanding legal standards of corporate governance as a condition for attracting more extensive shareholding. To the extent that cross-listing in the US subjects the firm to the jurisdiction of US laws, such cross-listing shifts a firm's legal presence. It "bonds" the firm to US corporate governance standards even if the firm has no operational presence there (Coffee, 1999; Stulz, 1999). Such bonding should attract more minority shareholding, broaden the shareholding base, and decrease the cost of capital, benefits that are especially valuable to emerging-market firms with more growth opportunities. So, emerging-market firms are more likely to leapfrog legally so they can obtain these bonding benefits.

We test hypotheses derived from our legal leapfrogging framework by analyzing the likelihood of US cross-listing in 7,453 firms domiciled in 22 emerging-market countries from 1996 to 2007. This sample covers different regions, including the Middle East–North Africa region with Turkey and Egypt and Southern Africa with South Africa and Zimbabwe. Consistent with our legal leapfrogging framework, we find that firms with high-growth opportunities but domiciled in emerging-market countries offering weaker legal protection are more likely to cross-list shares in the US. These core results prove robust to reasonable variation in model specification, estimation, and sampling strategies.

Our study contributes to management research on firm internationalization generally and to the leapfrogging research theme motivating this scholarly volume. First, we contribute a novel theory explaining why emerging-market firms shift their legal presence via cross-listing as a function of higher country- and lower firm-level factors. Our legal leapfrogging framework represents an advance on management theories of firm internationalization that highlight prospective host-country law (e.g., Bell et al., 2014) or firm-level growth opportunities (e.g., Filatotchev and Piesse, 2009) but do not articulate distinctive combinatorial effects on firm internationalization that might differ substantially from those of each in isolation. Legal leapfrogging is a "technology" relying primarily on intangible legal and financial rather than tangible inputs. Our study highlights which inputs and how they fit together. Our framework also represents an advance on related law and finance research assuming that all foreign firms have similar incentives to shift legal presence through cross-listing in the US to benefit from bonding with more protective legal regimes (e.g., Reese and Weisbach, 2002). Our framework instead incorporates an "institutional view" of strategy (Peng, 2003), highlighting distinctive incentives emerging-market firms (but not others) may have to internationalize their presence through cross-listing as a way to signal adherence to more demanding corporate governance standards than they face at home. With inclusion of this institutional dimension, our legal leapfrogging framework constructively refines the domain of bonding theory that scholars in law (e.g., Coffee, 1999) and finance (e.g., Stulz, 1999) may have earlier defined too broadly.

Second, we contribute new and novel empirical methods and evidence demonstrating robust support for hypotheses derived from our legal leapfrogging framework. For example, no previous empirical research in management or other fields has documented the "vanishing" legal system effects we demonstrate in our country-level analyses. We find and graphically illustrate with novel estimation methods (Zelner, 2009) that the higher likelihood of US cross-listing by foreign firms from emerging-market countries with less protective civil law systems vanishes to insignificance as rule of law strengthens even modestly in those same countries. This finding should prompt a reassessment of many other "results" in international management, law, and other fields suggesting that firms respond to differences in a country's legal system no matter the consistency with which laws from those different systems are applied (e.g., Flores, Aguilera, Mahdian, and Vaaler, 2013). We also confirm important findings about combinatorial effects of country-level legal and firm-level effects on emerging-market cross-listing tendencies. Again, no previous empirical research has documented the consistently significant and positively magnifying effects of higher firm-level growth opportunities on US cross-listing by emerging-market firms operating under different legal system and rule of law scenarios. This finding should prompt more frequent modeling of growth opportunities individually and in combination with other factors explaining firm internationalization, whether operational or non-operational and legal in dimension.

Third, we contribute important practice and public policy insights related to firm motivations to leapfrog legally via listing abroad. Executives managing US and foreign share exchanges around the world have a very practical interest in understanding why and how firms differ in terms of motivation to shift their legal presence internationally via cross-listing. As Coffee (2002) notes, for example, foreign firm listings on the New York Stock Exchange (NYSE) grew from only 96 in 1990 to 434 or approximately 15 percent of all NYSE listings in 2000. Over the same period, hundreds more foreign firms established US cross-listings traded off exchanges and "over the counter" via broker dealers. Various US legal reforms to corporate governance standards in the 2000s prompted some foreign firms to de-list but others to become new cross-listings after the same reforms. Our study advances policy debates about US legal reform and financial market competitiveness by sorting out why foreign firms have responded differently to such policy trends based on their home-country institutional context and growth opportunities. Our study also advances business practice by suggesting how executives at US exchanges and brokerage houses might tailor proposals for cross-listing to emerging-market firms—likely to be more interested in the benefits of shifting legal presence to bond with US corporate governance standards—differently than they would for firms from other countries.

Fourth and more broadly, we contribute to academic debates in international management (e.g., Siegel, 2009) and law (e.g., Aguilera and Williams, 2009) that have questioned the effectiveness of cross-listing as a means for foreign firms to change relevant corporate governance standards. Our study answers their questions as it clarifies conditions when cross-listing to bond is more and less likely. Evidence derived from our legal leapfrogging framework and emerging-market country institutional context points to the practical effectiveness of cross-listing. Thus, we advance an important academic debate by responding to bonding skeptics and defining specific conditions when emerging-market firms are more likely to implement this strategy. Those conditions are readily apparent in many African countries today, suggesting that African firms throughout the continent are more likely legal leapfroggers in the near term.

THEORY AND HYPOTHESES

Theoretical explanations of firm internationalization typically emphasize the role of country-level variation in geography, natural resources, labor costs, market size, and income (e.g., Wheeler and Mody, 1992). Strategic management perspectives on this topic also encompass lower-level firm characteristics that may influence internationalization tendencies on their own or in combination with country-level factors (e.g., Martin, Swaminathan, and Mitchell, 1998). For example, Henisz and Macher (2004) theorize that firms in high-technology industries choose countries for investment based in part on country-level wealth, technological capability, and policy stability. But the firm's current product mix and previous experience in the country also matter on their own and in interaction with country-level factors.

Such cross-level theorizing comports with an institutional view of strategy, which explains performance differences among firms through analysis of distinctive combinations of firm capabilities and higher-level structural factors in the economy often given to evolutionary change. For example, Peng (2003) offers alternative explanations for the success of firms operating in China and other prominent emerging-market countries of the 1990s and 2000s based on differences in firms' capabilities to adapt to economic liberalization and privatization policies. Cuervo-Cazerra and Dau (2009) exemplify such a cross-level approach when they document higher performance by local firms in Latin American countries experiencing structural reforms. Reforms have differential performance effects because of distinctive agency relationships benefiting state-owned enterprises compared to local privately owned firms; in addition, performance of both types of firms has been compared to firms controlled by foreign multinational enterprises (MNEs).

We take a similar cross-level perspective in developing our theoretical framework of legal leapfrogging factors. We identify two country-level factors and a third firm-level factor to explain general and firm-specific motivations for this legal (but not necessarily operational) shift in presence. Weak home-country legal protections discourage potential investors from shareholding. Cross-listing addresses this problem by shifting the legal presence of the firm and subjecting it to additional rules adding investor protection. Based on the objective of substantially and demonstrably improving investor protections, we focus on cross-listings by emerging-market firms in the US, which is widely considered to offer the strongest investor protection, particularly to minority shareholders (Coffee, 2002; Reese and Weisbach, 2002; Doidge et al., 2004). These factors motivate our theoretical framework and related hypotheses about legal leapfrogging tendencies.

Country-Level Factors

Our theoretical framework follows law and finance research in assuming that countries with legal systems based on common law provide stronger investor protection and thus weaker incentives for domestic firms to shift legal presence through cross-listing. We add to that analysis rule of law, the gauge of confidence in and adherence to legal rules, and their fairness and predictability for economic and social interactions. We see these two country-level factors as foundational to understanding corporate governance standards generally and the protection of shareholder interests, particularly minority shareholder interests, more specifically. Their foundational status makes them relevant to comparative analyses which emerging-market firms make according to our framework, no matter the extent of any legal shift abroad.

Legal system

As legal researchers note (Coffee, 1999; Reynolds and Flores, 2003; Ribstein, 2005), countries with legal origins in Anglo-American common law generally give the judiciary more independence from partisan political branches of government, permitting judges to exercise discretion in interpreting and applying legal principles equitably. Common law systems also provide private individuals greater access to courts for the adjudication of contract and property rights disputes, and thereby promote the development of case law precedents to guide economic behavior with less uncertainty and lower transaction costs. By contrast, countries with legal origins in Continental European civil law put judges under greater scrutiny by partisan political branches of government, greater reliance on specific legal and procedural codes rather than principles of discretion and equity, and a preference for state regulation over private litigation and case law to settle disputes and guide economic behavior.

Law and finance research documents links between country legal systems and financial market development (La Porta, Lopez-de-Silanes, Shleifer, and Vishny, 1998) and the strength of investor protections (Shleifer and Vishny, 1997; La Porta, Lopez-de-Silanes, Shleifer, and Vishny, 1999; Dyck and Zingales, 2004). Specifically for corporate governance issues, La Porta and colleagues (1999) document greater ownership concentration and insider block-holding in civil law countries, while Dyck and Zingales (2004) document that individuals pay a larger control premium to acquire firms in these same countries. This empirical evidence is consistent with the argument that civil law systems offer weaker legal protections to investors, particularly minority investors. Thus, local firms have fewer small, outside shareholders, and prospective majority investors are willing to pay more to acquire firms from civil law countries where they can more easily "tunnel" wealth to themselves (Johnson, La Porta, Lopez-de-Silanes, and Shleifer, 2000).

Management research has paid greater attention to distinctions between common and civil law systems to theorize about cross-country differences in corporate governance regimes affecting how local firms choose top managers, treat employees, and raise capital (Aguilera and Jackson, 2003). These legal distinctions inform empirical studies of local firm ownership structures, asset management, and financial performance in civil law country contexts (Hoskisson, Cannella, Tihanyi, and Faraci, 2004; Miguel, Pindado, and de la Torre, 2004). They also document changes in the behavior of firms from civil law countries once oversight standards, investors, and related individuals from common law countries are introduced. Oxelheim and Randøy (2005) analyze 187 firms operating in the 1990s and domiciled in civil law countries of Scandinavia. They find that chief executive officers are paid more, but also discarded faster when such firms are listed on US, United Kingdom (UK), or other common law country (e.g., Canada) exchanges and have directors from such countries. Adoption of another legal system through cross-listing and corporate governance reform helped explain both the higher executive pay and career peril in these "internationalized" Scandinavian firms.

Birkenshaw, Braunerhjelm, Holm, and Terjesen (2006) analyze geographic relocation patterns during the 1990s of 35 MNE corporate headquarters historically based in Sweden. Foreign relocation of MNE corporate headquarters is positively and significantly linked to MNE reliance on foreign investment, often from the US and UK.

These findings again illustrate how differences in a firm's home-country legal system shape firm behavior and prompt stronger incentives for legal leapfrogging through cross-listing. To wit, managers in emerging-market firms will have greater incentives to employ this strategy when common law protections are missing at home.

Hypothesis 1: Firms from emerging-market countries with common law legal systems cross-list less in the US than firms from emerging-market countries with civil law legal systems.

Rule of law

Our theoretical framework assumes that countries with stronger rule of law, no matter their common law or civil law system origins, provide greater investor protection and lower incentives to cross-list on US financial markets for bonding purposes. World Bank researchers investigating public governance quality and corruption trends (Kaufmann, Kraay, and Zoido-Lobatón, 2000; Kaufmann Kraay, and Mastruzzi, 2009, 2010) define rule of law as one gauge of confidence in and adherence to rules, their fairness, and predictability for economic and social interactions. Rule of law is a gauge related to private contract enforcement and property rights, the police, and the courts, as well as the likelihood of crime and violence. Thus, the quality of any country's rule of law requires examination of both legal "inputs," such as police training and judicial procedures, and "outputs," such as the extent and consistency of lawfulness in private economic transactions.

Although less emphasized in extant bonding research, management scholars have long been interested in the impact of rule of law on investment in non-industrialized country contexts. In the 1970s, Vernon (1971) described an "obsolescing bargain" problem for MNEs doing business in the developing world. Investment agreements between MNEs and host-country governments were vulnerable to opportunistic breach and renegotiation by host-country governments with little concern for the sanctity of MNE contract or property rights. As Hoskisson, Eden, Lau, and Wright (2000) note, similar concerns about the predictability and enforcement of contract and property rights in emerging-market countries have prompted new streams of research since the 1990s on optimal MNE investment timing in privatizing industries (Doh, 2000) and MNE investment under varying degrees of host-country policy uncertainty (Delios and Henisz, 2000). A recurring prescriptive implication for MNEs has been to achieve some minimal level of geographic scope in operations. The credible threat of shifting operations between countries would constrain host governments considering contractual breach or outright expropriation, what Vernon (1971) described as keeping "sovereignty at bay."

Law and development researchers cite weaker rule of law in emerging markets as the basis for "dysfunctional public order" in investing by wholly domestic players (McMillan and Woodruff, 2000). A shift to private ordering and extra-legal investment assurances through family or community relationships may be feasible (e.g., Vaaler, 2011), but such alternative investment assurances also narrow the range of potential investors. On the other hand, a competent and consistent public legal mechanism broadens the investment domain, including the domain of smaller, transient investment associated with minority shareholding (Arrighetti,

Bachmann, and Deakin, 1997). Firms from emerging-market countries with such mechanisms, no matter their legal system origin, will have less incentive to leapfrog legally via cross-listing in the US.

Hypothesis 2: Firms from emerging-market countries with strong rule of law cross-list less in the US than firms from emerging-market countries with weak rule of law.

Legal system and rule of law interaction

Law and finance research also provides substantial guidance in identifying individual factors for inclusion in our theoretical framework. It provides less guidance, however, about how these factors may interact, and what such interaction may mean for firms considering legal leapfrogging through cross-listing. One view assumes that the legal system accelerates the development of stronger rule of law. Mahoney (2001) highlights the value of judicial discretion in developing better adherence to rule of law in the resolution of commercial disputes. Similarly, La Porta and colleagues (1999) opine that the choice of common law represents a decision to limit and distribute state power that could be used to change basic property and contract rights important to investors. Priest (Priest, 1977; Priest and Klein, 1984) highlights the beneficial interactive impact of legal system and rule of law from a different angle. Common law's adversarial adjudication process tends to result in the survival of efficient rather than inefficient rules for resolving commercial disputes.

Another view treats rule of law development as less tethered to a legal system. Other factors could prompt stronger rule of law. Pistor, Raiser, and Gelfer (2000) document several legal protections beneficial to investors in countries with civil law systems, but they are based on well-articulated written securities regulation (e.g., in Germany) rather than common law traditions of broad judicial discretion. Beck, Demirgüç-Kunt, and Levine (2003) document deeper and broader financial markets in civil law countries with more sophisticated legal rules and well-funded courts. Stronger rule of law springing from national culture, legal acumen, and/or budgetary priority provides the basis for better-written articulation of legal rights and obligations no matter the legal system in place. Law enforcement, rather than content, has been shown to have greater impact on the tendency of firms to act in the interests of investors (Defond and Hung, 2004) and their ability to obtain financing (Pistor et al., 2000). Stronger rule of law reduces the extent of legal ambiguity and the potential benefits deriving from the greater judicial discretion associated with common law legal systems.

We hold to neither view regarding how they interact but note that both views share a conclusion that greater clarity and predictability renders the civil or common law nature of any country's legal system less important. If so, then legal system differences between home and prospective host country should matter less for emerging-market firms looking to leapfrog legally via US cross-listing.

Hypothesis 3: As rule of law strengthens, the impact of common law versus civil law legal system differences on the likelihood of emerging-market firm cross-listing in the US diminishes.

Firm-Level Factors

Growth opportunities

Comparison of home- versus prospective host-country legal protections jumpstarts an explanation for a firm's incentives to shift legal presence. It does not end it, at least in strategy research that emphasizes individual firm rather than collective country characteristics. Individual firm-level factors also matter on their own and in interaction with country-level institutions. Recall that the purpose of cross-listing to bond is to assure potential investors, particularly minority investors, that the cross-listing firm will respect laws more protective of their interests than laws in the firm's home country. Why then might some firms have greater need for investment, particularly minority shareholding investment, than others? One answer from law and finance research (Doidge et al., 2004) is firm growth opportunities, that is, contingent capacity to grow profitably where the key contingency is access to external (international) capital at reasonable cost. Firms with stronger growth opportunities confront a more significant and pressing need for access to the capital prospective minority investors could provide. From a resource-dependence perspective, such firms would be at a relatively more substantial power disadvantage vis-à-vis potential minority shareholder investors—as compared to firms with weaker growth opportunities—and would therefore be more willing to take actions that better protect minority investor interests (Pfeffer and Salancik, 1978). Firms with multinational operational presence are typical candidates for high-growth potential. Theories of the multinational corporation dating back to Hymer's seminal work (1976 [1960]) often assume that they have technologically based advantages promising enhanced performance abroad notwithstanding other liabilities of foreignness they may also incur (Zaheer, 1995).

From a law and finance perspective, Doidge and colleagues (2004) model the decision by foreign firms to cross-list abroad (in the US) as a decision by wealth-maximizing firm insiders—managers or closely-related family and institutional block holders. They assume that these insiders can extract wealth from the firm as it is currently funded at home or as a cross-listed firm with additional funding from foreign investors. Domestic legal protections permit greater rates of wealth extraction compared to rates after (US) cross-listing and adoption of stronger legal protections. But the firm may be forgoing an opportunity to grow with additional financing through cross-listing. If growth opportunities are strong (weak) then decreased ability to expropriate firm wealth after cross-listing is (not) sufficiently compensated for by the increase in overall firm wealth facilitated by additional funding. Doidge and colleagues suggest (but do not test whether) their model has special application to emerging-market firms that often exhibit high growth potential limited by domestic capital availability.

Management research on so-called "real options" complements this insight. Kogut (1985) was probably first to articulate the contingent value of firm multinationality using terminology from options research more familiar to finance. Unlike wholly domestic firms, multinational firms can "exercise" an option to shift production or other operations geographically in response to near-term threats and opportunities. Tong, Reuer, and Peng (2008) and Reuer and Tong (2010) summarize 25 years of management research analyzing different internationalization strategies, including international joint ventures and alliances, as efforts to create growth opportunities not available in the home market. Growth opportunities limited by access to external financing likely have greater value for firms from emerging-market countries where domestic debt and equity markets are typically less developed (Hoskisson et al., 2000; Douma, George, and Kabir, 2006).

Corporate governance research in management highlights costs of listing on foreign exchanges, including costs in meeting new formal regulatory requirements, informal political costs, governance issues related to what to disclose to foreign shareholders, and other costs related to new stakeholders (Aguilera, Filatotchev, Gospel, and Jackson, 2008). But growth opportunities may render such costs less daunting. Indeed, if growth opportunities are strong, then additional compliance costs may seem inconsequential compared to the advantages of broader shareholding through more minority shareholders, greater liquidity, and perhaps better oversight of management. Cross-listing promises such near-term effects. It acts as a strategy for signaling firm quality (Siegel, 2005) in a market also including many "lemon" firms (Akerlof, 1970). In these ways, both law and finance and related strategy and management research points to when and how emerging-market firms with stronger growth opportunities will also be more inclined to leapfrog legally via US cross-listing.

Hypothesis 4: Firms from emerging-market countries with better growth opportunities cross-list more in the US than firms from emerging-market countries with weaker growth opportunities.

Country- and firm-level interactions

Previous law and finance research again provides little guidance about how firm-specific factors such as growth opportunities may interact with country-level factors also relevant to firm decisions about whether to shift their legal presence abroad. Management research, however, does provide a guide based on how it has modeled other interactions between firm-level capabilities and country-level institutions. Consider, for example, international management research. One prominent theory of (operational) internationalization comes from Dunning (1977), who articulated an "eclectic paradigm" comprised of interacting country-level locational factors and firm-specific technological capabilities. Country-level factors such as rich natural resources or tax breaks for foreign investors act as complementary enhancements magnifying firm-specific advantages related, say, to specialized knowledge or technology. There are also negative complements. Henisz and Macher (2004) theorize and then document that country-level institutions rendering investment policies less predictable deter investment with a magnified deterrence effect for foreign firms with better technological capabilities.

We can build on such logic to theorize about how firm-specific factors may complement and magnify country-level effects on decisions to shift their legal presence abroad. We have already explained why firms with stronger growth options are more likely to shift legal presence via US cross-listing—better access to investment, particularly minority shareholding investment vital to realizing faster growth and profitability net of compliance costs. When such firms are currently domiciled in home countries with less protective legal systems and/or rule of law, lost contingent valued is magnified, and US cross-listing is even more attractive. In our context, wanting legal protections for an emerging-market firm with strong growth opportunities means domicile in a country with a civil (not common) law legal system and weak (not strong) rule of law. This combination of country- and firm-level characteristics leads to the highest likelihood of emerging-market firm leapfrogging legally via US cross-listing.

Hypothesis 5: As firm-specific growth opportunities improve, the impact of country-level insti-tutional factors on cross-listing by emerging-market firms in the US is magnified.

METHODS

Equation Terms and Measures

To gain initial insight on empirical support for our legal leapfrogging theoretical framework and hypotheses, we define and estimate three equations. We define and estimate Equation 11.1 to test country-level factors in our framework (Hypotheses 1–3). We define and estimate constrained and unconstrained versions of Equation 11.2 to test, respectively, firm-level factors (Hypothesis 4) and country-firm cross-level factors (Hypothesis 5) in our framework. We begin with Equation 11.1 designed to test country-level factors in our legal leapfrogging framework:

$$Y\left(US\ Cross-Listing_{iklt}\right) = \alpha + \sum_{j=1}^{j=7} \beta_j\ Country\ Controls_{klt-1} + \beta_8\ Common\ Law_{kl}$$

$$+\beta_9\ Rule\ of\ Law_{klt-1} + \beta_{10}\ Common\ Law*Rule\ of\ Law_{klt-1}$$

$$+\sum_{v=1}^{v=5} \omega_v\ Year_t + \sum_{\delta=1}^{d=5} Region_l + \varepsilon_{iklt} \tag{11.1}$$

This equation explains variation in the outcome variable, *US Cross-Listing*, the likelihood of US cross-listing by a firm *i* domiciled in emerging-market country *k* from region *l* in year *t*. The *i* subscript is an index of emerging-market country firms in our sample running from 1 to 7,453. The *k* subscript is an index running from 1 to 22 for 22 emerging-market countries in our sample. The *l* subscript is an index running from 1 to 6 for six regions (Africa, East Asia, Europe, Middle East, Latin America, and South Asia) where these emerging-market countries are located. The *t* subscript is an index running from 1 to 6 for six years where comparable dependent variable information is available (1997, 1999, 2001, 2003, 2005, and 2007). Right-hand-side independent variables are either fixed across these six years or vary over time, in which case they are lagged by one year to *t*-1 (1996, 1998, 2000, 2002, 2004, and 2006).

Table 11.1 provides information on all terms in Equation 11.1, including variable names, description, whether they are time varying, their data source, and their predicted sign (if not a dependent variable). The dependent variable in Equation 11.1 is *US Cross-Listing*, a 0–1 indicator variable taking the value of 1 if firm *i* from country *k* (and region *l*) in year *t* is listed in the US, and 0 otherwise. We defer to our discussion of data sources and sampling strategy below, including description of alternative means by which foreign firms can list in the US.

The right-hand-side coefficients to be estimated in Equation 11.1 are denoted by Greek letters—β, ω, and δ. β coefficients for seven country-level control variables (*Country controls*) follow from previous empirical research in management (Birkenshaw et al., 2006; Vaaler and Schrage, 2007) and law and finance (La Porta et al., 1998; Reese and Weisbach, 2002). These controls are designed in part to explain *US Cross-Listing* linked to motivations other than to shift legal presence for bonding purposes. Other motivations to cross-list include overcoming local capital market limitations and increasing investor recognition (Foerster and Karolyi, 1999; Errunza and Miller, 2000), increasing liquidity (Amihud and Mendelson, 1986), aligning sources of corporate finance with corporate strategies such as starting an employee stock option plan (Rock, 2001), increasing sales, making new investments or acquisitions (Saudagaran, 1988; Saudagaran and Biddle, 1995), or entering faster-growing markets (Vaaler and Schrage, 2007).

Table 11.1 Variable definitions, data sources, time variance, and hypothesized relationships used in analyses of country-level determinants of US cross-listing

Variable name	Description	Time variant	Source	Expected cross-listing impact
US Cross-Listing	Indicator variable taking value of 1 (and 0 otherwise) if firm is listed on a US exchange as a Level I ADR (including Rule 144A ADR), Level II–III ADR, or direct listing	Yes	Bank of New York (2010); OTC Markets (2010)	Dependent variable
Level II–III US Cross-Listing	Indicator variable taking value of 1 (and 0 otherwise) if firm is listed on a US exchange as a Level II or III ADR or direct listing	Yes	Bank of New York (2010); OTC Markets (2010)	Dependent variable
Market presence	Per capita US dollar value of goods and services exported from country to US, measured in hundreds of US dollars	Yes	ITC (2010)	Positive
Capital Availability[a]	Availability of capital to entrepreneurs in country, measured on scale of 0 to 10 (higher values indicate greater availability)	Yes	Milken Institute Capital Studies Group Capital Access Index (Angkinand et al., 1999–2007)	Negative
Share Market Liquidity	Natural log of US dollar value of shares traded on all country exchanges divided by average market capitalization of listed firms	Yes	World Bank (2016)	Negative
Economic Growth	Growth in country gross domestic product over previous year as a percentage	Yes	World Bank (2016)	Negative
Anti-Director Rights[b]	Strength country shareholder rights vis-à-vis firm insiders, measured on a scale of 1 to 6 (higher values indicate stronger rights)	No	La Porta et al., 1998	Negative
Liability Standards[c]	0–1 index indicating strength of public firm liability standards under country securities laws (higher values indicate stronger standards)	No	La Porta et al., 1998	Negative
Disclosure Rules[d]	0–1 index indicating strength of financial and accounting disclosure standards for home-country firms (higher values indicate stronger standards)	No	La Porta et al., 1998	Negative
Common Law	Indicator variable taking value of 1 (and 0 otherwise) if firm home country is common law jurisdiction	No	Reynolds and Flores, 2003	Negative

Variable name	Description	Time variant	Source	Expected cross-listing impact
Rule of Law	Standardized measure $(0,\sigma)$ of confidence in and adherence to national rules, their fairness, and predictability for interactions related to private contract enforcement and property rights, the police, and the courts, as well as the likelihood of crime and violence	Yes	Kaufmann et al., 2000, 2009, 2010	Negative
Firm Size	Natural log of US dollar value of total firm assets	Yes	Worldscope, 2021	Positive
Firm ROA	Net firm income divided by total firm assets	Yes	Worldscope, 2021	Positive
Firm Leverage	Total firm liabilities divided by total firm assets	Yes	Worldscope, 2021	Positive
Tobin's Q	Ratio of sum of market capitalization and total assets minus book value of shareholders' equity over total assets (higher values mean better growth opportunities)	Yes	Worldscope, 2021	Positive

Note: ADR = American depository receipts; ROA = return on assets. [a] *Capital Availability* measures are created through assessment of seven components: macro-economic environment, institutional environment, financial industry development, equity market development, bond market development, international funding, and "alternative sources of capital" (e.g., family savings rates). [b] *Anti-Director Rights* measures are created by examining and adding 1 when each of the following six provisions exist in the company law or commercial code of a country as reviewed in 1995: (1) shareholders can mail their proxy vote to the firm; (2) shareholders are not required to deposit their shares prior to the general shareholders' meeting; (3) cumulative voting or proportional representation of minorities on the board of directors is allowed; (4) a mechanism for providing relief to aggrieved minority shareholders exists; (5) the minimum percentage of share capital entitling a shareholder to call for an extraordinary shareholders' meeting is less than or equal to 10 percent; and (6) shareholders have rights waived only by shareholders' vote. We assume that each provision empowers smaller shareholders against large bloc shareholders and senior firm executives and board members typically better positioned to direct firm resources. [c] *Liability* measures equal the arithmetic mean of three other scores based on review of country securities laws in 1993: (1) a score for liability standards applicable to the share issuing firm and its directors; (2) a score for liability standards for the distributor of firm shares; and (3) a score for liability standards for the accountant advising firms. [d] *Disclosure* measures are created by examining and rating companies' 1990 annual reports for their inclusion or omission of 90 items. These items fall into seven categories: (1) general information; (2) income statements; (3) balance sheets; (4) funds flow statements; (5) accounting standards; (6) stock data; and (7) special items. Higher scores indicate greater accounting disclosure by country firms. A minimum of three companies in each country were studied. The companies represent a cross-section of various industry groups: industrial companies represent 70 percent and financial companies represent the other 30 percent.

Four country controls account for these other motivations. They vary across countries, k, and within countries over time, $t-1$: *Market Presence* is the per capita US dollar value of goods and services exported to the US, measured in hundreds of US dollars. It controls for alignment motivations to cross-list (e.g., Saudagaran and Biddle, 1995). *Capital Availability* is the availability of capital for entrepreneurs measured on a scale of 1 (low availability) to 10 (high availability). This measure includes capital available from both domestic and foreign investors, including foreign direct and portfolio investors. It controls for capital scarcity and investor recognition motivations to cross-list (Foerster and Karolyi, 1999). *Share Market Liquidity* is the natural log of the US dollar value of shares traded daily on all country share markets divided by average share market capitalization. It controls for liquidity motivations to cross-list (Amihud and Mendelson, 1986). *Economic Growth* is percentage of annual gross domestic product growth. It controls for market growth motivations to cross-list. The likelihood of cross-listing should increase with greater *Market Presence* but decrease with greater *Capital Availability*, *Share Market Liquidity*, and *Economic Growth*. Essentially, better economic and financial conditions back home decrease the need for shifting legal leapfrogging via US cross-listing.

Previous law and finance research (La Porta et al., 1998) identifies three additional controls related to specific substantive corporate governance provisions in the home country. They include home-country rights of shareholders vis-à-vis firm insiders (*Anti-Director Rights*) measured on a scale of 1 (weak rights) to 6 (strong rights), public firm liability standards under home-country securities laws (*Liability Standards*), and financial and accounting disclosure standards for home-country firms (*Disclosure Rules*), both measured as a 0 (weak standards) to 1 (strong standards) index. All three variables derive from a review of legal provisions between 1990 and 1995, the year before we started collecting country- and firm-level data in 1996. All three should be negatively associated with *US Cross-Listing*. Stronger substantive corporate governance conditions back home decrease the need for legal leapfrogging via US cross-listing.

Controlling for these specific provisions should give us better precision in assessing residual variation in *US Cross-Listing* tied to the foundational legal system and rule of law strength.[1] We follow La Porta and colleagues (1998) and identify the legal system of each country in our sample based on classifications provided by Reynolds and Flores (2003). Thus, another β coefficient estimates the impact of *Common Law*, a 0–1 dummy that takes the value of 1 for common law countries and permits assessment of Hypothesis 1. Another β coefficient estimates the impact of *Rule of Law*, a standardized measure $(0,\sigma)$ of country k's rule of law in year t and permits assessment of Hypothesis 2. Higher measures indicate stronger rule of law. Yet another β coefficient estimates the impact of interaction effect of *Common Law* and *Rule of Law* measure (*Common Law*Rule of Law*), thus permitting assessment of Hypothesis 3. This interaction term permits us to partition rule-of-law effects within a given legal system consistent with our theoretical framework. We also include ω coefficients to estimate time and δ coefficients to estimate geographical region effects on *US Cross-Listing*. 0–1 *Year* and *Region* "dummy" variables pick up unspecified and idiosyncratic time and regional effects. Consistent with good practice, one "referent" category of each set of dummies is omitted. The omitted referent year is 2007 while the omitted referent region is Latin America.

In Equation 11.2, *US Cross-Listing* is again a 0–1 dummy indicating whether a firm is cross-listed in the US. On the right-hand-side of Equation 11.2 the same seven country controls (*Country Controls*), year dummies (*Year*) and region dummies (*Region*) are included as in Equation 11.1. We then add three new β coefficients to estimate. They capture firm-related factors that may affect US Cross-Listing. Again, they are lagged one year $(t-1)$. *Firm Size* is the logarithm of annual total assets in US dollars. *Firm ROA* is firm i's annual net income divided by total assets. *Firm Leverage* is firm i's annual total liabilities over total assets.

---

[1]   Indeed, certain strategies for cross-listing may limit the application of certain substantive corporate governance conditions related to, say, *Anti-Director Rights*. For example, a common strategy for cross-listing by foreign firms via establishment of a Level I American Depository Receipt (ADR) program limits foreign firm exposure to US federal regulatory provisions related to the public and private enforcement of such rights. The same Level I ADR, however, does submit the foreign firm to service of process in the US, the jurisdiction of US courts, and the application of US civil and criminal procedures founded on strong common law and rule of law principles.

Research by Reese and Weisbach (2002), Doidge and colleagues (2004), and Piotroski and Srinivasan (2008) suggests that firm size, profitability, and leverage prompt managers to consider cross-listing to raise additional capital and present a more favorable profile to potential investors. Accordingly, we expect these three factors will increase the likelihood of a US listing by an emerging-market firm seeking to legally leapfrog from their home country to the US.

A constrained version, Equation 11.2, is used to test the firm-level factors in our framework:

$$Y(USCross - Listing_{iklt}) = \alpha + \sum_{j=1}^{j=7} \beta_j Country\ Controls_{klt-1} + \sum_{m=8}^{m=10} \beta_m Firm\ Controls_{iklt-1}$$

$$+\beta_{11} Tobin's Q + \sum_{v=1}^{v=5} \omega_v Year_t + \sum_{\delta=1}^{d=5} Region_l 11. + \varepsilon_{iklt} \tag{11.2}$$

This constrained version of Equation 11.2 is used to assess Hypothesis 4 and the direct impact of firm growth opportunities with the inclusion of *Tobin's Q*. This variable measures the ratio of the sum of market capitalization and total assets minus the book value of shareholders' equity over total assets (Hawn and Ioannous, 2016). Higher values indicate better growth opportunities.

Finally, an unconstrained version, Equation 11.3, is used to test the country-firm cross-level factors in our framework:

$$Y(USCross - Listing_{iklt} = \alpha + \sum_{j=1}^{j=7} \beta_j Country\ Controls_{klt-1} + \sum_{m=8}^{m=10} \beta_m Firm\ Controls_{iklt-1}$$

$$+\beta_{11} D1_{kl} + \beta_{12} D2_{kl} + \beta_{13} D3_{kl}$$

$$+\beta_{14} Tobin's Q * D1_{iklt-1} + \beta_{15} Tobin's Q * D2_{iklt-1} + \beta_{16} Tobin's Q * D3_{iklt-1}$$

$$+\beta_{17} Tobin's Q * D4_{iklt-1} + \sum_{v=1}^{v=5} \omega_v Year_t + \sum_{\delta=1}^{d=5} Region_l + \varepsilon_{iklt} \tag{11.3}$$

In the unconstrained version, Equation 11.3, we replace *Common Law*, *Rule of Law*, and *Common Law*Rule of Law* interaction terms with β coefficients for three dummy variables to facilitate the interpretation of interaction effects between firm-specific growth opportunities and country-level legal institutions. *D1* is set equal to 1 if a firm *i* is domiciled in an emerging-market country *k* with strong rule of law (i.e., *Rule of Law* scores in the top two thirds of all countries sampled) and common law system, and 0 otherwise. *D2* is set equal to 1 if the firm is in a strong rule of law country with a civil law system. *D3* is set equal to 1 if the firm is in a weak rule of law country with a common law system (i.e., *Rule of Law* scores in the bottom third of all countries sampled). *D4*, the referent (omitted) category, indicates firms domiciled in countries with weak rule of law and civil law system—the "weakest" scenario for investor protection. All three dummy terms should exhibit negative signs relative to the referent category since that is where country-level factors are most likely to prompt cross-listing. Interacting each of these dummies with *Tobin's Q* permits assessment of Hypothesis 5 and the magnified effects of higher-level institutional protections as firm-specific growth opportunities increase.

Estimation Strategy

Given the discrete measurement of dependent variables in Equations 11.1–11.3, we employ logistic regression. Tests of Hypotheses 1–3 focus on signs and statistical significance of three terms in Equation 11.1: *Common Law* (H1: $\beta_8 < 0$) *Rule of Law* (H2: $\beta_9 < 0$) and *Common Law*Rule of Law* (H3: $\beta_{10} > 0$). Tests of Hypothesis 4 focus on signs and statistical significance of the *Tobin's Q* term in Equation 11.2 (H4: $\beta_{11} > 0$). Tests of Hypothesis 5 focus on signs and statistical significance of the four *Tobin's Q*D* interaction terms in Equation 11.3: (H5: $\beta_{16} > \beta_{14}$ and $\beta_{17} > \beta_{15}$ when legal system is held constant; $\beta_{15} > \beta_{14}$ and $\beta_{17} > \beta_{16}$ when rule of law strength is held constant). These coefficient comparisons imply that *US Cross-Listing* is more sensitive to the positive cross-listing impact of *Tobin's Q* in common law countries with weak versus strong rule of law (*Tobin's Q*D3>Tobin's Q*D1*) and in civil law countries with weak versus strong rule of law (*Tobin's Q*D4>Tobin's Q*D2*) (H5: $\beta_{16} > \beta_{14}$ and $\beta_{17} > \beta_{15}$). These coefficients also imply that *US Cross-Listing* is more sensitive to the positive cross-listing impact of *Tobin's Q* in strong rule of law countries with civil law versus common law systems (*Tobin's Q*D2>Tobin's Q*D1*) and in weak rule of law countries with civil law versus common law systems (*Tobin's Q*D4>Tobin's Q*D3*) (H5: $\beta_{15} > \beta_{14}$ and $\beta_{17} > \beta_{16}$).

Sampling Strategy and Data Sources

Consistent with our theory, we are interested in cross-listing tendencies among firms domiciled in emerging-market countries. Using World Bank categorizations (World Bank, 2021), we define emerging-market countries as those in the lower-middle and higher-middle income country categorizations in 1996, our first year ($t-1$) of observing country- and firm-level characteristics prior to the first year of *US Cross-Listing* observation (t) in 1997. Our Worldscope database provides information on firm controls running up to the mid-2000s.

The resulting base sample comprises 7,453 distinct firms domiciled and listing shares on domestic exchanges in 22 emerging-market countries and potentially cross-listing shares in the US from 1997 to 2007: Argentina, Brazil, Chile, Colombia, Egypt, Greece, Hong Kong, India, Indonesia, Israel, Malaysia, Mexico, Pakistan, Peru, Philippines, South Africa, South Korea, Sri Lanka, Thailand, Turkey, Venezuela, and Zimbabwe. On average, these firms appear 3.59 times in our sample and we have 26,773 firm-year observations to analyze. No one country dominates the sample. Malaysia has the most firm-year observations at 3,973 (14.84 percent) followed by South Korea at 3,862 (14.42 percent) and Hong Kong at 3,812 (14.24 percent). Nor does one industry dominate. The most-represented industry classification is Worldscope's "chemical and allied products" industry with 1,779 observations (6.65 percent), followed by "food and kindred products" at 1,626 (6.07 percent) and then "electrical and electric equipment" at 1,351 (5.05 percent).[2]

---

[2] These classifications appear to be roughly equivalent to two-digit Standard Industrial Classifications.

We follow other empirical studies (e.g., Doidge et al., 2004) that sample and sort US cross-listings based on sponsored Level I, II, and III American depository receipts (ADRs), including those issued under SEC Rule 144A, and any direct listings by foreign firms. ADRs are the principal means for foreign firms to cross-list in the US. Palmiter (2002) provides useful background information on ADRs. They are receipts for shares issued abroad. ADR prices are quoted in US dollars and trade in the US like domestic shares. ADRs in any form imply consent to US jurisdiction in disputes, exposing foreign firms to the risk of US criminal prosecution for legal violations (e.g., price fixing). Level I ADRs are commonly used to give US investors access to existing securities of foreign issuers but cannot be used to raise new capital. Level I ADR programs set up costs averaged about $25,000 in the early 2000s. As academics (e.g., Benos and Weisbach, 2004), jurists (e.g., *Pinker* v. *Roche*, 2002; *In Re: Volkswagen*, 2017), and legal practitioners (e.g., Norton, Rose, and Fulbright, 2009) have noted, sponsored Level I ADRs can subject foreign firms to US securities fraud liability (e.g., under SEC Rule 10b-5), to US jurisdiction to hear such claims, to US federal rules of criminal and civil procedure to process in a timely manner such claims, and to the formation of plaintiff classes often greatly magnifying a foreign firm's legal liability under such claims.[3] Level I ADRs limit foreign firm requirements to comply with other important federal securities regulatory provisions such as those under the 1933 Securities Act and 1934 Securities Exchange Act.

Level II ADRs are traded on US exchanges (e.g., NYSE) and are commonly used by firms seeking greater liquidity and investor recognition. Level II ADRs subject foreign firms to all Level I ADR obligations and compliance with SEC registration requirements under the 1934 Securities Exchange Act. Level II ADR programs averaged about $1 million to set up in the early 2000s. Level III ADRs permit foreign firms to raise new equity capital in a public offering in the US. Level III ADRs subject foreign firms to all Level I–II ADR obligations and liability provisions of the Securities Act of 1933 dealing with share offerings. From a legal liability perspective, foreign firms cross-listing as Level III ADRs are equivalent to domestically domiciled, publicly listed US firms. Set-up costs for Level III ADRs averaged about $1.5 million in the early 2000s.[4]

Typically, researchers sample from all sponsored ADRs (including those issued under US SEC Rule 144A) and any direct listings by foreign firms. Researchers then often split the sample into Level I ADRs (including Rule 144A ADRs) and Level II–III ADRs (including direct listings). The first sampling strategy identifies all foreign firms potentially shifting their legal presence. The second split sampling strategy identifies foreign firms potentially shifting to bond more (i.e., Level II–III ADR) or less (i.e., Level I ADR) with US corporate governance standards. Our empirical investigation accounts for both strategies.

---

[3]   The January 2017 *In Re: Volkswagen* decision by Judge Charles Breyer highlights the importance of Volkswagen's sponsorship of Level I ADRs in concluding that liability for US securities fraud may apply to the German automaker notwithstanding recent US Supreme Court decisions limiting the extra-territorial application of US securities laws (e.g., *Morrison* v. *National Australia Bank*, 2010). Thus, we do not treat a firm as cross-listed if it has an unsponsored ADR.

[4]   Benos and Wesibach (2004) analogize these three legal shift strategies to swimming: ADR Level I firms "toe" the waters of US corporate governance; ADR Level II firms "wade" into those waters; and ADR Level III firms effectively "swim" in the same waters of US corporate governance as domestically domiciled, publicly listed US firms.

Our principal source of US cross-listing information comes from the Bank of New York (2021). We also review listings at OTC Markets, a private organization providing quotes on more thinly traded shares that may not be listed on an organized exchange in the US (OTC Markets, 2010). We review listings on NYSE, NASDAQ, and OTC Markets (again) for information on direct listings by foreign firms. We also note ADR or direct share de-listings and unsponsored (by the foreign firm) ADRs, which are dropped from our sample.

Data sources for the seven country-level controls in Equations 11.1–11.3 come from several sources: US International Trade Commission (USITC, 2021) (*Market Presence*); World Bank's World Development Indicators (2021) (*Share Market Liquidity, Economic Growth*); the Milken Institute Capital Studies Group Capital Access Index (Angkinand et al., 1999–2007) (*Capital Availability*); and La Porta and colleagues (1998) (*Anti-Director Rights, Disclosure Rules, Liability Standards*). The Milken Institute Capital Access Index is available only from 1998. We also use 1998 values for 1996. Results excluding 1996 are consistent with those reported below. Data sources for the three firm-specific controls (*Firm Size, Firm ROA, and Firm Leverage*) and *Tobin's Q* come from Worldscope (2021). The *Common Law* variable comes from La Porta and colleagues (1998) and Reynolds and Flores (2003), while the *Rule of Law* variable comes from the World Bank's Governance Matters database developed by Kaufmann and colleagues (2000, 2009). The *Rule of Law* variable measure is reported biannually from 1996 to 2002 and then annually. We observe the measure biannually from 1996 to 2006. This *Rule of Law* variable measure is an index constructed from more than 20 different component indicators of rule of law, ranging from components measuring the fairness and speed of the judicial process, to the enforceability of contracts, quality of property rights, the respect for law, and confidence in judges and the judicial system. Indicator variables used in Equation 11.3 (*D1–4*) are derived from *Common Law* and *Rule of Law* variables.

RESULTS

Descriptive Statistics and Pair-Wise Correlations

Descriptive statistics and pair-wise correlations are reported in Table 11.2. The mean value of the dependent variable, *US Cross-Listing*, is approximately 0.04 (3.80 percent) when defined as US cross-listing in any form, and approximately 0.01 (0.52 percent) for US cross-listing at ADR Level II–III. Other descriptive statistics comport with intuition about emerging-market countries and firms. For example, the mean for *Economic Growth* (country gross domestic product growth) is 0.08 (8.14 percent) with a standard deviation of 0.13, indicative of wide variation not unsurprising when our time period of study includes both years of sustained economic growth (e.g., 1996) and economic crisis and contraction (e.g., 1998) in emerging markets. The mean value on the *Common Law* dummy (0.51) indicates a roughly 50–50 split between firms in our sample from common law (e.g., India) and civil law (e.g., Brazil) countries. The *Rule of Law* mean score is 0.39, thus just above the zero mean for the larger sample of all countries analyzed by Kaufmann and colleagues (2000, 2009), again with substantial variation given the standard deviation of 0.65.

Pair-wise correlations in Table 11.2 fall within reasonable ranges and generally follow the intuition of our study. For example, pair-wise correlations with *US Cross-Listing* in any form (column 1) and on a more restricted ADR Level II–III basis (column 2) suggest that firms are

Table 11.2   *Descriptive statistics and pair-wise correlations*

	Mean	Std. dev.	1	2	3	4	5	6	7	8	9	10	11	12	13	14
1. US Cross-Listing	0.04	0.19														
2. Level II–III US Cross-Listing	0.01	0.27	0.94**													
3. Market Presence	6.36	5.94	−0.02**	−0.02**												
4. Capital Availability	6.22	1.01	−0.06**	−0.06**	0.75**											
5. Share Market Liquidity	1.72	0.38	−0.08**	−0.11**	0.15**	0.22**										
6. Economic Growth	0.08	0.13	−0.01*	−0.02*	−0.04**	−0.20**	0.16**									
7. Anti-Director Rights	3.32	1.32	0.02**	0.02**	0.26**	0.42**	0.04**	−0.09**								
8. Liability Standards	0.55	0.20	−0.11**	−0.11**	0.27**	0.31**	0.25**	−0.06**	0.33**							
9. Disclosure Rules	0.72	0.22	−0.09**	−0.10**	0.48**	0.63**	0.37**	−0.08**	0.46**	0.41**						
10. Common Law	0.51	0.50	−0.05**	−0.06**	0.39**	0.52**	0.25**	−0.09**	0.65**	0.14**	0.75**					
11. Rule of Law	0.39	0.65	−0.05**	−0.05**	0.57**	0.77**	0.34**	−0.09**	0.29**	0.21**	0.42**	0.26**				
12. Firm Size	11.95	1.84	0.23**	0.23**	0.04**	−0.04**	0.01	−0.02**	−0.07**	−0.09**	−0.10**	−0.13**	0.03**			
13. Firm ROA	0.00	0.18	0.04**	0.04**	−0.08**	−0.09**	0.02**	0.12**	−0.00	−0.07**	−0.02**	−0.00	−0.03**	0.20**		

	Mean	Std. dev.	1	2	3	4	5	6	7	8	9	10	11	12	13	14
14. Firm Leverage	0.53	0.35	0.01	0.01	−0.13**	−0.13**	0.05**	−0.05**	−0.10**	−0.02**	−0.09**	−0.09**	−0.12**	0.12**	−0.45**	
15. Tobin's Q	1.30	1.06	0.01†	0.02**	−0.02**	−0.01	0.03**	0.03**	0.10**	0.04**	0.02**	0.07**	0.03**	−0.20**	−0.15**	0.21**

Note: The two dependent variables are *US Cross-Listing*, a 0–1 term where 1 denotes listing in the US as an ADR Level I, II, III, or direct listing (including a listing under Rule 144A) and 0 denotes no US listing by a firm from one of 22 emerging market countries observed biannually from 1997 to 2007: Argentina, Brazil, Chile, Colombia, Egypt, Greece, Hong Kong, India, Indonesia, Israel, Malaysia, Mexico, Pakistan, Peru, Philippines, South Africa, South Korea, Sri Lanka, Thailand, Turkey, Venezuela, and Zimbabwe. *Level II–III US Cross-Listing* is a 0–1 term where 1 denotes listing in the US as an ADR Level II–III or direct US listing by a firm from the same 22 emerging-market countries observed biannually from 1997 to 2007. † p<0.10; * p<0.05; ** p<0.01.

less likely to cross-list when capital at home is more available, when domestic share markets have greater liquidity, when domestic liability and disclosure standards are more rigorous, and when they are smaller, less profitable firms. They are also less likely to cross-list when they have more protective common law and stronger rule of law domestically.

Core Analyses

Table 11.3 reports results from logistic regression estimations of Equation 11.1 with country-level determinants of *US Cross-Listing*. Column 1 reports results with country-level controls only. Standard errors are clustered on country. Four terms exhibit expected signs at commonly accepted levels of statistical significance. US cross-listing is more likely for firms from emerging-market countries with more US trade (0.055, p<0.01) and lower capital access (−0.179, p<0.05), slower economic growth (−0.692, p<0.10), and weaker liability standards (−1.155, p<0.01) back home. Only *Country Anti-Director Rights* exhibits a contrary sign at statistically significant levels (0.221, p<0.01).

Columns 2–5 sequentially add country-level terms tied directly to our theoretical framework and Hypotheses 1–3. Column 2 adds *Common Law*, which enters with a negative sign, but is not statistically significant at conventional levels, thus lending no support on its own for Hypothesis 1. Column 3 drops *Common Law* and adds *Rule of Law*, which is negative and statistically significant (−0.377, p<0.01), consistent with Hypothesis 2. Inclusion of both terms in column 4 yields results supporting both Hypothesis 1 and Hypothesis 2. *Common Law* (−0.460, p<0.05) and *Rule of Law* (−0.504, p<0.01) terms both enter with negative signs at significant levels. Country-level institutional factors related to legal system and enforcement positively and significantly affect the likelihood that an emerging-market firm will leapfrog legally to the US via cross-listing.

Column 5 adds to Equation 11.1 the *Common Law*Rule of Law* interaction term used to test Hypothesis 3. It enters positively and significantly (1.853, p<0.01). Consistent with Hypothesis 3, we observe that stronger rule of law diminishes the importance of legal system effects on US cross-listing likelihood. Another way to interpret these results is that the *Common Law* coefficient (β_9) captures the marginal impact on US cross-listing by firms from emerging-market countries with weaker rule of law. If *Rule of Law* score is set to 0—close to the *Rule of Law* sample mean of 0.39—the net impact on *US Cross-Listing* is fully captured by the *Common Law* coefficient estimated alone. As *Rule of Law* scores sink below 0, the linear combination of *Common Law* and *Rule of Law*Common Law* ($\beta_9 + \beta_{10}$) becomes increasingly negative. As *Rule of Law* scores exceed the sample mean, the same linear combination of *Common Law* and *Rule of Law*Common Law* yields less negative net effects on US cross-listing likelihood.

The non-linear nature of logistic regression means that interpretation of this interaction will benefit from re-analysis based on alternative simulation methods originally developed by King and colleagues (2000) with modifications by Zelner (2009), permitting illustration of simulation results. Using Zelner's (2009) "intgph" Stata procedure, we simulate US cross-listing likelihood among individual firms given different legal system and rule of law states. We set continuous (dummy) variables at their mean values, except for *Rule of Law*, *Common Law*, and *Rule of Law*Common Law* terms and graph expected changes in the likelihood of US cross-listing given increasing levels of *Rule of Law*. Results from this procedure are illustrated in Figure 11.1.

Table 11.3   Core regression results I: country-level determinants of US cross-listing

Empirical models →	(1) Country controls	(2) Country controls, common law	(3) Country controls, rule of law	(4) Country controls, common law, rule of law	(5) Country controls, common law, rule of law interaction
Variables ↓	Logit	Logit	Logit	Logit	Logit
Market Presence (β_1)	0.055**	0.057**	0.046**	0.052**	0.040**
	(0.010)	(0.010)	(0.010)	(0.010)	(0.012)
Capital Availability (β_2)	−0.179*	−0.178*	0.035	0.117	−0.133
	(0.085)	(0.084)	(0.108)	(0.112)	(0.113)
Share Mkt Liquidity (β_3)	0.051	0.053	0.167	0.223*	0.165†
	(0.098)	(0.099)	(0.105)	(0.112)	(0.099)
Economic Growth (β_4)	−0.692†	−0.700*	−0.761*	−0.832*	−0.386
	(0.354)	(0.353)	(0.358)	(0.355)	(0.337)
Anti-Director Rights (β_5)	0.221**	0.231**	0.243**	0.303**	0.326**
	(0.046)	(0.052)	(0.047)	(0.057)	(0.059)
Liability Standards (β_6)	−1.155**	−1.212**	−1.020**	−1.240**	−2.181**
	(0.292)	(0.316)	(0.275)	(0.289)	(0.347)
Disclosure Rules (β_7)	0.062	0.062	0.589†	0.779*	0.423
	(0.313)	(0.313)	(0.352)	(0.380)	(0.389)
Common Law (β_8)		−0.089		−0.460*	−1.642**
		(0.165)		(0.199)	(0.234)
Rule of Law (β_9)			−0.377**	−0.504**	−0.531**
			(0.107)	(0.125)	(0.125)
Common Law* Rule of Law (β_{10})					1.853**
					(0.149)
Region dummies	Yes	Yes	Yes	Yes	Yes
Year dummies	Yes	Yes	Yes	Yes	Yes
N	26,773	26,773	26,773	26,773	26,773
Pseudo R^2	0.093	0.093	0.095	0.095	0.110

Note: Columns 1–5 report point estimates and standard errors (in parentheses) and related outputs from binary logistic regression analyses of country-level factors affecting US cross-listing by firms from 22 emerging market countries observed biannually from 1997 to 2007. See Table 11.2 for the list of countries sampled. The dependent variable is *US Cross-Listing*, a 0–1 term where 1 denotes listing in the US as an ADR Level I, II, III, or direct listing and 0 denotes no US listing by firm i from country k in year t. Pseudo R^2 refers to the pseudo coefficient of correlation for binary logistic regression estimations. Regression results for year dummies and region dummies are not reported but are available on request. † $p<0.10$; * $p<0.05$; ** $p<0.01$.

The trend line in Figure 11.1 plots expected changes in the probability of an individual firm cross-listing in the US given a shift in home-country legal system from civil to common law and then increasing rule of law strength. Upper and lower bands are placed around that trend line based on a 5 percent level of statistical significance. The trend line indicates additional support for our general argument that a firm's home-country legal system is most salient when rule of law is weak, but that such legal system effects diminish as rule of law strengthens. A shift from civil to common law significantly decreases the likelihood of US cross-listing

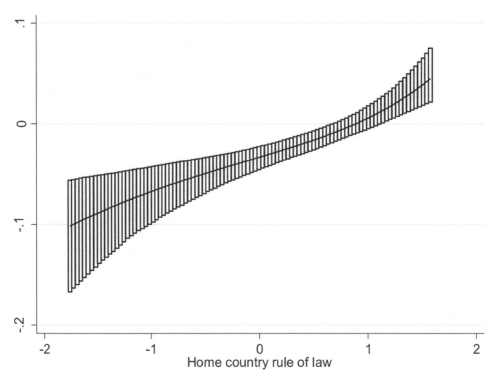

Note: The non-linear trend and confidence intervals (95 percent) from binary logistic regression-based
simulations of home-country rule of law effects on US cross-listing by firms from 22 emerging-market countries
observed biannually from 1997 to 2007. See Table 11.2 for the list of countries sampled. We simulate changes in
the likelihood of US cross-listing in any form (y-axis) as home-country rule of law strengthens (x-axis) and given
a change in the home country's legal system from civil to common law.

*Figure 11.1   Core regression results II: simulated interaction term results for
country-level determinants of US cross-listing*

until *Rule of Law* reaches approximately 0.70 on the x-axis of Figure 11.1. When *Rule of
Law* exceeds 1.20 on the x-axis, a shift from civil to common law legal system increases
(not decreases) firms' tendencies to leapfrog legally via cross-listing in the US. These results
underscore the importance of assessing aspects of country-level institutions individually and
in interaction.

Table 11.4 reports results from estimations of Equations 2 and 3 including both country-
and firm-level determinants of *US Cross-Listing*. Column 1 reports the estimation results
for Equation 11.2, that is, with country- and firm-level controls and *Tobin's Q* only. Again,
standard errors are clustered on country. Two of three firm-level controls enter significantly,
one with the expected positive sign (*Firm Size* = 0.667, p<0.01), but one with a significantly
negative rather than expected positive sign. Emerging-market firms are less (not more) likely
to cross-list when more leveraged (−1.041, p<0.01). *Tobin's Q* enters with a positive sign
at commonly accepted levels of statistical significance (0.263, p<0.01). Firms with better

growth opportunities are more likely to leapfrog legally through cross-listing in order to access capital permitting the realization of such opportunities. This support for Hypothesis 4 persists in column 2 when we add the country-level rule of law-legal system dummies (*Tobin's Q* = 0.247, p<0.01).

Table 11.4   *Core regression results III: country- and firm-level determinants of US cross-listing*

Empirical models →	(1) Country controls, firm controls, Tobin's Q	(2) Country controls, firm controls, Tobin's Q, dummies	(3) Country controls, firm controls, Tobin's Q, dummies, Tobin's Q *dummies	(4) No region fixed effects	(5) No year fixed effects	(6) No region or year fixed effects
Variables ↓	Logit	Logit	Logit	Logit	Logit	Logit
Market	0.032**	0.046**	0.047**	0.050**	0.037**	0.046**
Presence (β_1)	(0.010)	(0.013)	(0.013)	(0.009)	(0.012)	(0.009)
Capital	−0.149†	−0.063	−0.052	−0.427**	−0.012	−0.404**
Availability (β_2)	(0.089)	(0.093)	(0.093)	(0.071)	(0.089)	(0.064)
Share Mkt	−0.155	0.037	0.008	0.190†	0.069	0.249*
Liquidity (β_3)	(0.099)	(0.110)	(0.111)	(0.112)	(0.097)	(0.100)
Economic	−0.423	−0.641†	−0.623	−0.925*	−1.323**	−1.758
Growth (β_4)	(0.387)	(0.380)	(0.380)	(0.361)	(0.288)	(0.260)
Anti-Director	0.252**	0.405**	0.402**	0.515**	0.349**	0.508**
Rights (β_5)	(0.049)	(0.067)	(0.067)	(0.041)	(0.067)	(0.040)
Liability	−1.256**	−2.716**	−2.772**	−2.635**	−2.593**	−2.759**
Standards (β_6)	(0.338)	(0.522)	(0.524)	(0.277)	(0.528)	(0.269)
Disclosure	−0.194	−1.614**	−1.669**	−1.210**	−1.484**	−1.275**
Rules(β_7)	(0.348)	(0.512)	(0.514)	(0.288)	(0.529)	(0.288)
Firm	0.667**	0.657**	0.658**	0.655**	0.652**	0.647**
Size (β_8)	(0.022)	(0.022)	(0.022)	(0.021)	(0.021)	(0.021)
Firm	0.071	0.236	0.185	0.265	0.082	0.145
ROA (β_9)	(0.420)	(0.429)	(0.419)	(0.402)	(0.407)	(0.385)
Firm	−1.041**	−0.938**	−0.967**	−0.910**	−0.990**	−0.927**
Leverage (β_{10})	(0.179)	(0.177)	(0.173)	(0.167)	(0.173)	(0.166)
Firm	0.263**	0.247**				
Tobin's Q (β_{11})	(0.031)	(0.031)				
D1 (Str Rule,		−0.632**	−0.302	−0.122	−0.170	−0.069
Com Law) (β_{12})		(0.231)	(0.267)	(0.239)	(0.264)	(0.238)
D2 (Str Rule,		−0.600**	−0.351†	−0.331†	−0.316	−0.284
Civ Law) (β_{13})		(0.144)	(0.199)	(0.192)	(0.200)	(0.194)
D3 (Wk Rule,		−3.067**	−3.790**	−3.166**	−3.557**	−3.174**
Com Law) (β_{14})		(0.552)	(0.754)	(0.672)	(0.763)	(0.684)
Tobin's Q*			0.197**	0.227**	0.188**	0.221**
D1 (β_{15})			(0.039)	(0.038)	(0.039)	(0.039)

Empirical models →	(1) Country controls, firm controls, Tobin's Q	(2) Country controls, firm controls, Tobin's Q, dummies	(3) Country controls, firm controls, Tobin's Q, dummies, Tobin's Q *dummies	(4) No region fixed effects	(5) No year fixed effects	(6) No region or year fixed effects
Variables ↓	Logit	Logit	Logit	Logit	Logit	Logit
Tobin's Q*			0.262**	0.285**	0.252**	0.265**
D2 (β_{16})			(0.051)	(0.049)	(0.052)	(0.050)
Tobin's Q*			0.826**	0.756**	0.770**	0.710**
D3 (β_{17})			(0.225)	(0.225)	(0.229)	(0.229)
Tobin's Q*			0.450**	0.426**	0.382**	0.356**
D4 (β_{18})			(0.095)	(0.093)	(0.100)	(0.098)
Region dummies	Yes	Yes	Yes	No	Yes	No
Year dummies	Yes	Yes	Yes	Yes	No	No
N	26,773	26,773	26,773	26,773	26,773	26,773
Pseudo R^2	0.228	0.235	0.236	0.230	0.232	0.225

Note: Columns 1–6 report point estimates, standard errors (in parenthesis), and related outputs from binary logistic regression analyses of country- and firm-level factors affecting US cross-listing by firms from emerging-market countries observed biannually from 1997 to 2007. See Table 11.2 for the list of emerging-market countries sampled. The dependent variable is *US Cross-Listing*, a 0–1 term where 1 denotes listing in the US as an ADR Level I, II, III, or direct listing and 0 denotes no US listing by firm i from country k in year t. Regression results for year dummies and region dummies are not reported but are available on request. † p<0.10; * p<0.05; ** p<0.01.

In column 3 we re-estimate with the unconstrained Equation 11.3. We replace *Tobin's Q* with the interaction of *Tobin's Q* and the four dummies, *D1*, *D2*, *D3*, and *D4* (as in Equation 11.3). Recall that the interaction terms assess the sensitivity of *US Cross-Listing* to *Tobin's Q* in common law countries with strong rule of law (*Tobin's Q*D1*), civil law countries with strong rule of law (*Tobin's Q*D2*), common law countries with weak rule of law (*Tobin's Q*D3*), and civil law countries with weak rule of law (*Tobin's Q*D4*). All four terms are positive and significant consistent with earlier results indicating a greater likelihood to cross-list in the US as emerging-market firm growth opportunities improve.

Testing Hypothesis 5 based on Equation 11.3 requires two comparisons of the interaction terms. First, we hold constant legal system and compare differences in the impact of *Tobin's Q* as home-country rule of law goes from weak to strong. For firms from emerging-market countries with a common law system the test reduces to whether *Tobin's Q*D3* (0.826, p<0.01) is greater than *Tobin's Q*D1* (0.197, p<0.01). A Wald test indicates that the *Tobin's Q*D3* is larger and that this difference is significant at the 1 percent level, thus supporting Hypothesis 5. For firms from emerging-market countries with a civil law system, those differences reduce to whether *Tobin's Q*D4* (0.450, p<0.01) is greater than *Tobin's Q*D2* (0.262, p<0.01). Again, a Wald test indicates that *Tobin's Q*D4* is larger. This time the difference is significant at the 10 percent level, again supporting Hypothesis 5. The quality of higher-level institutional factors becomes more important in explaining legal leapfrog likelihood via US cross-listing as emerging-market firm growth opportunities increase.

Second, we test Hypothesis 5 by holding rule of law strength constant and then varying the legal system. For firms from emerging-market countries with strong rule of law, the difference in *Tobin's Q* effect on *US Cross-Listing* reduces to whether *Tobin's Q*D2* (0.262, p<0.01) is greater than *Tobin's Q*D1* (0.197, p<0.01). For firms from emerging-market countries with weak rule of law, the same difference reduces to whether *Tobin's Q*D4* (0.450, p<0.01) is greater than *Tobin's Q*D3* (0.826, p<0.01). Neither comparison is, thus lending no support for Hypothesis 5 regarding legal system. Although not illustrated here, these *Tobin's Q*D* interaction results and related comparisons are confirmed in alternative simulation analyses (King, Tomz, and Wittenberg, 2000; Zelner, 2009). This pattern of findings persists across columns 4–6 of Table 11.4 when we drop region effects (column 4), drop year effects (column 5), and drop both (column 6). The effect of firm-specific growth opportunities on legal leapfrogging likelihood does not differ in response to changing country-level factors related to legal system. From a broader perspective, results in Table 11.4 suggest that interaction effects between country- and firm-level factors are significant, but not uniformly so. Each country-firm combinatorial effect in a cross-level framework such as ours merits close scrutiny.

Robustness Analyses

Core regression results in Table 11.4 largely support Hypotheses 1–4 and lend partial support to Hypothesis 5. But these core regression results might be sensitive to reasonable variation in model specification, sampling, and estimation strategies. Table 11.5 reports results from eight variations that largely confirm our core results. Although not reported here, results from all eight of these robustness studies are confirmed with simulation methods applied earlier to our country-level estimations (King et al., 2000; Zelner, 2009).[5]

Alternative measures of anti-director rights and common law

The *Anti-Director Rights* and *Common Law* terms in our cross-level models of *US Cross-Listing* could be the source of measurement bias meriting remeasurement with alternatives. Aguilera and Williams (2009), Aguilera and Jackson (2010), and Spamann (2010) note both terms as important to the law and finance empirical research agenda, but also raise reasonable criticisms of both as originally developed by La Porta and colleagues (1998). The *Anti-Director Rights* measure they developed drew largely on assessments of corporate and securities law texts in the mid-1990s (e.g., Reynolds and Flores, 2003). Later research by Spamann (2010) remeasured the same *Anti-Director Rights* term for 1997 and 2005 based also on interviews and surveys of local attorneys in those same countries, and found substantial

---

[5]   In addition to robustness results discussed in this section of the study, we obtain results consistent with core regression results in Table 11.4 when we re-estimate Equation 11.1 and Equation 11.3 after doing the following: (1) replace the *Anti-Director Rights* variable measure with an alternative shareholder protection measure developed by Guillén and Capron (2016); (2) replace the *Rule of Law* categorization with an alternative categorization based on business perceptions of judicial efficiency used by La Porta and colleagues (1998); (3) add a control variable for the percentage of shares held by firm insiders; (4) add a control variable for firm cross-listing in countries other than the US or UK; and (5) add a control variable for the number of acquisitions of US firms by firms from each sampled country. Details regarding these results are available from the authors on request.

Table 11.5　Robustness results: country- and firm-level determinants of US cross-listing

Empirical models →	(1) Spamann measure of anti-director rights	(2) Klermann et al. measure of legal system	(3) Adding foreign sales	(4) Control of corruption	(5) Estimating with post-SOX sub-sample only	(6) Developed countries	(7) Accounting for different cross-listing levels	(8) Accounting for different cross-listing levels, adding UK, foreign sales
Variables ↓	Logit	Logit	Logit	Logit	Logit	Logit	Logit	Logit
Market Presence (β_1)	0.029*	0.129**	0.025	0.028*	0.023	−0.030**	0.041**	0.023
	(0.014)	(0.016)	(0.020)	(0.013)	(0.021)	(0.009)	(0.013)	(0.019)
Capital Availability (β_2)	0.162†	0.065	0.272*	0.007	−0.183**	0.086	−0.058	0.339*
	(0.092)	(0.112)	(0.139)	(0.092)	(0.123)	(0.139)	(0.092)	(0.132)
Share Mkt Liquidity (β_3)	−0.258*	−0.001	−0.063	0.107	0.133	−1.266**	−0.017	−0.198
	(0.112)	(0.120)	(0.225)	(0.110)	(0.170)	(0.239)	(0.110)	(0.235)
Economic Growth (β_4)	−0.296	−0.959*	−0.039	−0.696†	−1.533*	1.820**	−0.645†	0.272
	(0.392)	(0.457)	(0.587)	(0.376)	(0.707)	(0.649)	(0.380)	(0.619)
Anti-Director Rights (β_5)	0.174*	0.518**	0.494**	0.311**	0.370**	0.087†	0.408**	0.394**
	(0.072)	(0.081)	(0.107)	(0.063)	(0.108)	(0.046)	(0.066)	(0.103)
Liability Standards (β_6)	−1.397**	−1.286†	−3.447**	−1.020**	−2.450**	0.178	−2.593**	−2.638**
	(0.369)	(0.663)	(0.776)	(0.326)	(0.753)	(0.245)	(0.500)	(0.722)
Disclosure Rules (β_7)	−0.721	−3.474**	−2.175*	−0.644†	−0.905	−0.973*	−1.379**	−1.842*
	(0.461)	(0.512)	(0.846)	(0.352)	(0.909)	(0.446)	(0.500)	(0.801)
Firm Size (β_8)	0.666**	0.612**	0.653**	0.674**	0.703**	0.778**	0.665**	0.623**
	(0.022)	(0.023)	(0.032)	(.0.022)	(0.031)	(0.020)	(0.021)	(0.032)
Firm ROA (β_9)	0.066	0.433	1.235	0.027	0.597	−2.078**	0.182	1.306†
	(0.418)	(0.407)	(0.775)	(0.405)	(0.412)	(0.174)	(0.413)	(0.770)
Firm Leverage (β_{10})	−1.082**	−1.003**	−0.870**	−1.035**	−1.155**	−0.945**	−0.926**	−0.852**
	(0.174)	(0.186)	(0.255)	(0.178)	(0.267)	(0.142)	(0.170)	(0.250)
D1 (Str Rule, Com Law) (β_{12})	0.234	−0.928*	−0.246	−0.423	0.103	1.208**	−0.354	0.060
	(0.255)	(0.416)	(0.448)	(0.264)	(0.399)	(0.201)	(0.263)	(0.463)
D2 (Str Rule, Civ Law) (β_{13})	−0.293	−0.498*	−0.141	−0.692**	−0.388	0.522**	−0.369	−0.157
	(0.204)	(0.142)	(0.352)	(0.176)	(0.310)	(0.162)	(0.193)	(0.342)

Empirical models → Variables ↓	(1) Spamann measure of anti-director rights	(2) Klermann et al. measure of legal system	(3) Adding foreign sales	(4) Control of corruption	(5) Estimating with post-SOX sub-sample only	(6) Developed countries	(7) Accounting for different cross-listing levels	(8) Accounting for different cross-listing levels, adding UK, foreign sales
	Logit	Logit	Logit	Logit	Logit	Logit	Logit	Logit
D3 (Wk Rule, Com Law) (β_{14})	-2.654**	-4.694**	-3.119**	0.326	-3.250**	2.338**	-3.594**	-2.370**
	(0.717)	(0.813)	(0.797)	(0.321)	(1.064)	(0.421)	(0.730)	(0.790)
Tobin's Q* D1 (β_{15})	0.194**	0.161**	0.134**	0.264**	0.252**	0.401**	0.219**	0.166**
	(0.039)	(0.044)	(0.049)	(0.045)	(0.058)	(0.027)	(0.039)	(0.049)
Tobin's Q* D2 (β_{16})	0.276**	0.271**	0.361**	0.294**	0.369**	0.377**	0.280**	0.436**
	(0.050)	(0.052)	(0.097)	(0.048)	(0.072)	(0.033)	(0.049)	(0.099)
Tobin's Q* D3 (β_{17})	0.827**	0.883**	0.503*	0.185**	0.896**	0.594**	0.771**	0.539*
	(0.218)	(0.246)	(0.235)	(0.062)	(0.288)	(0.123)	(0.201)	(0.229)
Tobin's Q* D4 (β_{18})	0.458**	0.414**	0.624**	0.376**	0.477**	0.396**	0.450**	0.669**
	(0.095)	(0.105)	(0.167)	(0.084)	(0.112)	(0.049)	(0.088)	(0.157)
Firm Foreign Sales (β_{19})			0.390*					0.350†
			(0.183)					(0.180)
Firm UK Listing (β_{21})								3.190**
								(0.340)
Region dummies	Yes	Yes	Yes	Yes	Yes	Yes	Yes	Yes
Year dummies	Yes	Yes	Yes	Yes	Yes	Yes	Yes	Yes
N	26,773	26,773	11,604	26,773	15,802	55,204	26,773	11,604
Pseudo R^2	0.291	0.227	0.226	0.234	0.255	0.252	0.210	0.221

Note: SOX = Sarbanes-Oxley Act. Columns 1-8 report point estimates, standard errors (in parenthesis), and related outputs from binary logistic regression analyses of country- and firm-level factors affecting US cross-listing by firms from emerging-market countries observed biannually from 1997 to 2007. See Table 11.2 for the list of emerging-market countries sampled. In columns 1–6 the dependent variable is *US Cross-Listing*, a 0–1 term where 1 denotes listing in the US as an ADR Level I, II, III, or direct listing and 0 denotes no US listing by firm *i* from country *i* in year *t*. In columns 7–8, the dependent variable is again *US Cross-Listing*, but this time a 0–1–2 term where 1 denotes listing in the US as an ADR Level I, 2 denotes listing in the US as an ADR Level II, III, or direct listing, and 0 denotes no US listing by firm *i* from country *k* in year *t*. Regression results for year dummies, region dummies, and cut points for ordered logistic regression results are not reported but are available on request. † p<0.10; * p<0.05 ; ** p<0.01.

variance in measures and rankings of anti-director rights strength compared to La Porta and colleagues.

The *Common Law* categorization La Porta and colleagues developed also draws criticism for being so coarse-grained that it "only partially account[s] for governance realities" (Aguilera and Jackson, 2010, p. 486). Perhaps responding to such criticism, Klermann, Mahoney, Spamann, and Weinstein (2011) develop an alternative categorization of country legal systems based on legal and colonial origins. Only countries with both Anglo-American legal *and* colonial heritage might merit categorization as pure *Common Law* under their approach.

We address the possibility, raised by these criticisms, of bias in our findings in columns 1–2 of Table 11.5. In column 1, we replace the *Anti-Director Rights* measure developed by La Porta and colleagues (1998) with a weighted value based on Spamann (2010): scores for 1996 are identical to Spamann's 1997 score; 2006 scores are identical to Spamann's 2005 score; scores for 1998, 2000, 2002, and 2004 are calculated using a weighted average of Spamann's 1997 and 2005 scores, with the weighting balance progressively shifting from 1997 to 2005 over time. This alternative *Anti-Director Rights* term again enters positively at commonly accepted levels of statistical significance (0.174, $p<0.01$). More importantly, inclusion of this alternative has no effect on the four *Tobin's Q*D* interaction terms, which remain positive, and exhibit the same pattern of differences consistent with earlier results, indicating support for Hypothesis 5 regarding rule of law but not legal system.

In column 2 we replace the *Common Law* categorization based on La Porta and colleagues (1998) with a more restrictive 0–1 *Common Law* dummy based on Klermann and colleagues (2011). Firms from only four countries in our sample have both Anglo-American legal and colonial heritage and take the value of 1 with this more restrictive *Common Law* dummy: Hong Kong, Malaysia, India, and Pakistan. Inclusion of this alternative again has no effect on the four *Tobin's Q*D* interaction terms, which remain positive and exhibit the same pattern of differences consistent with earlier core results, indicating support for Hypothesis 5 regarding rule of law but not legal system. Consistent results with these alternatives let us return to using the original *Anti-Director Rights* and *Common Law* terms based on La Porta and colleagues for all other estimations reported in Table 11.5.

Foreign sales presence

We next consider the possibility of omitted variable bias. One such source could be foreign sales. A firm's overseas growth opportunities may very well be correlated with its present business abroad. To address that possibility, we include in column 3 an additional control, *Foreign Sales*, which is measured as the percentage of total firm sales outside of the firm's domestic market. Requiring this information drops our sample size to 4,065 distinct firms and 11,604 firm years. This likely skews the sample in favor of larger firms more likely to be selling abroad. Even so, we still have substantial variation in country- and firm-level terms and sufficient estimation power.

Foreign Sales enters positively and significantly at commonly accepted levels (0.390, $p<0.05$). Firms selling more abroad are more likely to shift their legal presence via cross-listing. All four *Tobin's Q*D* interaction terms remain positive and exhibit the same pattern of differences consistent with earlier core results, indicating support for Hypothesis 5 regarding rule of law but not legal system.

Alternative governance quality indicators

Another source of bias could follow from model misspecification related to key constructs. Our four different *D* scenarios and related interactions are based on the measure of *Rule of Law* developed by Kaufmann and colleagues. However, Kaufmann and colleagues (2010) define five additional measures to proxy for broader "governance" quality: (1) voice and accountability; (2) political stability and absence of violence; (3) government effectiveness; (4) regulatory quality; and (5) control of corruption.[6] Perhaps any of these dimensions of governance explain variation in legal shift tendencies, not necessarily rule of law and the legal dimensions it purports to capture.

One way to assess whether emerging-market firms are responding to weakness in home-country *legal* institutions is to re-estimate *US Cross-Listing* with one of these alternative governance measures. In column 4 we replace *Rule of Law* as the basis for constructing the four *D* scenarios with *Control of Corruption*. It measures perceptions of the extent to which public power is exercised for private gain—including both petty and grand forms of corruption—as well as capture of the state by elites and private interests. Like *Rule of Law*, *Control of Corruption* is a standardized measure $(0, \sigma)$ for country *k* in year *t*, with a similar mean for our sample (0.39). This new public governance has particular importance for emerging-market countries in Africa where corruption in different forms is bemoaned as a drag on economic and institutional development.

*Tobin's Q*D* interaction terms in column 4 exhibit the same positive signs and significant levels, but differences in magnitude are no longer consistent with Hypothesis 5. The impact of better growth opportunities for a firm domiciled in an emerging-market country with poor controls on corruption and a less protective civil law system (*Tobin's Q*D4* = 0.376, p<0.01) is not significantly greater than for a similarly situated firm domiciled in an emerging-market country with strong controls on corruption (*Tobin's Q*D2* = 0.294, p<0.01). The impact of better growth opportunities for a firm domiciled in an emerging-market country with a common law system but poor controls on corruption (*Tobin's Q*D3* = 0.185, p<0.01) is not significantly greater than for a similarly situated firm with strong controls on corruption (*Tobin's Q*D1* = 0.264, p<0.01). Such contrasts with our core results provide further assurance that we have properly identified legal constructs in our cross-level model. Home-country scenarios based on differences in legal system and rule of law quality are in fact capturing *legal* dimensions of governance relevant to emerging-market firms, including those from Africa.

---

[6] Descriptions of these other five governance variables include (1) voice and accountability— the extent to which a country's citizens are able to participate in selecting their government, as well as freedom of expression, freedom of association, and a free media; (2) political stability and absence of violence—the likelihood that the government will be destabilized or overthrown by unconstitutional or violent means, including politically motivated violence and terrorism; (3) government effectiveness— the quality of public services, the quality of the civil service and the degree of its independence from political pressures, the quality of policy formulation and implementation, and the credibility of the government's commitment to such policies; (4) regulatory quality—the ability of the government to formulate and implement sound policies and regulations that permit and promote private-sector development; and (5) control of corruption—the extent to which public power is exercised for private gain, including both petty and grand forms of corruption, as well as "capture" of the state by elites and private interests (Kaufmann et al., 2010).

Changing US corporate governance standards

Another source of bias could be related to time. At one point in time, superior governance quality might justify the costs of legal leapfrogging. However, subsequent changes in either governance quality or costs could change the balance of this calculus and lead a firm to rescind its move–de-list in the US and thus "jump back" home legally. Time-varying country controls, time (year) dummies and a time-varying *Rule of Law* measure might account for legal leapfrogging and then jumps back home only partially. Such time-related concerns might matter for our study. In 2002, the US passed the so-called Sarbanes-Oxley Act (SOX), creating new or enhanced corporate governance standards for public company boards, management, and professional service firms providing advisory legal and accounting services.[7] Legal commentators like Butler and Ribstein (2006) derided SOX as a "debacle" that substantially increased the cost and complexity of US corporate regulation without substantially improving oversight and deterrence of corporate malfeasance. By "raising the rent" of US corporate governance (Ribstein, 2005) without raising quality, foreign firms would shift cross-listing to non-US alternatives such as the London Stock Exchange's (LSE) Alternative Investment Market (AIM).

Consistent with this view, Litvak (2007) documents significant negative financial returns to US cross-listed firms as SOX legislation passed through various Congressional committee and plenary votes. Piotroski and Srinisvasan (2008) find that smaller firms were more likely to list in the UK, particularly on the LSE's AIM, after passage of SOX. Georgieva (2009) finds that foreign firms are more likely to terminate ADR listings. These studies analyze the behavior of firms from a broad range of countries, rather than the emerging markets where bonding motivations are most prominent. We find that this focus matters.

Column 5 reports results from re-estimation of Equations 11.2 and 11.3 with a sub-sample of 6,614 distinct firms and 15,802 emerging-market firm years from the post-SOX period (2003, 2005, and 2007). *Tobin's Q*D* interaction terms remain positive and significant, while differences in coefficient magnitude are again consistent with Hypothesis 5 regarding rule of law but not legal system. Passage of SOX may have changed US cross-listing behavior by firms from a broad range of industrialized or less developed countries, but not among emerging-market firms—the group of firms we think more likely to cross-list in the US to shift legal presence. If SOX raised US corporate governance rent, then firms from emerging-market countries also perceived increasing corporate governance value from paying that rent through cross-listing.

Applicability of bonding hypothesis to developed-country firms

Our legal leapfrogging framework and hypotheses followed in part from assumptions about distinctive characteristics of emerging-market countries and firms. Indeed, our study was

---

[7]   SOX indirectly promoted new and arguably stronger standards of corporate governance relevant to emerging-market firms cross-listed as Level I ADRs even though such ADRs are not listed on a US exchange and are not subject to the full force of the US federal securities regulatory regime of which SOX became part in the early 2000s. For example, SOX mandated the creation of the Public Company Accounting Oversight Board (PCAOB). The PCAOB registers auditors, defines specific processes and procedures for compliance audits, inspects and polices conduct and quality control, and enforces compliance with SOX mandates. The PCAOB essentially created a new certification regime for the corporate auditing profession, a certification that matters for all cross-listed foreign firms, not merely those cross-listed as Level II or III ADRs and thus subject to the substantive provisions of SOX.

motivated in part by the failure of previous research to find strong support for the bonding hypothesis. Because we attributed such findings, at least in part, to a failure to test the theory in a context where it was most applicable, it is important to test whether the cross-listing behavior of emerging-market firms is indeed different from that of firms from wealthier, industrialized countries. To investigate that possibility, we again construct our four *D* scenarios based on combinations of *Common Law* and *Rule of Law*, replacing our sample of emerging-market firms with a sample of 15,674 distinct firms and 55,204 firm years domiciled in 20 wealthy, developed countries: Australia, Austria, Belgium, Denmark, Finland, France, Germany, Ireland, Italy, Japan, Luxembourg, Netherlands, New Zealand, Norway, Portugal, Singapore, Spain, Sweden, Switzerland, and the UK.

Column 6 reports results from re-estimation with these developed-country firms. We again see positive and significant coefficients on *Tobin's Q*D* interaction terms, but we also observe important differences. The *D1*, *D2*, and *D3* terms in column 6 are all positive and significant, a contrast with the generally negative signs on the same terms when estimated with emerging-market firms. Compared to firms domiciled in developed countries with the "weakest" investor protection (i.e., weak rule of law and civil law system), firms from other countries are more (not less) likely to cross-list in the US. This trend contradicts the basic idea of the bonding hypothesis as well as our framework, which builds on that idea to argue that firms are more likely to shift their legal presence to the extent that their home-country institutions provide fewer investor protections. These contrasts suggest that developed- and emerging-market firms have different motivations to cross-list on US markets—for example, greater coverage by stock analysts. For developed-country firms, US cross-listing patterns are inconsistent with bonding motivations. These contrasts vindicate our study's legal leapfrogging framework assumptions and sampling strategies.

Different cross-listing levels

Column 7 presents results indicating the robustness of our core results to changes in estimation strategy. Up until now, we have modeled the cross-listing decision as a 0–1 choice, when in reality foreign firms can choose different ADR programs costing less to set up but signaling less adherence to US governance standards (ADR Level I) or ADR programs costing and signaling more (ADR Levels II–III). To understand whether accounting for such gradation in cross-listing and commitment matters, we redefine *US Cross-Listing* as a 0–1–2 choice. It is 0 for no US cross-listing, 1 for an ADR Level I (or Rule 144A ADR) cross-listing, and 2 for an ADR Level II or III cross-listing (or direct listing). We then employ ordered logistic regression with all the independent variables in Equations 11.2 and 11.3. Results and inferences are substantially the same as those reported in core results. In particular, we find that *Tobin's Q*D* interaction terms exhibit signs, significance levels, and comparisons consistent with Hypothesis 5 regarding rule of law.

International competition for cross-listings

In column 8 we present results from a final robustness study that varies both estimation and model specification strategies. Scholars in law (e.g., Ribstein, 2005) and accounting (e.g., Piotroski and Srinivasan, 2008) have identified alternative corporate governance regimes thought to provide some, if not all, of the investor protections offered by US cross-listing. Prominent among these alternatives is the UK, the fount of common law traditions and the home of the LSE's AIM. Set up in 1995, the AIM seeks listings by smaller, foreign firms with the promise of less heavy-handed regulatory oversight than on the main market of the LSE or other prominent US markets. We ask whether accounting explicitly for this alternative cross-listing destination undermines our core results.

For our sample of firms, the average rate of cross-listing in the UK is low—0.03 percent, compared to 4 percent cross-listing in the US. We add to the right-hand side of Equation 11.2 a *Firm UK Listing* dummy taking the value of 1 when the emerging-market firm has a listing on any UK share market. We also include the *Foreign Sales* term and re-estimate with ordered logistic regression and the 0–1–2 measure of *US Cross-Listing* (column 9). *UK Listing* enters significantly and positively (3.190, p<0.01) meaning that emerging-market firms listing there are also more (not less) likely to list in the US as well. In any case, the *Tobin's Q*D* interaction terms continue to exhibit signs, significance levels, and comparisons supporting Hypothesis 5 regarding rule of law.

DISCUSSION AND CONCLUSION

Central Results and Implications

In this study, we sought to develop and test a cross-level theoretical framework to explain the impact of country- and firm-level factors prompting firms to leapfrog legally. For management as well as law and finance research, we also sought more refined sampling and estimation approaches to focus on when this prompting would be stronger and when the source of that strength might flow more from country- versus firm-level factors.

We see substantial progress in reaching these goals. Theoretically, we developed a cross-level framework highlighting the importance of two legal institutions influencing emerging-market firm decisions to leapfrog legally: legal system and rule of law. We showed how each mattered for these decisions individually and together. We also identified firm-level growth opportunities as a driver of legal leapfrogging, both individually and as an interactive complement with country-level institutions. To our knowledge, no previous research in management, law and finance, or other fields has identified and integrated these factors into a single theoretical framework designed to explain whether and how emerging-market firms choose to leapfrog legally to bond with foreign (US) corporate governance systems, increase investor protections, and benefit from broader, deeper capital flows.

We documented relatively broad-based support for this framework in the US cross-listing tendencies of more than 7,453 distinct firms domiciled in 22 emerging-market countries from 1996 to 2007. Perhaps most interestingly, we documented subtler interactions indicating when country-level legal system effects vanish with growing rule of law strength, and how both country-level factors increase in importance when interacted with firm-specific growth opportunities. These interaction effects lend deeper insight to how firms weigh different factors when considering whether and how to leapfrog legally. Such interaction effects may explain variation in other firm behavior relevant to international management research. In the 2010s, Flores and colleagues (2013) explained variation in US multinational corporation operational location based on whether the prospective host country has a common law system, but without also accounting for rule of law strength in the host country. Our study suggests that such "results" merit another look at inclusion of rule of law measures individually and in combination with terms representing the legal system.

These theoretical and empirical contributions matter for international management research in a world where firm location has more than just an operational dimension. If corporate domicile is no longer the sole determinant of corporate governance destiny, then international management research needs theoretical lenses and empirical evidence to guide our understanding of where and how firms might shift their presence non-operationally. We offered both types of guidance with the proviso that their primary relevance was for emerging-market countries and firms. This focus has benefits for related research in law and finance. It helps reconcile anomalous findings in previous law and finance research (Reese and Weisbach, 2002; Litvak, 2007) based on aggregating emerging-market and industrialized countries, even though firms from these two types of countries may have quite different motivations to shift their legal presence through cross-listing. Our focus is also timely for strategy research encouraging the development of theory and empirics tailored to emerging-market settings where basic institutions supporting a market economy, capital formation, and corporate governance regimes are less settled (Hoskisson et al., 2000), and where competitive advantage depends on being able to adapt firm resources and capabilities to the shifting rules of emerging markets (Peng, 2003; Cuervo-Cazzera and Dau, 2009).

We think our study is also important for interdisciplinary research that bridges strategy and law and finance. Aguilera and Williams (2009) characterize law and finance research as "inaccurate, incomplete, and important." We might revise that characterization applied to legal shift research as inaccurate and incomplete when applied without careful consideration of a firm's legal institutional context. But when carefully considered, we think a law and finance perspective on why and how legal leapfrogging occurs is quite useful. Emerging-market firms exhibit US cross-listing tendencies consistent with legal leapfrogging to bond with and benefit from US corporate governance standards. Our study identifies the country- and firm-level characteristics that make such a move for such a motivation more likely. In these ways, we respond to critics like Aguilera and Williams and advance an important academic debate in international management and international law and finance circles.

Our findings also matter for managerial practice and public policy. We find that emerging-market firms behave as if they are seeking out (not avoiding) more demanding corporate governance standards. As Siegel (2009) also concluded, cross-listing lets firms signal an organizational commitment to standards that investors, particularly minority shareholding investors, will find attractive. Neither the implementation of SOX in the US nor the establishment and growth of competing foreign financial markets, like the AIM in the UK, has diminished the attraction of such signaling.

Critics might respond that firms from emerging-market countries need not cross-list in the US to signal improved corporate governance standards. They can refrain from cross-listing and invest in improved corporate governance practices at home. No doubt some emerging-market firms make that choice, but not often, at least according to Aggarwal, Erel, Stulz, and Williamson (2010), who analyzed investments in firm-level governance quality by more than 1,500 firms from 22 Organisation for Economic Co-operation and Development countries and Hong Kong in 2005. Their analyses suggest that firm- and country-level governance strength complement each other. Managers invest more (not less) in their own firm's governance quality as home-country corporate governance standards strengthen. Accordingly, the signal sent by improving firm governance standards may be weaker for firms based in home countries with weaker governance regimes. Results from our study suggest, however, that such firms may be able to overcome such disadvantages posed by weak home-country governance by shifting the relevant context for assessing country-level corporate governance standards. The signal sent by investment in firm-level governance improvements is likely to be more convincing when such firms have an established legal presence in a country with stronger investor protections.

Limitations and Future Research Avenues

In noting the limited (to emerging-market countries and firms) domain of our study, we should also note other limitations. Our framework highlights two country-level factors and one firm-level factor in explaining why some emerging-market firms leapfrog legally. Other firm-level factors merit examination. Researchers may benefit from identifying tangible technologies, tangible products, and people underlying growth opportunities prompting legal leapfrogging. Researchers could also benefit from identifying interfirm factors affecting legal leapfrogging tendencies. International alliances might do so without the need for cross-listing (Siegel, 2009). Researchers may benefit from comparing cross-listing likelihoods for emerging-market firms with more or less insider ownership. Recall cross-listing to shift legal presence and bond is a strategy for broadening the ownership base with more minority owners. Given the same home country-level legal and firm-level growth characteristics, a firm with more extensive insider ownership may benefit more from cross-listing that broadens that ownership.

Other country-level factors may merit further study. Consider, for example, the cross-listing impact of two transient country-level factors, one random and the other planned. Focusing on the set of firms in our sample from the strongest (common law, strong rule of law) and weakest (civil law, weak rule of law) institutional environments we found that the effect of strong growth opportunities on the likelihood of cross-listing for firms from weak institutional environments was stronger when countries experienced currency crises and during election years.[8] Wald tests comparing parameter estimates for *Tobin's Q*D4* terms suggest that cross-listing likelihood-related growth opportunities magnifies following currency crises (currency crisis year *Tobin's Q*D4* = 0.575, $p<0.001$; non-currency crisis year *Tobin's Q*D4* = 0.277, $p<0.001$) and during election years (election year *Tobin's Q*D4* = 0.689, $p<0.001$; non-election year *Tobin's Q*D4* = 0.323, $p<0.001$). These preliminary findings merit additional research on transient country-level factors that apparently "trigger" emerging-market firm search for stronger institutional environments where they might leapfrog legally in response.

Cross-listing is not the only means to access more protective institutions for firm investors. We have already noted previous research identifying alternatives like recruiting foreign directors or changing corporate charters (Oxelheim and Randøy, 2005; Birkenshaw et al., 2006). In a study of Mexican firms in the 1990s, Siegel (2009) investigates the effectiveness

---

[8]   We use Equation 11.3 to analyze currency crisis and national election effects. We test Hypothesis 5 by splitting the sample into two groups—shock year and non-shock year—for each type of shock, respectively. Full results from these estimations are available from the authors upon request.

of international strategic alliances with US firms as a signal that local Mexican firms will provide better investor protections than domestic legal institutions provide. His point merits future research attention. Lavie and Miller (2008) document that enhanced firm performance through alliances diminishes with increasing alliance complexity. Perhaps non-operational leapfrogging abroad through international alliances exhibits a similar trend.

There is nothing to indicate that these leapfrogging strategies are mutually exclusive. Firms can pursue an "all-of-the-above" approach. This possibility raises interesting questions about sequencing. Cross-listing might lead or follow strategic alliances with foreign firms. Recruiting foreign directors from a given country might increase or decrease the speed of follow-on cross-listing. We highlight the importance of internationalization as a multidimensional concept with important legal as well as more conventional operational aspects. But a legal leapfrogging may itself be multidimensional. The legal locus of a firm can shift with changes in markets where its shares are listed and traded as well as with changes in its list of corporate allies and directors. Future research along these lines will benefit from closer integration of strategy and legal perspectives on whether and how firms are "located" abroad.

REFERENCES

Aggarwal, R., Erel, I., Stulz, R., and Williamson, R. 2010. Differences in governance practices between US and foreign firms: Measurement, causes, and consequences. *Review of Financial Studies 23*(3): 3131–3169.

Aguilera, R., Filatotchev, I., Gospel, H., and Jackson, G. 2008. An organizational approach to comparative corporate governance: Costs, contingencies, and complementarities. *Organization Science 19*(3): 475–492.

Aguilera, R., and Jackson, G. 2003. The cross-national diversity of corporate governance: Dimensions and determinants. *Academy of Management Review 28*: 447–465.

Aguilera, R., and Jackson, G. 2010. Comparative and international corporate governance. *Academy of Management Annals 4*(1): 485–556.

Aguilera, R., and Williams, C. 2009. Law and finance: Inaccurate, incomplete, and important. *BYU Law Review 6*: 1413–1434.

Akerlof, G. 1970. The market for "lemons": Quality uncertainty and the market mechanism. *Quarterly Journal of Economics 84*: 488–500.

Amihud, Y., and Mendelson, H. 1986. Asset pricing and the bid-ask spread. *Journal of Financial Economics 8*: 31–53.

Angkinand, A., Barth, J., Lee, C., Li, T., Lu, W., Malaiyandi, S., McCarthy, D., Phumiwasana, T., Sui, S., Trimbath, S., and Yago, G. 1999–2007. Capital access index 1998–2006 (various annual issues written by combinations of co-authors listed above). Los Angeles, CA: Milken Institute.

Arrighetti, A., Bachmann, R., and Deakin, S. 1997. Contract law, social norms and inter-firm cooperation. *Cambridge Journal of Economics 21*: 171–195.

Bank of New York. 2010. *BNY-Mellon American depository receipt archive*. New York: Bank of New York.

Bank of New York. 2021. *American depository receipt database*. New York: Bank of New York.

Beck, T., Demirgüç-Kunt, A., and Levine, R.. 2003. Law and finance: Why does legal origin matter? *Journal of Comparative Economics 31*: 653–675.

Bell, R., Filatotchev, I., and Aguilera, R. 2014. Corporate governance and investors' perceptions of foreign IPO value: An institutional perspective. *Academy of Management Journal 57*: 301–320.

Benos, E., and Weisbach, M. 2004. Private benefits and cross-listing in the United States. *Emerging Markets Review 5*: 217–240.

Birkenshaw, J., Braunerhjelm, P., Holm, U., and Terjesen, S. 2006. Why do some multinational corporations relocate their headquarters overseas? *Strategic Management Journal 27*: 681–700.

Butler, H., and Ribstein, L. 2006. *The Sarbanes-Oxley debacle: What we've learned; how to fix it.* Washington, DC: American Enterprise Institute.

Coffee, J. 1999. The future as history: The prospects for global convergence in corporate governance and its implications. *Northwestern University Law Review 93*: 641–708.

Coffee, J. 2002. Race towards the top? The impact of cross-listings and stock market competition on international corporate governance. *Columbia Law Review 102*(7): 1757–1831.

Cuervo-Cazurra, A., and Dau, L. 2009. Pro-market reforms and firm profitability in developing countries. *Academy of Management Journal 52*: 1348–1368.

Defond, M., and Hung, M. 2004. Investor protection and corporate governance: Evidence from worldwide CEO turnover. *Journal of Accounting Research 42*: 269–312.

Delios, A., and Henisz, W. 2000. Japanese firms' investment strategies in emerging economies. *Academy of Management Journal 43*: 305–323.

Doh, J. 2000. Entrepreneurial privatization strategies: Order of entry and local partner collaboration as sources of competitive advantage. *Academy of Management Review 25*: 551–571.

Doidge, C., Karolyi, A., and Stulz, R. 2004. Why are foreign firms listed in the US worth more? *Journal of Financial Economics 71*: 205–238.

Douma, S., George, R., and Kabir, R. 2006. Foreign and domestic ownership, business groups and firm performance: Evidence from a large emerging market. *Strategic Management Journal 27*: 637–657.

Dunning, J. 1977. Trade, location of economic activity and the multinational enterprise: A search for an eclectic approach. In B. Ohlin, P. Hesselborn, and P. Wikman (eds), *The international allocation of economic activity*. London: Macmillan pp. 395–418.

Dyck, A., and Zingales, L. 2004. Private benefits of control: An international comparison. *Journal of Finance 59*: 537–600.

Errunza, V., and Miller, D. 2000. Market segmentation and the cost of capital in international equity markets. *Journal of Financial & Quantitative Analysis 35*: 577–600.

Filatotchev, I., and Piesse, J. 2009. R&D, internationalization and growth of newly-listed firms: European evidence. *Journal of International Business Studies 40*: 1260–1276.

Flores, R., Aguilera, R., Mahdian, A., and Vaaler, P. 2013. How well do supranational regional grouping schemes fit international business models? *Journal of International Business Studies 44*(5): 451–474.

Foerster, S., and Karolyi, A. 1999. The effects of market segmentation and investor recognition on asset prices: Evidence from foreign stocks listing in the United States. Journal of Finance 54: 981–1013.

Georgieva, D. 2009. Does Sarbanes-Oxley Act chase away foreign firms? Evidence from terminated ADR programs. *Journal of International Business Research 8*(2): 1–15.

Guillén, M. F., and Capron, L. 2016. State capacity, minority shareholder protections, and stock market development. *Administrative Science Quarterly 61*(1): 125–160.

Hasan, I., Kobeissi, N., and Wang, H. 2011. Global equity offerings, corporate valuation, and subsequent international diversification. *Strategic Management Journal 32*(7): 787–796.

Hawn, O., and Ioannous, I. 2016. Mind the gap: The interplay between external and internal actions in the case of corporate social responsibility. *Strategic Management Journal 37*(13): 2569–2588.

Henisz, W., and Macher, J. 2004. Firm and country-level trade-offs and contingencies in the evaluation of foreign investment: The semiconductor industry, 1994–2002. *Organization Science 15*: 537–554.

Hoskisson, R., Cannella, A., Tihanyi, L., and Faraci, R. 2004. Asset restructuring and business group affiliation in French civil law countries. *Strategic Management Journal 25*: 525–539.

Hoskisson, R., Eden, L., Lau, C., and Wright, M. 2000. Strategy in emerging economies. *Academy of Management Journal 43*: 249–267.

Hymer, S. 1976 [1960]. *The international operations of national firms*. Cambridge, MA: MIT Press.

In Re: Volkswagen. 2017. *In Re: Volkswagen "Clean Diesel" Marketing, Sales Practices, and Products Liability Litigation*, Decision of the US District Court for the Northern District of California, Docket Nos. 1705, 1706, 1708 (Decided January 4). www.dandodiary.com/wp-content/uploads/sites/265/2017/01/volkswagen-order-on-motion-to-dismiss.pdf

ITC. 2010. *US International Trade Commission trade database*. Washington, DC: International Trade Commission.

Johnson, S., La Porta, R., Lopez-de-Silanes, F., and Shleifer, A. 2000. Tunneling. *American Economic Review Papers & Proceedings 90*: 22–27.

Kaufmann, D., Kraay, A., and Mastruzzi, M. 2009. Governance matters V. World Bank Policy Research Working Paper #7106. Washington, DC: World Bank.

Kaufmann, D., Kraay, A., and Mastruzzi, M. 2010. The worldwide governance indicators: Methodology and analytical issues. World Bank Draft Policy Research Working Paper, September. http://info .worldbank.org/governance/wgi/pdf/WGI.pdf

Kaufmann, D., Kraay, A., and Zoido-Lobatón, P. 2000. Governance matters: From measurement to action. *Finance & Development 37*(June): 10–13.

King, G., Tomz, M., and Wittenberg, J. 2000. Making the most of statistical analyses: Improving interpretation and presentation. *American Journal of Political Science 44*: 347–361.

Klerman, D., Mahoney, P., Spamann, H., and Weinstein, M. 2011. Legal origin or colonial history? *Journal of Legal Analysis 6*: 379–409.

Kogut, B. 1985. Designing global strategies: Profiting from operational flexibility. *Sloan Management Review 27*: 27–38.

La Porta, R., Lopez-de-Silanes, F., Shleifer, A., and Vishny, R. 1998. Law and finance. *Journal of Political Economy 106*: 1113–1155.

La Porta, R., Lopez-de-Silanes, F., Shleifer, A., and Vishny, R. 1999. Corporate ownership around the world. *Journal of Finance 54*: 471–517.

Lavie, D., and Miller, S. 2008. Alliance portfolio internationalization and firm performance. *Organization Science 19*: 623–646.

Litvak, K. 2007. The effect of the Sarbanes-Oxley act on non-US companies cross-listed in the US. *Journal of Corporate Finance 13*: 195–228.

Mahoney, P. 2001. The common law and economic growth: Hayek might be right. *Journal of Legal Studies 30*: 503–525.

Martin, K., Cullen, J., Johnson, J., and Parboteeah, K. 2007. Deciding to bribe: A cross-level analysis of firm and home country influences on bribery activity. *Academy of Management Journal 50*: 1401–1422.

Martin, X., Swaminathan, W., and Mitchell, W. 1998. Organizational evolution in the interorganizational environment: Incentives and constraints on international expansion strategy. *Administrattive Science Quarterly 43*: 566–601.

McMillan, J., and Woodruff, C. 2000. Private order under dysfunctional public order. *Michigan Law Review 98*: 2421–2458.

Melin, L. 1992. Internationalization as a strategy process. *Strategic Management Journal 13*: 99–118.

Miguel, A., Pindado, J., and de la Torre, C. 2004. Ownership structure and firm value: New evidence from the Spanish case. *Strategic Management Journal 25*: 1199–1207.

Moore, C., Bell, R., Filatotchev, I., and Rasheed, A. 2012. Foreign IPO capital market choice: Understanding the institutional fit of corporate governance. *Strategic Management Journal 33*(8): 914–937.

Morrison v. *National Australia Bank*. 2010. *Morrison* v. *National Australia Bank Ltd et al.* Decision of the US Supreme Court, Docket No. 08-1191 (Decided June 24). www.supremecourt.gov/opinions/ 09pdf/08-1191.pdf

Norton, Rose, Fulbright. 2009. Establishing a Level 1 American depositary receipt program. July. www .nortonrosefulbright.com/knowledge/publications/22176/establishing-a-level-1-american-depositary -receipt-program

OTC Markets. 2010. *OTC Markets (formerly Pink Sheets) listing archive*. New York: OTC Markets.

Oxelheim, L., and Randøy, T. 2005. The Anglo-American financial influence on CEO compensation in non-anglo-american firms. *Journal of International Business Studies 36*: 470–483.

Palmiter, A. 2002. *Securities regulation: Examples and explanations* (2nd edn). New York: Aspen Law and Business.

Peng, M. 2003. Institutional transitions and strategic choices. *Academy of Management Review 28*: 275–296.

Pfeffer, J., and Salancik, G. 1978. *The external control of organizations: A resource dependence approach*. New York: Harper and Row Publishers.

Pinker v. *Roche*. 2002. *Harold Pinker* v. *Roche Holdings, Ltd*. Decision of the US Court of Appeals for the Third Circuit, Docket Nos. 00-4318 and 01-1562 (Filed May 30). http://caselaw.findlaw.com/us -3rd-circuit/1355653.html

Piotroski, P., and Srinivasan, S. 2008. Regulation and bonding: The Sarbanes-Oxley act and the flow of international listings. *Journal of Accounting Research 46*(2): 383–425.

Pistor, K., Raiser, M., and Gelfer, S. 2000. Law and finance in transition economies. *Economic Transition 8*: 325–368.

Priest, G. 1977. The common law process and the selection of efficient rules. *Journal of Legal Studies 6*: 65–78.

Priest, G., and Klein, B. 1984. The selection of disputes for litigation. *Journal of Legal Studies 13*: 1–20.

Reese, W., and Weisbach, M. 2002. Protection of minority shareholder interests, cross-listings in the United States, and subsequent equity offerings. Journal of Financial Economics 66: 65–104.

Reuer, J., and Tong, T. 2010. Discovering valuable growth opportunities: An analysis of equity alliances with IPO firms. *Organization Science 21*: 202–215.

Reynolds, T., and Flores, A. 2003. *Foreign law: Current sources of codes and basic legislation in juris- dictions of the world* (2nd edn). Littleton, CO: F. B. Rothman.

Ribstein, L. 2005. Cross-listing and regulatory competition. *Review of Law & Economics 1*: 1–50.

Rock, E. 2001. Greenhorns, yankees and cosmopolitans: Venture capital, IPOs, foreign firms and US markets. Theoretical Inquiries in Law 2: 711.

Rousseau, D. 1985. Issues of level in organizational research: Multilevel and cross-level perspectives. In L. L. Cummings and B. Staw (eds), *Research in Organization Behavior* (Volume 7). Greenwich, CT: JAI Press, pp. 1–37.

Saudagaran, S. 1988. An empirical study of selected factors influencing the decision to list on foreign stock exchange. *Journal of International Business Studies 19*: 101–128.

Saudagaran, S., and Biddle, G. 1995. Foreign listing location: A study of MNCs and stock exchanges in eight countries. *Journal of International Business Studies 26*: 319–341.

Shleifer, A., and Vishny, R. 1997. A survey of corporate governance. Journal of Finance 52: 737–783.

Siegel, J. 2005. Can foreign firms bond themselves effectively by renting US laws? *Journal Financial Economics 75*: 319–359.

Siegel, J. 2009. Is there a better commitment mechanim than cross-listings for emerging-economy firms? Evidence from Mexico. *Journal of International Business Studies 40*: 1171–1191.

Spamann, H. 2010. The "anti-director rights index" revisited. *Review of Financial Studies 23*: 467–486.

Stulz, R. 1999. Globalization of equity markets and the cost of capital. Journal of Applied Corporate Finance 12: 8–25.

Tong, T., Reuer, J., and Peng, M. 2008. International joint ventures and the value of growth options. *Academy of Management Journal 51*: 1014–1029.

USITC. 2021. USITC trade database. Washington, DC: United States International Trade Commission. http://dataweb.usitc.gov/

Vaaler, P. 2011. Immigrant remittances and the venture investment environment of developing countries. *Journal of International Business Studies 42*(9): 1121–1149.

Vaaler, P., and Schrage, B. 2007. Legal system and rule of law effects on US cross-listing to bond by emerging-market firms. In G. Solomon (ed.), *Academy of Management Annual Meetings Best Papers*. New York: Pace University Academy of Management.

Vernon, R. 1971. *Sovereignty at bay: The multinational spread of US enterprise*. New York: Basic Books.

Wheeler, D., and Mody, A. 1992. International investment location decision: The case of US firms. *Journal of International Economics 33*: 57–76.

World Bank. 2016. *World development indicators*. Washington, DC: World Bank.

World Bank. 2021. *World development indicators*. Washington, DC: World Bank.

Worldscope. 2021. *Worldscope fundamental data*. New York: S&P Global Market Intelligence.

Zaheer, S. 1995. Overcoming the liability of foreignness. *Academy of Management Journal 38*: 341–363.

Zelner, B. 2009. Using simulation to interpret results from logit, probit and other nonlinear models. *Strategic Management Journal 30*: 1335–1348.

12. How intellectual property regimes and innovative infrastructure promote growth of Africa's technological market

Ashley Elizabeth Sperbeck

INTRODUCTION

According to the World Intellectual Property Organization (WIPO), intellectual property, "refers to creations of the mind, such as inventions; literary and artistic works; designs; and symbols, names and images used in commerce" (WIPO, 2021h). Intellectual property serves as the foundation of innovation in any economy, where government-granted rights incentivize discovery and creativity by providing creators with an opportunity to profit from the value of their innovative work. In exchange, the creative work is, after a given time period, made public so that others may build on and benefit from the original.

Laws protecting intellectual property reduce the transaction costs between inventors and industry by providing information about the quality of the invention without jeopardizing the ownership of the idea. Federal recognition of intellectual property rights in the United States (U.S.) began with the adoption of the Constitution on September 17, 1787, with Article I, Section 8 providing that, "[t]he Congress shall have Power … [t]o promote the Progress of Science and useful Arts, by securing for limited Times to Authors and Inventors the exclusive Right to their respective Writings and Discoveries."

Generally, four types of intellectual property exist to protect an innovative idea or invention, which include (1) a trade secret, (2) a trademark, (3) a copyright, and (4) a patent (USPTO, 2020a, 2020b). In the U.S., a "trade secret" may be defined as (1) information that has either actual or potential independent economic value by virtue of not being generally known, (2) has value to others who cannot legitimately obtain the information, and (3) is subject to reasonable efforts to maintain its secrecy (USPTO, 2020a). Trade secrets are thought to be complementary to patent protection. In the U.S., a "trademark" is a word, phrase, symbol, and/or design that identifies and distinguishes the source of the goods of one party from those of others (USPTO, 2020b). A "copyright" protects original works of authorship, including literary, dramatic, musical, and artistic works, such as poetry, novels, movies, songs, computer software, and architecture (USPTO, 2020b). A "service mark" is a word, phrase, symbol, and/or design that identifies and distinguishes the source of a service rather than goods. Some examples include brand names, slogans, and logos (USPTO, 2020b). A "patent" is a property right granted by the government of the U.S. to an inventor "to exclude others from making, using, offering for sale, or selling the invention throughout the United States or importing the invention into the

United States" for a limited time in exchange for public disclosure of the invention when the patent is granted (USPTO, 2020b).

Francis Gurry, Director General of the WIPO, believes that intellectual property is a key factor that generates growth for a country. Specifically, Francis Gurry asserted that, "[intellectual property] rights secure legal framework for investment in – and commercialization of – innovation and creativity, enabling firms, including innovative start-ups, to navigate the perilous process of transforming an idea into a commercially viable product and to compete with success in the global marketplace, while safeguarding the public interest" (Gurry, 2015). Further, Gurry explains that, "[t]he goal now [in Africa] is to put these IP tools to work in support of the economic objectives of African economies" (Gurry, 2015). This approach is applied throughout this chapter.

APPROPRIABILITY

Intellectual property rights have created particular debate in the context of economic development internationally. The economic well-being of a nation or region is linked closely to the availability of know-how and technology. Technological progress is an important determinant of productivity and income level. Developing countries usually face limitations in their indigenous innovation capabilities and, hence, foreign sources too often exploit that gap.

It should be appreciated that the term "appropriability" refers to the capacity of an organization to retain the added value it creates for its own benefit (Kay, 1995). Classic contributors to the concept of appropriability include Austrian political economist Joseph Schumpeter, American economist Kenneth Arrow, and David Teece (Winter, 2006). Whereas Schumpeter and Arrow were concerned with the broader implications of appropriability for society, Teece's concerns focused on questions of business strategy and economic organization. Teece's framework fills a gap in the previous theoretical discussion of appropriability.

In general, Teece explains that there are key issues involving the boundaries of the innovation itself and these issues have complex interdependence with the questions of appropriability and strategy (Teece, 1986, 2006). Based on this concept, Teece provides a framework that identifies factors to assess and determine which "party wins from innovation." The framework describes three fundamental building blocks: (1) the appropriability regime; (2) complementary assets; and (3) the dominant design paradigm (Teece, 1986). Each of these three building blocks will be discussed in turn herein.

Building Block 1: Appropriability Regime

According to Teece, a "regime of appropriability" includes environmental factors, excluding firm and market structure, that govern an innovator's ability to capture the profits generated by an innovation. This first building block is associated with protecting the idea or the innovation. Important considerations include intellectual property rights protection. The most important dimensions of the regime include: (1) the nature of the technology and (2) the efficacy of the legal mechanisms of protection. As such, both the strength of formal intellectual property rules and regulations will be assessed in each country, as well as the nature of relevant technologies.

Building Block 2: Dominant Design Paradigm

This second building block includes finding the dominant design for a product. In general, scientific and artistic evolution includes (1) a pre-paradigmatic stage or state and (2) a paradigmatic stage or state. The "pre-paradigmatic stage" refers to a time period before a scientific consensus has been reached, where there is no single generally accepted conceptual treatment of a phenomenon in a field. Distinctly, the "paradigmatic stage" begins when a body of theory appears to have passed the canons of scientific acceptability (Teece, 1986). In early stages of industrial development (e.g., the pre-paradigmatic stage), product designs are fluid and manufacturing processes loosely organized and experimental. Competition manifests itself among designs. After trial and error in the marketplace, one design begins to emerge as more promising than others (Teece, 1986). Once the dominant design emerges, competition shifts to the price and scalability of such design. Although the innovator is responsible for the initial scientific breakthrough, if imitation of the product is easy, the imitator or follower may reap additional benefits not recognized by the innovator. However, Christensen warns of the impact of "disruptive innovations" on successful businesses (Christensen, 1997).

Establishing a dominant design is influenced by collateral assets, such as marketing channels, which include the people, organizations, and activities necessary to transfer the ownership of goods from the point of production to the point of consumption, and brand image, government and industry regulations, and technological advances within the industry (Teece, 1986). As such, for this building block, our chapter focuses on the marketing channels and government regulations/regulatory bodies within the given country.

Building Block 3: Complementary Assets

This third building block is associated with the ability to quickly and successfully commercialize an innovative idea (Teece, 1986). Successful commercialization requires that the innovative know-how be utilized with other assets. Marketing, competitive manufacturing, production, sales, and after-sales support are obtained from "complementary assets" (Teece, 1986). Complementary assets are categorized as (1) generic, (2) specialized, or (3) co-specialized (Teece, 1986).

Generic assets, such as manufacturing facilities, are general-purpose assets that do not need to be tailored to the invention in question. Where specialized assets have a unilateral dependence between the innovation and the complementary asset, co-specialized assets have a bilateral dependence (Teece, 1986). For this third building block, this chapter assesses factors such as the average age of the population, internet accessibility, and average education level. These factors directly contribute to the skill/ability of a country to reach scale quickly with a new technology.

Examples: Appropriability Regimes

In a "tight" appropriability regime, if an innovator has strong intellectual property protection on the invention (such as a strong patent), such intellectual property protection will deny imitators from copying the invention. In examples where the assets are generic, the innovator may license the technology (Teece, 1986).

In the pre-paradigmatic phase of a "weak" appropriability regime, rivalry is focused on trying to identify the design that will become dominant (Teece, 1986). Here, production volumes are low and there is little to be gained in deploying specialized assets. As the leading design is clarified, volume of the product increases and opportunities for economies of scale will induce organizations to begin gearing up for mass production by acquiring specialized tools and equipment. In the paradigmatic phase of the weak appropriability regime, if the innovative product fails to adequately fit the market, the innovator must begin the design process again.

PROPOSED MATHEMATICAL FRAMEWORK

This chapter proceeds by utilizing Teece's framework to posit the following equations, which, when used, result in an analysis of each country's capabilities to succeed technologically. Equation 12.1 is the general framework provided by Teece.

$$Framework = A + C + D \qquad\qquad (12.1)$$

where the variable "A" is associated with the appropriability regime, the variable "C" is associated with the complementary assets, and the variable "D" is associated with the dominant design paradigm.

As explained previously, when assessing the appropriability regime, one must look at the legal mechanisms for intellectual property protection available in the country (e.g., organizations, laws, declarations, etc.), as well as the nature of the technology. If the technology is emerging, intellectual property protections may not be available yet within that country. As such, the variable "A" or the appropriability regime may be represented as such:

$$A = IP + T \qquad\qquad (12.2)$$

where the variable "IP" is associated with the scope of legal mechanisms of intellectual property protection available in the country and the variable "T" is associated with the nature of the technology.

As such, from Equation 12.2, two scenarios can occur. First, if there is a technology that would not qualify as an emergent (such as the concept of electricity), the variable "IP" is high and the variable "T" is low. In this first scenario, the resulting variable "A" is high. A second scenario applies if there is an emerging technology, such as a cancer vaccine. Since this technology is not yet fully developed or recognized by the broader scientific community, the variable "IP" is low and the variable "T" is high, resulting in a lower variable "A" than in the first scenario. In this second scenario, it is more difficult to secure intellectual property protection.

Next, the variable "C" takes into account factors such as production, sales, and marketing, which will be collectively known as "innovative infrastructure." This variable takes into account not only the physical and demographic infrastructure of the country, such as the age of the population (e.g., the potential workforce), but also its internet/communication capabilities, educational status, health concerns, etc.

Regarding the variable "D," one must assess the dominant design paradigm – whether the design is widely accepted, the various marketing channels available, government regulation, and technological advances in the given industry. As such, the variable "D" is defined as follows:

$$D = R + MC \tag{12.3}$$

where the variable "R" is associated with the government regulation and the variable "MC" is associated with the marketing channels available. As can be seen by Equation 12.3, the variable "D" is directly dependent upon the summation of the variable "R" and the variable "MC." Further, in cases where government regulation (e.g., the variable "R") is high, it is likely that the variable "MC" is also high. In cases where the government regulation (e.g., the variable "R") is low, it is unlikely that there will be established marketing channels available for the given technology.

Compilation of Equations 12.1, 12.2, and 12.3 results in the framework shown in Equation 12.4. This framework helps assess the ability of each country to make use of its strengths to contribute to Africa's fast-growing technological marketplace.

$$Framework = [(IP + T) + C + (R + MC)] \tag{12.4}$$

For each variable in Equation 12.4, a scale of −5 to +10 may be used. A score of −5 to −1 for a given variable indicates a negative or weak variable (e.g., "W"), a score of +1 to +5 indicates a neutral variable (e.g., "N"), and a score of +6 to +10 indicates a positive or strong variable (e.g., "S"). The chapter proceeds by discussing each country and then applying our proposed framework.

THE REPUBLIC OF KENYA

Framework: Variable "A"

Variable "IP"

Background
Kenyan intellectual property laws have a colonial heritage. Specifically, British intellectual property law was first introduced into Kenya to advance general imperialist interests. On becoming a British colony in 1897, the substance of the British common law, the doctrines of equity and the statutes of general application in Britain were extended to the colony. The copyright laws applied to Kenya were designed to protect the monopoly rights of British publishers in Kenya, restrict the growth of the publishing industry in the country, and provide censorship for publications that colonialists termed seditious or immoral (Chege, 1978). However, most of these laws have been updated through the new Kenyan Constitution (2010) and intellectual property work done at Strathmore University in Nairobi.

Subsequent to the establishment of the copyright protections, the first registered patent in Kenya dates back to 1932. However, Kenya had no independent intellectual property protection system until 1989. Under Section 54 of the Patents Registration Act Cap. 508, only a person who was a grantee of a patent in the United Kingdom or a person deriving his or her right from a grantee by assignment or any other operation of law could apply to have a patent registered (Odek, 2009). The Patents Registration Act Cap. 508 was repealed in 1989

Table 12.1   *Select intellectual property laws, declarations, organizations, and regimes*
             followed by each country

Intellectual property laws, declarations, organizations, and regimes	Kenya	Nigeria	South Africa
African Regional Intellectual Property Organization	Yes		
Patent Cooperation Treaty	Yes	Yes	Yes
Paris Convention for the Protection of Industrial Property	Yes	Yes	Yes
General Agreement on Tariffs and Trade	Yes	Yes	Yes
World Trade Organization	Yes	Yes	Yes
Dakar Declaration on Intellectual Property for Africa	Yes		
Agreement on Trade-Related Aspects of Intellectual Property Rights (TRIPS)	Yes	Yes	Yes
Declaration on TRIPS and Public Health	Yes	Yes	Yes
Industrial Property Act of 2001	Yes		

upon enactment of Industrial Property Act Cap. 509, which established the Kenya Industrial Property Office, the predecessor of the Kenya Intellectual Property Institute (KIPI) (KIPI, 2017). The Industrial Property Act Cap. 509 was repealed in 2001 when the current Industrial Property Act 2001 came into force (KIPI, 2017). Intellectual property laws, declarations, organizations, and regimes protect Kenya; some of these are described in Table 12.1 (ARIPO, 2010, 2015, 2018, 2019a, 2019b, 2019c; Banwo & Ighodalo, 2016; Brewster, 2011; KLR, 2012; Sheppard, 1999; Taubman, 2011; WHO, 2021; WIPO, 2021a, 2021b, 2021e, 2021f, 2021g; WTO, 2021a).

Analysis and conclusion
Although the "Index of Patent Rights" (Park & Wagh, 2002) shown in Table 12.2 suggests that Kenya is ranked below South Africa, Kenya's rank should be placed higher due to the strong intellectual property regimes in place. For example, in 2018, Kenya led the way with the quantity of patent applications received at both the national and regional (Harare Protocol) level and the quantity of industrial design applications (ARIPO, 2018). Based on the breadth of intellectual property protection available in Kenya, as well as the uptake in the quantity and type of applications being filed, Kenya's variable "IP" is strong (or "S"). However, given the fact that Kenya's total score in the Index of Patent Rights is lower than South Africa's by at least 1, the variable "IP" is assigned a score of 6.

Variable "T"
Emerging technologies continually blossom in Kenya. As an example, Nairobi, the capital and the largest city in Kenya, is home to thousands of businesses and major international organizations, including the United Nations Environment Programme, the United Nations Office at Nairobi (United Nations, 2021), IBM, Intel, and Microsoft. Situated in the south-central part of the country, Nairobi is not only an established hub for business and culture, but Kenya's $1 billion technology hub is home to more than 200 startups, hence, Nairobi has been coined "Silicon Savannah" (Bright & Hruby, 2015).

The first major technological success came in 2007 with the mobile phone-based money-transferring service M-Pesa (Jelassi & Ludwig, 2016; Safaricom, 2021) and the

Table 12.2   *Index of Patent Rights*

	Coverage	Duration	Enforcement	Membership in international treaties	Protection from restrictions on patent rights	Total
Argentina	1.00	1.00	0.67	0.67	0.00	3.33
Australia	0.86	1.00	1.00	1.00	0.33	4.19
Austria	0.71	1.00	1.00	1.00	1.00	4.71
Bangladesh	0.86	0.80	0.00	0.33	0.67	2.66
Belgium	0.71	1.00	1.00	1.00	0.33	4.05
Botswana	0.57	1.00	0.00	0.33	0.33	2.24
Brazil	0.71	1.00	0.67	0.67	0.00	3.05
Bulgaria	0.57	1.00	0.33	1.00	0.33	3.24
Canada	0.57	1.00	0.67	1.00	0.67	3.90
Chad	0.71	1.00	0.33	0.67	0.33	3.05
Chile	0.86	0.88	0.33	0.33	1.00	3.41
China	0.14	1.00	0.33	0.67	0.33	2.48
Colombia	0.57	1.00	0.67	0.67	0.33	3.24
Czechia	0.86	1.00	0.00	1.00	0.67	3.52
Denmark	0.86	1.00	0.67	1.00	0.67	4.19
Ecuador	0.71	1.00	0.67	0.67	0.67	3.71
Egypt	0.71	0.75	0.67	0.33	0.00	2.46
Ethiopia	0.00	0.00	0.00	0.00	1.00	1.00
France	0.71	1.00	1.00	1.00	0.33	4.05
Germany	0.86	1.00	1.00	1.00	0.67	4.52
Greece	0.86	1.00	0.67	0.67	0.00	3.19
Grenada	0.71	0.70	0.00	0.67	0.33	2.41
Guatemala	0.29	0.75	0.33	0.33	0.00	1.70
Guyana	0.43	0.80	0.00	0.33	0.33	1.90
Hong Kong	0.57	1.00	0.33	0.67	0.33	2.90
Hungary	0.71	1.00	0.67	1.00	0.33	3.71
India	0.14	0.70	0.33	0.67	0.33	2.18
Indonesia	0.57	0.70	0.33	0.67	0.00	2.27
Ireland	1.00	1.00	0.33	1.00	0.67	4.00
Israel	0.71	1.00	0.67	1.00	0.67	4.05
Italy	1.00	1.00	1.00	1.00	0.33	4.33
Japan	0.86	1.00	1.00	1.00	0.33	4.19
Jordan	0.86	0.80	0.33	0.33	0.67	2.99
Kenya	0.71	1.00	0.67	0.67	0.00	3.05
Madagascar	0.86	0.75	0.33	0.67	0.33	2.94
Mexico	0.86	1.00	0.33	0.67	0.00	2.86
Mozambique	0.00	0.00	0.00	0.00	0.00	0.00

	Coverage	Duration	Enforcement	Membership in international treaties	Protection from restrictions on patent rights	Total
Netherlands	0.71	1.00	1.00	1.00	0.67	4.38
New Zealand	1.00	1.00	0.67	1.00	0.33	4.00
Nicaragua	0.00	0.59	0.00	0.33	0.67	1.50
Norway	0.57	1.00	0.67	1.00	0.67	3.90
Pakistan	0.86	0.80	0.00	0.00	0.33	1.99
Peru	0.71	1.00	0.33	0.33	0.33	2.71
Poland	0.57	1.00	0.33	1.00	0.33	3.24
Romania	0.71	1.00	0.00	0.67	0.33	2.71
Russia	0.86	1.00	0.33	1.00	0.33	3.52
Senegal	0.57	1.00	0.33	0.67	0.33	2.90
Singapore	0.71	1.00	0.67	0.67	1.00	4.05
Somalia	0.86	0.75	0.00	0.00	0.67	2.27
South Africa	0.71	1.00	0.67	1.00	0.67	4.05
South Korea	0.86	1.00	1.00	0.67	0.67	4.19
Spain	0.71	1.00	1.00	1.00	0.33	4.05
Sri Lanka	0.71	0.88	0.33	0.67	1.00	3.60
Sweden	0.71	1.00	1.00	1.00	0.67	4.38
Switzerland	0.71	1.00	0.67	1.00	0.67	4.05
Thailand	0.57	1.00	0.67	0.00	0.00	2.24
Togo	0.57	1.00	0.33	0.67	0.33	2.90
Tunisia	0.57	1.00	0.00	0.33	0.33	2.24
Turkey	0.86	1.00	0.00	0.67	0.33	2.86
United Kingdom	0.86	1.00	0.67	1.00	0.67	4.19
United States	1.00	1.00	1.00	1.00	1.00	5.00
Venezuela	0.57	1.00	1.00	0.33	0.00	2.90
Zimbabwe	0.57	1.00	0.33	0.67	0.67	3.24

Note: It should be appreciated that the Index of Patent Rights (Park & Wagh, 2002) is used to rank patent regimes internationally. The index focuses on five criteria: coverage (the subject matter that can be patented); duration (the length of protection); enforcement (the mechanisms for enforcing patent rights); membership in international patent treaties; and restrictions or limitations in the use of patent rights. For each of these criteria, a country is given a score ranging from 0 to 1, indicating the extent to which the country shows strength for the given criteria. It should be noted that Nigeria has not been ranked using this index.

open-source software application and non-profit technology company Ushahidi. Ushahidi's mission is to help marginalized people raise their voices and those who serve them to listen and respond better (Ushahidi, 2021). Ushahidi uses crowdsourcing for social activism and public accountability, serving as an initial model for "activist mapping" – the combination of social activism, citizen journalism, and geospatial information (Ushahidi, 2021). Another startup, BRCK, connects off-the-grid schools to the internet through solar-powered routers and tablets (BRCK, 2021). Moreover, AB3D, turns electronic waste into affordable three-dimensional printers that generate artificial limbs (AB3D, 2021).

Kenya is one of the leading innovative countries in Africa. Recently, Kenya has been ranked top in Africa in terms of the government's artificial intelligence (AI) readiness, or how well placed a government is to take advantage of the benefits of AI in their operations and delivery of public services, according to the International Development Research Center and Oxford Insights (Oxford Insights, 2019). In fact, the Kenyan government created a Blockchain and AI Task Force in February 2018 to provide the government with recommendations on how to harness these emerging technologies (Future of Life Institute, 2021). Based at least on the aforementioned, the variable "T" is strong (or "S") and assigned a score of 8, as there is room for improvement.

Framework: Variable "C"

The variable "C" assesses the innovative infrastructure of the given country, which encompasses population age, internet/communication availability, and educational and health-care status. Although approximately 90 percent of primary school age children attend school in Kenya, a mere 26 percent of youth ages 14 to 17 attend secondary school (EPDC, 2012). While the education of individuals ages 14 and up is lacking, it was found that in 2018, the adult literacy rate of people ages 15 and above who can both read and write a short simple statement about their everyday life was 81.54 percent, a 2.8 percent increase from 2014 (Macrotrends, 2021). Despite a youthful population (e.g., the current median age in Kenya is 20 years old according to Worldometer, 2021a) and a strong literacy rate, it follows that simple literacy is not the only key to technological or economic advancement. In fact, most Kenyans struggle with poverty, with roughly a third of the population surviving on less than $2 a day. Based on this, the variable "C" is weak, "W," and is assigned a score of −3, as there is room for improvement on this front. Despite a mere 2.64 percent unemployment rate in 2019 in Kenya (Statista, 2020a), internet access and affordability remain the biggest challenges for the country's rural population, according to Irine Achieng, a community liaison officer for the Sustainable East African Research in Community Health (Fredrick, 2019).

Moreover, in 2009, the Kenyan government developed the East African Marine System (TEAMS) as an initiative to link the country to the rest of the world through a 5,500 kilometer submarine fiber optic cable connecting Mombasa in Kenya to Fujairah in the United Arab Emirates, with two fiber pairs and an upgradable system capacity of 5.6 Tbps. TEAMS increased East African broadband and led to the establishment of Kenya's Information and Communication Technology Authority (Fredrick, 2019).

Framework: Variable "D"

Variable "R"

Of particular note, Kenya is a member of numerous regional bodies. The KIPI is the main implementation and administration agency for industrial property in Kenya; its mandate is to consider and grant approval of selected applications for industrial property rights. Further, the Industrial Property Tribunal provides an appropriate and specialized dispute adjudication mechanism for industrial property rights such as patents, industrial designs, utility models, and technological innovations (Republic of Kenya, Ministry of Industrialization, Trade and Enterprise Development, 2020).

The Kenyan government's position on patents has been that intellectual property rights should be exercised for the mutual benefit of the intellectual property right holder and consumers (WIPO, 2021d). According to Mboi E. Misati, a senior patent examiner at the KIPI, "the TRIPS [Agreement on Trade-Related Aspects of Intellectual Property Rights] Agreement should ensure a balance of the rights and the duties of the rights holders *vis-à-vis* the poor" (KLR, 2012; TRIPS, 1994; WTO, 2005).

Since Kenya's main areas of concern include access to medicines to address public health, Kenya's position has been to encourage patent protection but to relax the law to facilitate research and development. Based on the foregoing, the variable "R" is strong, or "S," and is assigned a score of 8.

Variable "MC"

Not only does Kenya have numerous ports used for the import and export of goods, but use of e-commerce in Kenya has grown significantly over the last few years, especially among small and medium enterprises (ITA, 2022). Moreover, Kenya recently adopted a digital economy blueprint meant to further develop the information and communications technology sector and e-commerce activity. Further, the Kenya Communications (Amendment) Act of 2008 adopts the United Nations' Model Law on Electronic Commerce of 1996, which seeks to promote e-government and e-commerce by increasing public confidence in electronic transactions, promoting legal recognition of electronic records and electronic (digital) signatures, and imposing penalties for cybercrimes involving electronic records, transactions, and computer and telecommunications equipment.

According to the Kenyan Communications Authority first quarterly report for 2019/2020, the number of wireless broadband subscriptions grew by 4.1 percent in 2019 to reach 52.1 million subscriptions, marking a penetration level of 89.7 percent (ITA, 2021). Available data indicate that 2G and 3G cover 96 and 93 percent of the population, respectively (ITA, 2021).

Several factors fuel e-commerce growth in Kenya. In 2018, Kenya scored 82 out of 100 on the "online payment methods indicator" – one of the four measures the United Nations Conference on Trade and Development ("UNCTAD") uses to measure the readiness of a country to support an e-commerce explosion (ITA, 2021; UNCTAD, 2021). The Kenyan government's ambition for universal 4G coverage, alongside accelerated smartphone ownership, places Kenya as one of the fastest-growing e-commerce markets (ITA, 2021). Based on the strong access to marketing channels, the variable "MC" is assigned a score of 7.

Framework conclusion

Equation 12.4 is reproduced here for reference:

$$Framework = [(IP + T) + C + (R + MC)] \tag{12.4}$$

Both the variable "IP" and the variable "T" of Kenya are strong, or "S," showcasing Kenya's strong intellectual property regimes which may or may not be able to protect the ongoing emerging technologies, and have been assigned scores of 6 and 8, respectively. Although the variable "C" shows a youthful population, a majority of which are literate and can contribute to the workforce if opportunities are presented, poverty remains a concern. As such, the variable "C" is deemed weak or "W," and has been assigned a score of −3. Moreover, the variable "D" shows strong government regulation, as well as multiple marketing channels for innovators to promote their products or services. Both the variable "R" and the variable "MC" are strong or "S," and have been assigned scores of 8 and 7, respectively. Thus, Equation 12.4 becomes:

$$Framework = [((S) + (S)) + (W) + ((S) + (S))],$$

or

$$Framework = [((6) + (8)) + (-3) + ((8) + (7))],$$

which results in an overall score of 26.

Based on the framework, Kenya's strong intellectual property regimes may be unable to protect the vast quantity of emerging technologies. Further, Kenya's strong government regulation, marketing channels, and youthful population must battle against technological deterrents, such as a lack of internet connectivity in rural areas, which results in a lack of connectivity/networking among citizens and a lack of informational flow, as well as medical/health concerns. For example, Kenya has among the highest rates of HIV/AIDS and tuberculosis in the world, although mortality rates have declined since the early 2000s, particularly for HIV/AIDS (Sewankambo, 2018).

Additionally, Chinese companies have sought to increase internet access in these rural areas since innovations are centered in the cities, so the rural areas are passive recipients of improvements until networks and infrastructure become pervasive (Mbewa, 2021). President Uhuru Muigai Kenyatta posed a development blueprint, or "The Big 4 Agenda," which includes four factors focused on for improvement in Kenya, namely, food security, affordable housing, manufacturing, and affordable health care (Huduma Namba, 2021).

THE FEDERAL REPUBLIC OF NIGERIA

Framework: Variable "A"

Variable "IP"

Background
The intellectual property regime in Nigeria is a derivative of the nineteenth-century English common law and doctrines of equity. The first industrial property law in Nigeria was the Trademarks Proclamation of 1900, by which the United Kingdom Trade Marks Act was made applicable to the then Protectorate of Southern Nigeria (Oyebade, 2002). This was extended to the entire country following the amalgamation of the Southern and Northern Protectorates in 1914 (Oyebade, 2002).

Current scope of protection
The scope of Nigerian intellectual property laws covers patents, copyrights, industrial designs, and trademarks. Specifically, copyright law is governed by the Copyright Act of 1988, with its amendments of 1992 and 1999 being recodified in the Laws of the Federation of Nigeria of 2010 (Onoyeyan, 2018), the Trademarks Act of 1965 regulates trademark registration and practice in Nigeria (Lexology, 2019), and patents and designs are regulated by the Patents and Designs Act of 1970.

Although Nigeria is not a member of the African Regional Intellectual Property Organization, it serves as a member of numerous intellectual property regimes, as shown in Table 12.1. Out of these regimes, the TRIPS Agreement has significantly impacted Nigeria. In fact, Nigeria is one of the member states of the World Trade Organization that applies the articles of the TRIPS Agreement to enforce intellectual property rights internationally (Brewster, 2011). In general, the TRIPS Agreement helped shape Nigerian intellectual property laws in accordance with international standards, encouraging foreign investment, local education, and the creation of employment. TRIPS helps ensure that investments in research can reap financial rewards, as research allows the innovator to recoup the costs and expenses of research as well as resulting profits.

Nigerian intellectual property laws provide numerous remedies in the event of infringement, which include damages, injunctions (such as an *Anton Piller* injunction), and other forms of relief. "*Anton Piller* injunctions" prevent a person from destroying vital evidence in his or her possession that may be needed by the parties in a suit before the court. Further, *Anton Piller* injunctions compel a defendant to allow the plaintiff to enter the defendant's premises and to search, examine, remove, or copy documents that are relevant to the proceedings before court. These remedies are consistent with the provisions of the TRIPS Agreement in Articles 45 and 46 (TRIPS, 1994). Based on the aforementioned, the variable "IP" would receive a strong or "S" score. However, Nigeria was not ranked in the Index of Patent Rights, and as such, the score falls to a neutral or "N" score of 5.

Variable "T"

Kola Aina, Founding Partner at venture capital firm Ventures Platform, explained, "[i]t won't be government or grants that will solve Africa's problems. Entrepreneurs will drive the scale and scope of change" (Unikorn, 2021). Such optimism is supported by Nigeria and Kenya being the continent's top startup investment destinations, jointly accounting for 81.5 percent of investment received in 2019 (Kazeem, 2020). For its part, Nigeria ranked top both for number of deals done and for their value as startup investments increased nearly five-fold compared to 2018 (Kazeem, 2020).

Nigeria's information and communication technologies sector has grown from less than 1 percent of gross domestic product in 2001 to almost 10 percent today (Ramachandran & Obado-Joel, 2019). Nigeria has also surpassed South Africa to emerge as a premier investment destination with 55 active technological hubs raising a total of U.S. $94.9 million. By contrast, South Africa raised U.S. $60.0 million with 59 active startups (Ramachandran & Obado-Joel, 2019). Nigeria is also Africa's biggest technology market and accounts for 23 percent of internet users in Africa, with 122 million people online in December 2018 (The Borgen Project, 2022). It also has the largest number of telecommunications subscribers, with a teledensity figure of almost 90 percent (NCC, 2022). The growth of the tech sector offers new possibilities for employment and entrepreneurship among Nigeria's growing labor force.

Of particular interest, "Yabacon Valley," an area within Yaba, a suburb of Lagos and nicknamed after "Silicon Valley," is regarded as the leading hub for technical innovations and development in Nigeria. Yabacon Valley consists of a cluster of banks, educational institutions, technology, and startup companies that steadily attract angel investors, venture capitalists, enthusiasts, and media. Specifically, Co-Creation Hub ("Cc-Hub") located in Yaba and founded in 2010 provides a platform where technology-oriented individuals can share ideas to solve social problems (Cc-Hub, 2021a). Cc-Hub became Nigeria's first startup incubator, with investments from the Indigo Trust, Omidyar Network, MainOne Cable Company, and the Lagos state government (Cc-Hub, 2021b).

In 2011, former banker Seun Onigbinde co-founded BudgIT, a Nigerian civic organization that applies technology for citizen engagement with institutional improvement to facilitate societal change (BudgIT, 2021). Other innovative ventures include Iroko, Paystack, Kaymu, Interswitch, Carmudi, Jovago, HelloFoods, and Rocket Internet (Adeshokan, 2017; Paystack, 2021). In fact, Iroko launched IrokoX, a multi-platform Pan-African network for filmmakers, musicians, and other creative aspirants to produce, distribute, and monetize short-form content (Bright, 2016). In November 2020, Visa paid $200 million for a 20 percent stake in Nigerian payments processor Interswitch, making it Africa's first "fintech unicorn," or a startup company with a valuation over $1 billion (Interswitch, 2020; Kazeem, 2019; Marras, 2020).

The strength of Lagos lies in its engineering talent (The Business Year, 2018). Also, according to Startup Genome's 2017 report, globally, Lagos' ecosystem has the ninth highest rate of founders with an undergraduate degree (The Business Year, 2018). Yaba is physically proximate to the University of Lagos and Yaba College of Technology (The Business Year, 2018). Nonetheless, Lagos still has a long way to go on the global stage. In the first half of 2017, many questioned Lagos' viability as a startup tech hub, worried that its hype was disproportionate to the reality (The Business Year, 2018). The average early-stage funding for a Lagos startup is U.S. $77,800, one third the global average (The Business Year, 2018). As such, the variable "T" is strong or "S," receiving a score of 8, similar to Kenya.

Framework: Variable "C"

Nigeria is the most populous country in Africa with more than 208 million; it is the seventh most populous country in the world (Worldometer, 2021b). Moreover, the current median age of the population in Nigeria is approximately 18 years – the third largest youth population in the world after India and China (Worldometer, 2021b). Despite having guidelines, the educational system has never been fully implemented (Ekundayo, 2019) and though primary education is free and compulsory, approximately 10.5 million children are not in school (UNICEF, 2021).

In the second half of 2020, Nigeria's unemployment rate was 27.1 percent, the highest on record (Trading Economics, 2020). Even the quality of employment has deteriorated, with one in every two working Nigerians either unemployed or underemployed (Olurounbi & Soto, 2020). The Nigerian economy was expected to shrink 5.4 percent in 2020 – its worst contraction in nearly 40 years (Olurounbi & Soto, 2020). The COVID-19 pandemic appears to be a temporary blip in progress, from which Nigeria can recover with foreign assistance. As such, the variable "C" receives a neutral or "N" score of 4.

Framework: Variable "D"

Variable "R"
Numerous government regulatory agencies help police intellectual property matters. For example, the Nigerian Copyright Commission is the regulatory body charged with the responsibility of copyright administration in Nigeria (Dun & Bradstreet, 2021). Further, the

Trademarks, Patents and Designs Registry under the Federal Ministry of Industry, Trade and Investment is the regulatory body with regards to intellectual property (Nordea, 2021). The courts also play a recognizable role in the administration and enforcement of intellectual property. Since the TRIPS Agreement does not mandate member states to create a separate court for the enforcement of intellectual property rights, Nigeria has assigned such functions to the Federal High Court (Constitute Project, 2020). As such, the variable "R" is strong or "S," receiving a score of 7.

Variable "MC"

The Nigerian Ports Authority is a federal government agency that governs and operates the ports of Nigeria for the import and export of products. The major ports controlled by the agency include Lagos Port Complex, Tin Can Island Port, Calabar Port, Delta Port, Rivers Port, and Onne Port (Nigerian Ports Authority, 2021).

Further, Nigeria's economy is gradually becoming cashless, as digital payment and electronic banking are being implemented. At present, many transactions can be conducted electronically using digital financial service platforms (ITA, 2020). The successful adoption of electronic payments in Nigeria is encouraging the entrance of payment service providers, which see Nigeria as a promising market (ITA, 2020). The demand for electronic transactions has attracted payment facilitators from Europe and Asia who are investing in Nigerian electronic infrastructure projects. Online commerce and financial technology in Nigeria is strengthened by the fast-growing youth population, expanding consumer power and increased smartphone penetration. The current e-commerce spending in Nigeria is estimated at $12 billion, and is projected to reach $75 billion in revenues per annum by 2025 (ITA, 2020).

Moreover, in 2015, the federal government signed the Cybercrime Act of 2015 into law, with the goal being to protect e-business transactions, company copyrights, domain names, and other electronic signatures in relation to electronic transactions in Nigeria (ITA, 2020). Despite this advancement, internet fraud is still prevalent in Nigeria (ITA, 2020). As such, the variable "MC" receives a strong or "S" score of 6.

Framework conclusion

Similar to Kenya, the variable "T" of Nigeria is strong. However, Nigeria's variable "IP" is neutral, showcasing a potential inability of Nigeria's intellectual property regimes to protect emerging technologies. The variable "C" shows a youthful population, a majority of which are literate and can contribute to the workforce once the effects of the COVID-19 pandemic subside. Further, over 100 million Nigerians are currently connected to the internet, with 250,000 new subscribers logging on in the last quarter of 2019, according to data from the Nigerian Communications Commission (Russon, 2020). Access to the internet is fast becoming democratized, with more than 95 percent of internet users going online using mobile broadband, according to Coleago Consulting, a telecoms consultancy firm working in the African region (Russon, 2020).

The variable "D" shows strong government regulation, as well as multiple marketing channels for innovators to promote their products or services. As such, Equation 12.4 becomes:

$$Framework = [((N) + (S)) + (N) + ((S) + (S))],$$

or

Framework $= [((5) + (8)) + (4) + ((7) + (6))],$

which results in an overall score of 30.

Based on the framework, Nigeria's intellectual property regimes may be unable to protect the vast quantity of emerging technologies. Nigeria's positive criteria regarding government regulation, marketing channels, youthful population, and Internet accessibility must battle against unemployment and medical/health deterrents. Currently, the top ten causes of death in Nigeria include lower respiratory infections, neonatal disorders, HIV/AIDS, malaria, diarrheal diseases, tuberculosis, meningitis, ischemic heart disease, stroke, and cirrhosis (CDC, 2019). Moreover, Nigeria is still dependent largely on foreign nations for various technological and industrial needs.

THE REPUBLIC OF SOUTH AFRICA

Variable "A"

Variable "IP"

The intellectual property laws, declarations, organizations, and regimes followed by South Africa are depicted in Table 12.1. Interestingly, South Africa is a "non-examining" country, meaning that South Africa merely requires examination of the patent application for compliance with formal requirements; no substantive examination process occurs (WIPO, 2009). The Companies and Intellectual Property Commission (CIPC) – an agency of the Department of Trade and Industry in South Africa that functions to register and maintain trademarks, patents, designs, and copyrights – does not investigate the novelty or inventive merit on which the application was filed (CIPC, 2021). This places responsibility on the inventor or patent applicant for ensuring that the patent application is valid.

The role of a governmental patent or trademark examiner is essential, as the examiner safeguards the quality of the application by reviewing it to determine the scope of protection claimed by the inventor and the existence of previously issued patents or trademarks. Potential adverse consequences resulting from this non-examination include the granting of patents that fall into legally excluded categories and obstacles for further research and development in certain technical fields.

As an illustrative example, Section 25(2) of the South African Patents Act No. 57 of 1978 excludes computer programs from patent protection (Kisch IP, 2016). While Article 10 of the TRIPS Agreement mandates that computer software and data compilations are to be protected by copyright under the Berne Convention, it does not require that software programs be protected by patents (WTO, 2021b). Since the South African patent office does not examine applications, software patents may proceed through the path illegally.

The South African patent registration approach is 20 to 30 times cheaper than other patent regimes, resulting in frivolous and useless patents (Pouris & Pouris, 2011). Although foreign investors can protect their inventions in South Africa cheaply, South African investors are unable to protect their inventions abroad due to the high costs. These disadvantages are observable in the following study, where during the 1996–2006 time period South African universities and their academics applied for 280 patents at the CIPC and only 58 of these, a mere

Table 12.3   WIPO Intellectual Property Statistics for 2019

Country	Quantity of patents	Quantity of trademarks	Quantity of industrial designs
South Africa	1514	34670	3364
Kenya	372	6869	160
Nigeria		14657	

20 percent, were protected abroad (Pouris & Pouris, 2011). Moreover, according to WIPO, and as shown in Table 12.3, South Africa leads the way in the quantity of patents, trademarks, and industrial designs filed in 2019 (WIPO, 2021c, 2021d).

However, these statistics may appear confusing, as the quantity of intellectual property applied for in no way correlates to the quality of the patent, trademark, or industrial design applied for, since South Africa is a non-examining country.

Variable "T"

South Africa has one of the largest information and communications technology markets in Africa. Several international corporates operate subsidiaries from South Africa, including IBM, Unisys, Microsoft, Intel, Dell, Novell, and Compaq, among others. Furthermore, South Africa is a regional leader in biometric data, payment cards to deliver social security, and drones in mining (Chakravorti & Chaturvedi, 2019). Recent technological developments in 2020 in South Africa include the creation of 5G infrastructure, mobile application development to provide enhanced functionality in the fields of banking, shopping, and ordering food, and enhanced e-commerce platforms and services (Kahla, 2020).

Technological startups, such as Bank Zero, RapidDeploy, Aerobotics, Pineapple, and Droppa, are making headlines (Venture Burn, 2020). For example, RapidDeploy is cloud-based software that enables public safety officials to reduce emergency response times and improve situational awareness. Another example, Aerobotics, a Cape Town-based aerial data analytics platform, provides analytics for drone users in the agricultural sector. Based on the foregoing, the variable "T" is strong, or "S," with a score of 8.

Framework: Variable "C"

Currently, South Africa is home to over 59 million people (Worldometer, 2021c) with a median age of 27.6 years old (Worldometer, 2021c). Along with Nigeria, South Africa is one of the two largest economies in Africa. According to South Africa's General Household Survey of 2018, approximately 14.2 million students attended school (Republic of South Africa, 2021). Participation in education institutions was virtually universal (97.4 percent) by the age of 15 years (the last compulsory school age) and approximately three quarters (74.5 percent) of learners were still in school by the age of 18 (Republic of South Africa, 2021). Additionally, the percentage of learners that attended no-fee schools had increased from 21.4 percent in 2007 to 67.2 percent by 2018 (Republic of South Africa, 2021).

Despite impressive enrollment figures, more than three quarters of children aged nine in South Africa cannot read for meaning, with this percentage as high as 91 percent in Limpopo and 85 percent in the Eastern Cape, which may be a function of the educational system or parents who are illiterate themselves (Amnesty International, 2020). Moreover, it has been asserted that "South Africa has one of the most unequal school systems in the world. Children in the top 200 schools achieve more distinctions in mathematics than children in the next 6,600 schools combined" (Amnesty International, 2020). Based on these statistics, it is not surprising that the unemployment rate in South Africa in 2020 was approximately 28.48 percent (Statista, 2020b). As such, the variable "C" scores a neutral, or "N," score of 2.

Framework: Variable "D"

Variable "R"

Patents and trademarks in South Africa are regulated by the CIPC, which is responsible for registering companies, co-operatives, and intellectual property rights, promoting education and awareness of intellectual property law, promoting compliance with relevant legislation, enforcing relevant legislation, monitoring compliance with financial reporting standards, and making recommendations to the Financial Reporting Standards Council, etc. (CIPC, 2021).

Variable "MC"

Due to South Africa's numerous ports and harbors, South Africa serves as a regional hub and a supply base for neighboring countries. As such, the South African government views the country's ports and terminals as key engines for economic growth. South Africa is situated on one of the busiest international sea routes, critical for international maritime transportation, and its geographic location presents an opportunity for investing in a diversified maritime market. In fact, South Africa has been ranked 19th as a financial hub by the World Economic Forum, which also gave the country top scores for having an advanced transport infrastructure (IOL, 2019).

Framework conclusion

According to Park and Wagh's Index of Patent Rights (Park & Wagh, 2002), South Africa was ranked as having the 12th strongest patent regime in 2001 (Pouris & Pouris, 2011). However, this statistic appears to be outdated since, differing from Kenya and Nigeria, the variable "IP" for South Africa in Equation 12.4 is low due to the lack of patent examination. Coupled with the strong variable "T," South Africa has emerging technologies, or technologies whose development and/or practical applications are still largely unrealized, that may be inadequately protected due to the lack of strong intellectual property rights available. The variable "C" shows a youthful population capable of employment. However, unemployment numbers are staggering. Moreover, though the variable "D" shows a weaker government regulation (e.g., resulting in a score of −1), South Africa's multiple marketing channels and physical ports serve to promote and transport products, resulting in a variable "MC" score of "S," or 7. Thus, Equation 12.4 becomes:

$$Framework = [((W) + (S)) + (N) + ((W) + (S))],$$

or

$$Framework = [((-1) + (8)) + (2) + ((-1) + (7))],$$

which results in an overall score of 15.

Based on the framework, South Africa's positive criteria must battle against deterrents including a lack of strong intellectual property protection available, internet connectivity issues, an education system that underserves its youth, unemployment, and medical/health issues. In fact, South Africa has only 64 percent internet penetration, with broadband and mobile internet speeds below the global median (Chakravorti & Chaturvedi, 2019). South Africa must increase internet accessibility to a broader cross-section of its population and improve the quality of such access. Further, South Africa currently faces an HIV and AIDS epidemic and the COVID-19 pandemic, coinciding with a high burden of tuberculosis, high maternal and child mortality, high levels of violence and injuries, and a growing burden of non-communicable diseases (e.g., cardiovascular diseases, diabetes, chronic respiratory conditions, and cancer) (Maphumulo & Bhengu, 2019; Mayosi & Lawn, 2012; Odendaal, 2019; Pillay-van Wyk & Msemburi, 2016).

South Africa may technologically springboard itself if the policies of South African President Cyril Ramaphosa, including a "digital skills revolution" that focuses on the training of 1 million youth in data science and related skills by 2030, as well as embedding of digital subjects within basic education to enable human capital to match the rapid evolution of the digital economy (Odendaal, 2019), are committed to reform. A renewed educational platform that teaches literacy nationwide is also needed.

CONCLUSION

Our application of Equation 12.4 successfully utilizes Teece's framework as a building block. Based on the application of our Equation 12.4, Nigeria is deemed the strongest country able to contribute to Africa's fast-growing technological market, with an overall score of 30. Kenya comes in a close second with a score of 26 and South Africa comes in third with a score of 15. These results are expected, as Nigeria's strong government regulation, multiple marketing channels for innovators to promote their products or services, youthful population, and increased internet accessibility will allow it to succeed. This assumes the country safeguards the health of its population and reduces dependence on foreign nations for technological and industrial needs.

Kenya's position is less certain. Despite strong government regulation, marketing channels, and a youthful population, the country battles against weak intellectual property regimes and technological deterrents, such as a lack of internet connectivity in rural populations. This country is also in massive debt due to Chinese infrastructure loans for its Standard Gauge Railway and other projects. Government and private citizen corruption is a large problem, as well. These negatives deter informational flow among citizens as well as for medical/health concerns. If internet connectivity in rural areas increases, rural citizens will no longer be passive recipients of improvements. Furthermore, successful completion of the Jubilee Government's Big 4 Agenda will increase Kenya's score.

South Africa, for its part, must battle against deterrents, including a lack of strong intellectual property protection, internet connectivity issues, high unemployment, unequal education, and medical/health issues. South Africa may technologically renew itself if the policies of South African President Cyril Ramaphosa are committed to reform.

REFERENCES

AB3D. (2021). African Born 3D Printing. AB3D. www.ab3d.co.ke/

Adeshokan, O. (2017). The fall of Yabacon Valley. Ventures Africa. http://venturesafrica.com/features/the-fall-of-yabacon-valley/.

Amnesty International. (2020). South Africa: Broken and unequal education perpetuating poverty and inequality. www.amnesty.org/en/latest/news/2020/02/south-africa-broken-and-unequal-education-perpetuating-poverty-and-inequality/

ARIPO (African Regional Intellectual Property Organization). (2010). Swakopmund Protocol on the Protection of Traditional Knowledge and Expressions of Folklore.

ARIPO (African Regional Intellectual Property Organization). (2015). Arusha Protocol for the Protection of New Varieties of Plants within the Framework of the African Regional Intellectual Property Organization (ARIPO) and Regulations for Implementing the Arusha Protocol for the Protection of New Varieties of Plants within the Framework of the African Regional Intellectual Property Organization.

ARIPO (African Regional Intellectual Property Organization). (2018). ARIPO annual report of 2018.

ARIPO (African Regional Intellectual Property Organization). (2019a). About ARIPO. www.aripo.org/#:~:text=The%20African%20Regional%20Intellectual%20Property%20Organization%20(ARIPO)%20is%20an%20inter,technological%20advancement%20for%20economic%2C%20social%2C

ARIPO (African Regional Intellectual Property Organization). (2019b). Harare Protocol on Patents and Industrial Designs within the Framework of the African Regional Intellectual Property Organization (ARIPO) and Regulations for Implementing the Harare Protocol on Patents and Industrial Designs within the Framework of the African Regional Intellectual Property Organization (ARIPO).

ARIPO (African Regional Intellectual Property Organization). (2019c). Banjul Protocol on Marks and Regulations for Implementing the Banjul Protocol.

Banwo & Ighodalo (2016). Strengthening intellectual property rights and protection in Nigeria. www.banwo-ighodalo.com/grey-matter/strengthening-intellectual-property-rights-and-protection-in-nigeria?leaf=6

BRCK. (2021). Connecting Africa to the internet. https://brck.com/

Brewster, R. (2011). The surprising benefits to developing countries of linking international trade and intellectual property. *Chicago Journal of International Law*, 12(1), 1–54.

Bright, J. (2016). Iroko launches IrokoX online network to showcase Africa's creative talent. Tech Crunch. https://techcrunch.com/2016/09/09/its-time-for-african-talent/

Bright, J. & Hruby, A. (2015). The rise of Silicon Savannah and Africa's tech movement. Tech Crunch. https://techcrunch.com/2015/07/23/the-rise-of-silicon-savannah-and-africas-tech-movement/

BudgIT. (2021). About us. https://yourbudgit.com/about-us/

Cc-Hub (Co-Creation Hub). (2021a). About us. https://cchubnigeria.com/

Cc-Hub Co-Creation Hub). (2021b). CcHUB is 5: Foolishly creating the future. https://cchubnigeria.com/cchub-5-foolishly-creating-future/

CDC (Centers for Disease Control and Prevention). (2019). Global health: Nigeria. www.cdc.gov/globalhealth/countries/nigeria/default.htm

Chakravorti, B. & Chaturvedi, R. S. (2019). Research: How technology could promote growth in 6 African countries. *Harvard Business Review*. https://hbr.org/2019/12/research-how-technology-could-promote-growth-in-6-african-countries

Chege, J. W. (1978). *Copyright Law and Publishing in Kenya*. Kenya Literature Bureau.

Christensen, C. M. (1997). *The Innovator's Dilemma: When New Technologies Cause Great Firms to Fail*. Harvard Business Review Press.

CIPC (Companies and Intellectual Property Commission). (2021). Our functions. www.cipc.co.za/index.php/about/our-functions/

Constitute Project. (2020). *Nigeria's Constitution of 1999*. www.constituteproject.org/constitution/Nigeria_2011?lang=en

Dun & Bradstreet. (2021). *Nigerian Copyright Commission (NCC)*. www.dnb.com/business-directory/company-profiles.nigerian_copyright_commission_%28ncc%29.4d53afe87f42186bce906334407718e8.html

Ekundayo, O. O. S. (2019). Education in Nigeria is in a mess from top to bottom: Five things can fix it. *The Conversation*. https://theconversation.com/education-in-nigeria-is-in-a-mess-from-top-to -bottom-five-things-can-fix-it-112894#:~:text=Nigeria's%20education%20system%20is%20based ,of%20four%20years%20tertiary%20education

EPDC (Education Policy and Data Center). (2012). Education profiles. www.epdc.org/node/406.html

Fredrick, M. (2019). *Internet Access: How Rural Kenya is Keeping Pace*. Akademie. www.dw.com/en/ internet-access-how-rural-kenya-is-keeping-pace/a-47071209

Future of Life Institute. (2021). AI policy: Kenya. https://futureoflife.org/ai-policy-kenya/?cn-reloaded =1

Gurry, F. (2015). Intellectual property for an emerging Africa. *WIPO Magazine*. www.wipo.int/wipo _magazine/en/2015/si/article_0001.html

Hduma Namba. (2021). Contribution of Huduma Namba to the Big Four agenda. www.hudumanamba .go.ke/the-big-4/

Interswitch. (2020). The gateway to Africa's payment ecosystem. www.interswitchgroup.com/

IOL. (2019). SA climbs on WEF Global Competitiveness Index. www.iol.co.za/news/politics/sa-climbs -on-wef-global-competitiveness-index-34533898

ITA (International Trade Administration, U.S. Department of Commerce). (2020). Nigeria: Country commercial guide. www.trade.gov/knowledge-product/nigeria-ecommerce

ITA (International Trade Administration, U.S. Department of Commerce). (2021). Kenya: Country commercial guide. www.trade.gov/knowledge-product/kenya-ecommerce

ITA (International Trade Administration, U.S. Department of Commerce). (2022). Kenya country commercial guide. August 20. www.trade.gov/country-commercial-guides/kenya-ecommerce

Jelassi, T. & Ludwig, S. (2016). Digital business transformation in Silicon Savannah: How M-Pesa changed Safaricom (Kenya). IMD. www.imd.org/research-knowledge/for-educators/case-studies/ digital-business-transformation-in-silicon-savannah-how-m-pesa-changed-safaricom-kenya-/

Kahla, C. (2020). Four technological advances to benefit South Africans in 2020. *The South African*. www.thesouthafrican.com/technology/four-technological-advances-to-benefit-south-africans-in -2020/

Kay, J. (1995). Appropriability. *Foundations of Corporate Success: How Business Strategies Add Value*. Oxford Scholarship Online.

Kazeem, Y. (2019). Nigeria's top fintech company is set to be Africa's first home-grown unicorn with visa investment. *Quartz Africa*. https://qz.com/africa/1746031/visa-buys-stake-for-200-million-in -nigerias-interswitch/

Kazeem, Y. (2020). Startup funding in Africa broke more records in 2019. *Quartz Africa*. https:// qz.com/africa/1782232/how-much-did-african-startups-raise-in-2019/#:~:text=Annual%20venture %20capital%20investments%20in%20Africa&text=Nigeria%20and%20Kenya%20were%20the,of %20investment%20received%20in%202019

KIPI (Kenya Industrial Property Institute). (2017). About KIPI. www.kipi.go.ke/index.php/about

Kisch IP. (2016). The balancing act of patentability. www.kisch-ip.com/the-balancing-act-of-patentability

KLR (National Council for Law Reporting – Kenya Law Reports). (2012). *Industrial Property Act*. National Council for Law Reporting with the Authority of the Attorney-General.

Lexology. (2019). Requirements and procedure for patent registration in Nigeria. www.lexology.com/ library/detail.aspx?g=f0321f8b-0da4-4480-b424-ca31ca894726

Macrotrends. (2021). Kenya literacy rate 2000–2021. www.macrotrends.net/countries/KEN/kenya/ literacy-rate#:~:text=Adult%20literacy%20rate%20is%20the,a%202.8%25%20increase%20from %202014

Maphumulo, W. T. & Bhengu, B. R. (2019). Challenges of quality improvement in the healthcare of South Africa post-Apartheid: A critical review. *Curationis*, 42(1), 1901.

Marras, F. (2020). Fintech unicorns. *Fintastico*. www.fintastico.com/collections/fintech-unicorns/

Mayosi, B. M. & Lawn, J. E. (2012). Health in South Africa: Changes and challenges since 2009. *The Lancet*, 380(9858), P2029–P2043.

Mbewa, D. O. (2021). Konnect Project: Chinese company works to bridge digital divide between Africa, world. *CGTN AFRICA*. https://africa.cgtn.com/2021/05/23/konnect-project-chinese-company-works -to-bridge-digital-divide-between-africa-world/

NCC (Nigerian Communications Commission). (2022). Subscriber statistics. www.ncc.gov.ng/statistics
-reports/subscriber-data

Nigerian Ports Authority. (2021). Who we are. https://nigerianports.gov.ng/#

Nordea. (2021). Intellectual property in Nigeria. www.nordeatrade.com/en/explore-new-market/
nigeria/intelectual-property#:~:text=The%20Trademarks%2C%20Patents%20And%20Designs,with
%20regards%20to%20intellectual%20property

Odek, J. O. (2009). *The Kenya Patent Law: Promoting Local Inventiveness or Protecting Foreign
Patentees?* Cambridge University Press.

Odendaal, N. (2019). Government commits to digital skills revolution. *Creamer Media's Engineering
News.* www.engineeringnews.co.za/article/govt-commits-to-digital-skills-revolution-2019-07-26

Olurounbi, R. & Soto, A. (2020). Nigeria jobless rate climbs to highest in at least a decade.
Bloomberg. www.bloomberg.com/news/articles/2020-08-14/nigeria-s-jobless-rate-climbs-to-highest
-in-at-least-a-decade#:~:text=People%20walk%20through%20a%20market%20in%20Abuja%20on
%20June%203.,-Photographer%3A%20KC%20Nwakalor&text=Unemployment%20in%20Nigeria
%20surged%20to,with%20its%20fast%2Dexpanding%20population

Onoyeyan, G. (2018). Copyright law and photocopying practice in Nigeria. *Library Philosophy and
Practice*, 1–9. https://digitalcommons.unl.edu/libphilprac/2179?utm_source=digitalcommons.unl.edu
%2Flibphilprac%2F2179&utm_medium=PDF&utm_campaign=PDFCoverPages

Oxford Insights. (2019). Government Artificial Intelligence Readiness Index 2019. www.oxfordinsights
.com/ai-readiness2019

Oyebade, A. (2002). *The Transformation of Nigeria: Essays in Honor of Toyin Falola.* Africa World
Press.

Park, W. G. & Wagh, S. (2002). Index of Patent Rights. In J. Gwartney & R. Lawson (Eds), *Economic
Freedom of the World: 2002 Annual Report* (pp. 33–41). The Fraser Institute.

Paystack. (2021). Why choose Paystack? https://paystack.com/why-choose-paystack

Pillay-van Wyk, V. & Msemburi, W. (2016). Mortality trends and differentials in South Africa from
1997 to 2012: Second national burden of disease study. *Lancet Global Health*, 4(9), e642–e653.

Pouris, A. & Pouris, A. (2011). Patents and economic development in South Africa: Managing intellectual property rights. *South African Journal of Science*, 107(11/12), 1–10.

Ramachandran, V. & Obado-Joel, J. (2019). Reports: The new economy of Africa: Opportunities for
Nigeria's emerging technology sector. Center for Global Development. www.cgdev.org/reader/new
-economy-africa-opportunities-nigerias-emerging-technology-sector?page=0

Republic of Kenya – Ministry of Industrialization, Trade and Enterprise Development. (2020).
Industrial property tribunal. www.industrialization.go.ke/index.php/departments/state-department
-for-investment-and-industry/58-industrial-property-tribunal#:~:text=The%20Industrial%20Property
%20Tribunal%20was,property%20recognized%20by%20the%20Constitution

Republic of South Africa. (2021). Education. www.gov.za/about-sa/education

Russon, M. (2020). How internet access is improving in Nigeria. BBC News. www.bbc.com/news/
business-51377955

Safaricom. (2021). M-PESA mobile money transfer. www.safaricom.co.ke/personal/m-pesa

Sewankambo, N. K. (2018). HIV incidence and scale-up of prevention in western Kenya. *The Lancet
HIV*, 5(5), E204–E205.

Sheppard, D. F. (1999). Patent law in South Africa with particular reference to the TRIPS agreement.
Journal of World Intellectual Property, 2(4), 607–615.

Statista. (2020a). Kenya: Unemployment rate from 1999 to 2020. www.statista.com/statistics/808608/
unemployment-rate-in-kenya/#:~:text=Kenya's%20unemployment%20rate%20was%202.64,work
%20but%20cannot%20find%20jobs

Statista. (2020b). South Africa: Unemployment rate from 1999 to 2020. www.statista.com/statistics/
370516/unemployment-rate-in-south-africa/.

Taubman, A. (2011). *A Practical Guide to Working with TRIPS.* (pp. 1–250). Oxford University Press.

Teece, D. J. (1986). Profiting from technological innovation: Implications for integration, collaboration,
licensing and public policy. *Research Policy*, 15(6), 285–305.

Teece, D. J. (2006). Reflections on "profiting from innovation." *Research Policy*, 35(8), 1131–1146.

The Borgen Project. (2022). Gender inequality in Nigeria's tech industry. https://borgenproject.org/gender-inequality-in-nigerias-tech-industry/

The Business Year. (2018). Lagos: The next Silicon Valley. www.thebusinessyear.com/nigeria-2018/lagos-the-next-silicon-valley/focus

Trading Economics. (2020). Nigeria unemployment rate 2006–2020. https://tradingeconomics.com/nigeria/unemployment-rate

TRIPS. (1994). Agreement on Trade-Related Aspects of Intellectual Property Rights. April 15, Marrakesh Agreement Establishing the World Trade Organization, Annex 1C, 1869 U.N.T.S. 299, 33 I.L.M. 1197.

UNCTAD (United Nations Conference on Trade and Development). (2021). About UNCTAD. https://unctad.org/

UNICEF. (2021). Nigeria: Education. www.unicef.org/nigeria/education

Unikorn. (2021). Nigeria's tech startups defy the odds. www.unikorn.org/nigerias-tech-startups-defy-the-odds/

United Nations. (2021). United Nations Office Nairobi. https://unon.org/

Ushahidi. (2021). About Ushahidi. www.ushahidi.com/

USPTO (United States Patent and Trademark Office). (2020a). Trade secret policy. www.uspto.gov/ip-policy/trade-secret-policy

USPTO (United States Patent and Trademark Office). (2020b). Trademark, patent, or copyright? www.uspto.gov/trademarks-getting-started/trademark-basics/trademark-patent-or-copyright#:~:text=A%20trademark%20is%20a%20word,party%20from%20those%20of%20others.&text=Unlike%20patents%20and%20copyrights%2C%20trademarks,a%20set%20term%20of%20years

Venture Burn. (2020). Eight SA startups to keep an eye on in 2020. https://ventureburn.com/2020/01/eight-sa-startups-to-keep-an-eye-on-in-2020/

WHO (World Health Organization). (2021). The Doha Declaration on the TRIPS Agreement and Public Health. www.who.int/medicines/areas/policy/doha_declaration/en/

Winter, S. G. (2006). The logic of appropriability: From Schumpeter to Arrow to Teece. *Research Policy*, 35(8), 1100–1106.

WIPO (World Intellectual Property Organization). (2009). The economics of intellectual property in South Africa. www.wipo.int/ip-development/en/economics/1013.html

WIPO (World Intellectual Property Organization). (2021a). Berne Convention for the Protection of Literary and Artistic Works. www.wipo.int/treaties/en/ip/berne/

WIPO (World Intellectual Property Organization). (2021b). PCT: The International Patent System. www.wipo.int/pct/en/.b

WIPO (World Intellectual Property Organization). (2021c). Statistical country profiles: Kenya. www.wipo.int/ipstats/en/statistics/country_profile/profile.jsp?code=KE.

WIPO (World Intellectual Property Organization). (2021d). Statistical country profiles: South Africa. www.wipo.int/ipstats/en/statistics/country_profile/profile.jsp?code=ZA

WIPO (World Intellectual Property Organization). (2021e). Summary of the Paris Convention for the Protection of Industrial Property (1883). www.wipo.int/treaties/en/ip/paris/summary_paris.html

WIPO (World Intellectual Property Organization). (2021f). The Paris Convention for the Protection of Industrial Property. https://wipolex.wipo.int/en/text/288514

WIPO (World Intellectual Property Organization). (2021g). The PCT now has 153 contracting states. www.wipo.int/pct/en/pct_contracting_states.html

WIPO (World Intellectual Property Organization). (2021h). What is intellectual property? www.wipo.int/about-ip/en/

Worldometer. (2021a). Kenya population. www.worldometers.info/world-population/kenya-population/

Worldometer. (2021b). Nigeria population. www.worldometers.info/world-population/nigeria-population/

Worldometer. (2021c). South Africa population. www.worldometers.info/world-population/south-africa-population/

WTO (World Trade Organization). (2005). *Managing the Challenges of WTO Participation: 45 Case Studies*. Cambridge University Press.

WTO (World Trade Organization). (2021a). South Africa and the WTO. www.wto.org/english/thewto
_e/countries_e/south_africa_e.htm
WTO (World Trade Organization). (2021b). TRIPS Part II: Standards concerning the availability, scope
and use of intellectual property rights. www.wto.org/english/docs_e/legal_e/27-trips_04_e.htm

13. Africa's post-pandemic economic recovery: catch up, don't give up

Lyal White, Liezl Rees, and Nikitta Hahn

INTRODUCTION

The severity of the COVID-19 pandemic on the global economy is well documented. World gross domestic product (GDP) contracted by 3.1 per cent in 2020 (IMF, 2021a). Sub-Saharan Africa's decline was much more severe, with a −1.7 per cent contraction, precipitating the first continent-wide recession in 25 years, according to the International Monetary Fund (IMF, 2021b). Although lower than initially expected, it is a concerning reversal of Africa's developmental progress over the decade prior to 2020. According to the IMF (2022), global growth reached 5.9 per cent, with Africa recording 3.6 per cent in 2021. Global growth is projected to decline to 4.9 per cent in 2022, while Africa's growth is estimated to increase marginally to 3.8 per cent. However, per capita GDP is unlikely to recover to pre-crisis levels until 2025 (IMF, 2022). It is clear that recovery across the continent will not be linear; Africa is likely to present an increasingly disparate set of numbers and performance indicators across its 54 countries over the next few years.

Five key areas have been identified as being pivotal to post-pandemic recovery and progress across Africa. These are pervasive inequality, a lack of statistical data, the ability of African countries to connect to the digital economy, the future of work on a continent beset by vulnerable informal businesses and jobs, and poor levels of and access to quality education. The pandemic exposed and accentuated these issues globally. But nowhere has their impact been more severe, and more immediate, than in Africa, where a dramatic slowdown and even reversal of key development metrics not only undermines post-pandemic economic recovery but threatens to reverse decades of progress on an already underdeveloped continent. Despite these setbacks, the pandemic could potentially be the catalyst to accelerate and drive new and important changes in key areas of development, encouraging the progress of citizens and investors alike, and introducing a greater sense of urgency in government policymaking and reform.

The five countries covered in this chapter, given their geographic spread, represent a general trend across Africa, offering instructive lessons and experiences specific to the continent, while relevant to global development in general. They are Egypt, Ethiopia, Kenya, Nigeria, and South Africa. South Africa, Nigeria, and Egypt are the three largest economies in Africa. Collectively, they comprise more than 60 per cent of the continent's GDP (Table 13.1). Ethiopia, with almost 120 million people, has the second largest population in Africa (after Nigeria), and more than 70 per cent of its people are under the age of 30 (Bezu, 2017). Considered one of the most promising economies on the continent prior to the pandemic,

Table 13.1   *GDP percentage growth rates 2018–2022*

Country	2018	2019	2020 forecast	2020	2021	2022 forecast
Egypt	5.3	5.6	1.9	3.6	3.3	5.2
Ethiopia	7.7	9.0	2.6	6.1	2	8.7
Kenya	5.6	5.0	0.6	−0.3	5.6	6.0
Nigeria	1.9	2.2	−5.3	−1.8	2.6	2.7
South Africa	1.5	0.1	−6.4	−7.0	5.0	2.2
Brazil	1.8	1.4	−5.8	−4.1	5.2	1.5
United Kingdom	1.3	1.4	−10.4	−9.8	6.8	5.0

Note: Brazil and the United Kingdom have been included for comparative purposes.
Source: IMF Data Mapper (2022).

Ethiopia enjoyed consistently high growth for nearly 20 years, while Kenya is widely regarded as a champion of regional integration and innovation and has driven positive diplomatic engagement with both the East and West. Each of the five countries is a leader in its respective sub-region, and carries significant weight in terms of its economic size and trajectory, population, and political influence in the broader African context. A variety of factors, including demographics, geographical size, urbanisation, levels of development, and political systems not only distinguish them, but so do their unique challenges. The COVID-19 pandemic could potentially be the catalyst to accelerate and drive new and important changes in key areas of development, encouraging the progress of citizens and investors alike, and introducing a greater sense of urgency in government policymaking and reform.

AFRICA'S TRAJECTORY: KEY DEVELOPMENTS AND TRENDS EXPOSED OR ACCELERATED BY THE COVID-19 PANDEMIC

Africa's economic growth and development before COVID-19, the continent's trajectory over the pandemic period, and current pathway to recovery have not, and will not, be uniform across all countries. This is particularly true for the five countries discussed in this chapter. The economic and political state of each country before COVID-19 will determine the pace and nature of their recovery in the long term.

This highlights the fact that a single solution or approach to dealing with the pandemic, and a post-pandemic recovery, should not be uniform across the continent but rather country specific, as the performance of the five countries in this study, on the five key areas discussed in this section, will show.

Widening Inequality

Interventions to contain COVID-19 have exacerbated socioeconomic inequality on an unprecedented scale, both within and between people and countries. The impact of measures taken to manage the virus has been a watershed moment in history: COVID-19 could be the single biggest contributor to deepening inequality at a global scale. Africa is at the centre of this seismic shift. The enormous impact of the pandemic on progress across the continent became evident in 2020 when worldwide lockdowns resulted in output in Sub-Saharan Africa contracting by 3.7 per cent, with a per capita income decline by 6.1 per cent (World Bank, 2021c). The loss of an estimated 22 million jobs across the continent strongly propelled economic inequality with the most vulnerable members of society disproportionately affected, including informal workers, youth, women, and unskilled people (International Labour Organization, 2020).

Tables 13.2 and 13.3 capture the Gini coefficient, as well as the GDP per capita in current United States (US) dollar prices, across the five selected countries between 2019 and 2020. The Gini coefficient measures the income distribution across a country's population, while the GDP per capita averages the sum of a country's economic output per person. South Africa has the highest Gini coefficient rate of the five countries measured and it was the only country to experience a significant decline in GDP per capita. This shrunk by 15.2 per cent between 2019 and 2020.

Table 13.2   Gini coefficient values and GDP per capita

Country	Gini coefficient	GDP per capita 2019	GDP per capita 2020
Egypt	31.5 (2017)	3,019.1	3,547.9
Ethiopia	35.0 (2015)	855.8	936.3
Kenya	40.8 (2015)	1816.5	1,838.2
South Africa	63.0 (2014)	6,001.4	5,090.7
Nigeria	35.1 (2018)	2,229.9	2,097.1

Source: World Bank Data Repository.

Table 13.3   Population size and unemployment rates across selected African countries

	Population size (millions)			Unemployment (% of total labour force)		
	2019	2020	2021	2019	2020	2021
Africa	1 308,06	1 340,6	1 370,7	6.611	7.281	7.70
Egypt	110,39	102,33	104,26	7.84	9.167	9.30
Ethiopia	112,10	114,97	117,88	2.326	3.237	3.70
Kenya	52,57	53,78	54,99	5.01	5.729	6.60
Nigeria	200,96	206,14	211,40	8.53	9.714	9.01
South Africa	58,56	59,31	60,04	28.47	29.22	35.6

Source: Population: Macrotrends.net; Worldometers.info. Unemployment: Macrotrends.net; World Bank (2021a).

Egypt has the lowest Gini coefficient of the five and the second largest GDP per capita value, which increased by 17.5 per cent between 2019 and 2020. If not addressed urgently and decisively, the worsening inequality of opportunity will become a defining characteristic of Africa's socioeconomic landscape.

Egypt

Egypt's outlook for economic recovery is more favourable than it is for most parts of Africa. It was one of the few emerging market economies to maintain a positive economic growth rate during the pandemic. The country's relatively low Gini coefficient and growing GDP per capita hold promise for a more equal society. The government's focus on maintaining macroeconomic stability through the advancement of key structural reforms and bolstering of social safety nets helped to cushion the blow of pandemic-related income losses in 2020 (All Africa, 2021).

Ethiopia

Despite achieving double-digit economic growth for a decade prior to the onset of the pandemic, Ethiopia's growth trajectory has been undermined by conflict in the Tigray region, low per capita incomes, and widening inequality. COVID-19 and climate change also threaten the country's aspirations to reach lower-middle income status by 2025 (World Health Organization, 2021). According to the World Bank (2022), lower middle-income countries are those with a per capita income of between $1,036 and $4,045 per annum. Ethiopia, at $936 in 2021 and increasing at an annual rate of nearly 10%, should reach lower middle-income status well before 2025, barring any unforeseen economic events.

Kenya

Kenya has some of the highest levels of inequality in the world, with an extreme gap between the richest and poorest Kenyans. It has the second highest Gini coefficient after South Africa among the five countries under study. According to Oxfam, 8,300 people (fewer than 0.1 per cent of the population) are wealthier than the remaining 44 million people (the bottom 99.9 per cent) in the country (Oxfam, 2021). The number of extremely wealthy individuals in Kenya is growing at a rate faster than anywhere else in the world, and is projected to increase by over 80 per cent within the next ten years (Oxfam, 2021). The pandemic has highlighted the urgent economic interventions and reform required to ensure a more sustainable and equal society in Kenya.

Nigeria

Despite being the largest economy on the African continent in GDP terms, Nigeria's socioeconomic crisis has been exacerbated by COVID-19 in the wake of rising food prices, increasing poverty, and a lack of social safety nets. Nigeria's GDP per capita declined by 4 per cent from 2019 to 2020 (Table 13.2). In the months after COVID-19 hit the country, the oil price hit record lows, briefly falling below zero. As its economy is dependent on oil exports for the bulk of its revenues and foreign exchange, Nigeria struggled to regain momentum, entering into recession in late 2020, reversing three years of growth (White, 2021).

South Africa

In South Africa, current dysfunctional elements of the state apparatus have compounded the country's pre-existing problem of structural inequality. A tiny 0.1 per cent of the richest individuals in South Africa own more wealth and assets than the poorest 90 per cent of individuals combined (Business Tech, 2021). The country's GDP per capita declined by 15.2 per cent from 2019 to 2020 because of economic hardships before the pandemic (see Table 13.2).

South Africa's extreme disparity in wealth and lacklustre growth is compounded by unequal access to opportunities, education, and land ownership. The high level of youth unemployment – reaching an all-time high of 66.5 per cent in the first quarter of 2022 – is of particular concern (Trading Economics, 2021). In the second quarter of 2021, South Africa recorded unemployment of 34.4 per cent, its highest since 2008 and one of the highest rates in the world (Reuters, 2022). South Africa is a prime example of how the pandemic has further exacerbated endemic inequality and set the country up for a lasting crisis.

Africa's Data Deficit

According to Morten Jerven (2013), author of *Poor Numbers: How We Are Misled by African Development Statistics and What to Do about It*, one of the most pressing challenges facing African governments in planning and policy formulation is the poor quality of basic economic and social statistical data and analytical capabilities. Hard and accurate numbers are the foundation of policy decisions and choices:

> Reliable statistics, including estimates of economic growth rates and per capita income, are basic to the operation of governments in developing countries and vital to non-governmental organisations and other entities that provide financial aid to them. Rich countries and international financial institutions such as the World Bank allocate their development resources on the basis of such data. The paucity of accurate statistics is not merely a technical problem; it has a massive impact on the welfare of citizens in developing countries. (Jerven, 2013)

From counting COVID-19 infections to the impact of the pandemic on local, national, and regional economies, the challenge of poor numbers and reporting has undermined the continent's response to the pandemic, and threatens to undermine its recovery. One of the consequences of the data deficit is that the full extent of COVID-19 in Africa is largely unknown. The situation is exacerbated by overburdened healthcare systems that often lack modern technology and efficient processes. Outdated census statistics have not helped matters, and many rural and outlying areas have not been captured in the COVID-19 data for infections and deaths.

The data crisis in Africa is not new. Almost half of the continent's population lives in a country where a national census has not taken place since 2009. The recommended time between censuses is ten years (*The Economist*, 2020). As Table 13.4 shows, two of the five countries in this study have not conducted a census in ten years or more. Ethiopia's last census took place 14 years ago, in 2007. It was only the third in the country's history, and the first to be documented and the results publicly disseminated (International Housing Survey Network, 2007). Around 30 per cent of adults in Sub-Saharan Africa have no formal identification, according to the Identification, Financial Inclusion and Development in Sub-Saharan Africa report produced by the World Bank and International Finance Corporation. The percentage is much higher among women, youth, and the very poor. This affects financial and economic inclusion, healthcare, education, and migration, among other things (Klapper et al., 2019). Data on births and deaths are also typically inaccurate or unavailable (*The Economist*, 2020). Overall, record keeping of population trends in Africa is dismal, leaving governments and policymakers to speculate where to build clinics and roads, and businesses where to invest in new markets (*The Economist*, 2020). Without credible data, African governments will continue to

Table 13.4   *Most recent national census date in selected countries*

Country	Census year
Egypt	2017
Ethiopia	2007
Kenya	2019
Nigeria	2006
South Africa	2022 (in process)

Source: Egypt: Population, Housing, and Establishments Census (2017); Ethiopia: Summary and Statistical Report of the 2007 Population and Housing Census (2007); Kenya: 2019 Kenya Population and Housing Census Reports; Nigeria: *The Conversation* (2021); South Africa: Stats SA (2021).

struggle to make appropriate plans to manage the COVID-19 crisis and others in the future, as well as to manage national planning and other initiatives on an ongoing basis.

The situation in the five countries under study can be extrapolated across the continent. In fact, given that the five are among the most developed in Africa, the situation is likely to be worse in many other nations. Reliable data need to be the foundation of planning for post-pandemic recovery, particularly given the fact that most African countries have high levels of informality in terms of business, migration, and residency.

A Regional Approach to Connectivity and Digitalisation

Connectivity is key to facilitating trade, economic activity, and growth. It determines the efficiency and capacity of a country to move goods, services, capital, and information internally and beyond its borders. African countries continue to lag in the development of connecting infrastructure, including roads, rail, ports, and telecommunications. This not only affects the efficiency of logistics, but the costs of doing business. The pandemic has exposed the extent of African countries' infrastructure deficits, forcing governments to critically assess where investments need to be made as they focus on immediate recovery and long-term economic development. It has also highlighted the importance of deepening regional integration.

Trading under the African Continental Free Trade Area (AfCFTA) began in January 2021, making Africa the largest free trade area in the world based on the number of member countries. Connecting 1.3 billion people across 54 countries, with a combined GDP of about $3.4 trillion, the AfCFTA has the potential to lift 30 million Africans out of extreme poverty and drive much needed reforms to boost inclusive economic growth by improving the movement of goods, services, people, and information (World Bank, 2020). However, there are many issues still being negotiated to make the first phase of AfCFTA fully operational (Thompson, 2021). The pandemic demonstrated that Africa's industrial production can be swiftly strengthened, and African industries can react to demand if given the opportunity to do so (White & Rees, 2021). While governments moved quickly to coordinate their response to COVID-19 and integrate their supply chains, African firms stepped up to address markets gaps created by the pandemic, which played a role in not just building local capacity but also strengthening regional value chains. In Ethiopia, for example, Ethiopian Airlines adapted to lower passenger numbers by repurposing passenger planes for cargo, while firms in the country's industrial parks retooled to manufacture personal protective equipment. AfCFTA is also a catalyst for the growth of small, micro, and medium enterprises. Among other interventions, negotiations for e-commerce and digital trade are set to be fast-tracked under the Africa-wide free trade pact, which will improve modernisation efforts and business competitiveness as well as market access.

The pandemic particularly highlighted Africa's dependence on imported pharmaceuticals. In 2018, 95.9 per cent of the continent's medicinal and pharmaceutical products were imported from outside its borders. Africa's vaccine sales are worth about $1.3 billion, within a global market estimated to be $33 billion. Despite this, the continent accounts for 25 per cent of the global demand. Africa's market share could be expanded to a projected $5.4 billion by 2030 – if it takes important steps such as overcoming access barriers, equitably addressing pricing issues, and introducing new products (including COVID-19 vaccines). Technological innovations along with progress made in addressing trade barriers, regulatory issues, and other key enablers could position Africa to compete with other emerging market vaccine manufacturers, such as Brazil and India. The development of vaccine production capabilities in these countries is an important underpinning of Africa's early-stage bio economy roadmap (Gennari et al., 2021). However, developing this bio economy is not a simple process; it is a complex undertaking involving multiple role players, from pharmaceutical companies to multilateral development partners such as the African Union and African Development Bank. Supportive regulations and an enabling environment for manufacturing need to be in place, which should include basics such as regular power supply, cold storage facilities, and efficient supply chains.

Improved integration across Africa is therefore an important plank in the development of an Africa-based pharmaceutical capacity and needs to be supplemented by a proactive policy agenda both nationally and regionally. Strengthening trade facilitation will improve collaboration between countries and enable them to scale production if the products can be moved easily, cheaply, and quickly around the continent. One of the issues that needs to be tackled in Africa is poor and uneven access to the internet and the quality and reliability of access (Bower, 2021). The shift to online working, teaching, shopping, and other activities as a result of lockdowns has highlighted the need for greater attention to the information and communications technology (ICT) sector generally.

According to the United Nations Economic Commission for Africa, less than one in five households on the continent has access to the internet, which is a constraint to economic growth (Internet Society, 2021a). Estimates by Google and the International Finance Corporation show the internet economy has the potential to contribute up to US$180 billion to Africa's GDP by 2025 (Internal Finance Corporation, 2021). Two metrics – growth in active internet users and cost of mobile data – illustrate the levels of digital connectivity in Africa and highlight the need for tackling constraints to build a more connected and inclusive Africa. As Table 13.5 demonstrates, the five countries in this study need to address constraints in telecommunications if they are to benefit from the internet economy. Penetration rates vary between 68.2 per cent in South Africa to a dismal 25 per cent in Ethiopia. This, in turn, is affected by the high cost of mobile broadband data, limiting access for poorer Africans. Table 13.6 shows the cost of mobile broadband data, using 2 Gigabytes of data as a percentage of gross national income (GNI) per capita.

Table 13.5   *Percentage of individuals using the internet in 2010 and 2022*

Country	2010	2022
Egypt	21.60	71.9
Ethiopia	0.75	25
Kenya	7.20	42
Nigeria	11.50	51
South Africa	24.00	68.2

Source: 2010 figures are based on reports from the International Telecommunication Union and 2022 figures are based on a DataReportal study (Kemp, 2022).

Table 13.6   *Cost of mobile broadband data (2 GB) as a percentage of GNI per capita (US$, 2021)*

Country	% GNI per capita	US$
Egypt	1.09	$3,20
Ethiopia	5.34	$3,26
Kenya	3.12	$4,64
Nigeria	2.00	$2,99
South Africa	2.32	$11,25

Source: ICT Price Baskets Dashboards, International Telecommunication Union (2021).

Egypt: digital reform, but less freedom

Internet penetration in Egypt was 71.9 per cent in January 2022, the best performance out of the five countries (Kemp, 2022). This is indicative of significant investments made in telecommunications infrastructure by the Egyptian government in recent years.

The Inclusive Internet Index 2021 outlines the current state of internet inclusion across 120 countries in four categories: availability, affordability, relevance, and readiness. It shows that Egypt climbed five places to 73rd overall following the government's recent moves towards digital transformation (Daily News Egypt, 2021). However, most of Egypt's telecommunications infrastructure is owned by Telecom Egypt, a state-owned company. This gives the authorities the power to suspend the internet and decrease speeds to serve the government's agenda, which has occurred on several occasions (Freedom House, 2020). A study by Freedom House (2020) found that at the end of March 2020, 546 websites were blocked by the authorities, infringing on the rights of people to access information. The affordability of mobile broadband data in Egypt in 2020 was 1 per cent of GNI per capita, well below the 2 per cent rate recommended by the Broadband Commission for Sustainable Development – a joint initiative of the International Telecommunication Union (ITU) and the United Nations Educational, Scientific and Cultural Organisation to promote internet access. If Egypt is to participate meaningfully in the digital economy, continued investment must be made in its telecommunications infrastructure to expand internet access and improve its reliability and freedom (OECD, 2020).

Ethiopia: coming out of digital isolation
Ethiopia is one of the least connected and most digitally isolated countries in the world. The percentage of people using the internet in Ethiopia was a mere 25 per cent as of January 2022 (Kemp, 2022). This is a substantial increase from 2010, when less than 1 per cent of the population used the internet, but is far from optimal in a country of almost 120 million people and has significant repercussions for innovation and inclusive economic growth. Furthermore, the affordability rate[1] of mobile broadband data was the highest out of the five countries at 9.52 per cent of GNI per capita in 2020. This is more than four times the 2 per cent rate recommended by the Broadband Commission (ITU, 2021b).

Part of the problem is a lack of telecommunications infrastructure in rural areas where almost 80 per cent of people live. The country's unreliable electricity supply and regular power outages, as well as poor internet speeds, limit access further (Freedom House, 2020). In an effort to address these problems, about US$40 million of a 2019 US$300 million World Bank loan has been earmarked for expansion of the sector (Freedom House, 2020). Despite Ethiopia's commitment to reform its ICT sector through partial privatisation, the country periodically shuts down the internet and social media in response to political criticism and crisis. For example, the government implemented a three-month shutdown in parts of Orōmīya State from January 2020 due to conflict between government forces and a faction of the Oromo Liberation Front (Freedom House, 2020).

Furthermore, more than a quarter of Ethiopian adults do not have a proper identity card or bank account, and only 49 per cent have a mobile connection – all essential for participating in the digital economy (Navis & Moore, 2019). The Ethiopian government has a long way to go in equipping the country with the necessary infrastructure, tools, and skills to integrate and participate effectively in the digital economy to leverage, among other things, the potential of its large youth population (Schneidman, 2021).

Kenya: urban advances versus rural poor
Despite a high mobile penetration rate of more than 110 per cent, and the widespread use of mobile money, only 42 per cent of Kenya's population used the internet in 2022 (Kemp, 2022). This is largely because 70 per cent of the population live in rural areas, with only 17 per cent of these individuals having access to the internet due to severe telecommunications infrastructure and electricity constraints (Mugendi, 2020). In terms of the affordability of mobile broadband data, at 3.31 per cent of GNI per capita, Kenya is slightly above the rate recommended by the Broadband Commission, but it is still prohibitively expensive for a large part of the population (ITU, 2021). The Kenyan government has invested substantially in the broadband connectivity provided by four undersea fibre optic cables off the country's coast, including Seacom, Teams, Eassy, and Lion2 (International Trade Administration, 2021).

Overall, while internet access has continued to improve in Kenya, particularly in major urban centres, cost and infrastructure challenges continue to limit internet quality and speed of connections in rural areas. Despite these challenges Kenya's capital, Nairobi, has become known as the Silicon Savannah, a name drawn from Silicon Valley in the US, because of its status as a regional leader in internet connectivity and ICT infrastructure investment (International

---

[1]   The affordability rate is measured by the ITU as the share of income spent on telecommunication and internet services, expressed as a percentage of monthly GNI per capita.

Trade Administration, 2021). Analysts predict continued growth in Kenya's ICT sector, which will translate into job opportunities in key industries, such as financial services, retail, manufacturing, healthcare, agriculture, and tourism (Switzerland Global Enterprise, 2021).

Nigeria: big plans, poor implementation

Internet penetration in Nigeria stood at just 51 per cent of the population in January 2022 (Kemp, 2022). Given the country's population of more than 200 million people, this makes it one of the largest populations of internet users in Sub-Saharan Africa at just over 105 million people. The number of mobile connections was 82.4 per cent (Kemp, 2022). Despite the large number of connections, low internet penetration has been attributed to the high cost of internet adoption in rural areas, poor quality services, and inadequate infrastructure – unreliable power supply is a major issue for stable internet access (Udegbunam, 2020). In 2019, Nigerian households reported receiving about 9.5 hours of electricity per day (Freedom House, 2020). In terms of the affordability rate of mobile broadband data, at 1.71 per cent of GNI per capita, Nigeria is slightly below the rate recommended by the Broadband Commission. In 2020, the Nigerian government introduced a new National Broadband Plan 2020–25, which aims to expand broadband penetration to 70 per cent of the population by 2025 (Freedom House, 2020). The government has implemented a temporary policy to waive charges for laying fibre optic cables on federal highways until December 2022 to make it cheaper for internet service providers to install this infrastructure across the country (Kazeem, 2020).

Like Kenya, Nigeria is a centre of financial innovation, and revenues from the fintech sector are expected to reach $544 million in 2022, up from $153 million in 2017 (Monteiro, 2021). Nigeria is home to several African unicorns – companies with a valuation of $1 billion and more. They include Flutterwave, a payment company founded in 2016 that helps businesses to build customisable payments applications, payments platform Interswitch, founded in 2002, and e-commerce company Jumia (Collins, 2021). If Nigeria, and other African countries, are to achieve sustainable and inclusive economic growth, they need to encourage the growth of innovative companies offering appropriate and affordable products and services that also improve efficiencies and address longstanding challenges within countries and across borders (Hyde, 2021).

South Africa: good coverage, high cost

Internet penetration in South Africa reached 68.2 per cent as of January 2022 (Kemp, 2022). The majority of suburbs in urban centres, such as Cape Town, Johannesburg, Pretoria, and Durban, have fibre optic cables, with projects to roll out public Wi-Fi in metropolitan areas and towns across the country having been relatively successful (Freedom House, 2020). The least connected individuals are typically those living in rural areas. In general, internet speeds and reliability are good compared to the other four countries. However, regular power cuts by the state-owned power supplier, Eskom, have increasingly interrupted services over the past decade (Grootes, 2019). The cost of data in South Africa is high, at 2.5 per cent of GNI per capita, which equated to $10.21 per 1.5 gigabytes in 2020. This is unaffordable for individuals earning less than $500 per month – about 40 per cent of the population (Freedom House, 2020). Following the release of an inquiry by the Competition Commission into the data service market in 2019, the country's leading two internet service providers, Vodacom and MTN, agreed to reduce data costs and increase the number of zero-rated websites accessible on their networks, including universities, schools, and some job portals (Freedom House, 2020). The internet offers countries the means to participate in the global, digital economy. Overall, the five countries in this study, with low penetration rates, high data costs, and unreliable services, need to invest significantly in not only telecommunications infrastructure but also electricity and appropriate regulations in order to increase access to local and global digital products and services. This is critical for sustainable and inclusive development economic growth in the post-pandemic era (World Bank, 2021c).

The Future of Work in Africa: Leveraging the Informal Economy

In the wake of the spread of COVID-19 across the world, digital technologies have been in the ascendancy (World Bank, 2021b). In the workplace, trends in remote working and e-commerce were accelerated across almost all sectors and have changed demands globally for certain skills and labour (McKinsey Global Institute, 2021). The pandemic forced businesses, workers, and consumers to embrace new technologies at short notice. This trend towards the more ubiquitous use of online and digital platforms will outlast the pandemic, but effective participation in this new economy will require more investment in supporting infrastructure and skills. These new approaches pose a significant challenge for industries and jobs dependent on physical, on-site interactions and, most significantly in Africa, those in the informal sector (McKinsey Global Institute, 2021).

For Africa, the implications of this disruption have been profound and underlined the digital divide that existed before the pandemic. According to the ITU's 'Measuring digital development' report (2021a), 90 per cent of people in developed regions have access to the internet compared to just 33 per cent of Africa's population, with the biggest access challenges existing in rural areas. Furthermore, a mere 50 per cent of African households in urban areas have internet access at home, and just 15 per cent in rural areas (ITU, 2021a). Only 17 per cent of Africans in urban areas have such access to a computer, while in rural areas it is a low 2 per cent (ITU, 2021a). This has serious implications for the adoption of work-from-home models for those in formal employment and for access to online learning. Table 13.7 outlines the coverage of internet access and computer availability at a household level for the five countries in this study.

Table 13.7   Percentage of households with computer and internet access

	Computer at home	Year of data	Internet access at home	Year of data
Egypt	70.2	2020	73.0	2020
Ethiopia	5.0	2016	15.4	2016
Kenya	8.8	2019	17.9	2019
Nigeria	6.4	2018	15.2	2017
South Africa	22.7	2019	63.3	2019

Source: ITU (2021a).

Just over 70 per cent of households in Egypt have a household computer, and 73 per cent have access to the internet from home, compared to Ethiopia, Kenya, and Nigeria, where less than 10 per cent of the population has a computer and access to the internet from home is less than 20 per cent in all three countries (ITU, 2021a). South Africa also performs poorly on both measures, with 63.3 per cent of the population able to access the internet from home and 22.7 per cent having access to a home computer (ITU, 2021a). Efforts need to be made to ensure the informal sector in Africa, which accounts for more than 80 per cent of non-agricultural jobs and more than 60 per cent of urban employment, does not get left behind in this digital shift (Given & Karlen, 2020). Informal jobs and businesses are typically insecure, low in productivity, have unskilled owners and workers, and lack ready access to credit, basic services, and high-value markets (Given & Karlen, 2020). A World Bank survey conducted between April and June 2020 found that 56.3 per cent of respondents with informal urban jobs in Nigeria stopped working because of COVID-19 and 39.2 per cent in rural areas, demonstrating the vulnerability of this market segment (Weber et al., 2020). Table 13.8 outlines the percentage of people working in the informal sector in the five African countries in this study.

Table 13.8   Percentage of individuals working in the informal sector

	Percentage of informal-sector employment	Year of data
Egypt	63	2020
Ethiopia	90	2016
Kenya	80	2019
Nigeria	84	2018
South Africa	20	2019

Source: Egypt: Middle East Institute (2020); Ethiopia: African Union (2008); Kenya: *Friedrich Ebert Stiftung* (2020); Nigeria: Centre for the Studies of the Economies of Africa (2020); South Africa: *The Conversation* (2019).

Ethiopia, Nigeria, and Kenya have an exceptionally high proportion of informal to formal jobs of the countries in this study. Policy interventions to improve the welfare and skills of workers, boost productivity of small-scale businesses, and create jobs are essential (International Labour Organization, 2020). The future of work in Africa is not about growth in formal-sector jobs and full-time employment; it is about people working multiple 'gigs' or jobs, for entities that are formalised as far as possible (Ng'weno & Porteous, 2018). It is important to see how to leverage digital technologies and platforms to make the nature of informal work more productive and qualitative for workers (Ng'weno & Porteous, 2018). This will require giving more people access to digital technologies to give them greater access to information and improved customer reach through social media (World Bank, 2021b).

Research indicates that the adoption of new technologies in Africa not only creates new jobs, it also improves worker productivity. Both informal and formal businesses on the continent that adopted digital technologies prior to the pandemic, such as smartphones, digital payment platforms, and management systems, demonstrated improved productivity levels, increased profits, and higher wages and employment over the period (World Bank, 2021b). Building on the digital components of their businesses, these companies were able to ramp up activities and increase sales and employment. For example, Nigeria's online retailer, Jumia, had a more than 50 per cent increase in transactions in the first half of 2020, from 3.1 million to 4.7 million, compared to the first six months of 2019 (World Bank, 2021b).

According to the United Nations, Africa's working-age population will grow by 224 million by 2030 and 730 million by 2050 (United Nations, Department of Economic and Social Affairs, 2019). Insufficient formal wage jobs are being created to absorb new entrants, and as a result, the informal sector will continue to grow. In order to reverse this trend and reset prevailing economic structures built on informality and a reliance on natural resources, African governments must fast-track policies and investments to improve the ecosystem for entrepreneurs, while also expanding connectivity, fostering innovation, and improving access to finance (World Bank, 2021c). Simultaneously, the general lack of digital skills to meet the requirements of the growing global digital economy needs to be addressed (Wallace-Stephens & Morgante, 2021).

As companies work to achieve sustainability and profitability in the rapidly changing business landscape, boosting productivity and reaching new customers requires employees to have different skills and new ways of thinking (London School of Economics and Political Science, 2021). Governments must invest heavily in education, especially in science, technology, engineering, and mathematics, to improve available skills to drive new digital economies (World Bank, 2021b).

According to the World Economic Forum, digital skills (incorporating computer skills, basic coding, and digital reading) have become core competencies, which are necessary to allow people to actively participate in the digital economy. This highlights the need for both the government and private sector in African countries to prioritise the reskilling and upskilling of workers. In Figure 13.1, which measures digital skills over a three-year period, Ethiopia, Nigeria, and South Africa fall below the world median score of 4.20, while Kenya and Egypt

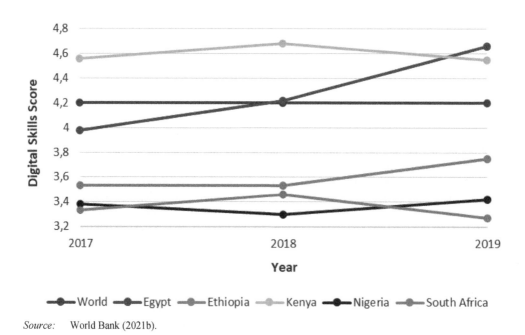

Source: World Bank (2021b).

Figure 13.1   Digital skills among active population, 2017–2019

surpass it. South Africa has the lowest year-on-year average growth of 0.7 per cent (World Bank, 2021b).

Given the future of work in a digitally led context, it is critical for Africa to foster new skills and employment pathways to not only effectively participate in the digital economy, but to unlock the vast opportunities on offer. Making drastic improvements in school curricula and tertiary education, as well as providing access to high-quality educational institutions, will be critical to address current skills gaps and meet the requirements of business in the future. The following section considers the future of education in Africa in more detail through the prism of the countries in this study.

The Impact of COVID-19 on Education in Africa

Economic modernisation and the future world of work is defined by increasing connectivity. This demands equal access to education at all levels and improved literacy levels. Access to inclusive education will determine Africa's ability to capitalise on the opportunities of digitisation. This is essential to narrow the digital divide between Africa and other regions, and to maintain competitiveness in the global economy.

Prolonged school closures resulting from COVID-19 lockdowns held back access to quality education in Africa for millions. According to a UNICEF report, 'Are children really learning?' (2022), as the pandemic entered its third year in 2022, 23 countries were yet to fully open schools, impacting 405 million school children. Forced school closures and low rates of internet access at home have resulted in children aged 7–14, notably in Sub-Saharan Africa, demonstrating the lowest rates of foundational reading skills globally (UNICEF, 2022). While online learning has been fast-tracked because of the pandemic, it presents a significant challenge to African students who cannot access this medium of education because of a lack of access to the internet, electricity, relevant equipment, and no digital skills. At the onset of the pandemic, only 29 per cent of higher education institutions in Africa were able to move online in a shift to emergency remote teaching, compared to 85 per cent in Europe (Koninckx et al., 2021). To safeguard Africa's future, a resilient, inclusive, and integrated economic system that fosters productive learning environments through accessible innovative solutions and technological advances is imperative. The future of education in Africa relies on reducing the digital learning divide and building critical digital and literacy skills.

Egypt: pushing online education

Egypt has a relatively high literacy rate of 71.2 per cent for adults aged 15 years and older, compared to other African countries (World Bank, 2021a). It also has a comparatively low number of children out of school, as well as a high number of students enrolled in vocational education programmes and pre-university education. Prior to the onset of the pandemic, the country's education sector was constrained by historically low budgetary spending on education, inefficient allocation of educational resources, as well as high unemployment rates among higher and tertiary education graduates (Biltagy, 2021). The rapid acceleration of the digital economy has enabled the introduction of innovative and sustainable interventions to address structural educational issues. In a bid to respond to growing digital education needs and address educational inequality, Egypt and the United Arab Emirates have collaborated in a new online school launched in March 2021 (Egypt Independent, 2021). The Digital School (https://thedigitalschool.org/), the first of its kind, is an Arab online school that aims to reach 1 million disadvantaged students by 2026, as well as progressively improve the quality of online education across the board (Egypt Independent, 2021).

Ethiopia: poor access to education

Ethiopia has a low literacy level, with only 51.1 per cent of adults aged 15 years and older considered to have adequate literacy skills (World Bank, 2021a). Eight months of school closures as a direct response to COVID-19, which affected 26 million children, have widened the gap between rich and poor (Bizuwork & Sewunet, 2020). Government interventions to support distance learning for students have been implemented, but this leaves disadvantaged students by the wayside, as they often cannot access the required technology or learning materials and often lack support and assistance at home (Bizuwork & Sewunet, 2020). Although digital education is at an early stage in Ethiopia due to limited infrastructure and spending, the government has begun implementing its digital transformation strategy. A collaboration between the Ministry of Innovation and Technology and the Internet Society seeks to expand connectivity and internet access to rural areas, as well as develop and implement digitisation strategies in key growth sectors (Internet Society, 2021b). Ethiopia has already started using blockchain technology in education for identification and record-keeping purposes. Other benefits are providing real-time verification and access to grades, boosting the quality of education nationwide, and creating employment opportunities (Mesmar, 2021). However, challenges for online education remain, including access and cost issues, particularly for those in rural areas.

Kenya: tackling educational inequality

2020 has been described as a lost year in education for impoverished Kenyan students following the closure of schools for nine months. The impact of COVID-19 on the education system could potentially worsen already low literacy rates in the country, currently at 81.5 per cent for adults aged 15 years and older (World Bank, 2021a). Prolonged school closures, interrupted learning, and inaccessible learning materials have left disadvantaged children vulnerable to child labour, child marriage, and teenage pregnancy.

The extreme economic divide at a national level is evident in students' varied performance. Students that were able to continue learning throughout the pandemic improved on their positive examination results of previous years, while 53 per cent of rural students showed significant declines in their levels of mathematics knowledge and comprehension (Zaman, 2021). The extreme inequalities exposed by the pandemic gave Kenyan officials the impetus to rapidly connect students digitally through the launch of DigiSchool, a digital literacy programme developed by the Ministry of Information, Communications and Technology. Using a multi-stakeholder approach, it aims to equip learners with the necessary skills for virtual instruction and digital learning (DigiSchool Kenya, 2021). This multi-pronged programme addresses infrastructure and broadband challenges, the upskilling of teachers, and provides digital content for online learning. Microsoft has also partnered with the Ministry of Education in Kenya in the Global Partnership for Education initiative to expand digital education and advance data competency through data science (Microsoft, 2021).

Nigeria: private solutions to digital access

Nigeria's education system has suffered from a range of challenges that predate the pandemic, such as adult literacy rates at a low 62 per cent (World Bank, 2021a). Eight months of school closures prompted the introduction of alternative technology-based methods of learning. More than 70 per cent of state governments said they had implemented learning alternatives such as television and radio broadcasts of lessons in a 'learn from home' approach. Electricity cuts, lack of access to technology and a lack of teaching professionals during lockdowns meant many children were unable to participate in home schooling (Azubuike, 2021). The pandemic also disrupted the distribution of educational material, particularly to rural and impoverished areas.

On the upside, the private sector is developing partnerships to boost access to digital education for Nigerian children. Private partnerships and learning interventions by the likes of Microsoft have led to the training of 18,000 secondary school teachers in digital literacy, while financial institutions and telecommunications operators are working to improve digital access to educational systems and internet connectivity (Ogundare, 2021). Local innovation hubs have also provided internet solutions to ensure that as many students as possible have access to virtual education (Oladunjoye, 2020). Building digital literacy skills across the country, utilising available technologies, as well as bolstering internet access and educational material are all playing a role in keeping Nigerian students connected.

South Africa: a slow move online

South Africa's downward trajectory of adult literacy continues to threaten the future progress of the country. Literacy rates decreased from 94.4 per cent in 2015 to 87 per cent in 2017 (World Bank, 2021a). Schoolchildren in South Africa are nearly one year behind where they otherwise would be because of pandemic-related school closures (UNICEF, 2021). With relatively sophisticated digital infrastructure and access, South Africa has failed to utilise the opportunity provided by digital education, and the country needs to adopt a more innovative approach to ensure that impoverished learners are not left behind. High data costs and lack of access to educational software have hampered the ability of existing higher education institutions to take real advantage of the opportunity to advance digital transformation among South Africa's youth, who are future participants in the global digital economy (Mabolloane, 2021).

CONCLUSION

The impact of the COVID-19 pandemic is arguably more significant in Africa than elsewhere, given the continent's demographic dynamics, underdevelopment, and inequality. Deeper global inequality threatens to be the most obvious and consequential impact of the pandemic, given the interconnected nature of the world and its people today. Africa is at the centre of this, and its growth trajectory hinges on addressing the recent socioeconomic shockwaves comprehensively and universally.

As was the case with Africa's economic growth and development before COVID-19, the continent's trajectory over the pandemic period, and subsequent pathway to recovery, has not, and will not, be uniform across all countries. This is particularly true for the five countries discussed in this chapter. The economic and political state of each country before COVID-19 will determine the pace and nature of their recovery in the long term. Egypt, for example, is expected to recover to pre-pandemic levels of growth in 2022 – about 5.2 per cent – on the back of renewed business confidence and increasing investment, especially as international tourism recovers.[2] However, Egypt must address challenges around uneven digital access and the modernisation of education to ensure continued growth in the long term. The recovery of the Ethiopian economy hinges on crucial reforms, such as the liberalisation of strategic sectors as well as the management of sociopolitical tensions. In the immediate future, economic growth should return to pre-pandemic levels reaching about 9 per cent by 2022; but the long-term implications of COVID-19 in Ethiopia depend heavily on so-called 'non-economic' factors associated with education and political stability. As one of the least connected and most digitally isolated countries in the world, it is critical that the government invests in the required infrastructure, tools, and skills, so that Ethiopia may integrate and effectively participate in the digital economy. Kenya recovered faster than the other economies in 2021, given its strong economic standing before the pandemic, as growth rates averaged 5.7 per cent from 2015 to 2019, along with its deep connectedness to global markets. In 2022, the economy is expected to grow by around 6 per cent. However, widening inequality, particularly around education and economic inclusion, may undermine Kenya's progress in the longer term.

Structural deficiencies are likely to hamper recovery in Nigeria. Growth projections in 2022 remain modest, at around 2.7 per cent, as the economy remains dependent on oil prices and investment is constrained by an onerous regulatory environment (Games, 2021). Nigeria needs to increase the contribution of the non-oil sector to exports and revenue generation to offset volatility in the oil sector. This would improve Nigeria's long-term prospects and build on its existing assets of a large and youthful population and an innovative and entrepreneurial business sector. Urgent policy reforms are needed to address the challenge of Nigeria's exceptionally high proportion of informal to formal jobs, and improve the welfare and skills of the country's workers, boost productivity of small-scale businesses, and create new jobs relevant to the digital economy.

Finally, South Africa's slow recovery remains a concern for its citizens, and for the continent at large. The South African economy contracted sharply by 6.4 per cent in 2020, with pre-COVID-19 levels of output and productivity only likely to increase in late 2023 (National Treasury Budget Review, 2021). COVID-19 has exposed structural flaws in South Africa's economy. While reforms to address constraints to growth have been avoided until now, they can no longer be delayed. Proper recovery depends on addressing the severe social constraints and prevailing divisions that exist, particularly around inequality and education.

As discussed, the pandemic has accentuated a range of issues, from poor data and access to information to high levels of informality in the private sector, and relatively low digital connectedness, not to mention inequality and poor education systems. African governments have an enormous task ahead of them on several fronts in rebuilding their economies as the pandemic retreats. Broadly, these include recouping lost gains following mediocre continental growth over the past decade, and the devastating impact of the pandemic, to bridging divides that threaten to undermine past progress and set the continent even further back in its development. It is imperative that future growth in Africa is inclusive and that the rebuilding process makes countries more competitive and resilient. The key driver in this regard is equal

---

[2]   For a country overview see www.worldbank.org/en/country/egypt/overview#1 and https://africa incmag.com/2020/08/12/egypts-economy-may-rebound-to-6-5-in-2021-new-imf-forecast-shows.

access to the digital economy. Without this, the economic, social, and cultural divides between Africa and the rest of the world will widen. The nature of recovery and the reforms adopted for sustainable and competitive economic inclusion will be essential to predicting the shape of recovery and progress in the post-COVID-19 era. This will distinguish those that used the crisis as an opportunity to reset their structures and trajectories from the rest.

In conclusion, the question remains: Will countries use this pandemic as an opportunity to implement necessary reforms and changes, or will they continue to hesitate and muddle their way through the precarious balance of economic competitiveness and progress as they prioritise political expedience over clear-sighted policy?

REFERENCES

African Union. (2008). Study on the informal sector in Africa. Labour and Social Affairs Commission of the African Union. https://au.int/sites/default/files/newsevents/workingdocuments/26936-wd -lsc_exp_4_vi-informal_economy_version-a1.doc

All Africa. (2021, 23 July). Egypt: IMF–SBA with Egypt achieved major targets during COVID. https:// allafrica.com/stories/202107230527.html

Azubuike, O.B. (2021, 2 June). Education, digital skills acquisition and learning during COVID-19 in Nigeria. Africa Portal. www.africaportal.org/features/education-digital-skills-acquisition-and -learning-during-COVID-19-nigeria

Bezu, S. (2017, 18 April). Ethiopia can convert its youth bulge from a political problem into an opportunity. *The Conversation.* https://theconversation.com/ethiopia-can-convert-its-youth-bulge-from-a -political-problem-into-an-opportunity-75312

Biltagy, M. (2021, April). How did COVID-19 pandemic impact education in Egypt? Euro-Mediterranean Economists Association. https://euromedeconomists.org/download/how-did-COVID-19-pandemic -impact-education-in-egypt/?wpdmdl=11061&refresh=6123d7e00c7791629738976

Bizuwork, D., & Sewunet, Z. (2020, 4 December). Schools reopening restores normalcy to children amid lingering COVID-19 risks. UNICEF. www.unicef.org/ethiopia/stories/schools-reopening-restores -normalcy-children-amid-lingering-COVID-19-risks

Bower, U. (2021, May). Making Egypt's post-COVID growth path more sustainable. European Commission. https://ec.europa.eu/info/sites/default/files/economyfinance/eb066_en.pdf

Business Tech. (2021, 4 August). New data shows what it takes to be in South Africa's richest 10%. *Business Tech.* https://businesstech.co.za/news/wealth/510822/new-data-shows-what-it-takes-to-be -in-south-africas-richest-10

Collins, T. (2021, 10 March). Flutterwave becomes Africa's fourth $1bn unicorn. African Business. https://african.business/2021/03/technology-information/flutterwave-becomesafricas-fourth-1bn -unicorn

The Conversation. (2021, 9 December). Nigeria's census has always been tricky: Why this must change. https://theconversation.com/nigerias-census-has-always-been-tricky-why-this-must-change-150391

Daily News Egypt. (2021, 21 April). Egypt jumps 5 places on Inclusive Internet index 2021: IDSC. https://dailynewsegypt.com/2021/04/21/egypt-jumps-5-places-on-inclusive-internet-index-2021-idsc

DigiSchool Kenya. (2021). About us. www.digischool.go.ke

The Economist. (2020, 9 May). Lacking data, many African governments make policy in the dark. www .economist.com/middle-east-and-africa/2020/05/07/lacking-data-many-african-governments-make -policy-in-the-dark

Egypt Independent. (2021, 17 March). Egypt, UAE announce new certified online learning platform. https://egyptindependent.com/egypt-uae-announce-new-certified-online-learning-platform

Freedom House. (2020). Freedom on the net 2020. https://freedomhouse.org/country/egypt/freedom-net/ 2020

Games, D. (2021, 21 April). Nigeria looks to build back after pandemic havoc. African Business. https:// african.business/2021/04/trade-investment/nigeria-looks-to-build-back-after-pandemic-havoc

Gennari, T., Holt, E., & Kaplow, L. (2021). Africa needs vaccines. What would it take to make them here? McKinsey and Company. www.mckinsey.com/industries/pharmaceuticals-and medicalproducts/ ourinsights/africa-needs-vaccines-what-would-it-take-to-make-them-here?

Given, M., & Karlen, R. (2020, 3 December). Supporting Africa's urban informal sector: Coordinated policies with social protection at the core. World Bank Blogs. https://blogs.worldbank.org/africacan/ supporting-africas-urban-informal-sector-coordinated-policies-social-protection-core

Grootes, S. (2019, 9 December). Twelve years of loadshedding: Written starring and directed by the ANC. *Daily Maverick*. www.dailymaverick.co.za/article/2019-12-09-twelve-years-of-load-shedding -written-starring-directed-by-the-anc

Hyde, P. (2021, 30 August). Nigeria's fintech frenzy: Onwards and upwards. *Forbes Africa*. www .forbesafrica.com/cover-story/2021/08/06/nigerias-fintech-frenzy-onwards-and-upwards

IMF. (2021a, April). Regional economic outlook for Sub-Saharan Africa: Navigating a long pandemic. www.imf.org/en/Publications/REO/SSA/Issues/2021/04/15/regional-economic-outlook-for-sub -saharan-africa-april-2021

IMF. (2021b, October). World economic outlook: Recovery during a pandemic. www.imf.org/en/ Publications/WEO/Issues/2021/10/12/world-economic-outlook-october-2021

IMF. (2022, January). World economic outlook update: Rising caseloads, a disrupted recovery, and higher inflation. www.imf.org/en/Publications/WEO/Issues/2022/01/25/world-economic-outlook -update-january-2022

Internal Finance Corporation. (2021). e-Conomy Africa 2020. Google and International Finance Corporation.www.ifc.org/wps/wcm/connect/e358c23f-afe3-49c5-a509-034257688580/e-Conomy-Af rica-2020.pdf?MOD=AJPERES&CVID=nmuGYF

International Housing Survey Network. (2007). Population and housing census of 2007. https://catalog .ihsn.org/index.php/catalog/3583

International Labour Organization. (2020, 17 September). The future of work in the digital economy. / www.ilo.org/global/about-the-ilo/how-the-iloworks/multilateral-system/brics/2020/WCMS_771117/ lang--en/index.htm

International Trade Administration. (2021, September 30). Kenya – country commercial guide: Information, communications and technology (ICT). www.trade.gov/country-commercial-guides/ kenya-information-communications-and-technology-ict

Internet Society (2021a, 6 July). Internet exchange points are critical to improving internet access and lowering connectivity costs in Africa. www.internetsociety.org/news/press-releases/2021/internet -exchange-points-are-critical-to-improving-internet-access-and-lowering-connectivity-costs-in-africa

Internet Society. (2021b, 10 June). The Ministry of Innovation and Technology and the Internet Society sign new pact to advance digital economy in Ethiopia. www.internetsociety.org/news/press-releases/ 2021/the-ministry-of-innovation-and-technology-and-the-internet-society-sign-new-pact-to-advance -digital-economy-in-ethiopia

ITU (International Telecommunication Union). (2021a). Measuring digital development: Facts and figures 2021. www.itu.int/en/ITUD/Statistics/Documents/facts/FactsFigures2021.pdf

ITU (International Telecommunication Union). (2021b). Measuring digital development: ICT price trends 2020. www.itu.int/en/ITUD/Statistics/Pages/ICTprices/default.aspx

Jerven, M. (2013). *Poor Numbers: How We Are Misled by African Development Statistics and What to Do about It*. New York: Cornell University Press.

Kazeem, Y. (2020, 7 September). Nigeria is trying to bridge internet inequality and boost access by cutting expensive red tape. Quartz Africa. https://qz.com/africa/1900348/nigeria-waives-right-of-way -charges-to-boost-internet-access

Kemp, S. (2022, February 15). Digital 2022. DataReportal, various countries. https://datareportal.com/ reports/digital-2022

Klapper, L., Ansar, S., Hess, J., & Singer, D. (2019, March). Identification, financial inclusion and development in Sub-Saharan Africa. World Bank Group. https://openknowledge.worldbank.org/ handle/10986/18078

Koninckx, P., Fatondji, C., & Burgos, J. (2021, 19 May). COVID-19 impact on higher education in Africa. OECD Development Matters. https://oecd-development matters.org/2021/05/19/COVID-19 -impact-on-higher-education-in-africa

London School of Economics and Political Science. (2021, 16 March). Event. www.lse.ac.uk/Events/2021/03/202103161400/work

Mabolloane, P. (2021, 3 August). Data costs and online access high on list of obstacles to online learning for South African students. *Daily Maverick*. www.dailymaverick.co.za/opinionista/2021-08-03-data-costs-and-online-access-high-on-list-of-obstacles-to-online-learning-for-south-african-students

McKinsey Global Institute. (2021, February). The future of work after COVID-19. www.mckinsey.com/featured-insights/future-of-work/the-future-of-work-after-COVID-19

Mesmar, D. (2021, 27 April). Ethiopia overhauls its education system with IOHK blockchain partnership. Global Educational Supplies and Solutions. www.gesseducation.com/industry-news/ethiopia-overhauls-its-education-system-with-iohk-blockchain-partnership?page=8

Microsoft (2021, 2 August). Microsoft to partner with Kenya and governments across Africa to transform education for millions of students. Microsoft News Center. https://news.microsoft.com/en-xm/2021/08/02/microsoft-to-partner-with-kenya-and-governments-across-africa-to-transform-education-for-millions-of-students

Monteiro, L. (2021, 12 August). 3 promising FinTech start-ups to watch out for in Nigeria. IBS Intelligence. https://ibsintelligence.com/ibsi-news/3-promising-fintech-start-ups-to-watch-out-for-in-nigeria

Mugendi, J. (2020, 15 December). Challenges in implementing digital technologies in rural Kenya. Engineering For Change. www.engineeringforchange.org/news/challenges-implementing-digital-technologies-rural-kenya

National Treasury Budget Review. (2021). www.treasury.gov.za/documents/National%20Budget/2021/review/FullBR.pdf

Navis, K., & Moore, W. G. (2019, 12 August). Here's what Ethiopia needs to become Africa's next tech hub. Center for Global Development. www.cgdev.org/blog/heres-what-ethiopia-needs-become-africas-next-tech-hub

Ng'weno. A., & Porteous, D. (2018, 15 October). Let's be real: The informal sector and the gig economy are the future, and the present, of work in Africa. Center for Global Development. www.cgdev.org/publication/lets-be-real-informal-sector-and-gig-economy-are-future-and-present-work-africa

OECD. (2020, 27 November). OECD digital economy outlook 2020. www.oecd.org/digital/oecd-digital-economy-outlook-2020-bb167041-en.htm

Ogundare, F. (2021, 29 April). Nigeria: Lagos partners Microsoft, trains 18,000 teachers on digital literacy. All Africa. https://allafrica.com/stories/202004290587.html

Olundjoye, B. (2020, 22 October). Making online education accessible to all in Nigeria. Pulitzer Center. https://pulitzercenter.org/stories/making-online-education-accessible-all-nigeria

Oxfam. (2021). Kenya: Extreme inequality in numbers. www.oxfam.org/en/kenya-extreme-inequality-numbers

Reuters. (2022, 29 March). South Africa's unemployment rate hits new record high in Q4 2021. Reuters. www.reuters.com/world/africa/south-africas-unemployment-rate-hits-new-record-high-q4-2021-2022-03-29/

Schneidman, W. (2021, 15 June). Ethiopia, human rights, and the Internet. Brookings. www.brookings.edu/blog/africa-in-focus/2021/06/15/ethiopia-human-rights-and-the-internet

Switzerland Global Enterprise. (2021, September). Silicon Savannah: Tapping the potential of Africa's tech hub. Switzerland Global Enterprise. www.sge.com/en/article/global-opportunities/20213-c6-kenya-tech-hub-fint1

Thompson, F. (2021, 28 July). Delay expected as deadline looms for AfCFTA rules of origin talks. Global Trade Review. www.gtreview.com/news/africa/delay-expected-as-deadline-looms-for-afcfta-rules-of-origin-talks

Trading Economics. (2021). South Africa youth unemployment rate. https://tradingeconomics.com/south-africa/youth-unemployment-rate

Udegbunam, O. (2020, 4 November). 58% of Nigerians unable to access internet – survey. *Premium Times*. www.premiumtimesng.com/news/top-news/424547-58-of-nigerians-unable-to-access-internet-survey.html

UNICEF. (2021, 22 July). Learners in South Africa up to one school year behind where they should be. www.unicef.org/press-releases/learners-south-africa-one-school-year-behind-where-they-should-be

UNICEF. (2022). Are the children really learning? https://data.unicef.org/resources/are-children-really-learning-foundational-skills-report/

United Nations, Department of Economic and Social Affairs. (2019). World population prospects 2019. https://population.un.org/wpp/Publications/Files/WPP2019_VolumeI_ComprehensiveTables.pdf

Wallace-Stephens, F., & Morgante, E. (2021, 2 August). Pathfinding: The future of work in Sub-Saharan Africa. The RSAorg. www.thersa.org/reports/future-of-work-sub-saharan-africa

Weber, M., Palacios-Lopez, A., & Contreras-Gonzalez, I. M. (2020, 18 November). Labor market impacts of COVID-19 in four African countries. World Bank Blogs. https://blogs.worldbank.org/opendata/labor-market-impacts-COVID-19-four-africancountries

White, L., & Rees, L. (2021, 3 September). Benefits of Africa's free trade bloc could boost post-pandemic recovery. *Business Day.* www.businesslive.co.za/bd/opinion/2020-09-03-benefits-of-africas-free-trade-bloc-could-boost-post-pandemic-recovery

White, T. (2021, 16 April). Figure of the week: COVID's impacts on the Nigerian extractive sector. Brookings. www.brookings.edu/blog/africa-in-focus/2021/04/16/figure-of-the-week-covids-impacts-on-the-nigerian-extractive-sector

World Bank. (2020, 27 July). The African Continental Free Trade Area. www.worldbank.org/en/topic/trade/publication/the-african-continental-free-trade-area

World Bank. (2021a, April). *Africa's Pulse.* Volume 23. https://openknowledge.worldbank.org/bitstream/handle/10986/35342/9781464817144.pdf

World Bank. (2021b). GCI 4.0: Digital skills among population.

World Bank. (2021c, January). Global economic prospects. https://pubdocs.worldbank.org/en/389631599838727666/Global-Economic-ProspectsJanuary-2021-Analysis-SSA.pdf

World Health Organization. (2021). Ethiopia. https://covid19.who.int/region/afro/country/et

Zaman, M. (2021, 24 July). After COVID-19, let's reimagine education in Kenya. UNICEF. www.unicef.org/kenya/stories/after-COVID-19-lets-reimagineeducation-kenya

Index